THE WORTH OF
WOMEN'S WORK

SUNY Series on Women and Work
Joan Smith, Editor

THE WORTH OF WOMEN'S WORK

A *Qualitative Synthesis*

Anne Statham, Eleanor M. Miller, and Hans O. Mauksch, *Editors*

STATE UNIVERSITY OF NEW YORK PRESS

Published by
State University of New York Press, Albany

© 1988 State University of New York

For more information, address State University of New York
Press, State University Plaza, Albany, N.Y., 12246

Library of Congress Cataloging-in-Publication Data

Statham, Anne.
    The worth of women's work.

    (SUNY series on women and work)
    Incldes index.
    1. Women—Employment—United States. I. Miller,
Eleanor M., 1948-   II. Mauksch, Hans O. III. Title.
IV. Series.
HD6095.S73 1987   331.4'0973   87-6472
ISBN 0-87706-591-0
ISBN 0-88706-592-9 (pbk.)

10 9 8 7 6 5 4 3 2

Contents

Foreword

The scholars and advocates who gathered at Wingspread in October, 1985 came together because they believe there is a critical relationship between research and public policy. In the 80's only certain kinds of research — the overnight, instant polls and the numbers games from the BLS or Census Bureau are given attention from the media and from politicians. Decision makers seem to be out of touch with the more arduous and longterm research — the qualitative work done by scholars. Although polls and vast statistical counts can be useful, the fact is qualitative research should be the food of policymakers and should, in turn, be fed by them. The energy to change our society's attitudes and policies toward women in the workplace and the leadership to overcome resistance to change has to come from strong convictions that only result from a deep understanding of people and their problems. That is one important role of qualitative research.

Research agendas are often affected by the mood of policymakers. Today, for example, the work of women's advocates is hampered by a climate of opinion which says that working women's problems have been solved, that sex discrimination has been eliminated or vastly reduced, and that women have equal opportunity and are free to choose their economic futures. The ideology of individualism and laissez-faire is rampant. Our country's minorities, especially blacks and Hispanics, are subject to the same rhetoric of false cheer and misplaced optimism. This is not to say that working women have made no economic progress in the past two decades, but rather that there are still serious problems facing women that cannot be solved by individual effort alone.

The papers delivered at this conference hold the proof of our still-discriminatory wage system, of our lack of response to the child care crisis, and of an educational system that still projects for women little choice other than traditionally-female, low-paid work or the high risk, rose-covered cottage. This research eloquently tells us we must challenge our institutions more fervently than ever before, and we must not be held hostage by these hard political times. This is the research that policymakers should be hungry for. This research describes the world of working women — women who work in nursing homes, become police officers, sell sex for a living, clean homes, or type letters. The dedicated field work represented by the papers connects us to these women workers and tells us crucial information: who they are, what their goals are, and what risks they'll take to improve their lives. These papers are subjective while numbers are objective, and there are those who would rather not know the truths with faces and names to them.

Through combining the efforts of advocates and academics, we really can help working women in this country. Grassroots women are honest in their testimony about their own lives, but they don't have the tools or the structures to carry their concerns and needs far beyond their own communities. But the tools and the structures are there — advocates have them, and scholars have them. We understand the paths of communication and we can use them on their behalf. The voices of women workers can be heard in this collection of qualitative research papers. The reader must reflect on what is here and discover the congruent themes that will lead to even stronger designs for policy.

For the scholar this book is an opportunity to broaden the audience for research. For the advocate it is more dramatic. Much of advocacy for women is reactive and uses struggle to maintain the level of commitment to civil rights established over 20 years ago. This research comes as passionate evidence to support our efforts. By integrating qualitative research with concerns on advocates' agendas, we can develop more effective policy strategies.

The 34 million women who are in the pink- and blue-collar work force — sales workers, service workers, factory and clerical workers — have a simple agenda. They want decent wages and benefits; they want affordable child care and dependent care; they want training and education for advancement in their jobs; and they want decent and dignified working conditions. They have said it over and over again — with different accents and in different ways, but it is always the same. These desires are not new nor are they greedy. As Bella Abzug says, "It is shocking that as women, we have to beg to contribute our labor to society. We have to beg for family support systems, decent wages, and the dignity to do what men have always done." I agree, it is shocking.

The joining of NCWW and the scholars whose work is presented here attempts to show that policy and scholarship do, in fact, intersect, although there has often been a tug of war between the two. Policy people have resisted adapting their agendas to the realities of research findings, while academics often want just a few more years to make sure that the longitudinal study confirms the original latitudinal one. The truth is that in the next few years, we will need each other more than ever. It is not acceptable to make policy via the media, or because it is an election year, or based on a short-term economic analysis or to satisfy a military neurosis. It is an insult to those who need our help so badly.

The common denominator is that we are all advocates for improving the status of working women. We each have different tasks to do. Some will do research, some will do public education, some will write legislation, and some will organize people at the community level. We will all do what we do best. In this book, you will be touched by women's lives. Let each of us also be motivated to take action.

ALEXIS HERMAN
CHAIR, NATIONAL COMMISSION ON WORKING WOMEN

Acknowledgements

Many individuals and organizations have contributed significantly to this volume. Without the substantial financial and moral support of the Johnson Foundation, the host for the Wingspread Conference where the authors gathered and presented preliminary drafts of their papers, this volume would never have been possible. Rita Goodman, a vice president with the Foundation, and Kay Mauer, conference coordinator, were particularly helpful in this regard. The conference was co-sponsored by the National Commission on Working Women (Sandra Porter, Executive Director) and the University of Wisconsin-Parkside Women's Studies Program (Teresa Peck, Coordinator). Their support and input was, again, immensely important. Financial support was also given by the University of Wisconsin-Parkside's Program Development Fund (Alan Guskin, Chancellor and Mary Elizabeth Shutler, Vice Chancellor) and by the American Sociological Association (William D'Antonio, Executive Officer) in the form of two grants from the Committee on Problems in the Discipline. Input was received from several individuals in the planning of the conference and overall project, among them Timothy Diamond, Mary Margaret Fonow, Jane Hood, Sandra Porter, Laurel Richardson, and Mary Romero. Sandra Porter contributed significantly to the actual structure and process of the conference, and LuAnn Simpson and Terri Eisenbart acted as student assistants. Other participants contributed scholarly and policy expertise at the conference. Arlene Kaplan Daniels was most helpful in the early stages of gathering these individuals together. She participated along with Joan Acker, Ellen Bravo, Kay Clarenbach, Alice Cook, Judith Dilorio, Heidi Gottfried, Harriett Engel Gross, Ruth Needleman, Anne Nelson, Sandra Porter, and Judith Wittner. High quality clerical assistance was given by Alice Beezat, Pat Jones, Pat Nennig-Hayes, Debbie Ritchie-Kolberg, Pat Ondishko, Jennie Peshut, Marge Reiman, Marge Rowley, Zona Selensky, Vickie Skoczynski, Celita Thompson, and Luella Vines and editorial assistance by Gabrielle Kleinman, Catherine Loeb and Meredith Ross. Financial and in-kind support in the actual publication of the work was provided by the Social Science Research Facility of the University of Wisconsin-Milwaukee (Swarnjit Arora, Director) and the Office of Assistant Dean of Letters and Science, G. Richard Meadows also of that institution. And, of course, the respondents in these studies, who shared so willingly of their lives, made this all possible on the most basic level. Finally, we wish to thank the contributors, who cooperated so beautifully, and our spouses — Michael Zupan, Dale Jaffe, and Roberta Mauksch — who have us support in our individual lives that enabled us to finish this project.

Part I

INTRODUCTION
AND ANALYSIS

CHAPTER 1

Women's Approach to Work:
The Creation of Knowledge

ANNE STATHAM, HANS O. MAUKSCH, ELEANOR M. MILLER

This book began as a dream, progressed through a conference, and became reality as a secondary analysis of qualitative studies. A major driving force behind the project was the desire to integrate a significant number of studies of women's labor force experiences, moving beyond the simple accretion of information to a search for themes, unifying concepts and analytic insights. In this sense, the individual studies included in this volume became sources of information *and* units of analysis in the search for unifying sets of concepts illuminating the work of women.

The information contained in these studies was first presented at a conference called "Women and Work: Integrating Qualitative Research" held at the Wingspread Conference Center in Racine, Wisconsin, in October of 1985. It was here that we began our first real work of synthesizing — rather than simply aggregating — our findings about women at work. We listened to one another's papers and received feedback from each other as well as from participating academic and policy specialists. In our discussion, we searched for the structure of concepts that would provide the synthesis binding these studies together. Some concepts, such as the "seamlessness" of women's work and private lives, as well as that of a "woman's approach to work," emerged immediately and powerfully at the conference. Others, such as the importance of unequal power and bonding in work relationships, have occurred to us in our more recent analysis of the papers. We are confident that the concepts we have derived will be useful for those looking at the book from either a sociology of women or a sociology of work perspective.

It is more than coincidental that all of the studies presented here use qualitative methodologies. This is the second driving force for this project. In essence, the book represents a model for integrating qualitative research, a much-needed step in that research tradition. Qualitative approaches present a unique opportunity to do the integrating described above. While other (more qualitative) methods offer their own strengths, qualitative analyses provide particularly complex, rich views of life and fertile sources for synthesis. Thus, our conceptual model relies heavily on the use of qualitative methodology, since conceptual creation is, after all, one of its major strengths.

The third motivating concern that inspired the conference and that is explored in this book is the conviction that these studies, these issues, and these methodologies have direct relevance to the shaping and assessing of social policy. To the extent that these studies succeed in demonstrating perspectives and factors distinct to the sociology of work, and to the extent that these studies distinguish between what is peculiar to women's work and what is not — to that extent can this project contribute a frame of reference for assessing policies, their assumptions, and their consequences. As shown eloquently in the following pages, the intent of policies formulated on the macrosociety level may not translate effectively on the microlevel of individual and group experiences. The link between social science data and the formation and implementation of policies is a pervasive concern of social scientists. Yet, there is some uneasiness within sociology about the applicability of social science knowledge to policies bearing on "real life." Since policy development requires access to information synthesis, the approaches represented in these projects may facilitate continuity between problem, data, and solutions. The obstacles to effective communication between knowledge producers and applied practitioners became evident during the Wingspread Conference; we often work without knowledge of the other's sources. Both predictive analysis and life-related understanding need development and commitment if we are to convey information effectively to those who seek to affect the structure and process of actual lives.

KNOWLEDGE OF WORKING WOMEN

Much new knowledge about women's work experience has been gained in recent years. The information that has accumulated tends to be quite dramatically split into broad-scale demographic studies and survey data, on the one hand, and smaller-scale qualitative research, on the other. The former approach provides knowledge about trends, relationships between variables, and patterns applicable to large groups of women. Yet this type of knowledge has failed to yield any real understanding of the lives behind the numbers. In contrast, the isolated, idiosyncratic qualitative studies have peered deeply into women's lives, but their findings have not been generalizable or couched in terms of broader concepts.

Some of the puzzling problems women encounter in the workplace are not easily understood; their solutions will undoubtedly only be found by incorporating a qualitative approach, at least in part. For instance, Reskin (1984) has advocated the collection of case study material to supplement existing demographic data on sex segregation in the labor force. Labor force segregation is a terribly intractable problem, regardless of other gains women have made, and survey data provide few insights into why this is so. We need to know more about what women are thinking and feeling, what obstacles they find when trying to enter nontraditional occupations. A similar strategy is also being proposed in the area of comparable worth (Olendahl, Palmer and Ratner 1980). Here again, in-depth data are needed to inform us of the specific processes operating to devalue women's jobs and/or individual responses to those processes. This information would help us understand the societal trends we are already aware of.

INTEGRATING QUALITATIVE RESEARCH

The situation with the qualitative tradition is just as troubling as that with the larger scale approach, albeit for different reasons. Here we have a wealth of insightful data gathered through painstaking methods, which provide remarkable insight into particular work situations yet has not been synthesized into larger themes and coherent statements about women's work situation in general. The samples in these studies are typically small and unsystematic. A single researcher is rarely able to gather updated information from other samples because of time constraints. Also, the settings are often very different. These studies, then, tend to exist in isolation, a problem endemic to all qualitative approaches. Indeed, there is no intellectual tradition of drawing on these approaches to look for the universal characteristics necessary for building theory. Our project provides a mechanism for moving beyond the level of single studies.

Those who use qualitative approaches have typically embraced some form of interpretive sociology—symbolic interaction, ethnomethodology, phenomenology — which questions the positivist notion that we can anticipate social structures and set out to measure them with standard survey techniques, ignoring the individual's perspective in the process. Giddens (1976), Barnes (1974), and Glaser and Strauss (1967) have argued that the logico-positivistic research tradition so prevalent in sociology generates a sociology alien to the "lay" person, indeed to much of "real social life." These theorists argue that to produce more valid results we must begin our analysis at the level of the individual, taking his or her definition of the situation into account, otherwise we are left to work with preconceived notions or categories that may have no meaning to the individual, producing useless information in the end. Even Marxists, particularly feminist Marxists (Smith 1974; Jaggar 1983), make the same claim. This claim may well be true, but taking an interpretive approach has its own problems. With it, it becomes difficult to move to the more general level of structure and pattern.

Theorists differ in the extent to which they see this problem as correctable or endemic. Huber (1973), for instance, sees interpretive perspectives as hopelessly compromised by the social fact that certain definitions carry more weight in determining common understandings than others. Giddens (1976) emphasizes the continuous feedback endemic to these perspectives, arguing that they *become* relativism, that there is never an end to the need to analyze background expectations. Lofland (1970), on the other hand, joins Glaser and Strauss (1967) in arguing that researchers using this framework have simply not gone far enough with their methods, that they have engaged in "analytic interruptus." All argue for a mechanism to discover and account for patterned, structured aspects of society as well as for individual reactions.

Attempts to solve this problem are varied. One solution is to combine quantitative techniques with qualitative methods. The Iowa School of symbolic interactionism, for instance, uses symbolic interaction as the basis for positivistic (quantitative) survey research. However, many question the extent to which this approach remains interpretive. Giddens advocates a blending of interpretive and structural perspectives as a way of "explicating divergent forms of life," giving structure to individual agency in a way absent from previous work. He argues that our assessments must begin with an "immersion in the form of life" (p. 161–62) we wish to study, something qualitative researchers do best.

A third approach advocated by Glaser and Strauss and later by Lofland, called *comparative analysis*, is a method of deriving mini-concepts from case studies and attempting to apply them across diverse settings ("divergent forms of life"). In this way, structures or patterns become apparent as they apply beyond a single setting. In getting to structure, Glaser and Strauss suggest the development of formal grounded theory, a theory built from results from narrower substantive areas (possibly studies by different researchers).

We are using a variant of this latter approach. Several of us have independently completed qualitative studies of women in specific occupations. From our data, we have written papers that deal with previously agreed-upon topics, a process that has sensitized us to common patterns in the various settings. Because we have looked at diverse settings of a single type — occupations — we believe it likely we will find common, or easily contrasted, factors to exist across these settings. Hence, we are beginning the work called for by many interpretive sociologists.

THE POLICY RELEVANCE

Issues surrounding women's labor force participation are of practical as well as theoretical interest. Many serious problems are faced by women in the work force. Equally important are the contributions women make to the workplace that go unnoticed. From the beginning of this project, we have been concerned that our findings be given attention in both applied and academic circles. The issue of policy relevance was a serious consideration at the Wingspread Conference where these papers were first presented. As we groped our way toward distilling and synthesizing the commonalities in these separate pieces of research, we continually asked ourselves what the implications were for the "real lives" of women. In this sense, we ended where we began, wanting to probe deeply into the lives of women, hoping to gain clearer knowledge.

The recommendations that we derive are based on long and detailed looks into women's lives. In contrast to those obtained from more quantitative approaches, our results do not emerge as extremes. Rather, we see many of the nuances, the in-between and conditional situations and reactions. Hopefully, our results will be useful in their more detailed depiction of the difficulties women face.

RELEVANCE TO OTHER AREAS OF INQUIRY

The central focus of the volume involves an intersection of the sociology of work and occupations and the sociology of women. The explorations and findings reported are also significant for other areas of study. Observations about the involvement of women in work, the variations of meanings, and the notion of the "seamlessness" of women's work and private lives have bearing on the literature on the life cycle, particularly on timing and phasing throughout life.

An area of research that can be informed by the studies gathered here and that also has much to contribute to the sociology of women and work can be found in the literature on minority groups. In many significant ways, data on women can be fruitfully examined within the framework of minority group analysis. The utility of examining the status of women in America from a minority group perspective was suggested very early in an appendix to one of the classical studies of Blacks in America (Myrdal 1944, App. 5). The use of the minority group analysis is, in many instances, significant in explaining problems women have in the workplace and values assigned to those activities defined as "women's work." For example one collection of essays focusing on occupations with primarily female membership came to the conclusion that working groups identified as female can, at best, attain "semi-professional status" (Etzioni 1969) — a finding consistent with those of comparable research on minority group employment.

Finally, our findings contribute to the field of stratification a new awareness of how individuals function in both prestigious and degraded positions. Perhaps most significant in this regard is the evidence that occupants of degraded statuses find ingenious ways of enhancing their self- perceptions, and maintaining control of their work settings.

THE PLAN OF THE BOOK

The book is divided into five sections, the first containing this introduction and a secondary analysis — a synthesis — of the disparate findings. Next come the original papers, revised after conference presentation, and grouped into three parts. Part II includes reports of women in traditionally female occupations performing the "caretaker" role. These occupations — nursing assistant, domestic worker, janitor, and street hustler — are held by women who work hard for their living at the lower end of the socioeconomic scale. Part III presents reports of higher-status women in traditional female professions (nursing, teaching, counseling, and administration in female-typed fields). Interestingly, we find these women to also be dealing with status issues. Papers in part IV report on women in traditionally male occupations (police work, management, direct sales, factory work). Here, the socioeconomic status is mixed, though many issues cut across the various status levels included. In Part V we consider the policy relevance of our findings and then conclude by assessing their implications for the field of qualitative research.

REFERENCES

Barnes, Barry. 1974. *Scientific Knowledge and Sociological Theory*. London: Routledge and Kegan Paul.

Etzioni, A. 1969. *The Semi-professions and Their Organization*. New York: Free Press.

Giddens, Anthony. 1976. *New rules of sociological method: A positive critique of interpretative sociologies*. New York: Basic Books.

Glaser, Barney and Anslem Strauss. 1967. *The Discovery of Grounded Theory: Strategies for Qualitative Research*. New York: Aldine Publishing Company.

Huber, Joan. 1973. "Symbolic interaction as a pragmatic perspective: The bias of emergent theory," *American Sociological Review* 38:274–84.

Jagger, Allison. 1983. *Feminist Politics and Human Nature*. Totowa, N.J.: Rowman and Allenheld.

Lofland, John. 1970. "Interactionist imagery and analytic interruptus," In *Human Nature and Collective Behavior: Papers in Honor of Herbert Blumer*, edited by Tamotsu Shibutani. Englewood Cliffs, N.J.: Prentice-Hall.

Myrdal, Gunnar. 1944. *An American Dilemma: The Negro Problem and Modern Democracy*. New York: Haysen.

Olendahl, Terry, Phyllis Palmer, and Ronnie Ratner. 1980. "The pay-equity conference: 'Comparable worth' research issues and methods," In *Manual on Pay Equity: Raising Wages for Women's Work*. edited by Joy Ann Grune. Washington, D.C.: Committee on Pay Equity.

Reskin, Barbara. 1984. *Sex Segregation in the Workplace: Trends, Explanations, Remedies.* Washington, D.C.: National Research Council.

Smith, Dorothy. 1974. "The social construction of documentary reality," *Sociologial Inquiry* 44:257–68.

CHAPTER 2

The Integration Work: A Second-order Analysis of Qualitative Research

ANNE STATHAM, ELEANOR M. MILLER, HANS O. MAUKSCH

This chapter comprises what we consider to be the heart of the study, our major contribution to the enterprise of qualitative research. Here, we have analyzed the papers, treating them as bits of qualitative data much as interviews, field notes, and diaries were used in the original studies. By doing this, we see much more clearly the coherence among apparently disparate findings. The most striking conclusions we have drawn were not at all apparent to us from our more cursory view before beginning our analysis in earnest. Some coherencies were beginning to take shape — but had not taken such clear form — in the preliminary analyses that took place at the conference. It is in this later work that we see the true worth of the qualitative approach used systematically: its ability to highlight subtle, sometimes opaque connections. In doing so, we also make our greatest contribution to the study of women's labor force behaviors, for that is the substance of our conclusions.

In all 13 studies presented here, qualitative data provide a rich look into the lives of the women, and the men, studied. The researchers did focused interviews, participant observation, and asked their respondents to keep diaries. Using a variety of methods, they gathered their data from close range, coming to know their respondents and their settings quite well. In addition, the researchers often had personal experiences to draw upon in understanding and interpreting what they saw. Seven conceptual themes emerged as most striking from our analyis, themes used to give us a coherent view of women's work exerience across various occupational, race, and social classes. They are: 1) maintaining autonomy and control; 2) maintaining dignity; 3) handling asymmety in relationships; 4) dealing with degradation and devaluation; 5) approaching work in a "woman's" way; 6) managing relationships in the workplace; and

11

7) the seamlessness of life. These are the issues or qualities all of the women were most frequently concerned with.

ISSUES ON THE JOB

Autonomy and Control

Autonomy and control in the work setting are the job characteristics discussed most consistently across the studies. Both the authors and their respondents recognized the importance of autonomy in determining job attractiveness and satisfaction. For example, Collins asserts that degree of autonomy determines the extent to which a job is a profession. However, the professional standing of a job is not a perfect predictor of job satisfaction (Pavalko, 1987). The situation is really much more complex. For one thing, degree of autonomy varies greatly across the job status hierarchy and does not necessarily correlate with the job/profession distinction. As Martin (p. 208) points out, Stewart and Cantor's (1974) job classification scheme based on the autonomy or discretion held by job occupants was intended to be a true *alternative* to the more traditional job/profession scheme. She argues that

> . . . The fact that the police officer at the lowest level of the hierarchical organization has enormous discretionary decision-making authority . . . [is] . . . what makes policing unique and a "male" occupation (p. 208).

Martin argues that this discretion, or autonomy makes police work a desirable occupation, despite the fact that:

> Police officers are blue collar workers with mediocre prestige working in the public service sector with professional aspirations but little recognition as a "profession" (pp. 207–8).

Others stressed the importance of autonomy for their respondents. Miller, talking about street hustlers, observes that these women obtain " . . . a sense of independence, excitement, and autonomy . . . that . . . persons who labor in the world of legal work rarely enjoy." (p. 127) And Romero reports that the domestic workers she interviewed "identified themselves as professional housekeepers" (p. 87), while Hood's custodial workers viewed themselves as "'trained professionals' . . . [who] really knew how to clean" (p. 102). None of these workers had high status jobs nor would they be classified as professionals by most schemes (Pavalko 1987). Yet, they spoke more often of the autonomy (and resulting control) they had acquired in their work settings than women in what would ordinarily be thought of as higher status jobs that more closely approached "professional" types. If frequency of mention is a measure of the salience of a particular characteristic, then autonomy is certainly at the forefront of our respondents' concerns.

In fact, the *loss* of professional status and resulting "lack of power, autonomy, and status" was a major concern of the teachers Spencer interviewed (p. 168), and the *lack* of professional status and control over their work was problematic for the genetic counselors Rothman and Detlefs interviewed (p. 155-56). Both groups of women desired to be recognized for what they considered to be professional capabilities and performance. Related to this, the managers Statham interviewed bemoaned their lack of time for autonomous "planning" activities and their heavy involvement in "doing" or "fighting fires" instead (p. 229).

Relatively high levels of dissatisfaction seemed to exist among the women with higher status jobs. Why would they be less satisfied with jobs that supposedly provide more autonomy? Perhaps their expectations are greater — because of their alternatives or anticipatory socialization. Women with different levels of expectations may see fewer alternatives. For example, in talking about the street hustlers she interviewed, Miller notes that "These women have little education, almost no work experience, and few market skills. They are fully cognizant of the sorts of employment possibilities open to them" (p. 127). There may also be some rationalization involved. Hood (p. 102) refers to Hughes' idea that "people who do dirty work protect honorific self-conceptions from those who threaten to weaken them. . . " (Hughes 1974, 280). The more degraded the work, by societal standards, the more motive to present one's work in a positive light.

However, there seems to be more involved than rationalization or differing expectations. These workers discussed very specific mechanisms they used to bring their work under their control and provide themselves with autonomy in the workplace. There is considerable evidence here that *action* was occurring, in addition to altered perceptions. By using these mechanisms, they were able to transform what might be degrading, "dirty work" into "good work." As Hood puts it:

> Good work allows for autonomy and expression of oneself. Good work elevates and nurtures, and does not belittle or undermine a person. Good work allows one to take pride in accomplishments and to work independently most, if not all, of the time (p. 97).

How is it that workers in jobs ordinarily considered to be degraded turn them into good work? From the accounts reported in this book, it is through their own individual agency. What follows are the specific mechanisms they use to do so.

Determining content of work. Workers who are somehow able to determine the content of their work felt most in control. This was easier to do if supervisors were not immediately present. For this reason, private house workers preferred to work when their employers were not home.

All of the informants preferred to work alone in the house (Romero, p. 119).

(How do you feel about working in a house by yourself? Do you get lonesome?) "No, I like it . . . I don't think I ever liked people watching me all the time . . ." (Glenn p. 71).

And Hood reports the dissatisfaction the women custodial workers felt when they were switched from night to day shift.

. . . they felt worse because of the tension of working around so many people . . . a union stewart [explained] . . . "You don't see no finished job. You don't see nothing . . . You can't do it. You can't work with wall-to-wall people" (p. 101).

Closeness of supervision, and resulting constraints on the ability to control work content, was a critical factor in other jobs as well. Spencer reports that:

. . . teachers are often treated in infantile ways . . . Principals can assign teachers such duties as monitoring restrooms or detention rooms, can enter and observe classrooms without notifying teachers, and can schedule meetings without consulting teachers. In a few cases, principals go through teachers' desk drawers and grade their lesson plan books (p. 174).

Diamond reports a similar situation for nurse's assistants.

In two of the homes we were explicitly not allowed to sit by the patients. Should the Board of Health appear, or one of the occasional physicians drop in, this would appear as loafing. We were told to keep moving, unless we were charting, for to keep moving is to look busy (p. 48).

And Rothman and Detlefs perceive closeness of supervision among the genetic counselors they interviewed ("they [are] . . . answerable to both physicians and to program and hospital administrators") as a source of dissatisfaction to them (p. 155). Sometimes control is felt even in the absence of one's supervisor. Connelly and Rhoton say of the direct sales workers they interviewed

Within the direct sales normative structure, a paradox exists. The worker is viewed to be free . . . yet within both organizations, workers experience extensive normative constraints. Codes of dress exist, one is trained in set routines . . . They . . . limit the workers' options (p. 256).

This causes problems for many workers. The presence of autonomy is appreciated. As Statham reports, managers liked the autonomy they *did* have to accomplish things, though women managers, in particular, would have sometimes liked to have had more direction (p. 238).

However, there were certain areas of work open to worker control, and successfully executing this control was a source of much satisfaction. The genetic counselors in Rothman and Detlefs' study were immensely pleased that they had ". . . no interference, no doctor with a capital *D* giving a diagnosis, saying things that are an anethma to the patient . . . " (p. 157). or in other ways interferring with the *internal* workings of the counseling session. Though they had little influence on the "large structure . . . the parameters of their work . . . " they had secured this basic bit of autonomy for themselves. While Rothman and Detlefs viewed this as "autonomy by default" (p. 157), saying the doctors were not really *interested* in what happened during the counseling sessions, both genetic and abortion counselors viewed this autonomy as one of the most satisfying aspects of their jobs.

The ability to set and adhere to one's own standards was mentioned by several groups of workers as being very important. Concerning domestic workers, Romero says that the women she talked with perceived that they had:

> . . . responsibility for maintaining the employers' homes. Maintenance involved bringing the employer's house up to a standard that would then be maintained on a daily basis (p. 82). . . . [This] planning and organizing work permitted the domestic to feel like her own boss (p. 85).

As one of her respondents put it "Once the person learns that you're going to do the job they just totally leave you to your own" (p. 85). Glenn reports a similar finding:

> The employer may signify at the beginning what needs to be done, but the worker organizes the work to accomplish the tasks in the time allotted . . . The job was done when the tasks were accomplished to their own satisfaction (p. 72).

The worker has certain external standards she seeks to uphold. As one of Glenn's respondent's said "I tell them I have a certain way I want to work" (p. 101). And the custodial workers Hood interviewed:

> . . . described strong proprietary feelings about "their" areas . . . Several female workers complained of how difficult it was to inherit another worker's area . . . if the area had not been "kept up like it should" . . . They had their own standards and . . . took pride in leaving their areas in good condition after a night's work (p. 98).

Related, sometimes integrally involved, in these struggles to maintain standards is the necessity of controlling the pace and routine of one's work. Hood's respondents enjoyed being able to "pace their own work" (p. 98), as did Romero's and Glenn's. Glenn reports an effort on the part of employers akin to industrial speed-up when employers would attempt to add tasks if workers occasionally finished early.

> In order to finish everything, the worker was forced to do everything faster . . . some women maintained control . . . by defining and enforcing their own

standards . . . If they worked extra time, they did not want to be paid, if they
accomplished it in less time, they reserved the right to leave (p. 73).

Romero reports that women:

> who achieved a degree of autonomy in their work environment were often
> able to substitute the use of mental labor for physical labor. Planning and
> organization was essential for maintaining the house . . . in the most efficient
> manner (p. 85).

The mechanisms available to these women to achieve autonomy depended largely upon the structural features of their jobs. Domestic workers used
their flexibility to pressure employers to give them autonomy. Selection was
important here. As Glenn puts it:

> Over half of the women mentioned autonomy . . . as the main advantage
> of their work . . . This is in part the result of workers selectively retaining
> employers who are willing to leave them alone . . . By working for several
> employers, . . . they . . . were freer to quit one . . . (p. 71).

These women used the same techniques to pressure employers about their
wages. Not all workers have the flexibility to change employers. Those with
perhaps the least autonomy were the Hispanic women working in the border
factories studied by Fernandez Kelly and Garcia. Here, workers had no control over *who* they worked for — or *when*. The industry seemed attracted to
this type of worker because they constituted a labor force that would expand
and contract at the whim of the employer (pp. 280-81). These workers had no structural position from which to insist upon different treatment. They had no viable
alternatives.

Other mechanisms can be used to gain autonomy. Hood (p. 147) describes
the use of "cultivating techniques," in which custodial workers switched to day
work got to know the schedules and preferences of those in the offices they
cleaned, reducing the friction over interruptions.

Maintaining Dignity

Struggles for autonomy and control — and the achievement of them —
provided workers with a major source of dignity on their jobs. Other factors
were also powerful contributors. Their commitment to their jobs, the extent
to which they perceived their jobs as important, the extent to which they enjoyed doing their jobs were among these factors. To some extent, these factors
were related to the status or professional standing of their jobs. The administrators Collins spoke with were interviewed because they had been recommended as "leaders in their fields" (pp. 187-88). They took pride in their
achievements.

> An overwhelming number of the rewards mentioned were intrinsic to the jobs they hold . . . Most frequently the women seemed to be describing the pleasure of mastery and accomplishment . . . They talked about "doing something that worked," . . . "seeing projects completed," . . . "seeing others I've helped accomplish things" . . . (p. 192).

Clearly, there was a wide range of factors giving these workers a sense of dignity on their jobs.

> Women managers . . . enjoyed their positions . . . [though] they perceived strict limits on how far they could go . . . (p. 230).

Statham reports that a class distinction existed here, that women managers saw themselves as in a group separate from secretaries.

> [They] expressed a desire to distance themselves from the secretarial role . . . Said one, after working through an adjustment to a newly created job, "I would never go back to the secretarial ranks again." She felt she had "grown beyond that" (p. 231).

A desire for this status distinction is also seen in the *lack* of it among teachers, as reported by Spencer: "[Teachers] have to engage in such demeaning tasks as monitoring bathrooms and performing janitorial duties in their classrooms" (p. 174). This also occurred among nurses, as reported by Corley and Mauksch:

> Nurses undertook cleaning, fixing clogged commodes, washing beds . . . they were dissatisfied with this approach because it took time away from giving care to patients . . . [T]hey . . . do unskilled jobs like floor scrubbing because even domestic staff will not consent to be bullied (p. 142).

To the extent workers can move away from these "menial" tasks, they derive more dignity from their jobs. Even workers in jobs of relatively low status are able to do this. As mentioned in the last section, Romero's respondents (domestic workers) attempted to move from purely physical labor to a combination that included "mental labor" (organizing and planning), a source of great satisfaction to them (p. 85). Diamond also talks about the "thought work" the nurse's assistants he studied engage in, work that confers a certain amount of dignity (p. 48–49) — though it may go unrecognized.

Other perceptual mechanisms are also available, many of them related to the process of "honorific self concept" protection discussed by Hughes (1958). In talking about street hustlers, Miller says:

> Only when one frames these activities as illegal work rather than as crime can one understand . . . those who engage in them (p. 111) . . . Hustling for them is simply "illegal work" that underclass people often engage in just as upper-class people spend their time doctoring or lawyering (p. 128).

Hence, they do not see it simply as crime, but mostly as work. Romero describes strategies used by domestic workers to "minimize the personal cost of being a domestic."

> The women . . . attempted to eliminate the stigma attached to the occupation by making a distinction between maid and housekeeper . . . Identifying themselves as professional housekeepers . . . emphasizes the domestics' special skills and knowledge (p. 87).

These domestic workers also focused on the benefits of their working for their families, particularly in providing "extras" that their husband's earnings did not permit. In several instances, the families seemed to simply deny the fact that the woman was working (pp. 88-89), resolving the status question altogether. Another focus strategy, previously mentioned, was discussed by Hood (p. 98). The custodial workers she interviewed focused on the finished product of their labor, taking great pride in that.

These strategies, in addition to efforts aimed at maintaining autonomy and control, provided the women working in these settings with a certain amount of dignity. However, there were other factors that threatened their sense of dignity and esteem.

Asymmetry in Relationships

Many of these workers reported difficulties stemming from the asymmetrical nature of their relationships with others in the workplace. Often, social placement determined the asymmetry. For instance, many of these women dealt with men who were their superiors. This combination of gender and occupational dominance made it extremely difficult for the women to hold their own. "Rank" was pulled with varying results. One result was the "dumping" of work onto others, as observed by a secretary in Statham's study talking about men's relationsips with women managers and secretaries who said that "Men can get away with dumping their work onto someone else and walking out the door" (p. 231). This was also observed by Corley and Mauksch in their study of nurses: "The theme of "dumping" tasks onto nursing was very prevalent in comments about physicians" (p. 143). This seemed to happen because those in the situation were "counting on the underdog to fill the gaps" . . . (p. 141).

In the informal Amway family, the husband often pushes work onto the wife. Connelly and Rhoton note that

> The Amway woman is more often than not unmotivated to participate . . . [s]he often anticipates the extra work of their involvement — the products that need to be transported and the paperwork that needs to be filled out and transmitted (p. 249).

The ability — and tendency — for male managers to exploit women factory workers is also evident in Fernandez Kelly and Garcia's depiction of life in the border factory. "Frequently women are hired because they are bearers of highly replaceable, tractable and inexpensive labor" (p. 281).

And Hood (p. 103) describes efforts on the part of custodial workers to bring asymmetrical relationships with managers and those whose offices they cleaned (professors, administrators, etc.) into a closer state of symmetry — by their use of "cultivating techniques."

This theme is repeated in the dominating role physicians are reported to take in relationships with social workers, counselors, nurses, and nurse's assistants. As Rothman and Detlefs say about genetic counselors:

> Asked how doctors treat them, some were satisfied, some not: "I can't generalize. Some definitely respect what I have to say and my abilities, and some talk around me, over me — don't view me as a separate entity" . . . "A lot of doctors treat you like nurses. And they treat the nurses like subhumans" (p. 156).

The situation with abortion counselors was less ambiguous.

> Counselors must constantly affirm their worthiness to the professionals at the abortion clinic . . . [One of them said] "usually the social worker is on the bottom of the totem pole" . . . when it comes to professional respect, I don't find it readily available to social workers (p. 225).

In cases where power was given to the social worker, it entailed what Rothman and Detlefs call "autonomy by default."

> One of the counselors expressed it this way. "In some respects, because they don't take social serves and counseling seriously, it really gives you an opportunity to create your own situations" (p. 161).

Diamond (p. 48), as previously noted, discussed the nurse's assistants tendency to "keep moving," to look busy, least a Board of Health member or physician happen along and catch them "loafing." And Corley and Mauksch noted the traditional perception of nurses as "the physician's hand-maiden" (p. 136).

Principals definitely played a dominating role in the lives of teachers; again, the principals were usually men. As Spencer argues:

> Male domination in administrative positions means a hierarchical arrangement in which decisions in schools are made by males and carried out by females — a situation comparable to clerical workers and managers. In both situations, relationships between those in control and the workers became strained and impersonal and contacts between them decrease . . . managers capitalize on the sterotype that women want to please . . . orders given to women are disguised as personal requests that they find it difficult to refuse (p. 171).

Miller describes the male domination women street hustlers experienced in relating to their "men."

> The beatings and sexual assults female street hustlers received at the hands of their "men" . . . [and others] . . . were numerous (p. 125) . . . "Men" would simply not permit women to [solo] hustle . . . All who attempted solo hustling . . . did so only once . . . it was . . . a sort of stand for independence . . . [that] was . . . short lived (p. 119).

Other women encountered power differentials, resulting in problems in dealing with men as *peers*. Here, dominance was not built into the relationships, as with those described above, yet the men might act even more vicious if they were feeling particularly threatened. For example, Collins describes a nursing administrator having an encounter with a physician in which he said "You and your boss say you are an administrative person but you are a nurse to me and no nurse is going to tell me what to do." (pp. 195-96). This physician was obviously having difficulty making the transition from a dominant/subordinate relationship to one between peers. Martin discussed that policemen were having similar difficulties.

> Policewomen face interactional dilemmas because as police officers they are expected to behave with other police officers according to the norms governing relations among peers; as women they are expected to adhere to norms governing male-female relationships (p. 213).

Here again, past status inequities (based on gender) interfere with the participants' ability to form egalitarian peer relationships in the present. The policemen responded by reinforcing their "macho" culture of "raunchy" language, jokes, and gossip about the women that forced women into either a "whore" or "nice girl" mode of behavior, enhancing the woman's position as a "token" (p. 206).

Problems of asymmetry can also arise in relationships between women in the workplace, particularly if authority differences are reinforced by class or ethnic distinctions. This is seen most vividly (and discussed most explicitly) in Glenn's study of Japanese-American domestic workers. As she sees it, a major task facing these women is the necessity for balancing the personalism and asymmetry inherent in the mistress/domestic relationship.

> Personalism pervades all aspects of the employer-employee relationship (p. 65) . . . Despite the intimacy, however, there remained a not-quite surmountable barrier of status, reinforced by cultural and racial differences (p. 67). . . . [Said one woman] "Only a few families treat you real well," . . . (p. 68).

Glenn chronicles particular implications of this asymmetry for the worker: "In an asymmetrical relationship, the lower-status person has to be attuned to the feelings and moods of the higher-status person" (p. 68).

Diamond also notes a kind of status distinction in women-to-women relationships, those between the nurse's assistants and nursing home patients. Here, however, domination is achieved partly by depersonalizing the situation.

> The first assignment as the day begins is usually expressed like this. "Diamond, today you have beds 206 to 230." This did not refer to the beds I was to make, but to the people who occupied them (p. 45) . . . The rush is on to finish breakfast by 8:30, so there is pressure when one has to help several people to eat. The luck of the draw was noted in the question, "How many feeders you got today?" (p. 45).

As he saw it, this approach enabled the workers to see the patient as "an object of scorn," and to get on with their work.

Statham notes a different type of situation. Between women managers and secretaries there were actually fewer status distinctions than between men managers and their secretaries, though the status differences were there. Certainly, there was less domination and more concern that the secretary develop her own career. One secretary said "I think women are much more respectful of their secretaries . . . more appreciative of the things they do" (p. 232). And Statham observed "Women managers . . . were . . . seen as more supportive of the secretary as an individual with a career path of her own" (p. 233).

Perhaps the difficulty in separating secretarial from managerial work — and the racial and cultural homogeneity — makes status distinctions less pronounced. It is also possible that men, as a group, would (or do) maintain even greater status distinctions between domestic workers and nursing home patients than these female mistresses and nurse's aides described above.

Degradation/Devaluation

For some of these workers, the occupation itself was viewed as degraded. As workers, they would have encountered problems with devaluation or degradation regardless of their sex. This class effect is seen in the analyses of the political economy of the nursing home (Diamond), the border factory (Fernandez Kelly and Garcia), the abortion clinic (Rothman and Detlefs), and domestic work (Glenn). The implications are described vividly by Diamond:

> What happens when this web of social relations is placed into the contemporary terms of market discourse? (p. 49) . . . Concrete human relations get changed when they are transformed into the documentary reality of commodities . . . The reality of local, everyday reality is transformed — annihilated, actually (p. 50). . . . In the process of transforming these social relations into tasks, caring work is turned into a commodity (p. 51).

This process of depersonalizing the relationship degrades both the worker and the patient. Neither feels that their caring *work* or their caring *needs* are recognized.

> After these caring relationships are filtered . . . there emerge . . . separate in-
> dividuals ("beds") with sicknesses which demand discrete units of health care,
> and menial workers to feed, transport, and toilet them . . ." (p. 51).

Similar implications of the profit motive are seen in abortion clinics. As
Rothman and Detlefs says:

> A few of the counselors . . . explicitly stated the "business" end of abortions
> as the cause of the limitation in their role. . . . "This is a profit-oriented clinic
> . . . profit-oriented rather than woman-oriented" (p. 161).

Other authors discussed the workers' position in our political economy
more generally. Fernandez Kelly and Garcia describe the previously mentioned
need for high-tech factories to find an easily contractable work force to maintain their competitive edge. Glenn notes the ease with which domestic workers
can be manipulated in a situation that provides no structural guarantees for
workers' rights. Workers in such positions often face demands for hard physical
labor. As Glenn says

> Workers were expected to scrub floors on their hands and knees, wash clothes
> by hand, and apply elbow grease to waxing and polishing . . . the physical
> demands of the work are apparent in [their] descriptions. At least two women
> . . . felt their bodies or health had been wrecked . . . " (p. 60).

The strain of combining work and family demands were particularly tiring, a fact also noted by Hood in her description of third shift custodial workers
who existed in "a permanent state of exhaustion" (p. 99). And health problems that resulted from work involvement were reported by Miller in her study
of street hustlers (pp. 124–125).

Workers in jobs with little structural protection could be assigned demeaning tasks, given low wages, and, in the case of the street hustlers interviewed by Miller (p. 125), beaten by the "men" they were supposedly working
for. It was difficult for these women to find recourse for these difficulties. Some
protections help. Domestic workers are now covered by minimum wage laws,
so their salaries have improved relative to other workers, though they are
still quite low and the laws are unenforceable outside institutional settings.
Diamond describes a coworker who reacted to her wages within such a protected setting:

> . . . with a shriek after looking at her first paycheck — take-home of $209,
> after two weeks of work including a weekend. "$209?", she asked with a sense
> of shock, "How do they expect us to live on $209?" (p. 41).

Minimum wage does not necessarily guarantee a living wage. And Fernandez Kelly and Garcia describe the "balkanization of the work force" in high-
tech industries, where workers are purposely sought who will be unlikely to

unionize and, hence, unlikely to push for wage increases and other reforms. Even among the custodial workers Hood studied who belonged to the AFSCME union, several reported working a second job to support their families adequately (p. 278, p. 93).

Of course, it is not possible to separate totally these concerns about degradation and devaluation from gender. They are not class issues alone. Often, work is devalued *because* it is seen as women's work. And women within male-dominated occupations often find themselves devalued or degraded.

Concerning the first issue, the devaluation of "women's work," Diamond addresses the issue of "caring work."

> There is another dimension of what nursing assistants and others do that I will call caring work . . . yet this dimension (of caring) is invisible in the language of business and medicine, and is written out of the charts (p. 48).

As Collins puts it, "It is time to ask the questions, how much do we care about caring and are we willing, as a society, to offer respect and a living wage to those who do it for us?" (p. 200).

Following this argument, certain types of work are set aside for women to do and then the work is neither recognized nor fully rewarded. Glenn notes the fact that "Since the nineteenth century, domestic work has been an economic ghetto for women of color" (p. 57). Domestic work, which is women's work — women of color — is perceived to be "on the lowest status rung".

Occupations also *lose* status as they change from being male dominated to female dominated. Rothman and Detlefs note this transition for the genetic counselor.

> Genetic counseling had undergone a status decline (p. 152) . . . In the early part of this century . . . it was carried out by physicians, usually pediatricians, who were counseling parents of children born with birth defects (Sorenson, Swazey, and Scotch 1981) (p. 152) . . . Today's genetic counselors have a masters of science degree in human genetics and counseling . . . Almost all are women (p. 153) . . . A number of women go into genetic counseling because it is the "next best thing" to a career in medicine (p. 154).

Here, we see a higher status occupation serving as a "woman's ghetto." Admittedly, its status fell as it became more heavily female. A similar trend was noted by Spencer with regard to teachers. As the occupation became more heavily female, teaching came to take on conditions of:

> . . . low pay and . . . lack of control over [the] workplace. The conditons under which teachers work are [now] more similar to those of blue-collar workers than to those of professionals (p. 171).

Though Martin's account of policemen's desire to keep women out of their occupation does not explicitly discuss fears of status loss, that is certainly implied.

> The policeman's opposition to female officers is based on concerns about the disruptive effect of women on the division of labor, the work norms, the work group's solidarity, and on the sexist ideology that undergirds their definition of the work as "man's work" (p. 209).

In our culture, "men's work" is more highly regarded.

Having made it into male-dominated occupations, women face further barriers that are in themselves degrading. Statham describes the ". . . limitations on women's [manager] advancement; in all three institutions there was a definite point beyond which women could not move" (p. 226).

Salary differentials also existed, as discussed by Statham (p. 227) and Collins (p. 195). The administrators Collins talked with also discussed the general "reluctance to hire and promote women," as well as "prejudice against hiring a woman . . . [that] comes from the community" (p. 195). Statham also describes difficulties women managers had in having their competencies recognized, perhaps because of misunderstandings about gender-specific approaches to management (discussed more fully below). Martin notes other factors in the policewoman's work setting making it difficult for her to obtain recognition, including "limited assignments, instruction, . . . overprotection, . . . performance pressures" (p. 211).

These findings suggest that women generally face attempts to devalue or denigrate their work efforts. This is true for women in both high status and low status jobs, though certainly the combination of low status job *and* female status intensifies pressures toward degradation.

AS WOMEN WORK

The previous themes in this chapter describe issues both men and women encounter in the workplace. The following three themes emerged as issues that were peculiar to women workers. One issue concerns the question of whether there is a style of working unique to women. This issue was addressed directly by several of our authors. Related to that is the importance of bonding or relationships in the workplace and the question of whether this is in fact any more important or prominent for women workers. The true nature of this aspect of work is examined quite closely. Finally, we explore the seamless quality of these women's lives.

A Woman's Way

Several of the papers provide a direct comparison between men and women workers in the same occupation, permitting us to ask the sensitive yet intriguing question of whether or not the sexes dffer in their approaches to work. In considering this issue, one must confront the notion that women have traditionally been considered to be more people-oriented and less task oriented in their work than men. We did find some evidence that women are emphasizing the personal or relationship aspects of their jobs. Collins says:

> From these interviews with top women administrators in female fields, it is clear that the women have maintained the female socialized values of nurturance and the importance of the relationship (p. 200).

Connelly and Rhoton find that:

> Mary Kay [predominantly female] is different from Amway [predominantly male] in some important ways . . . Nurturance, caring for others, appears as a predominant theme in Mary Kay work (p. 261).

These traits are often used against women, as Spencer observes: "Managers capitalize on the stereotype that women work to please others and are more sensitive and honest and less mercenary than men" (p. 171).

Corley and Mauksch amplify this insight in their study of nurses.

> The commitment to client shown by nurses is defined as fitting into a female stereotype and, thus, as a natural by-product of a female role . . . A set of characteristics which would otherwise earn applause and prestige, can be neutralized, if not trivialized, when identified with the presumed natural consequences of low status attributes (p. 136).

"Typical" or expected female behavior can also work to their advantage, as Martin points out about the police. "Effective officers of both sexes appeal to "sex appropriate behavior" on the part of citizens as well as respect for the officer's authority to gain citizen cooperation" (p. 215).

However, our findings in total suggest that person orientation is not the primary or major type of orientation women take to their jobs. For example, Collins follows her observations about the importance of nurturance and relationship with a further observation about the importance of task. "They have enjoyed the opportunity to influence their organization and to make things happen" (p. 200).

Among the three papers directly comparing men and women workers, (Hood, Martin, and Statham), women's concern with task accomplishment is evident. Hood concludes that women custodial workers ". . . related more personally to their jobs than men did . . . [N]ot being able to do their work properly affected the women more negatively than it did the men" (p. 101).

The secretaries that Statham interviewed perceived that women managers actually do more of the work. "Women are the motivators and organizers, the ones with the organization and energy . . ." (p. 238).

Statham concluded that the women managers were both:

> ... task-engrossed, person invested ... [and] men [were more] image-engrossed, autonomy invested ... [The women] focus on getting the task done and investing in the development of others partly to that end ... [The men] talk more about the importance of their work for the organization than they do about actually doing the work (pp. 236–237).

The emphasis of the men on power and organizational position (image) is reiterated in Hood's observations of men custodial workers. In their reactions to a shift change, she noted that:

> Comments about custodians' powerlessness in their attempts to deal with management or that the "union was weak," were far more typical of male custodians than of the women (p. 101) ... The males' objections focused on hierarchy, patterns of domination ... (p. 101).

And Connelly and Rhoton find that:

> Amway [predominantly male] emphasizes one's position within the hierarchical chain of command even in the routine work of placing orders (p. 261) ... [while] Mary Kay work ... [has a] less rigid hierarchical structure [and] ... ambivalence regarding exploitation (p. 261).

All of this is not to say that relationships were *not* important to these women. Rothman and Detlefs noted that many genetic counselors told them "I like to work with people" (p. 154), and Hood allowed that ". . . females' concerns were expressed in terms of network, relationships and ability to care for their areas and their families" (p. 101).

Rather, women may be blending task and person involvement in unique and effective ways not previously recognized in the workplace, as stressed by Statham.

> The [differences found] call for a drastic rethinking of the distinction between task and people orientations in the management literature (p. 240) ... Women may not be managing *inadequately*. They may simply be doing so *differently*. The existence of these alternative approaches may represent strengths, not weaknesses, a fact which must be recognized in the literature and by those doing the evaluating. Otherwise, important contributions women can make to the art of managing will be needlessly lost (p. 240).

Women may have a unique style, but that style has apparently not yet been delineated in the literature. Performing in this different way, however, may not come easily. Martin quotes Spradley and Mann (1975, 6) as saying ". . . [I]t is often easier for a society to allow women to occupy new roles than to allow them some new style on performance within these roles" (p. 208).

However, many of these women themselves may not be aware of the women's movement, which may offer alternative self perceptions. As Miller says about the street hustlers she interviewed, "[They] were much more likely to define their own personal problems in terms of racial prejudice and discrimination or general social inequality than in terms of sexual inequality" (p. 125).

And Collins said about the hospital administrators:

> [Some] seem to have forgotten they were nurses. Their identification with their profession and with other women was difficult to discern. In one instance, a woman told me that she doubted her experiences could be applicable to other women . . . I remember feeling sad for her that she had lost so many connections in her life (p. 199).

Bonding/Relating at Work

These studies permit us to look at one aspect of women's supposedly unique style — the interconnection between task and people concerns — in some detail. For all of these workers, bonds were established in the workplace with client, peer, or supervisor; maintaining these relationships became a critical part of the work day. This concern was blended with the motivation to effectively accomplish the task. Statham emphasized the connection between the two realms. ". . . these women (managers) were *not* perceived as being *primarily* people-oriented. Their dedication and commitment to accomplish the *tasks* was thought to be equally important" (p. 238).

Their people orientation was apparently used to foster task accomplishment:

> The women's people orientation was seen as a way of accomplishing the task (p. 239) . . . Women managers believed personalized attention made their subordinates more effective and productive. [One of them said] "I feel that if my people are happy, they are going to do a better job for me and they do" (p. 239).

Diamond posits an even more integral tie between bonding and task accomplishment in the workplace.

> There is a special knowledge and skill involved in the caring work . . . There is the mental work . . . There is the emotional work . . . What distinguishes these is that they are social relations, not tasks (p. 48) . . . The work is not a set of menial tasks, but a set of social relations in which the tasks are embedded (p. 49).

In fact, the social relationship can considerably ameliorate the impact of a menial task. One of the nurse's assistants Diamond worked with put it this way. ". . . Some shit don't stink . . . It depends on if you like 'em and they like you, and if you know 'em pretty well . . . If you like 'em, it's like your baby" (p. 49).

"Cultivated relationships" could also produce tangible rewards. The custodial workers Hood interviewed reported that such techniques:

> . . . could . . . yield birthday and Christmas presents . . . Helping a faculty member move a file cabinet, or watering plants while someone was on vacation could mean a ten dollar tip or a fifth of scotch. One supervisor claimed that the workers in his section "made out like bandits" at Christmas (p. 103).

But even here, personal relationships seemed to foster task accomplishment. ". . . However . . . the custodians at Urban University used cultivation primarily in order to manage their work environment rather than as a means of gaining material reward" (p. 103).

Miller also found the instrumental and personal integrally bound together in the relationships the street hustlers she interviewed had with their "men." While these "men" were definitely business associates, Miller found that:

> For these women the personal side of the relationship far outweighed the business side in importance. As a matter of fact, one of the most common reasons for a "woman" to leave a "man" was when some occurrence made it obvious that the relationship, from his point of view, was entirely for business purposes. On such occasions, women would say: "He wasn't nothing' but a pimp . . ." (p. 115).

Interpersonal relationships were also an important feature of the domestic worker's situation. As Glenn puts it:

> Mutual trust and compatibility are important because employer and employee are thrown together in a situation in which there is little privacy. The worker has access to the most intimate regions of the household where she may become privy to family secrets. The worker, in turn, is open to constant scrutiny by her employer. A sense of mutual obligation (a carry-over of feudal values) also colors the tie between employer and employee (p. 66).

Relationship skills are also important in police work, as dealing with citizens is a major part of the required tasks. Again, it seems to be a matter of managing relationships in which tasks are embedded. As Martin says:

> Police officers face recurrent uncertainties in relating to citizens . . . [They] cannot depend on citizens to accept police definitions of the situation and must deal with denials, accounts, and efforts to activate irrelevant statuses . . . Although all officers occasionally face . . . deference refusals, such situations continually threaten interactions for policewomen who must find ways to turn them to their advantage, minimize their occurrence, and limit their effects on the officer's control of the situation (p. 214).

These workers find themselves using relationships with supervisors or clients to enhance their job performance. Both Romero and Glenn reported that their respondents relied upon personal networks for finding jobs. Glenn says:

> The importance of the personal can also be seen in the women's preference for personal introduction for job placement. Personal placements were seen as a more reliable way of finding a compatible, trustworthy employer than more impersonal means, such as ads (p. 66).

And Romero found that:

> In acquiring most of these jobs, the women relied upon "word-of-mouth." Their resources for information on job openings included husbands, sisters, cousins, friends, and neighbors. Thus, their networks were usually confined to the Chicano community. Women reported that family members usually assisted in obtaining employment as a domestic (p. 81).

In addition, Romero reported that these networks provided job training for younger women.

> Unique to the younger woman's introduction to domestic service was an apprenticeship period in which they accompanied a relative or friend. Two women would work together for a certain period of time (several days or weeks) until the newcomer decided she was ready to take on her own employers on a regular basis (p. 81).

Miller also found networks to be important sources of "occupational" information for Milwaukee street hustlers.

> Most street hustling is carried out in the context of deviant street networks . . . Such a network has fluid boundaries . . . and can be activated for relatively short or for extended periods of time (p. 112) . . . [Its] major function is to facilitate street hustling as an income-producing strategy . . . [They] often focus on a particular sort of street activity . . . [and provide] information about opportunities to make money on a hustle and potential threats about one's ability to do so . . . (p. 113).

But networks do more than this. As Miller found "In addition to being a source of information, deviant street networks may be a source of socio-emotional support, self-esteem, and courage" (p. 113). This type of supportive network also exists among the police. Martin says that:

> The policeman's "working personality" is shaped by the presence of danger and the potential for violence. These lead to a generalized suspiciousness and to isolation from the community . . . Set apart from the public . . . officers turn to their occupational community for support (p. 208) . . . [Also], close punitive control systems . . . have led officers to protect themselves from an

unpredictable public and their own officers through a cohesive, informative occupational community . . . (p. 209).

Hence, it is particularly devastating for women recruits to be excluded from these networks. If women are better at maintaining such relationships once begun, it will ultimately be to their advantage in the workplace.

In some instances, it seems that relationships were more satisfying (and productive) when women alone were involved. For example, Martin noted that among policewomen:

> One apparently successful approach is temporary sex segregation in training and initial assignment. In several instances where women were trained separately or assigned to work alone or together, and could not manipulate, compete with, or rely on men, they acquired the skills necessary to perform well (p. 218) . . . [This] benefitted the women who were reported to be "more self-reliant, utilize their own judgement, and make their own decisions." It also helped them gain the respect of their male counterparts who were "impressed by the many strengths displayed by the women" (p. 219).

And Statham noted a tendency for more satisfying relationships between women managers and their secretaries.

> Women secretaries (and the women managers themselves) felt that women managers formed better relationships with their subordinates. They were seen, first of all, as being more considerate (p. 231) . . . [as] better appreciat[ing] and respect[ing] their skills and capabilities (p. 232), . . . as more supportive of the secretary as an individual with a career path of her own (p. 233).

However, other authors noted a great deal of conflict in woman-to-woman relationships. This was particularly true in Glenn's accounts of the power struggle between the domestic worker and her mistress. And Diamond notes the depersonalized nature with which women nurse's assistants treat women nursing home patients. However, he sees the social structure pushing both parties in this direction.

> In the process of making people into nursing home patients and workers their social characteristics become blurred (p. 44) . . . The organization is based . . . on the separation of . . . women from women . . . Revolution, in this domain, can only be built up from models of women caring for women which are not intruded on by the capitalist patriarchal processes of commodification. To develop a caring-centered language and philosophy of nursing based on social needs, we will have to look to models of women living and tending to women (p. 46).

Rothman and Detlefs make the point that even if relationships between women are ostensibly harmonious, they may in fact be exploitative.

> When the [abortion] counselor does her work well, she gives the client the experience of being treated "as a person," . . . [I]n doing her job well, the counselor participates in her own and her client's exploitation. The point is most clearly illustrated in the profit-making clinics, which remain organized around profits, and counselors are used only to the extent that their presence contributes to profit (p. 164).

It seems, then, that maintaining relationships is an integral part of these women's work lives. However, this concern is not done in isolation from task accomplishment, but is rather a necessary aspect of doing the work. This insight brings home in full force the notion in Diamond's paper that work is not a list of tasks to be accomplished but a series of relationships to be managed. The work tasks are embedded in these relationships.

The Seamlessness of Life

The lives of these women had a remarkably seamless quality about them. Their lives are not composed of easily discernible, discrete compartments, as conceptualized by early role theorists. In contrast, the separate realms of their lives were interwoven, interdependent and mutually reinforcing. Perhaps Hood puts it most vividly in her discussion of the implications of a shift change for the custodial workers she interviewed.

> . . . [M]oving to day work . . . had far-reaching personal consequences for the personal and family lives . . . [T]he "single" managerial decision to move the custodians to day shift had far from simple consequences for the work lives of Millie Jones and her coworkers. This paper describes the kaleidoscopic effects of that change as it rippled through the[ir] lives (p. 95).

In adjusting to the shift change, the women workers in particular found themselves making major changes in other aspects of their lives, since all parts of their lives were tightly woven together.

Other authors make similar points. Some note the overlap in tasks performed in the work and family setting. This could cause overload in several ways. First, women need variety in their lives. Spencer talks about the teachers she interviewed.

> The seamless, overlapping quality of home and school was a particular problem for elementary teachers who had children, as they came home to the same kind of work they experienced at school. Talking only to small children during all one's waking hours created a need to have adult interaction and conversation . . . Yet, married teachers with children rarely spent any of their time away from their families because they felt guilty about leaving their children with baby-sitters (pp. 179-180).

Domestic and custodial workers also found themselves extending their work activities at home. Cleaning, either their own or others' spaces, comprised an enormous part of their total work activity. The same could be said of others in caretaker positions, such as nurses and nurse's assistants, though perhaps to a lesser degree.

The interdependence was problematic in another way: the role overload or time commitment involved. As Spencer says:

> While working women in general have been described as having a double day of work, I found that many teachers had a triple day of work. They taught all day, did most of the housework (including childcare), and then did more school work such as grading paper (p. 179).

Romero reports a similar phenomena among the domestic workers she interviewed ". . . Women working six to seven hour days, five days a week as domestics, experienced the common 'double day' syndrome known to many working mothers . . . " (p. 88). In fact, domestics appreciated the flexibility in their work situations largely because it allowed them:

> . . . to fulfill family obligations without major disruptions at home or work. [One of them said] "You can change dates . . . you can go later, and work later, just as long as you get the work done" . . . [and another said] "Most of the people I've worked for like kids, so I just take the kids with me. It's silly to have to work and pay a sitter" (p. 84).

The women Glenn interviewed noted how much simpler this juggling of schedules had become since domestics began cleaning different homes every day. One woman described her work schedule, many decades earlier, with a single family.

> It began at 6:30 in the morning when she left home to catch a trolley. She arrived at work just before 8:00, then "Wash the breakfast dishes, clean the rooms, make lunch, and clean up. Go home. Back at 5:00 to help with cooking dinner and then do dishes. Come, go, and back again. It was very hard. I had to take the trolley four times" (p. 59).

These domestic workers also found overlap between the two spheres in their search for jobs. As previously mentioned, family members often put them in touch with prospective employers. Miller noted a similar tendency for some of the street hustlers she inteviewed.

> Among female street hustlers in Milwaukee there are three analytically distinct, although occasionally intersecting, paths that lead to involvement in street networks. The first is related to membership in a particular domestic network . . . which seems directly or indirectly responsible for the recruitment of black women . . . despite . . . often heroic efforts . . . to prevent this from happening . . . especially . . . when there is some degree of intersection between domestic networks and deviant street networks (p. 115).

There was another way in which work and family realms intersected for these street hustlers, and that involved the care of children.

> ... Women who had children before being recruited were more likely to sustain contact with their families/households of orientation ... In every instance, [the] women ... either arranged for a familial network member to care for the child(ren) or were forced by the members of their households as well as by the realities of their lives to make such arrangements (p. 117).

These connections made them vulnerable to pressures from family members that could have a major impact on their work lives.

> ... [T]hese caretakers are in a position to inform the authorities of their whereabouts and activities should they decide it is in their interest ... to ... "slow down" a woman who is perceived to be moving "too fast" ... Caretakers also attempt to control their former female charges when they think they are in physical danger [i.e., nervous breakdown, drug addictions] (p. 118).

Children may also lead a women to place herself in danger of arrest.

> Several women interviewed described situations in which they were "on the run" ... and had returned home to see children on their birthdays or other special occasions or when they heard they were ill. This sort of behavior sometimes led to their arrest (p. 120).

As Miller puts it "children ... are often used to manipulate female street hustlers."

The conflict between work and family experienced by many women was summarized by Collins.

> Nearly all of the women mentioned that balancing their career and family responsibilities was currently a concern or had been in the past ... although a third of the women ... had never married ... [They] mentioned ... responsibilities for aging and ill parents (p. 197) ... Being a wife can affect one's career life adversely ... A nursing director who is single herself said, "A wife has two full time jobs. I don't know how they (her nursing staff) do it" (p. 197).

Collins says it for many of the women described in these chapters; they emphasize "their search for balance between their work and family lives" (p. 200).

The conflict implied in the search for balance between work and family can also emerge as a conflict between the demands of the family/feminine/private realm and the work/professional realm. Martin reports that the policewomen she interviewed tended to experience this conflict and resolve it by acting one of two ways on the job: by emphasizing the feminine ("the deprofessionalized woman") *or* the professional ("the defeminized woman"), As she puts it:

*Police*women view their female status as irrelevant to the job. They emphasize their "professionalism" and strong adherence to police norms and values including assertiveness, the willingness to use violence, the rule of silence, and physical support of the partner. They strive to achieve a high number of arrests, derive work satisfaction principally from law enforcement activities, and have made it clear they do not want to be "overprotected" by male officers (p. 216) . . . [They] are critical of . . . the female officers . . . they term "feebles" or "mediocres." . . . *Police*women are not comfortable on street patrol or with the task of controlling citizens' behavior. They are concerned about their own physical limitations, are fearful of injury, and believe street patrol is a threat to their femininity which is important on the job as well as off. They acquiesce to the sterotypic roles of mother, sister, seductress, pet (pp. 216-17) . . . They do not desire promotion . . . but rather seek administrative, clerical, or community service assignments or hope to leave policing in the near future (p. 217).

CONCLUSIONS

Our findings point to many aspects of women's work lives previously unappreciated or underemphasized. One point is that work *requires* the management of relationships. This concern is not an "extra" that women *choose* to emphasize over task accomplishment. Rather, task accomplishment depends upon the management of relationships. The job is a series of relationships to be managed rather than a list of tasks to be performed. As Diamond said, the tasks are embedded in relationships.

This dual emphasis is seen in women's attempts to gain autonomy, deal with degradation or subordination, and maintain their dignity. It is also seen in our discussion of women's unique approach to work. Perhaps women are simply more attune to this connection in their work; perhaps it has simply not been adequately explored among male workers. The literature on work and occupations has yet to take a hard look at the intersection between task and gender.

A second major point to be gained from this analysis is the remarkable facility many of these women show in maintaining dignity — often against incredible structural odds. Feelings of accomplishment and worth, satisfaction with one's working conditions, dignity and self-motivation do not seem to depend so much upon the professional standing and prestige of one's job as measured by traditional standards, as upon the amount of autonomy and control one can garner in the workplace. In some respects, this control may actually increase as traditional job prestige declines (and, perhaps, involvement in a bureaucracy increases). Whatever her position, autonomy and control are important predictors of the pleasure of work. This may partially explain common findings, perplexing to some, that women's job satisfaction remains relatively high despite their generally less desirable jobs.

The flexibility these workers had at work enhanced their ability to balance the ever-conflicting demands of work and family life. We were struck by the seamless quality of these workers' lives. One set of skills was relevant to many parts of life. And the demands of each realm inevitably impinged on the other.

Simultaneously, these diverse qualitative case studies suggest that many commonly held beliefs about women and work must be reexamined in light of the insights they provide. Ultimately, they pose questions for our entire conceptualizations of work and occupations.

REFERENCES

Hughes, E.C. 1958. *Men and Their Work*. Glencoe, IL: The Free Press.

——— 1974. Comments on "Honor in dirty work," *Sociology of Work and Occupations* 1:284–287.

Pavalko, R. 1987. *The Sociology of Occupations and Professions*. Itasca, IL: F. E. Peacock Publishers.

Sorenson, J.R., J. Swazey, and N. Scotch. 1981. *Birth Defects*. 17:191–192.

Spradley, J.P. and B. Mann. 1975. *The Cocktail Waitress: Women's Work in a Man's World*. New York: Wiley.

Stewart, P. and M. Cantor. 1974. *Varieties of Work Experience*. Cambridge, Mass.: Schenkman.

Part II

DOING WHAT COMES NATURALLY? THE CARETAKER ROLE

CHAPTER 3

Social Policy and Everyday Life in Nursing Homes: A Critical Ethnography*

TIMOTHY DIAMOND

INTRODUCTION

This is a preliminary report on a sociological research project in which I worked as a nursing assistant (or nurses' aide) in a series of nursing homes in the United States. Here, long-term care systems are being developed along the organizational model of business and nursing homes are considered an industry. This study focuses on the ongoing creation of that industry. It does so from the standpoint of the everyday life of some of the people inside, especially nursing assistants and patients. The study starts with my own situated experience and those of my coworkers, links these experiences to the social organization of nursing homes, and places these experiences and this social organization within the context of larger social and economic policies.

I began the project by attending a vocational school which trains nursing assistants. After completing the training, I worked full time in three nursing homes for a period of just under two years. The primary objective in undertaking the participant observation project was to get to know personally nursing assistants and patients over time, and to experience everyday life in different kinds of homes. This initial analysis describes some aspects of that everyday life and links them to social and political forces beyond them.

*This paper is part of a forthcoming book and first appeared in 1986 in *Social Science and Medicine*. The research was funded under grants from the Midwest Council for Social Research in Aging and the Retirement Research Foundation. Their support is gratefully acknowledged.

Some of the roots of this study are in medical sociology, especially that based in critical approaches to health care institutions (Friedson 1970; Gill and Twaddle 1979; Doyal 1979; Stacey 1982; Davies 1979; Campbell 1981). Gerontological research has also been informative (Neugarten 1982; Estes *et al* 1984; Ingman *et al* 1979; Luken 1987; Peterson and Quadagno 1985; Kayser-Jones 1981; Gubrium 1975; Newton 1979; Walker 1983; John 1984; Brents 1984). Ethnographic research in health care settings has been part of the background literature as well (Goffman 1961; Emerson and Warren 1983; Glaser and Strauss 1967). Feminist literature has been conceptually essential (Jaggar 1983; Harding and Hintikka 1983; DiIorio 1980). Almost all nursing home workers and most nursing home residents are women. both substantially and methodologically, the writing of Dorothy Smith has been especially instructive (1974, 1979, 1981). Smith suggests a method of critical ethnography, drawn from Marx and Engels' outline of the materialist method (1947) in which researchers begin with actual situations of people and link these activities to more general characteristics of the society. It is a method for exploring macropolitical forces in the micropolitical moments of their everyday execution.

AN INTRODUCTION TO NURSING ASSISTANT WORK

The owner of our vocation school stood tall in his three-piece suit on that first night of class as he welcomed the new nursing assistant trainees with a mix of medical and military imagery: "Welcome to the firing line of health care." We were recruits in an area of work that is being formalized as a new profession. While the job of nurses' aide has existed for many years, it is now being organized for nursing homes and home health care. By 1990 nursing assistants will constitute one of the largest and fastest growing occupational groups in the U.S. (Alexander 1983). While their work is supervised by the more highly trained registered nurses and licensed practical nurses, nursing assistants are by far the largest group of workers in nursing homes. Although some men do the work, almost all nursing assistants are women.

In the training course, we learned that we were to become members of the health care team, a part of the noblest of professions. We learned elementary biology, and how we were never to do health care without first consulting someone in authority; and we learned not to ask questions but to do as we were told. As one of the students, a black woman from Jamaica used to joke, "I can't figure out whether they're trying to teach us to be nurses' aids or black women."

Most of the students laughed at the joke; most were black women. The majority of the nursing assistants I met throughout the research were nonwhite. As a white man it was not always easy to explain to the people I met why I was studying and working this way. The director of the school turned out to be one of the last white men I was to see in this work, except for administrators and some patients. While men may own and direct nursing homes, it is not a white man's land inside. So my place in this world was continually at issue, and I explained it in different ways to my classmates and to many of the nursing assistants and patients. I told them I was doing research, and most were supportive. It was not as easy with administrators, however. Initially, I indicated on my job applications that I was a researcher interested in studying nursing homes. The people reading the applications were, I inferred, not nearly as supportive, for not once was I offered a job. They seemed not to value research from this vantage point. Eventually, I began to emphasize my training as a nursing assistant rather than as a researcher. Using this strategy, I was soon employed. I was not alone as a man, yet as one of the very few white men, my presence was never without suspicion. It was one of the administrators who first expressed the general skepticism of my presence when he asked, "Why would a white guy want to work for these kind of wages?"

It was a shock when I finally began to work and experience the conditions to which he was referring. Deborah Saunders (all names in this paper are fictitious), a coworker, expressed the situation with a shriek after looking at her first paycheck, "take-home pay of $209, after two weeks of work, including a weekend. $209?", she asked with a sense of shock; "How do they expect us to live on $209?" Deborah's complaint was no idle grumbling over low pay. She was expressing, and indeed living, a contradiction present in certain emerging forms of wage labor. In some service sectors, occupied overwhelmingly by women, pay rates fall below the actual cost of subsistence (Beechey 1978). This appeared to be the case for many nursing assistants with whom I worked. Many, if not most, were sole supporters of a family. At $104.50 per week, which is $3.50 per hour minus deductions (15 cents above minimum wage), they often complained about not having enough money for essentials — food, rent, utilities, transportation, and their children's needs. In short, the wage creates poverty; the newly professionalized health care workers earn less than family subsistence even with a full time job. The feminization of poverty, in this case, seems to extend to full time workers. Solange Ferier from Jamaica summarized it, "You know, Tim, I done this job for six years in my country. One thing I learn when I come to the States — you can't make it on just one job." Most of the nursing assistants I met work more than one job if they can, and live in hope of overtime. Even a full time job at slightly over minimum wage is not enough. 'Minimum' wage turns out to be an abstraction; it may make sense to policymakers and economists, but it is considerably less than minimum in these people's lives. The policies that name these wages as 'minimum' are far removed from the everyday contingencies that this pittance involves.

ECONOMIC POLICY AND THE PATH OF POVERTY

I worked in both private and state-subsidized homes. From the conversations I had with patients in these homes I conclude that in the U.S. there is an economic life course involved in being a long-term patient. Meeting people in different homes disrupted my image of nursing home life as a static existence. One does not 'end up' in a nursing home; one proceeds on a path that is the consequence of social policy and the embeddedness of nursing homes within the organizational model of business and industry. In the U.S., care is based on ability to pay. Long-term patients tell about living through the phases of Medicare, private resources (if any), bankruptcy, and public aid. Given the present economic arrangements for long-term care, a patient moves along a path; the more time in long-term care, the poorer one becomes.

There are two types of nursing homes, distinguished by the hours of 'skilled' nursing compared with those of 'intermediate' care that is provided. I worked in both types. Medicare enters at the beginning of an acute health crisis and pays most of the bill. Yet this is a short-term, rehabilitation-centered program: it has time, sickness, and dollar limits. This is the United States' only federal program for long-term care, but it is actually a very short-term program: one is supported only for a matter of months. It is probably more correct to say that the U.S. has no federal long-term program, except for Medicaid, which is funded in part by the states. Medicaid, a form of public aid, pays a nursing home for care only after a patient has become indigent. Since long-term care can mean years, indigence is frequently a part of nursing home life.

Many patients told me of their fears as those last weeks of Medicare drew near and, for example, that "damn hip wouldn't heal." Every day Grace DeLong asked me to hand her her checkbook and bank statements. At the time she had $10,000 in life savings, having worked as a secretary all of her life. She stared at the book for long periods every day, as though to clutch those savings. She lived fearing that they would be drained from her. She had seen it happen to others. Nursing homes are expensive. Costs vary by home from $1500 to $3000 per month. Medicare lasts only a matter of months, after which patients are on their own, relying on whatever personal resources are available through insurance supplements and savings. As mentioned above, most insurance policies, like Medicare, pay only when one is classified as in need of skilled care. Joyce Horan was nervous that insurance people would visit her; she was afraid they would see she was better enough to be reclassified as only needing 'custodial' or intermediate care, be dropped from the rolls, and probably sent to a different ward or home.

Jim McCheever was not so lucky. Jim was 78 years old, had an inoperable brain tumor, and was surely dying. He lasted only six months so in some ways he was not even a long-termer. Right to his death, Jim remained sturdy, stoic, and, for the most part, continent. Unfortunately, this worked to his disadvantage. It was determined that he did not need skilled nursing care, and so was not eligible for Medicare. The social policy is that the government will help based only on a strict criterion of medical need. Increasingly, a patient's illness must be such that it fits into one of the predefined categories that are part of the emerging 'prospective payment' systems. Jim did not fit into any category. I knew his family well enough to learn that, because of this, it cost his 78-year-old widow over $17,000 to pay for his care during his last six months. Living through long-term care means feeling constant insecurity over having to pay to live in a home, while at the same time realizing the impossibility of doing so for long. It is a journey toward indigence. Grace DeLong, seeing it coming, and clenching her checkbook, used to go on and on in her fear; her pleas were quite high-pitched and frenzied, "Get me out of here! I can't stay here! I've got to get out of here!" A passer-by or someone who had only a fleeting contact with her might interpret her clamor as senile ranting. But she was afraid of losing that $10,000. She had no one at home to care for her, and felt trapped.

There are many patients who really do need to stay in nursing homes. Some, like Grace, simply have no other place to go; some are confused and unable to cope with life on their own; some are sick or weak or frail; some have run out of money. Many enter a nursing home by a combination of these forces. Some of these people may regain strength and maintain a relatively high level of physical and psychological functioning; then they are placed in intermediate wings or floors or in separate facilities. Although patients' psychic or physical states may stabilize, their economic base never does.

When resources are depleted, there is public aid. In the abstract language of government, Medicare and Medicaid are two different 'support systems' for older people. In actuality, living through these policies, they are sequential: a person moves from one to the other and it is a movement toward becoming a pauper. Under Medicaid, the government, partly federal, partly state, pays the nursing home a per capita fee for care. It is not exactly correct to say that a patient 'receives' this public aid; it is closer to say that she or he is 'on' Medicaid. The state pays the nursing home, not the patient. What the nursing home gets currently amounts to about $1500 per month. What the patient receives of this is about $25 per month, or less than a dollar a day. This is a severe economy, even for bedridden patients. Personal items, phone calls, cigarettes, coffee from the machine — and $25 is gone by the middle of the month. On public aid, nursing home life is the life if a pauper.

Contrary to the popular image of rest or retirement, nursing home life is not an economically stable situation. This became evident in conversations I had with people who linked the experience of private-pay and public aid in their own lives. The women and men I met at the expensive home started out in the posh two lower floors. When their money had run out, they were moved to the public aid wings, there to receive noticeably inferior care. There was a certain pressure within the home that many residents complained about. The management had made it clear that they preferred more short-term Medicare patients, since these patients were worth more. One could feel a murmur of fear among the public aid patients that many would be asked to leave or go to another home. No doubt this would happen to some. I know because I met women and men in the poor homes who had started as private pay residents in other homes and had been forced to leave them. Meeting them made me understand that there is a distinct economic progression in nursing home life — the longer one stays the more impoverished one becomes, and the more unstable one's environment becomes.

Frequently, nursing homes are approached in our thinking as though they were a series of separate places: the idea is to find a good one, or a good model and eliminate the bad ones. To live in long-term care, however, may well refer to homes in a series rather than *a* home. One does not live in just 'a' home, but moves through a system — a maze of different wards, floors, and homes.

The relationship these people have to the society, then, is precarious even before one begins to consider their physical or psychological conditions. These organizational disruptions (moving from one home or ward to another) are beyond the internal workings of a particular home and something about which anyone inside, including those with authority, can do little. They are a by-product of current social policies related to long-term care. These policies themselves breed a fear that derives directly from living in the society. When Grace was screaming "I've got to get out of here!", she was screaming not just at the nursing home, but also at her society beyond it. I came to change my image of nursing home life as a static enterprise. It is not sitting in a chair 'doing nothing.' Rather than being passive, it is always a process. The policies that shape this environment inform every moment of nursing home life. Each person is situated somewhere on an overall turbulent path. Each person sits in a chair, or lies in a bed, often appearing motionless, but is moving and being moved, however silently, through the society.

THE EVERYDAY MAKING OF PATIENTS

Another image of passivity that I carried into the research related to preconceptions I had about patients. Having 'ended up' in a nursing home, I thought of them as recipients of someone else's acts, acted upon rather than acting. Patients are formally defined into the organization in a passive way: that is, they are named in terms of diseases, and their basic record of care — the chart — is all about what health care goods and services are rendered to them, about what is done to them, not about what they themselves do. It appears as a passive existence to outside observers, visitors who get snapshot views and carry snapshot imagery of people 'just sitting.' Working in the local reality of everyday relations dissolved that image. From here there is another way of thinking about nursing homes that conceives of patients as actually quite active. The question might be asked, "What kind of work is involved in surviving in a nursing home?" The notion of passive runs close to making patients objects, which, at worst, leads to the ongoing presumption that "they are out of it," and even at best leads only to questions like, "What can we do for them?" Yet as one gets to know patients it becomes clear that almost all are thinking, conscious people, however fragile and intermittent that consciousness might be. This point of departure presumes patients to be present, actively aware, conscious, at some level — participants in the setting, not just acted upon, and struggling to be at the helm of their own consciousness, even with all the appearances to the contrary.

I say 'struggle' because there can develop within nursing homes an impersonal ethos in which frail, senile patients are assumed to be 'out of it.' They are inserted into an impersonal mode with pervading notions that their minds are 'gone.' Yet, getting to know people in their ongoing lives, it becomes evident that being in long-term care is not just a passive existence. It is also very active. It takes a lot of effort.

Nursing homes are medical environments. They are not short-term hospitals for these people, yet still they operate on the organizational model of a hospital. When one enters a nursing home, a chart is slid into its slot, there to record the units of health care one receives — all related to the first page of the chart, the diagnosis, or sickness category. One is a patient, treated in an environment that mimics a hospital, with its spotless, sanitized floors, its PA system blaring, its white-uniformed staff, its air of emergency.

In our daily round of work, as in the schooling, the texts and the manuals, nursing assistant work was defined in a task-centered, physical way. The first assignment as the day began was usually expressed like this, "Diamond, today you have beds 206 to 230." This did not refer to the beds I had to make, but to the people who occupied them. The first task was to wake the residents, get them up if at all possible, and prepare them for breakfast and medications. This was the hardest part of the day for many nursing asssistants, and a source of continual sharing of jokes and complaints. It was hard because it was so hard for the residents, and something they fought against, so the first moments of the day were often spent in conflict. "Work all my life waiting for retirement," Ms. Black used to grumble, "and now I can't even sleep in the mornings." I used to try to explain to her that this was a hospital — at least we followed hospital regimens here — but at 7 A.M. that made little sense to her, or to me.

After the patients were awakened, those who were able to leave their beds were transported to the dayroom for breakfast. Some residents could not perform all the complex tasks of eating, and had to be helped. The rush was on to finish breakfast by 8:30, so there was pressure when one had to help several people eat. The luck of the bad draw was noted in the question, "How many feeders you got today?" 'Feeder' referred to a patient who needed help eating. The one who is doing the eating becomes the object in this term, the object of feeding, and under the pressure of time, an object of scorn. Buried underneath this pressured moment, however, was the act of feeding a frail, sick person — a delicate process, requiring much skill. To learn the extremely slow pace of an old person's eating, or how to vary portions and tastes, how to communicate nonverbally while feeding — these are refined skills, but unnamed, indeed suppressed, by the dictates of the organization.

After breakfast, the 'menial' tasks began that would occupy the assistants until lunch: showers or bed baths, toileting or bed pans, changing beds, taking vital signs, continually charting it all. The body was recorded. 'Vitals,' a word drawn from the Latin word for 'life,' was a continual activity. As the work is lodged in our current vocabulary, it is part of a medical regimen, meaning blood pressure, temperature, pulse, and respiration. Since many people had identical vital signs day in and day out for all their years of residency, this procedure seemed more like a ritual than a requirement of health care, at least to residents, who frequently mocked it, "I guess you got to make sure I'm alive again today, eh?" 'Vitals,' in the homes, meant physical life, not biography, emotions, or social milieu.

It seems hardest of all for these people to cope when their behavior is called a disease, when that link between this confused present and that known past is severed. Yet even to be placed on certain wards and floors is to be treated as mentally impaired. Meanwhile, a constant life in a total institution is a source of confusion (Goffman 1961) especially for older people. At the very time of their life when they are struggling to maintain their own cognitive abilities and sanity, they become enmeshed in a cultural ethos that says they are "going through their second childhood" or they are "out of their minds." Many residents express anger at this ethos, but a nursing home is not a place where anger is spoken about or permitted. Patienthood is an engulfing identity and, over time, many residents seem to become resigned in the face of its power.

Yet, sometimes the anger has a clear social and political content. Ms. Black had been a math teacher. At 74, when I met her, she was confined to a wheelchair and had lived through the economic pathway to the public aid phase. She was furious that, as a result, she had lost complete control over her Social Security check. It was absorbed by the institution as partial payment. She would sit in her wheelchair in the hall and yell, "Where's my Social Security? Get me the administrator! I want my Social Security checks!" Once or twice the administrators did stop by to explain to her that her check was only part of what it cost to keep her there. That was not an adequate explanation for her. She would get frantic in her fury, trying to move beyond the logic of that answer, trying to reclaim control over the old-age support to which she had contributed all her working life. When she yelled too much, the health care staff took over to calm her, sometimes through chemical means. Her anger was then charted in ways congruent with the world of patienthood: "Ms. Black was acting out again today."

Although a nursing home is often a chaotic and angry place, there are within each home and within most patients pockets of creativity, of insightfulness, or competence. Patients are active participants in the setting in complex, humorous, and gracious ways. "And how are you today?", a visiting volunteer or physician or minister would ask Mary Ryan, frequently in a voice too loud. "Oh . . . fine . . . " she would respond, though very slowly." . . . And you?" Mary was being polite, as she always was to outsiders. She was not fine, she was miserable. She complained about her restraints all day, and after the visitors were gone, she would complain about them once again. The question "And how are you today?" from a stranger had very little to do with her ongoing life. But in this snapshot visit and irrelevant question, she graciously carried on the conversation, as we all do, with "Fine, thanks. And you?" Meanwhile, the visitors, unaccustomed to her slow, spacey manner (for they lived their lives at a much faster pace than she), and full of presumption about the institution, walked out the door with a vaguely focused sympathy: "Poor Mary — a shame she's so out of it."

While they no doubt mean well, many of the visitors, like the above, will never be more than strangers, at least emotionally, to the patients. Some patients have friends within the nursing home, but for the most part the home, too, is a gathering of strangers, people alone with others. Some sit next to each other for months and years and do not talk to each other, often do not even know each others' names. One can look out on a room where 40 or 50 people are eating and hear little or no conversation. Residents seem alienated from one another. Ties to the world, even the local world, diminish as the overwhelming passification process of patienthood sweeps over. People curl in socially, as they are continually remade into patients.

'Curl in,' however, does not mean passivity. Life inside the home is neither rest nor passive nothingness; it is a repository of effort. It is passive only to outsiders, who with snapshot methods, create a 'them' and a 'we,' and create a passivity. In our creation of images and concepts of passivity, what the patients do while sitting there doing nothing is outside our understanding. Meanwhile patients in long-term care are actively engaged in the work of being a patient.

As a historical process, this creation of the impersonal mode of patienthood is accelerating. Soon nursing homes in the U.S. will be reimbursed on the basis of an abstract, quantified index, just as hospitals now are on the basis of diagnostic related groups. This index will be derived in a purely mechanical fashion, based on what is called activities of daily living, the components of which are the time it takes to feed, transport, and toilet any given patient. The patient as a subject in this process is further obliterated, becoming the acted upon, encased in a discourse of crude behaviorism.

It is also a discourse based on the isolation of individuals. A patient is not defined or diagnosed or written about in terms of social relations in or out of the home, but in terms of sickness. At the end of the evening, Claudia Moroni, age 66, used to go to visit her mother, Maria, age 88; by an odd set of circumstances, both were residents of the home, though on different floors, separated by different medical categories. Then they were told that they could no longer visit at night. It seems Claudia became too fond of crawling into the bed with her mother, and cuddling with her. The report of this decision appeared on their separate charts in this way: "Claudia is no longer allowed to visit her mother after 8:00 P.M. At night they practice lesbianism."

This was not the only time I encountered references to 'lesbianism' as a taboo in nursing homes. However, I mention this incident at the conclusion of this section not to raise the issue of homophobia, but to illustrate the separation of relational units, the isolation of individuals as individuals, that seems to be an essential part of making people into patients. Each person is defined as a separate unit, to be treated, charted, and charged. The power of the medical model is such that for some, like Claudia's mother, every act is interpreted as a manifestation of disease. Patients seem to expend considerable effort holding fast against the force of these ideas.

THE INVISIBILITY OF CARING WORK

In one home it was emphasized repeatedly that the two most important tasks nursing assistants had to accomplish were to make sure patients were available to take their medications and to be sure that everything we did was charted. "If It's Not Charted," read a large sign behind the nurses' station, "It Didn't Happen."

Nursing assistants are trained in and judged in terms of the performance of physical tasks, like taking blood pressure and pulses, giving bed pans, and turning, showering and feeding patients. When these tasks are accomplished, they are coded and recorded in the all-important link between that work and the outside world — the chart. Recording tasks on the chart fits them into the overall organizational scheme of things, called health care. In terms of this participation, what nursing assistants do is considered unskilled.

I found the work that nursing assistants do far more complex than a conception of 'unskilled' or 'menial' would imply. Much of what they do does not fit into the chart as it is constructed at present. This other, nonphysicalist dimension of what nursing assistants, and others might do might be called *caring work* (Finch and Groves 1983; Diamond 1984a). The social relations involved in holding someone as they gasp for breath fearing that it might be their last, or cleaning someone, or laughing with them so as to keep them alive, feeding them or brushing their teeth, helping them hold on to memories of the past while they try to maintain sanity in the present — these are constant, essential, and difficult parts of the work. They are unskilled and menial practices only if nursing assistants are presumed to be subordinates in a medical world. Yet this caring work is invisible in the language of business and medicine, and is written out of the charts. On the chart it is physical life that is monitored and recorded.

Formally, nursing assistants' tasks have nothing to do with talking with patients. It is, in fact, probably more efficient not to converse. In two of the homes we were explicitly not allowed to sit with patients. Should the Board of Health appear, or one of the occasional physicians drop in, this would appear as loafing. We were told to keep moving, unless we were charting, for to keep moving is to look busy. Supervisory nurses are under considerable pressure to see that all tasks get charted, and that all the patients' units of health care are properly recorded.

Yet there is work beyond this merely physical work that remains invisible and unmentioned. There is a special knowledge and skill involved in caring work. It begins with being in touch with someone else's body, and its need for constant, intimate tending. There is the mental work, much of which is only obvious when it is not done, as when someone turns up poorly dressed, or becomes incontinent when it was the nursing assistant's job to insure against it. There is much more emotional work — holding, cuddling, calming, grieving. There is a great deal of thought work — tending to one patient, thinking of another. What distinguishes this kind of work is that it involves social relations, more than simple tasks. The tasks themselves are only part of wider social relationships, though the only part that gets documented in the formal language and record keeping of the work. In the charting process (but not before), these tasks become the reality of the job, and become separated from social relations.

The lesson that nursing assistants' tasks are performed within the context of social relationships was taught me best by Mary Gardner, a fourteen-year veteran of nursing assistant work. It was she who told me, in all seriousness, that "some shit don't stink." I asked her to explain a bit more what she meant. As she was teaching me how to make a bed, she made it perfectly clear: "It depends on if you like 'em and they like you, and if you know 'em pretty well; it's hard to clean somebody new, or somebody you don't like. If you like 'em, it's like your baby." A bit later she made reference to a man with whom she had had to struggle every day: "But now take Floyd, that bastard, that man's shit is foul." Through her explanation it became clear that the work is not a set of menial tasks, but a set of social relations in which the tasks are embedded.

At this point in the development of nursing homes, the social relations of caring work which contextualize these patients' and nurses' aides lives are relegated to an oral tradition. They are not incorporated into the textbooks or charts or reimbursement schemes. They are erased from the formal record. Or perhaps they do not happen at all. For, in this environment, if it's not charted, it didn't happen.

THE COMMODIFICATION OF CARE

As systems of long-term care develop in advanced capitalist societies, they increasingly come to be defined in terms of business. The nursing home industry is supposed to be a business based on care. 'Care' is the basic stock-in-trade, that which is advertised, bought, and sold. There seems to be a question at this historical moment that is still worth asking, even as nursing homes proceed on what looks like an inexorable course toward corporatization. Can caring be a business? What happens when this web of social relations is placed into the contemporary terms of market discourse? How does day-to-day care for human beings get turned into a commodity?

One day, in a lecture to the workers on our ward, the administrator of one of the homes reprimanded the nursing assistants with a dictum commonly heard in staff meetings: "I hope I don't have to remind you," he said, "that a nursing home is a twenty-four-hour-a-day, three-hundred-sixty-five-day-a-year business." He took for granted that he was operating a business, and was chiding us to be more productive in those terms. Business was a taken-for-granted reality for him. Yet the business model is not a natural fact, but a historically specific mode of organization. The everyday work of human caring and the social relation between career and patient is molded into the language of business costs, beds, profit margins, cost-accountability, turnover, bottom lines. The power of this logic is such that these terms are made to seem reality itself, and dominate everyday life in the homes.

Nursing homes are major growth corporations, growing in rate of profit, and becoming increasingly private, and multinational in ownership. It is an industry, also, that is being built from a world system of labor. The abstract dictate of multinational capital to search for ways of reducing labor 'costs' creates a situation in which Third World nurses, usually trained in their own countries, are imported to work in First World nursing homes. Nursing is becoming a part of the world economy (Diamond 1984b). In the U.S., for example, supervisory nursing is often done by Filipino nurses. These women and men are well-trained medically in their own country, although in a markedly different culture than that of the U.S. In the daily life of a nursing home, this creates some chaos, both in terms of the nurses' difficulties with the colloquial language and customs of the States, and in terms of their often bitter feeling of exploitation, since working conditions for them are not what they were told when recruited. Yet their difficulties with the cultural tradition and language is of little consequence to the formal order of the organization, which requires only that they are adequately trained in the profession and science of health care. That a nursing staff can be in charge by virtue of this training, but unable to understand the social customs or slang of a patient, is not even considered a paradox in the business terms which dictate the employment of foreign nurses. By the time this 'capital-labor' relation is translated into cost effectiveness for the corporation, the day-to-day chaos it creates has become invisible.

Concrete human relations get changed when they are transformed into the documentary reality of commodities, when care is encoded in reimbursement concepts. The local reality is erased from the view of those whose contact with nursing homes is mediated by these abstract business terms. One of the key notions that facilitates this translation is cost accountability. To make sense in the language of cost-accountability, units of service have to be coded into dollars and cents, care into units of care. One day during our clinical training we had completed all our assigned tasks and had returned to our instructor to see what our next order might be. After some reflection the R.N. instructor suggested, "Why don't you go do some psychosocial stuff?" Hearing this pseudo-scientific notion for the first time, one of the student trainees (whispering 'moron' under her breath) whipped back, "What do you mean, talk to them? What do you think we've been doing all day?" We had continually conversed with our patients while tending to them. Now we were receiving a new, distinct managerial directive and it could fit into the cost-accountability of the administrative logic, like vitals or showers. Now we could go talk to (or, rather, "do some psychosocial stuff with") the patients and it could be entered into the records as a discrete nursing task, and be separately charted and charged under the heading of hours of nursing care.

For another example, in one home, Saturday night dinner almost always consisted of one cheese sandwich and watery tomato soup. This dinner was carefully recorded and open for inspection, with one slight twist. The administrative heading that this meal comes under is nutrition, for which we have units of measurement. Each tray had a card on it with the amount of protein and carbohydrates that the food purportedly contained; we had to turn in the cards after every meal. So the records showed that each resident got x grams of carbohydrates and y grams of protein — what becomes in that frame of reference a nutritionally balanced meal. The State Board of Health inspected one day, and the rumor was that they were particularly concerned with nutrition on this visit. The inspection consisted of examining the computerized records. We passed the inspection.

In each of these examples, the reality of the local, everyday life is transformed — annihilated, actually. The administrator's admonition to us that this was a business was certainly correct, more than I imagined when he spoke it. In this language people are market phenomena. It begins in defining people as bodies. The body is conceptualized and treated and recorded in a quantitative way compatible with reimbursement. Terms like beds, costs, turnovers and profit margins are taken for granted as part of nursing home life. These are economic units. The discourse of nursing home life becomes subsumed under that of nursing home management.

Generating a commodity involves transforming a good or service from its everyday meaning as a support of social relationships into an abstract meaning for private profit. Even more than hospitals, which operate with high technology, nursing homes throughout the Western world depend on caring work as a means of profit. In order for commodities to be created, social relations must be redefined. In the process of transforming these social relations into formal tasks caring work is turned into a commodity. Caring work is turned into discrete and quantifiable tasks; these then become the nuts and bolts that allow nursing homes to run as enterprises for profit. The caring relations are coded into measureable and cost-accountable tasks: talk into 'psychosocial stuff,' emotional into technical, the cheese sandwich into units of protein, quality into quantity. The cheese sandwich is disconnected from the world, or, rather, is transformed from something it may or may not be (i.e., good food) into what it must be: units of costable measurement. Measures are scattered throughout the chart, linking the ongoing daily care to business and, in the process, remaking it.

One of the dangers of this transformation is that the local reality of patients' lives can become invisible and the caring relations remain implicit and unnamed. After these caring relations are filtered into the documentary reality (Smith 1974) what emerges in their place are separate individuals ("beds") with sicknesses, which demand discrete units of health care, and menial workers to feed, transport and toilet them — tasks which are all measured in time units required to execute the tasks. The charts record individuals broken down into units of costable measuement; these units can then be built back up as commodities. Life inside the home can then be talked about in terms congruent with any other capitalist organization producing a product for profit. This is the logic of commodities, a logic that informs every moment in the day-to-day production of nursing home life.

CONCLUSION

This study is about alternatives within nursing homes, not alternatives to them. None of this discussion leads to the conclusion that nursing homes should not exist. They could, however, be radically reorganized. I presume that it is preferable that people with common needs for nursing care live in groups rather than alone, and that it is preferable that a society provide nursing homes rather than insist that those people be taken care of by kin (Finch and Groves 1983). As a result of the forthcoming rise in the population of old people, dependency/caretaking relations will be an increasing feature of social life (Walker 1983). In this study, just as patients and nursing assistants constitute its empirical base, I propose that they be considered a vital voice in nursing home research and political action. They know a lot about how they would like their lives to be different, and analysis of their situation can provide concrete bases for change. Their everyday life provides the counterlogic against which to evaluate the industry, profit logic in which it is encased, and a point of departure for deconstructing it.

The starting point for the counterlogic is the presupposition that patients are conscious of and active in the world in which they live, and active in its daily construction. It is not a situation of passivity. There is action, resistance, some expressed need; this is a point from which change might proceed. This is different from policy directed toward nursing home life from the outside in. It is different because in this procedure the people and their relations — not the homes — are the units of analysis. Approaching the analysis in this way is to move away from a sociology of structures, and toward one grounded in people's actual everyday situations. The discussion of the pathway to proverty offered an example of the results of this change of focus. In the lived experience of current policy, it is not a question of designing good homes and sanctioning bad ones, but of designing a policy that will stabilize the turbulent path that is now beyond most patients' control.

This is a historical period in which there is great need for an overall long-term care policy. I arrive at this conclusion from talking with many patients who were shocked and confused upon arriving in their nursing home(s). They were frightened of their future precisely because of the absence of existing social policy that would enable them to predict it. They were lost in a society that has little or no national long-term care policy.

The research objective here is to to start with everyday situations and link them to social policy. I would argue that many social policies now do not reflect an understanding of their consequences for everyday life. In this procedure one gets to know people over time and studies how their lives are shaped by policies. This necessarily involves a redefinition of who constitutes the social actors in social policy to include not only those who make policies, but also those who live them out. To include the latter is to conceptualize nursing home patients not just in terms of their sicknesses, but also as social and political beings, and to listen to their world, even its babble, for its social and political significance.

Nursing assistants and patients are not classes of people who are essentially silent and passive. They communicate ideas and emotions with specific social and political content — content which is tied directly to the conditions of the organization and, in turn, to the society. Nursing assistants wonder why after 40 hours of work they still have to seek overtime just to survive; they wonder why the work they do, even if it is tending to someone during their last days, or even to their deaths, is still dismissed as menial and unskilled. Residents frequently express a desire to reclaim control over their own social security checks, and wonder why after paying into social security all their lives they are now reduced to public aid; they wonder why they have to be hungry again one hour after their Saturday night dinner; and why the staff is so convinced that they are crazy. These are questions that permeate life on a ward. They are derived from social conditions. The method of analysis I am suggesting involves seeing these people within the context of these social conditions as political participants in the ongoing production of everyday life, though at the present time caught in a set of relationships over which they have little or no control.

From the accounts of the people with whom I spoke, it became clear that living through current Medicare policies creates its own insecurities, while living through Medicaid is to face the life of a pauper. In addition, these policies give rise to economic instability and often residence not in 'a' home, but in a series of different wards, floors and homes. These policies can be reconstructed, and one way to begin is to explore how they disrupt everyday life.

I also raise issues concerning minimum wage, conceptions of nursing assistant work, the encasement of the hospital environment over time, passive versus active conceptions of patients' lives, the social relations of caring work, and the task-centered quantitative focus of current business-centered organizational models. All of these issues are drawn from everyday experiences (Smith 1981).

In this method research is not teleological, that is, it does not seek the answer to the perfect nursing home. The object, rather, is to work toward empowerment for those whose lives become objectified in this context. One does not lay out a utopia and work backwards. Nor does one deconstruct commodification *en masse*, as a whole; it is deconstructed word by word proceeding from the everyday activity, the local reality, of the people encased by it.

Current patients and nursing assistants tell us that the lives they are living now portend what is to follow. They are in a way pioneers. How much of their knowledge gets recorded depends in large part on how effectively researchers bridge the worlds of the everyday and its larger contexts and cultivate the methods for giving them speech. When we get to know patients and nursing assistants as social and political participants, they offer a different perspective on Social Security, Medicaid, caring work, nursing, and old age. The issues I raise in this study grow out of just a few of the societal relations being lived out in nursing homes, there for us to learn about, or, more to the point in terms of this method, there for the women and men inside to teach.

REFERENCES

Alexander, C.P. 1983. "The new economy," *Time* May 30:62–70.

Beechey, V. 1978. "Women and production: A critical analysis of some socio-logical theories of women's work." In *Feminism and Materialism: Women and Modes of Production*, edited by A. Kuhn and A. Wolpe. Boston: Routledge & Kegan Paul: 155–197.

Brents, B.H. 1984. "Capitalism, corporate liberalism and social policy: The origins of the Social Security Act of 1935," *Mid-American Review of Sociology* 9:23–40.

Campbell, M. 1981. "Social organization of knowledge research on nursing," Paper presented at International Nursing Conference: *Research—A Base For the Future?* University of Edinburgh.

Diamond, T. 1984a. "Caring work," *Contemporary Sociology* 13:556–558.

Diamond, T. 1984b. "Elements of a sociology for nursing: Considerations on caregiving and capitalism." *Mid-American Review of Sociology* 9:3–21.

DiIorio, J. "Nomad vans and lady vanners: A critical feminist analysis of a van club." Ph.D. dissertation, The Ohio State University, 1980.

Doyal, L. 1979. *The Political Economy of Health.* London: Pluto Press.

Estes. C., L.E. Gerard, J.S. Zones and J.J. Swan, eds. 1984. *Political Economy, Health and Aging.* Boston: Little, Brown.

Emerson, R. and C. Warren (eds). 1983. "Trouble and the politics of contem-porary social control institutions," *Urban Life*, Special Issue, Volume 12.

Freidson, E. 1970. *Profession of Medicine.* New York: Dodd Mead.

Finch, J. and D. Groves, eds. 1983. *A Labour of Love: Women, Work and Caring.* Boston: Routledge & Kegan Paul.

Glaser, B. and A. Strauss. 1967. *Awareness of Dying.* Chicago: Aldine.

Gill, D.W. and A. Twaddle. 1977. "Medical Sociology: What's in a name?" *In-ternational Social Science Journal* 29:369–389.

Goffman, E. 1961. *Asylums.* Garden City, N.Y. Doubleday.

Gubrium, J. 1975. *Living and Dying at Murray Manor.* New York: St. Martin's.

Harding, S. and M.B. Hintikka, eds., 1983. *Dis-covering Reality.* Boston: Reidel.

Ingman, S., C. Mac Donald and R. Lusky. 1979. "An alternative model in geriatric care," *Journal of the American Geriatric Society* 27:279–283.

Jaggar. A. 1983. *Feminist Politics and Human Nature.* Totowa, N.J.: Rowman and Allanheld.

John, R. 1984. "Prerequisites of an adequate theory of aging: A critique and reconceptualization." *Mid-American Review of Sociology* 9:79–108.

Kayser-Jones, J.S. 1981. *Alone and Neglected: Care of the Aged in Scotland and the United States.* Berkeley, CA: University of California.

Luken, P. 1987. "Social identity in later life: A situational approach to understanding stigma," *International Journal of Aging and Human Development,* forthcoming.

Marx, K. and F. Engels, 1947. *The German Ideology,* edited by C.J. Arthur. New York: International Publishers.

Neugarten, B.L., ed. 1982. *Age or Need:? Public Policies for Older People.* Beverly Hills, CA: Sage.

Newton, E. 1979. *This Bed My Center.* London: Virago.

Peterson, W.A. and J. Quadagno, eds. 1985. *Social Bonds in Later Life: Aging and Interdependence.* Beverly Hills, CA: Sage.

Smith, D. 1974. "The social construction of documentary reality," *Sociology Inquiry* 44:257–276.

——. 1979. "A sociology for women," In *The Prism of Sex* edited by J.A. Sherman and E.T. Beck. Madison, WI: University of Wisconsin: 135–187.

——. 1981. "The experienced world as problematic: A feminist method," *Twelfth Annual Sorokin Lecture.* Saskatoon: University of Saskatchewan.

Stacy, M. 1982. "Who are the health care workers? Patients and other unpaid workers in health care," Paper presented at the International Sociological Association Conference. Mexico City.

Walker, A. 1983. "Care for elderly people: A conflict between women and the state," In *A Labour of Love: Women, Work, and Caring,* edited by J. Finch and D. Groves. Boston: Routledge & Kegan Paul: 106–128.

CHAPTER 4

A Belated Industry Revisited: Domestic Service among Japanese-American Women

EVELYN NAKANO GLENN

Since the end of the nineteenth century, domestic service has been an occupational ghetto for women of color. Native whites shunned it because of its degraded status, preferring even the worst industrial jobs to domestic servitude (Addams 1896; Watson 1937). This left the field open to those who had little choice, including large numbers of black, Chicana and Asian-American women. These women were forced into wage employment by the uncertainty of husbands' and fathers' earnings, yet were excluded from most industrial and white collar jobs by a race and sex stratified labor market.

Despite their image as a "successful" minority, Japanese women were no exception: they faced the same restrictions as other women of color. Prior to World War II they were barred from employment in offices and stores, and excluded from manufacturing firms and government. Thus, many turned to private household work. In 1940 over half of all employed Japanese-American women in the San Francisco Bay area, foreign and native born, were employed as domestics (U.S. Census 1943). Even after World War II, when the more virulent forms of anti-Asianism had abated, Japanese-American women remained disproportionately concentrated in this category.

This discussion draws upon material from a larger study of Japanese-American women domestic workers in the San Francisco Bay area (Glenn 1986). In that study, I examined the experiences of three generational cohorts: pre-1924 immigrants (issei), the first American born generation (nisei) and post-World War II immigrants (war brides). Qualitative data were obtained through open-ended inteviews with 48 women. These were comprised of fifteen issei, aged 65 to 91; nineteen nisei, aged 48 to 84 (of whom 12 had been raised exclusively in the United States and 7 had spent part of their childhood in Japan — the latter referred to by the special term *kibei*); and 12 war brides, aged 41 to 55. Fourteen *issei*, two *kibei* and one war bride were interviewed in Japanese, the remainder in English. An initial interview of one to three hours and a follow-up of half an hour to two hours was obtained from each participant. The interviews covered immigration and/or childhood marriage, employment history, experiences at work, attitudes about work, relations with employers, family and household arrangements, and health issues. Supplementary information was also obtained from informant interviews with 30 men and women who were long time residents; by attending church functions, senior center gatherings, other group meetings and functions, and informal social events; and from the U.S. Census and a few early surveys, community directories, church histories, and newspaper files.

HISTORICAL BACKGROUND

Just as all other forms of work have been transformed by the advance of capitalism, so has the organization and structure of household employment. Thus the image of domestic service as static and unchanging, is belied by the dramatic alterations in both conditions and content of work during the past hundred years.

The most significant change has been the shift from live-in service to day work. Prior to the twentieth century servants in the United States, who were primarily young single women, resided with their employers (Katzman, 1978). Black, Chicana, and Japanese-American domestics differed from earlier native and European-American servants in that they were usually married and lived out. Only a few *nisei* I interviewed had worked as live-in "school girls" before marriage. One who did so in the 1930s echoed the complaints of earlier generations of European immigrant domestics who reported that the lack of boundaries and being constantly "on call" interfered with their freedom (Salmon 1897). She recalled she had to go straight home from high school every afternoon. She undertook one major cleaning task such as dusting or ironing, then prepared supper and cleaned up afterwards. After this, she was supposed to be free to study. However, her employer frequently expected something extra: babysitting when they went out, preparing and serving dinner to guests, or tutoring the children in their homework. Dinner parties on week nights were a special bane:

> Dinner would be at 8:00, and they'd have some guests who passed out from drinking. Finally, at 10:00, she'd say, "Could you send for dinner?" I remember I put the serving dishes in the oven to wash the next day. By the time you finished serving and washing, I'd have to do homework after midnight . . . I was a terrible student — I'd fall asleep in class.

While some live-in domestics liked being included in the household and treated as a member of the family, many found the combination of constraints on their freedom and lack of restraints on employers' demands in residential service onerous. Live-in service also interfered with married women's family responsibilities. Thus, other things being equal, Japanese women preferred day work positions.

Until the 1930s, full time nonresidential positions with one employer were fairly common. Women worked either as all-around household help for middle class families employing only one servant, or as "second girls" in multiservant households, performing a variety of tasks under the direction of a housekeeper. Full time positions gave workers stable employment, set hours, and a chance for a private life. But this was a restrictive arrangement. To provide all-around services, they had to put in an extended day, which typically began with breakfast clean up and ended with clean up after the evening meal. The day was broken up by an afternoon break, during which the *issei* usually returned home to prepare a meal or do chores. A domestic worker I interviewed described her typical work day, which began at 6:30 in the morning when she left home to catch a trolley. She arrived at work just before 8:00, then:

> Wash the breakfast dishes, clean the rooms, make lunch, and clean up. Go home. Back at 5:00 to help with cooking dinner and then do the dishes. Come, go, and back again. It was very hard. I had to take the trolley four times.

Partly because of the extended hours in full time domestic jobs and partly because of the greater availability of day jobs, all the married women in the study eventually turned to day work. They worked in several different households for a day or half-day each week and were paid on an hourly or daily basis. The work day ended before dinner, and schedules could be fitted around family responsibilities. Many women worked part time, but some women pieced together a 40 or 48 hour week out of a combination of full and half-day jobs. These women preferred all day jobs because they disliked having to rush to complete two houses in a day, as well as having to travel between them. However, full time day positions were not always available, and women had to settle for ten or twelve half-day jobs. Most of the homes in which the Japanese day workers were employed were modest. In San Francisco, many employers live in apartments and do not need or cannot afford more than a few hours of outside help each week.

Historically, the content and definition of domestic service has shifted along with the changes in the economy and the family. Prior to the industrial revolution, the work of servants in America was not very different from the work of other members of the household. Since most goods consumed in the home were still produced there, a major portion of servants' duties consisted of what would today be considered production, including spinning, cultivation, food preservation, manufacturing consumables, such as soap and candles, as well as household implements (Salmon 1897). Similarly, in preindustrial Japan, servants were engaged as extra hands in household production. In prosperous farm families, for example, servants were used as laborers in the field or in silkworm cultivation (Embree 1939).

With industrialization, domestic service came to refer to a narrower set of activities: namely, "personal services which resist packaging or mechanization" (Chaplin 1978, 99). More specifically, it referred to care and maintenance activities: cleaning, laundry, preparing and serving meals, child care, and the overseeing of these. Today, domestic employment is defined in terms of a loosely-conceived set of "domestic" activities taking place in a particular setting — the household. Interestingly, even though the main core is made up of housecleaning and laundry, women categorized as domestics perform a variety of other tasks, which include not only productive activities, but also expressive functions. For example, companionship was an important aspect of the work in many situations, particularly in situations where a woman had worked for an elderly employer for many years.

Overall, the most important duty is cleaning, and, especially (in the earlier period) laundry. Before World War II, laundry and housecleaning were two equally time-consuming household chores. Employers frequently hired different workers for the two sets of tasks. Laundry was viewed as less skilled and more menial, and was often assigned to women of color, such as the Japanese (c. f., Katzman 1978). Two *issei* and one *nisei* mentioned taking in laundry at home while their children were young and they were unable to go out to work. Ironing was also a specialty of some *issei*. Many *issei*, however, did both laundry and housecleaning, and both were arduous because of the low level of household technology. Cowan (1976) suggests that the availability of household help slowed the adoption of labor-saving devices by middle class housewives. The *issei*'s accounts confirm this by showing that employers stressed hand labor. Workers were expected to scrub floors on their hands and knees, wash clothes by hand, and apply elbow grease to waxing and polishing. Some sense of the work and of the typical routines in the pre-war period is conveyed by Mrs. Murakami's description of her routine, when she began work in 1921.

> When we first started, people wanted you to boil the white clothes. They had a gas burner in the laundry room. I guess you don't see these things any more — an oval-shaped boiler. When you did day work, you did the washing first. And if you were there eight hours, you dried and then brought them in and ironed them. In between, you cleaned the house from top to bottom. But when you got to two places, one in the morning and one in the afternoon, you do the ironing and a little housework.

The physical demands of the work are apparent in this description. At least two women — one *issei* and the other *nisei* — felt their bodies or health were wrecked by the strain of combining this kind of hard labor with heavy responsibilities at home.

THE CHARACTER OF DOMESTIC WORK

The most striking features of domestic work — and these are linked — are its preindustrial character and its degraded status. The shift from live-in service to day work can be viewed as contributing to the modernization of domestic work, so that it more closely corresponds to industrialized labor. Work and non-work life are clearly separated, and the basis for employment becomes more clearly contractual, *i.e.*, the worker sells a given amount of labor time for an agreed-upon wage. Yet as long as the work takes place in the household, it remains fundamentally preindustrial — "the belated industry" as Addams (1896) called it. While industrial workers produce surplus value which is taken as profit by the employer, the domestic worker produces only use value (Braverman 1974). In a society based on a market economy, work that produces no exchange value is devalued (Benston 1971). While industrial workers are integrated into a socially organized system of production, the household worker remains atomized. Each domestic performs her tasks in isolation, and her work is unrelated to the activities of other workers. Finally, whereas the work process in socially organized production is subject to a division of labor, task specialization, and standardization of output, domestic labor remains diffuse and nonspecialized. The work consists essentially of whatever tasks are assigned by the employer.

Although household work has escaped forms of degradation found in industry — detailed division of labor, machine pacing, and standardized procedures (Work in America 1973) — it ironically shares negative characteristics of deskilled industrial jobs; it involves almost exclusively manual labor, provides few challenges, and offers little chance to learn new skills, advance, or gain recognition.

Research on housewives suggests that those doing domestic work may respond much like workers in industrial jobs. A sample of English housewives complained about monotony (doing the same thing over and over); fragmentation (doing a series of unconnected tasks); mindlessness (thinking of things other than the task at hand); excessive pace (rushing from one task to the next); and social isolation (being alone in the house too much) (Oakly 1974). Paid domestic work may be even more alienating than unpaid housework for the family. The tasks that are hired out tend to be the most physical and least creative tasks: scrubbing floors rather than baking cakes. Unlike the housewife, the domestic does not even get to enjoy or use the final product of her labors, the clean kitchen, shiny furniture, etc. Moreover, by selling her labor, the domestic employee is stripped of the rationalization available to the housewife that the work is being performed purely for the sake of "love" or other higher motives.

These characteristics of housework indicate some areas of similarity to lower level manual occupations, but do not fully account for its exceptionally low status. Why is domestic service typically ranked below even the most routine machine tending jobs? Skill, or rather the lack of it, might be a possibility; however, as Caplow (1954) suggests, there is ambiguity about the extent of skills required. Leslie (1974) points out that public attitudes about the skills of servants have always been contradictory. Since at least the late nineteenth century, employers have been vocal in their demands for good experienced help and lamented what they saw as deteriorating standards. Quite possibly, it is because "domestic skills were familiar and therefore easy to ignore" (Leslie 1974, 82). Thus, Caplow (1954) suggests that the "real" reason for the low status of domestic work is not skill, but rather the belief that personal service (by which I take Caplow to mean personal subordination) is inherently degrading. In addition, housework involves what Hughes (1958) calls "dirty" work, literally in that it deals with dirt and figuratively in that it is considered distasteful and therefore is sloughed off onto subordinates by those in higher status positions.

ON THE JOB

Against this backdrop, a major task of the analysis is to discover how the worker finds meaning and satisfaction, dignity, and self-esteem from work that most people consider unchallenging at best and repugnant at worst. The resolution of these issues for these women was found in the dialectic between the multiple forms of oppression they experienced and the strength, determination, and grit they developed in order to gain control and autonomy in their lives.

The oppressions they faced were numerous. First, the work itself was very hard. As stated above, several women felt they had "used up [their] bodies" over the course of their work lives. While 12 women indicated that they generally disliked the work, 6 pointed specifically to the fact that it was too heavy, that it was a strain and required too much effort; "I don't like to clean house, too heavy, you know" (Mrs. Takagi); "I don't like it; it's hard work" (Mrs. Tajima). Preferred tasks tended to be those that were more creative (e.g., arranging flowers, baking cookies), skilled (sewing or nursing), service-oriented (e.g., care of elderly), more circumscribed (cleaning bathrooms), or less strenuous (ironing). The disliked aspects were for the most part the heavy physical work, such as scrubbing floors and washing windows.

The physical, demanding nature of the job remained despite the technological inventions many of these women had witnessed over the course of their working lives. The women said they had to work steadily and quickly, as shown in such remarks as, "You can't let things go," "You can't stop and take a break too long," "I don't want to get behind," "You have to keep watch all of the time," "You want to finish that place in four hours . . . you can't fool around." To completely clean a house or apartment in four hours requires a fast and constant pace that makes the work tiring. Thus, Mrs. Uchikura, who was accustomed to heavy work as a charwoman in a hospital, nevertheless, said, "Doing hospital work is easier than doing housework. Housework you have to work as hard as you can. You have to clean everything. Scrub." Mrs. Frankel describes domestic work as "hard — healthwise, it's hard labor." Mrs.

Inaba, another war bride, said that even though she had done her own housework for fifteen years, the first time she went out and did four straight hours of housecleaning in someone's home, she was exhausted.

Thus, despite the improvements in household technology and decreased size of households, domestic work remains a physically demanding occupation. The women described the work as not very complicated in that it involved skills that they learned while growing up or that are easily acquired on the job and 9 of the women described the work as "easy," "just play." Nevertheless, they also reported that the volume of work and the pace at which it must be done was arduous. It takes them some time and experimentation to learn techniques to get the work done quickly and to minimize strain.

Another problem these women faced had to do with pay and benefits. Because of its atomization, domestic work remained invisible and was not subject to regulation until after World War II. Domestic workers were excluded from protections won by industrial workers in the 1930s, such as Social Security and minimum wages. While sporadic attempts were made to organize domestics in large cities, such efforts rarely succeeded in reaching more than a small minority, and Japanese-American women appear never to have been part of any efforts to do so. Thus, there was no collectivity representing their interests. It goes without saying that they received none of the benefits accorded organized workers, such as sick days or paid vacations. If a worker did not work, she got no pay, and when the employer went out of town, the worker was put on unpaid leave. (The issei, of course, never took vacations themselves.)

Because there were no industry standards, wages varied according to idiosyncratic factors. Informants and subjects reported that the going rate for day workers around 1915 ranged from 15 cents to 25 cents an hour. The top rate rose to around 50 cents an hour by the late 1930s. Full time domestics earned between 20 and 35 dollars a month in 1915, while school girls earned from 2 to 5 dollars a week. I was unable to find wage data on other semiskilled occupations in the Bay Area, but other studies have found that domestic wages during this period compared favorably with those of factory, sales, or other low-level female occupations (e.g., Katzman 1978).

Some of the variation in wages can be attributed to market factors. Wealthier and larger households were expected to pay more. The rate in some communities was higher than in others, probably due to the balance of labor supply and demand. For example, Alameda had a higher proportion of Japanese seeking domestic work and had among the lowest wages. Still, what is striking is the seeming arbitrariness of wages. Some workers were willing to work for less than the going rate, and some employers were willing to pay more than they had to to get a worker.

It may be useful to examine the process by which wages were set in individual cases. Generally, the employer made an offer and the worker either accepted it or looked for another job at a higher wage. While the shortage of workers established a floor for wages, the effect was not uniform. What employers offered depended a great deal on personalistic factors. Sometimes the worker benefitted, if the employer especially wanted to keep her for personal reasons. At other times, employers used their knowledge of the worker's personal situation to push wages down. Both of these elements are evident in Mrs. Takagi's story. Her employers liked her and paid her more than the going rate. However, during the depression, employers cut back on help, and Mrs. Takagi couldn't find enough work to fill the week. One employer knew about her plight and offered her an extra day's work if she would take a cut in pay.

> She said to me, "I tried another girl, because you get the highest wages. I tried a cheaper one, but she wasn't good. She never put the clothes away and never finished the ironing . . . What do you think — take three dollars and fifty cents and I'll keep you. I'll give you two days a week." I wanted the money — I was trying to save money to get my son [from Japan]. So, I said, "Fine." She said, "I'll never tell anybody." Here a month later, she told every friend . . . Everybody said, "You're working for so and so for three dollars and fifty cents and here you're getting four dollars." See that's the way all the jobs were. A lot of people worked for two dollars and fifty cents, so I was just crying.

Mrs. Takagi weathered this crisis and did not have to take cuts from the others, but she felt humiliated at being caught out, and she still smarts at recalling the incident.

Today, domestic work still lags behind industrial employment in worker protection and benefits, but at least they are now covered by Social Security and federal and state minimum-wage laws (Women's Bureau 1975). Some observers feared the *issei* would not apply for benefits because of past bad experiences with the government and their negative attitudes about welfare. Contrary to expectation, the *issei* were not reluctant to apply for their rightful benefits once they were given information and instructions.

As for current wages, women in this study were earning more than the federal minimum wage — many substantially more. However, as in the past, the range of wages is wide. Despite the privatized nature of domestic work, most workers are aware of the going rate, since their friends tend to work in the same field. Thus, some workers knew they were receiving less than the market rate, while a few indicated that they were earning more. Workers also sometimes accepted different rates from different employers. In all these cases, both interpersonal dynamics and "human capital" (*i.e.*, value of skills, strength, speed, etc.) were factored into the calculations.

Since most of the women had worked for the same employers for some time, problems arose, not so much from starting pay, as from the lack of raises. Once a woman was in a job, she tended to stay on at the same wage at which she started. Generally, the women reported that it was easier to start a new job at higher wages than to get a raise on the old one. Only half of the women indicated employers gave them automatic raises. The personal nature of the relationship made it difficult for them to ask for a raise. Sometimes it was because the employer was elderly or ill and relied on the worker, but the most common reason mentioned by the women was more general feelings about the personal nature of the relationship with the employer, "She's so nice that I don't like to ask." If they ask and are refused, they'll feel hurt and have to leave. Even if it is granted, the employer might be resentful. Even Mrs. Kadoi, who said she asked for raises every two or three years, said, "Certain people are so nice, it's hard to ask. So, I'm going to wait for the right time to come." Thus, even though workers are in sufficient demand that employers cannot take advantage of them as they might have before the war, they can exploit the workers' feelings of obligation and the pervasive norm of "niceness" to keep wages down. This is apparent in Mrs. Loring's case, where she describes her employer as "more like a friend." She noted that she had not received a raise in seven years. "They never offered a raise, but they're so nice . . . like at Christmas . . . she, the doctor [her husband] gave me some money and told me to buy something."

The converse situation can also occur. The employer may offer higher than market wages because she is especially attached to the worker or prefers her company. Mrs. Inaba, a war bride, started working for one woman in the early 1960s at 15 dollars for a six-hour day; by the mid-1970s, she was getting 20 dollars for three or four hours. She explained:

> They gave that to me because [she said]: "You do it just so, you're very particular." She doesn't care about the money. "Any amount, if it's you." So, the money part was good. But my body was used up.

In another case, an *issei*, Mrs. Nishimura, said she was already getting more than the average ($4.50 an hour), and yet:

> They're offering to raise my salary. But I tell them that since I'm old, I'm very slow. They say I'm doing a good job, though. A very good job, I'm told — although I really shouldn't say this. And I'm such an all-purpose person. I can do anything . . . sewing, everything. So they are eager to have me work.

CONTRADICTIONS IN THE EMPLOYEE/EMPLOYER RELATION

As the above incident illustrates, the relation between employees and employers in domestic service is highly personalistic. This personalism coexists with an asymmetry that is also inherent in the relationship. The interaction between personalism and asymmetry creates many contradictions for the worker.

Personalism pervades all aspects of the employer/employee relationship. Employers are concerned with the worker's total person — her moral character and personality — not just her work skills. The domestics in the study, in turn, judge their employers on moral and characterological grounds. For example, they spoke approvingly of employers who were good Christians, neat and clean in their habits, intelligent, well-educated, and happy in their family life, and disapprovingly of those who were dirty or messy, lazy, insensitive, lax in disciplining children, disrespectful toward relatives, or who drank too much. The importance of the personal can also be seen in the women's preference for personal introduction for job placement. Personal placements were seen as a more reliable way of finding a compatible, trustworthy employer than more impersonal means, such as ads. Mutual trust and compatibility are important because employer and employee are thrown together in a situation in which there is little privacy. The worker has access to the most intimate regions of the household where she may become privy to family secrets. The worker, in turn, is open to constant scrutiny by her employer.

A sense of mutual obligation (a carry-over of feudal values) also colors the tie between employer and employee. The domestic is expected to demonstrate loyalty while the employer is expected to concern herself with the worker's welfare. This mutuality is viewed as a positive feature by some workers. Mrs. Yanari recalled that after the start of World War II, her employer urged her to come to live with her for protection. Mrs. Shinoda remembers her first employer's concern fondly.

> That lady was really nice. She would turn on the light and heat in my room and stay up, waiting for me to return. Usually, she would go to sleep early, but even if I returned late at night, she would wait up for me with the room heated up.

The tie is premodern in that obligations transcend purely economic or instrumental considerations. The commitments are usually lifelong and continue even when the terms of the original "contract" can no longer be fulfilled (the domestic can no longer perform the same duties or the employer can no longer afford to pay adequately). Thus, many elderly domestics, *issei* and *nisei*, report that they are treated with special consideration by long-time employers. They are picked up and brought home from work and released from heavier duties. Mrs. Kubota, a 72 year-old *kibei*, said:

> Now the places I go, because I'm old, they know I'm weak. So it's just a hobby. Talk, talk, and then going home, they take me home, because it's hard.

The obligation is reciprocated in that workers often maintain a life-time commitment to employers. Preretirement-aged women, who would like to cut back, also refuse to abandon their older employers. Mrs. Suzuki, a *kibei*, had been employed for over 20 years by an elderly retired professor; even though she wanted to spend more time babysitting for her daughter, she tried to go a half a day every month. By doing so, she was helping this woman maintain her independence:

> I don't charge too much. She's a professor, retired now, 84. I mop the floors and do things for her. She's very particular, so she doesn't want anyone else. So, I can't quit. I'm stuck. She's nice, so I don't mind helping her. Her family

is in Los Angeles. She has a family, but they don't help her. When her son comes, she says she's fine. She's blind, but doesn't tell him she's blind. She's afraid that he'll put her in a nursing home. So, I help her. My husband helps, too, doing her gardening. (Mr. Suzuki is a factory worker, not a gardener, by profession.)

For many women, the relationship with particular employers is analogous to family ties. They describe their situations as "just like a family thing," or say that their employers "treat me like a member of the family." For some *issei* and war brides, the tie is charged with emotional significance; it substitutes for kin ties that they never had or that were lost when they left Japan. Mrs. Takagi, an *issei*, was especially close to her second employer, Mrs. Cox, whom she describes in these terms:

> She was a Christian. Any time I came down with a sickness, she said, "Call a doctor." If I go to the hospital, she came every day. She was almost a second mother. If I didn't have her help, I would have been badly off. I went to Japan, and she gave me help with that.

Mrs. Howell, a 43 year-old war bride, has had two unhappy marriages, but gets a great deal of emotional succor from her elderly employers.

> I'm working for all German peoples. I'm working for one 97 year-old lady, 92, then 65, and I have one 70 and one 80. Old people look like my grandmother . . . I'm so comfortable because these people can give me love: I can give love. I enjoy every 4 hours that I'm working . . . My mamma died when I was young. That's probably why I like old people. I can depend on them; I can trust them. That probably means I didn't have enough love when I was young.

Despite the intimacy, however, there remained an insurmountable barrier of status, reinforced by cultural and racial differences. Thus, the familial attitude of the employer usually took the form of benevolent maternalism. Mrs. Fujii had an employer who pressed her with food or discarded clothing to take home. Other women reported similar gifts and bonuses (usually in lieu of higher wages). Even Mrs. Takagi, who formed close and long-lasting ties with her employers, recognized the employers' need to perform acts of "noblesse oblige." She said she had learned to accept gifts, including old clothes and furniture even when she didn't want them. Otherwise, the employer was apt to feel the worker was "too proud" and withhold further gifts and bonuses.

This feature of the employer/employee relationship, asymmetry, the traditional mistress/servant relation, exhibited in pure form the relation of superior to inferior. Servants dressed in distinctive uniforms to mark their station in life and used a different form of address when speaking to the mistress and guests. In many situations, including contemporary American society, the domestic belongs to a distinct and subordinate racial ethnic group. Thus, the domestic worker is set apart, not only by contrived badges of inferiority, but by physical and cultural differences. Differences may be perceived as even greater in the case of immigrants, who do not speak the dominant language or who may speak it with an accent. When social distance is great, the domestic may be treated as a "nonperson". Mrs. Kono complained bitterly about one employer she particularly disliked. "She didn't look at me as a human being. Her furniture, her house were more important."

Mrs. Takagi recalls that before the war, employers often displayed contempt. "Before the war, it was 'Jap' this, 'Jap' that," and employers fed domestics with table scraps." She recalls once being offered a lunch consisting of asparagus stalks whose tips had been bitten off by her employer's son.

Because of the stigma attached to domestic service, workers are sensitive to the implication that their employers consider them mere servants or housecleaners. Mrs. Suzuki complained that many employers "think they can do anything. Only a few families treat you real well. So many people, you work for them, and they treat you like a servant." The younger *nisei* and the war brides are more likely than the *issei* and older *nisei* to resent being treated as a menial. Mrs. Nishii says that perhaps because of her personality, she found it grating to work as a school girl. In contrast to her sister, who always seemed to be treated like one of the family, "I always worked for awful people."

> I used to rail when the son would bring his friends and ask me to teach them how to jitterbug, and he's say "This is our maid." I'd stand there and say I am *not* your maid! . . . I had to dress up in that maid's outfit when they had dinner parties. It was all part of it about how phoney these people were that I worked for. I suppose this was my way of surviving; I had such contempt for those people, because I thought they're so gauche.

Similarly, Mrs. Osborn declares that an attitude of superiority is what bothers her most about some employers.

> I'll never be rich. I don't care how much they are going to pay me, you know. I don't care. If there is an uncomfortable feeling or they think I'm just a housework person, I'm not going to work. Even if they pay me 50 dollars an hour, no! I [have to feel] comfortable working with that family.

In addition to those overt expressions of inequality, however, there were also more subtle and indirect expressions of asymmetry.

For example, in an asymmetrical relationship, the lower-status person has to be attuned to the feelings and moods of the higher-status person. Mrs. Fujii said that she could always tell when an employer was displeased because "I'm under and she's tops, so I could always tell what she's thinking. I think if I'm demanding of her (in the position of authority over her), then I probably won't feel what she wants to do." Mrs. Taniguchi, inadvertently provided an insight into how this sensitivity develops when she described her approach to domestic work:

At first, since I hadn't had much chance to enter Caucasian homes, I was a little frightened. But after I got used to it, it became very easy. And I concluded after working for awhile, that the most important thing in this type of job is to think of and be able to predict the feelings of the lady of the house. She would teach me how to do certain things in the beginning, but after a month or two, I gradually came to learn that person's likes, tastes, and ideas. So, I try to fulfill her wishes — this is only my way of doing it, of course, and so, for example, I'll change the water in the vase when it's dirty or rearrange the wilting flowers while I'm cleaning house. In that way, I can become more intimate with the lady the house in a natural way, and the job itself, becomes more interesting . . . sometimes I plant flowers in the garden without being asked . . . so then I'll start to feel affection even for that garden.

Although her employers may have appreciated Mrs. Taniguchi's aesthetic sensibilities, it is doubtful they were as aware of and responsive to her thoughts and feelings as she was of theirs.

The personalism and asymmetry in the employer/employee relations were complementary. The supposed inferiority and differentness of the domestic made it easy for the employer to be generous and to confide in her. The domestic was not in a position to hurt her or make excessive demands, and secrets were safe with someone from a completely separate social world. This complementarity between personalism and asymmetry, and the role of racism in promoting asymmetry, were shrewdly observed by Mrs. Okmaura, a 78 year-old *issei*, who noted:

There are some things you can talk freely about to other racial types. Those people just wanted to talk to someone; they didn't even care that I couldn't understand English, so I couldn't help them. They just wanted to complain about their son or their son's wife.

An informant suggested that the language barrier, though it hampered communication, may have contributed to the smoothness of relationships between the *issei* and their employers. The *issei* could not "hear" insulting or denigrating comments. One worker confirmed this by saying she had never minded being a domestic, but added that had she understood English, she might have gotten into quarrels with her employers. It does appear that the *issei* were less likely than the *nisei*, or war brides, to admit being bothered by the asymmetrical relationship with the employer. In addition to language, social and cultural differences may have helped to insulate the worker from directly feeling subordinated.

Ultimately, however, the personalism and asymmetry created contradictions in the employer/employee relationship. As Coser (1973, 32) put it, "The dialectic of conflict between inferior and superior within the household could never be fully resolved, and, hence, the fear of betrayal always lurked behind even the most amicable relationship between master and servant." The fear is evident in *issei* women's complaints about employers who distrusted them.

Mrs. Takagi once found money left under the corner of a rug. She carefully replaced the rug without touching the money or saying anything about it; she had been warned by her father-in-law that employers sometimes tested the domestic's honesty by leaving valuables about. Mrs. Taniguchi indignantly reported an incident in which she was suspected of dishonesty.

> There was a place I was working temporarily. They asked me whether I had seen a ring. I didn't know what kind of ring they meant, so I just told them, "no." I hadn't seen any ring while I was vacuuming. They sounded a little skeptical, saying it's strange I hadn't seen it. I felt insulted then, as though they were accusing me of something.

The conflict was also seen in the struggle between employer and employee over control of the work process. The employer attempted to exercise as much power as possible; the women reacted. Mrs. Kishi echoes the sentiments of many of the women when she said that her greatest dislike was an employer who was "*yakamashi*" (noisy, critical):

> Indeed, where they don't say too many things, the work is better. If they ask, "Have you done this? Have you done that? Do you understand?" There is that sort of place. Most people don't say such things because they know [better].

Some employers were suspicious that the worker would loaf or cut corners if she was not watched or monitored. Several women mentioned quitting jobs because the employer constantly checked up on them. Mrs. Fujitani complained about one woman.

> The lady was too particular, and she's always watching you, following you, whatever you're doing. And Japanese people, you know, aren't the kind that you have to keep their eye on you. They're honest . . . they work. So, I don't like anybody that has to follow me and see what I'm doing.

Mrs. Taniguchi stopped working for one woman who spied on her. She said most of her employers left the house while she worked. If they returned, they announced themselves loudly. In this case:

> The Mrs. would come in very quietly, without warning, so it made me feel as if she were spying on me to make sure I wasn't doing anything wrong. I disliked that a great deal.

GAINING CONTROL AND AUTONOMY

Despite the existence of multiple forms of oppression, these women showed remarkable ingenuity in gaining autonomy and control for themselves in the situation. The choice of day work can be seen as one means to gain greater autonomy. By working for several families, the domestics became less dependent on one employer, and so were freer to quit. Also, work hours could be adjusted to fit in with the workers' other interests and responsibilities. As Mrs. Tanabe said about her change from full time work with one employer to day work, "You're freer to yourself." It gave the women flexibility of hours and time off.

Over half of the women mentioned autonomy — being their own boss — as the main advantage of their work. In many cases, this is because the employer is out of the house or stays out of sight. This in in part the result of workers selectively retaining employers who are willing to leave them alone.

> (How do you feel about working in a house by yourself. Do you get lonesome?) "No, I like it . . . I don't think I ever liked people watching me all the time or where I have to communicate with other people I don't like. Housework, I'm my own boss. I feel so big. I feel free." (Mrs. Sentino, war bride)

When asked whether she ever felt alone or isolated, for example, Mrs. Tomita said, "No, I feel better when I'm alone. It's easier to work." Even when employers do not complain or interfere, their presence can be disturbing. They may want to chat, and this slows the work down. Working while the employer is visibly idle is also uncomfortable. Mrs. Kishi, a *kibei*, mentioned both aspects:

> (How do you feel about working alone?) Oh, it's easiest when they're not at home. If they're at home, sometimes she comes and talks and I can't work. If you're talking then, you're just resting." (When you do housework in someone else's home, you don't meet people. Do you like this or not?) I don't care, but I don't like it when people stay home. I like nobody home. More easy to work. Everything smooth. When people are at home, I'm so warm, and they're not doing anything. They just sit and say it's cold and put on the heater. It's so hot! (laughs).

And Mrs. Amano said.

> I liked it best when nobody was here. The places I worked . . . they went out. The children were in school and I was all by myself, so, I could do what I wanted. If the woman was at home, she generally went out shopping. I liked it when they didn't complain or ask you to do this or that. The places I worked, I was on my own. It was just like being in my own home, and I could do what I wanted.

Her sentiments were echoed by other women who say they strongly prefer employers who leave the house. Mrs. Kishi, an *issei*, said: "I don't like it when people stay home. I like nobody home. It's more easy to work—every thing is smooth."

Other women said they stayed with employers who left them alone and stayed out of their way. Mrs. Fujii, a *nisei*, said that one employer was so nice that she could not ask for a raise. When asked what was nice about her, she laughed, "You don't have to work very hard. (laughs uproariously) She leaves everything to me. I do whatever I want to do. She doesn't care." Mrs. Kadoi said her favorites are:

> Ladies that don't like housework . . . that house is easy to work for. Because then I can do the whole thing my way. I like to decorate, and so I like to re-arrange their furniture my way. Some people are particular, and then I don't touch it. But certain people I like to (have my way) and move it around.

Under these circumstances, workers have considerable latitude to devise their own routines. The employer may signify at the beginning what needs to get done, but the worker takes over organizing the work to accomplish the tasks in the time allotted. Mrs. Simeone, a war bride, was typical in that she had developed a general routine, but was also flexible enough to handle special requests.

> Usually, I go to the kitchen first. I wash everything, clean the refrigerator and oven, then mop. Whatever they ask me to wax, I do. I do each room, one at a time, dust and vacuum.

Another typical routine by an *issei*, Mrs. Uematsu for a four-hour day, was broken up by lunch.

> I usually dust first, but then there are places where I change the sheets. Every week change the sheets and then dust. Then vacuum. That takes 'til noon. Then I eat lunch. In the afternoon, I clean the kitchen, stove and clean the oven. It's not set. Today, if the oven is dirty, I clean the oven. Of course, every-where there's laundry, when you do day work.

Younger *kibei* and war brides were more likely to seize the initiative right from the beginning. The first day on the job, they announce they are trying out the job to see what needs to be done and how long it takes — much in the fashion of an expert consultant. Mrs. Kakoi said she never felt pressure because she always insisted on 6 hours:

> Certain people ask for a short time, but I usually ask for plenty of time. If they tell me they only want me for four hours, I tell them I have a certain way I have to work. I can't do it in four hours. Even a small house I work more hours. You need plenty of time to do it neat so you don't rush.

Having control over the tasks and timing was important. One way of gaining this control was to pick jobs, in the first place, according to the mix of activities. Other tasks that were enjoyed could also be added later. Mrs. Langer chose to work for the elderly, so she could make use of her nurse's train-ing. She stated, "I don't like housework, but I like to take care of people." She watched over her elderly employers when they bathe and felt rewarded when they told her she was no ordinary domestic.

These women also attempted to control employers' attempts to speed up their work pace. A common complaint voiced by the workers was that if they finished their work 10 or 15 minutes early, some employers demanded that they do something extra. Mrs. Kawai said, "Yes, I had some ladies say 10 minutes is 10 minutes, so find something to do!" Or, if the worker accomplished the agreed-upon task within the designated period, the employer added more tasks. In order to finish everything, the worker was forced to do everything faster.

Some women maintained control over the work by defining and enforcing their own standards; they insisted on working on the basis of tasks, rather than time. The job was done when the tasks were accomplished to their own satisfaction. If they worked extra time, they did not want to be paid; if they accomplished it in less time, they reserved the right to leave. Mrs. Osborn took this approach right from the start.

> . . . They leave a check, and when I'm finished, I pick it up. Sometimes I stay for fifteen minutes over, I'm not going to go after them to pay. I don't mind, if necessary, to work even two hours over. They don't have to pay, but they don't have to deduct, like a half hour [If I finish early].

The final recourse, when all else fails to bring around a recalcitrant or unreasonable employer, was to quit. Miss Ishida recalled such a situation.

> It kind of escalated. He was a bachelor, and when I first start to work, he did the washing. I did the ironing and putting away, because he didn't like to do it. But the longer I stayed, he kept leaving it. I didn't — can't — leave it, so I automatically did it. Then he got married, and I had a little more work to do, but I cut down on the housework because they didn't use all the house, so I skipped one week in some of the rooms that they never used. But that place I quit. No, I didn't really quit (laughs).

Because of demand for domestic help, workers can easily find another job with more favorable conditions or better pay.

SUMMARY

Managing both the job and relations with employers constitute major issues for the domestic. The personalistic, preindustrial character of the work and its degraded status create a series of dilemmas and contradictions. The lack of institutional structure means that domestics have considerable flexibility in arranging work hours, and the absence of industrial work discipline often means the worker can determine the pace of her work. Yet that same lack of structure and bureaucratic hierarchy and rules mean that workers are isolated, unprotected, and subject to arbitrary demands.

The personalism in the employer/employee relationship may leave some room for the worker to negotiate conditions or obtain favors; however that negotiation takes place within asymmetric power relations, reinforced by larger systems of class and race domination. In these circumstances involvement in personal relationships leaves the domestic vulnerable to exploitation. The employer can make demands based on feelings of affinity or in other ways use personal knowledge to their own advantage in the bargaining process. Gifts, favors, or even "niceness" bestowed by the employer in the guise of friendship are designed to raise the level of the worker's obligation and loyalty, thus disguising exploitation.

Beyond the actual conditions of work, the worker also contends with the symbolic meaning of their work. As one observer noted, domestic work is widely considered the "lowest rung of legitimate employment" (Caplow 1954). The low status accorded domestic service extends to the worker and stigmatizes her.

I have suggested that Japanese domestics contend with these conditions by struggling to maximize their autonomy and their control over their work. Their strategies include selecting and retaining employers who allow them scope to do the job as they see fit, seizing the initiative from employers, setting their own routines, and defining their own standards of work. These strategies keep employers at a distance and allow the workers to express their own individuality, thus allowing them to achieve a sense of satisfaction from what most consider menial work.

REFERENCES

Addams, Jane. 1896. "A belated industry," *American Journal of Sociology* 1:536–50.

Benston, Margaret. 1971. "The political economy of women's liberation," In *From Feminism to Liberation*, edited by Edith Hoskins Altback. Cambridge, Mass., and London: Schenckman, p. 199–210.

Braverman, Harry. 1974. *Labor and Monopoly Capital*. New York: Monthly Review Press.

Caplow, Theodore. 1954. *The Sociology of Work*. New York: McGraw-Hill.

Chaplin, David. 1978. "Domestic service and industrialization," *Comparable Studies in Sociology* 1:97–127.

Coser, Lewis. 1973. "Domestic servants: The obsolesence of a social role," *Social Forces* 52:31–40.

Cowan, Ruth Schwartz. 1976. "The industrial revolution in the home: Household technology and social change in the twentieth century," *Technology and Culture* 17:1–23.

Embree, John F. 1939. *Suye Mura: A Japanese Village.* Chicago: University of Chicago Press.

Glenn, Evelyn Nakano. 1986. *Issei, Nisei, Warbride: Three Generations of Japanese American Women in Domestic Service.* Philadelphia: Temple University Press.

Hughes, Everett C. 1958. *Men and their Work.* Glenco, Ill.: The Free Press.

Katzman, David H. 1978. *Seven Days a Week: Women and Domestic Service in Industrializing America.* New York: Oxford University Pess.

Leslie, Genevieve. 1974. "Domestic service in Canada, 1889–1920," In *Women at Work:* Edited by J. Aeton, P. Goldsmith, and B. Shepard. Ontario, 1850–1930. Toronto: Canadian Women's Educational Press. p. 71–126.

Oakley, Ann. 1974. *The Sociology of Housework.* New York: Pantheon Books.

Salmon, Lucy M. 1897. *Domestic Service.* New York: Macmillan. Stanford, CA: Stanford University Press.

U.S. Bureau of the Census. 1943. *Sixteenth Census of the Population, 1940: Population Characteristics of the Non-white Population by Race.* Washington, D.C.: U.S. Government Printing Office.

Watson, Amey. 1937. "Domestic service," *Encyclopedia of the Social Sciences* 5:198–206.

Women's Brueau, U.S. Department of Labor. 1975. *1975 Handbook of Women Workers.* Washington, D.C.: U.S. Government Printing Office.

Work in America. 1973. *A Report of a Special Task Force to the Secretary of Health, Education and Welfare.* Washington, D.C.: U.S. Government Printing Office.

CHAPTER 5

Day Work in the Suburbs: The Work Experience of Chicana Private Housekeepers*

MARY ROMERO

INTRODUCTION

Most research on domestic service begins with a set of assumptions based on the experience of European immigrant women. For these white, rural immigrant women, domestic service often represented a path to assimilation into the dominant American culture. As most foreign-born (and native-born) white domestics have historically been young and single, the occupation usually functioned as an interim activity between girlhood and marriage. Domestic service could also offer a first step toward employment in the formal sector and mobility into the middle class. Hence, domestic service became known as the "bridging occupation" (Broom and Smith 1963).

The experience of minority women differs radically. For women of color, domestic service has not resulted in social mobility but rather has trapped them in an occupational ghetto (Glenn 1981). Most minority women have not moved into other occupations as a result of their experience as domestics; instead, they have remained in domestic service throughout their lives. Minority women are usually married and work to support their families. Married black domestics have usually remained employed, whether they lived in or were day

*I am indebted to numerous persons who commented on the original version of this paper. Many of these people attended the conference on "Women and Work: Integrating Qualitative Research" (Racine, Wisconsin, 1985), where I presented the present version. In particular, I wish to thank Arlene Kaplan Daniels, Dee Ann Spencer, Judith Wittner, Evenly Glenn, and Sandra Porter. I also want to thank Frances Kleinman for her editorial comments.

workers, and they have not experienced intergenerational mobility (Lerner 1972; Katzman 1981; Rollins 1985); married Japanese-American (Glenn 1981) and Chicana domestics (Romero 1987) who were primarily day workers experienced some intergenerational mobility. Examination of the work histories of minority women domestics has led several researchers to abandon the traditional emphasis on assimilation and mobility and to focus instead on the actual work experience, particularly the employer/employee relationship.

Several researchers have documented the caste-like situation faced by generations of black women workers in the United States (Chaplin 1964; Katzman 1981). Their limited job opportunities in the South can be inferred from the fact that black servants were found even in lower middle class and working class white families. Better working conditions and higher wages attracted black women to Northern households. As factory and other job opportunities outside the home opened up for foreign-born white women, black women began to dominate the domestic occupation in the North. For a short period during the Depression, black women found themselves replaced by white domestics; but, in general, there were not enough white domestics to offer serious competition and the white women's positions as servants was short-lived. In 1930, 20 percent of household workers were native-born white and 41 percent, foreign-born white; by 1949, the proportion of foreign-born white had dropped to 11 percent. Moreover, while two-thirds of all black women were employed as domestics in 1930, this had only dropped to 50 percent by 1940. It was only after World War II that black women entered other fields in large numbers (Coley 1981).

The majority of Japanese-Amercian women working in the Bay Area prior to World War II were employed as domestics, a disproportionate concentration that persisted for more than one generation. Glenn's study (1986; 1981; 1980) of Japanese-American women in the San Francisco Bay Area identified several characteristics that made domestic service a port of entry into the labor market:

> The nonindustrial nature of the job, the low level of technology, and the absence of complex organization made it accessible; its menial status reduced competition from other groups who had better options; and the willingness of employers to train workers provided *issei* and *nisei* women with opportunities to acquire know-how and form connections outside the family and away from direct control of fathers and husbands (Glenn 1981: 381–82).

At the same time, successful generations of Japanese women became trapped by established pathways that provided access to the job in the beginning, but later separated them from other opportunities and resources. Consequently, Japanese women frequently continued to work as domestics even after marriage.

Because both domestic and mistress are women, their gender designates them as responsible for housework. In the case of white European domestics, the mistress frequently assumed a benevolent or even motherly role. However, this cannot be assumed with regard to minority women serving as domestics, as in this instance the mistress is in the position of delegating low-status work to women not only of a lower class but also of a different ethnic and racial group. In the case of black women, the domination/subordination pattern of the relationship grew out of attitudes developed during slavery that black servants were inferiors and nonpersons. Racism prevented white mistresses from assuming the surrogate mother role with their black domestics; instead, they adopted a benevolent role, treating the women as "childlike, lazy and irresponsible," hence requiring white governance (McKinley 1969).

In short, studies of black and Japanese-American women indicate that domestic service is not a "bridging occupation" offering transition into the formal sector. These studies have raised additional questions about minority women's experience as domestic workers. Rather than approaching domestic service in terms of acculturation and intergenerational mobility, researchers can approach the occupation from the worker's point of view. The following study explores domestic service as a serious enterprise with skills that have been either dismissed or ignored by previous researchers.

METHOD

This study is based on interviews with 25 Chicanas living in an urban western city. I conducted two- to three-hour open-ended interviews in the women's homes. I asked the women to discuss their work histories, particularly their experience as domestics. Detailed information on domestic work included strategies for finding employers, identification of appropriate and inappropriate tasks, the negotiation of working conditions, ways of doing housework efficiently, and the pros and cons of domestic work. The accounts included descriptions of the domestics' relationships to white middle class mistresses and revealed the Chicanas' attitudes toward their employers' lifestyles.

A snowball sampling method was used to identify Chicana domestic workers. Several current and former domestic workers I knew introduced me to other workers. Churches and social service agencies also helped to identify domestic workers in the community. In a few cases, community persons also assisted. The respondents ranged in age from 29 to 58. The sample included welfare recipients as well as working class women. All but one of the women had been married. Four were single heads of households; the other women were currently living with husbands employed in blue-collar occupations, such as construction and factory work. All of the women had children. The smallest family consisted of one child and the largest family had seven children. At the time of the interview, the women who were single heads of households were financially supporting no more than two children. Nine women had completed high school, and seven had no high school experience. One woman had never attended school at all. The remaining eight had at least a sixth-grade education.

RESEARCH FINDINGS

Work Histories

The majority of the women had been employed in a variety of jobs over their lifetimes. They had been farm workers, waitresses, factory workers, sales clerks, cooks, laundresses, fast-food workers, receptionists, school aides, babysitters, dishwashers, nurse's aides, and cashiers. Almost half of the women had worked as janitors in hospitals and office buildings or as hotel maids. About one-fourth of the women had held semiskilled and skilled positions as beauticians, typists, medical record clerks, and the like. Six of the women had worked only as domestics.

Only three women had worked as domestics prior to marriage; each of those three had worked in live-in situations in rural areas of the Southwest. Several years later after marriage and children, these women returned as day workers. Most of the women, however, had turned to nonresidential day work in response to a financial crisis; in the majority of cases, it was their first job after marriage and children. Some of the women remained domestics throughout their lives, but others moved in and out of domestic work. Women who returned to domestic service after employment elsewhere usually did so after a period of unemployment. Because of the flexible schedule, most of the women preferred housework to other employment during their children's preadolescent years. Many of the older women had returned to domestic service because the schedule could be arranged around their family responsibilities and health problems. For all of the women, the occupation was an open door: they could always find work as a domestic. Their experience as domestics had lasted from 5 months to 30 years. Women 50 years and over had worked in the field from 8 to 30 years, while 4 of the women between the ages of 33 and 39 had 12 years experience.

The women's opportunities in the labor market were apparently not significantly improved by working as domestics. No matter how intimate the relationship between employee and employer, the domestic was never included in a broader social network that might provide other job opportunities. As long as community resources were limited to low-paying; low-status positions, the women found it difficult to obtain employment that offered benefits and a higher salary. Still, it is important to keep in mind that horizontal mobility can make significant differences in the quality of one's life. As Becker noted:

> All positions at one level of work hierarchy, while theoretically identical, may not be equally easy or rewarding places in which to work. Given this fact, people tend to move in patterned ways among the possible positions, seeking that situation which affords the most desirable setting in which to meet and grapple with the basic problems of their work. (Becker 1952, 470).

While the women I interviewed preferred factory positions because of their pay and benefits, many found themselves hired during the peak season and subsequently laid off. Women unable to obtain regular factory positions usually remained in domestic service until they retired or health problems emerged. Most of their clerical experience was in community-based organizations. Only when jobs increased in the Chicano community — for instance, through CETA or bilingual education programs — did the women have an opportunity to develop skills useful in applying for jobs elsewhere. These programs usually freed the women from daywork as a domestic. Only after retirement or periods of unemployment did these women again return to daywork to supplement the family income.

FINDING DAY WORK

In acquiring most of these jobs, the women relied upon word of mouth. Their sources for information on job openings included husbands, sisters, cousins, friends, and neighbors. Thus, their networks were usually confined to the Chicano community. Women reported that family members usually assisted in obtaining employment as a domestic. For instance, one woman had been working in the fields with her family one day when her husband returned from the owner's home with a job offer to do housework. Sisters, cousins and in-laws frequently suggested housekeeping and willingly provided the contacts to obtain employers. Several women joined the ranks in response to a relative's need for a replacement during an illness, vacation, or family obligation. One woman started out with a cleaning agency. However, she quickly abandoned the agency, preferring to work independently. This pattern of using informal networks in job searches is consistent with other research findings on work (Reid 1972; Katz 1958).

Younger women's introduction to domestic service frequently began with an apprenticeship period in which they accompanied a relative or friend. Two women would work together for a certain period of time (several days or weeks) until the newcomer decided she was ready to take on her own employers on a regular basis. This training provided newcomers with an opportunity to acquire tips about cleaning methods, products, appliances, the going rate, advantages and disadvantages of charging by the house or the hour, and how to ask for a raise.

Most women found their first employers through the community network of other domestic workers. Later, new employers were added with the assistance of current employers who recommended their employees to friends and neighbors. Two women reported using ads and employment agencies along with relatives and friends. But most voiced a strong preference for the informal network. Recommendations and job leads from the informal network of family and friends provided women with a sense of security when entering a new employer's home.

In many ways these women demonstrated employment patterns similar to other working women in traditionally female occupations. Movement in and out of the labor market coincided with stages of family life. Husbands' unemployment, underemployment, or financial crisis were the major reasons for reentry into the work force. And, like most other women, domestic workers found employment in low-paying, low-status jobs. However, their ability to obtain immediate employment may distinguish them from other women who seek employment during times of financial crisis. These Chicana workers were unique in that they could always find employment as domestics. The challenge was to find a job *outside* domestic service.

Work Conditions of Day Work in the Suburbs

Most of the domestics interviewed for this study drove 20 to 60 minutes every morning to work. In two cases, the employer provided transportation. All of the women worked for non-Hispanic families. The usual arrangement was to work for one household per day; however, with an increase in the number of professional, middle class people living in smaller units, such as condominiums, cleaning two apartments a day had become a more common pattern. Exceptions in the present sample included two women working solely for parish priests and another woman working for one family five days a week. The average work week ranged from three to five days a week. Almost half of the women worked six- or seven-hour days, and the others worked half-days.

During the course of interviews, it became apparent that norms were changing regarding the type of tasks associated with general housekeeping. Older women with 20 or more years experience considered ironing, laundry, window cleaning, cooking, and babysitting as part of the job; however, none of the women currently employed as domestics identified such requests as the norm. Several current domestic workers and younger informants distinguished between "maid" work and "housekeeping" on the basis of these tasks. Glenn (1986) found similar trends. Twenty years ago, domestics service usually meant ten- to twelve-hour days and often included yard work and cleaning the cars or the garage. Today the work usually consists of vacuuming all the rooms (frequently moving the furniture), washing and waxing the floor, dusting, and cleaning the bathrooms and kitchen. Each home typically requires four to seven hours.

After the first two workdays in an employer's home, the women established a routine for housecleaning. For instance, the women would arrange a schedule to work around members of the employer's family who were at home. Domestics identified themselves as professional housekeepers with responsibility for maintaining the employer's home. Maintenance involved bringing the employer's house up to a standard that would then be maintained on a weekly basis. Domestics established a routine for incorporating extra tasks on a rotating schedule: for example, cleaning the refrigerator or oven once a month. The employer's cooperation in establishing a routine played an important part in the employee's decision to keep a particular job.

Most women earned between 30 and 65 dollars a day depending on the number of hours worked. Most women averaged 8 dollars an hour. Employers usually paid by cash or personal check each day the domestic came. A few paid by personal check once a month. Although none of the women received health care benefits, some employers offered other benefits. Four of the older women were paying into Social Security; this had been initiated by long-term employers who expressed concern over their employees' welfare. Paid vacations were another benefit obtained by women who had worked several years for the same employer. As with Social Security, a paid vacation was the exception rather than the norm. A few of the women received Christmas bonuses. None of the women received automatic annual raises. Because very few employers offered a raise, the women were forced to make the request. Since the only power the women had was to quit, the most common strategy was to pose an ultimatum to the employer — "Give me a raise or I'll quit." Sometimes a woman would announce to her employer that she had to quit because she faced a problem with transportation or childcare. In this instance, the hope was that the employer would offer a raise to keep the employee from quitting.

Most people clean house once or twice a week and assume the domestic's experience is comparable. However, the domestic's routine recurs everyday: carrying the vacuum up and down the stairs; vacuuming sofas and behind furniture; washing and waxing floors; scrubbing ovens, sinks, tubs, and toilets; dusting furniture; emptying wastebaskets; cleaning mirrors. Backaches from scrubbing and picking up toys, papers, and clothes are common. All of the work is completed while standing or kneeling. Beyond the physical demands of the job, many women faced the additional stress of having their work treated as non-work. Several domestics recalled occasions when employers' children or guests spilled drinks on the floor or messed up a room and expected the worker simply to redo her work. All of the women refused, pointing out that the work had already been completed. Although domestics are paid for housework, the job is treated no differently than housework done by housewives (Oakley 1974).

Maximizing Work Conditions

Housework itself offers few intrinsic rewards; therefore, women who choose domestic service over other low-paying, low-status jobs typically strive to maximize their working conditions. The women interviewed for this study put a great deal of thought into identifying ways to improve work conditions, and they had very clear goals in establishing conditions with employers.

Flexibility in their work time was the crucial factor for many of the women who wanted to be home with their children. As Mrs. Lopez[1] explains:

> I'd always try to be home when the children went to school and be home when they came home. . . . I would never leave my children alone. I always arranged with the ladies [employers] — always told them that I had children and that I had to come home early.

---

1. I have changed the subjects' names to protect their anonymity.

Domestic work allowed the women to arrange their own hours, adding or eliminating employers to lengthen or shorten the work week. Determining their own schedule allowed the women to get their children off to school in the morning and be back home when school was over. It also provided a solution for women with preschool age children:

> Most of the people I've worked for like kids, so I just take the kids with me. It's silly to have to work and pay a sitter; it won't work (Mrs. Montoya, age 33, 12 years' experience, mother of two).

> So that's mainly the reason I did it [domestic work], because I knew the kids were going to be all right and they were with me and they were fed and taken care of (Mrs. Cordova, age 30, 8 years' experience, mother of two).

Domestics were thus able to fulfill family obligations without major disruptions at home or work.

> You can change the dates if you can't go a certain day, and if you have an appointment, you can go later and work later, just as long as you get the work done. . . . I try to be there at the same time, but if I don't get there for some reason or another, I don't have to think I'm going to lose my job or something (Mrs. Sanchez, 54 years old, 18 years' experience, mother of six).

> That's one thing with doing daywork — if the children are sick or something, you just stayed home because that was my responsibility to get them to the doctor and all that (Mrs. Lopez, age 64).

Since the domestics worked alone and had a different employer each day, they could control the number of days and hours spent cleaning. Women who needed to attend to family responsibilities found employers for two or three days a week and arranged to clean the houses in five hours. In contrast, women whose major concern was money could work six days a week and clean two houses everyday. In order to control the number of days and hours worked, women established a verbal contract identifying what tasks constituted general housekeeping. This agreement was flexible and was adjusted to particular situations as they arose. As Mrs. Sanchez explained:

> Suppose one day they [the employers] may be out of town, and that day you go to work. You won't have much work to do, but you'll get paid the same. And then maybe some other time they're going to have company and you end up working a little more and you still get paid the same. So it averages about the same, you know, throughout the month (Age 54, 18 years' experience).

Maintaining a routine for accomplishing necessary tasks allowed domestics to control the work environment and eliminated the need for employers to dictate a work schedule. Once an agreement was made, the workers determined how quickly or slowly they would work. Contract work provided employees with considerable autonomy, as well as recognition of their skills by employers.

On the other hand, a few women found contracts inadequate in controlling the amount of work requested. Instead, they clearly stipulated the number of hours they would work. Then they would do as much work, at their own pace, as the time allowed. By establishing a set number of hours, the domestic forced the employer to choose particular tasks to be rotated each week.

Planning and organizing the work permitted the domestic to feel like her own boss. When the employer permitted, domestic work offered a variety of advantages not available in many other jobs. Key among these advantages was autonomy. Once the employee was no longer taking orders and receiving instructions about how to clean, she had the freedom to structure the day's work. Mrs. Portillo spoke about the importance of this job characteristic:

> Once the person learns that you're going to do the job, they just totally leave you to your own. It's like it's your own home. That's what I like. When you work like in a hospital or something, you're under somebody. They're telling you what to do or this is not right. But housecleaning is different. You're free. You're not under no pressure, especially if you find a person who really trusts you all the way. You have no problems (Age 68, 30 years' experience).

All of the informants preferred to work alone in the house. Women who achieved a degree of autonomy in their work environment were often able to substitute mental labor for physical labor. Planning and organization were essential for maintaining the house and arranging the work tasks in the most efficient manner. Several of the women were responsible for keeping an inventory of cleaning supplies as well as for maintenance of housekeeping equipment. It was not uncommon for the women to be called upon to rearrange furniture and fixtures. Therefore, autonomy in the work environment made it possible to unite the mental and manual labor involved in housework. Most of the women noted that this combination made the work more interesting and meaningful.

The Relationship between Mistress and Domestic

Class differences have always existed between mistresses and domestics; however, cultural differences are a relatively recent phenomenon in domestic service. Historically, mistresses have defined the employment of ethnic minority women as a benevolent gesture, offering to the less fortunate the opportunity to culturally and morally upgrade themselves. Mistresses frequently pry into or comment on domestics'personal lives without invitation. Sometimes they treat domestics like children. Racism is a reality of the job. Although many incidents are difficult to resond to, most women quit employers who make racist comments, such as "Chicanas have too many children" or "Chicanas lack ambition."

Several of the women in this study felt they were treated as cultural curiosities. Often mistresses would limit questions and discussion topics to Chicano culture and attempt to explain differences in their experiences as cultural. For instance, one woman recalled that an employer had decorated her house with Santos purchased on her annual trips to northern New Mexico. The employer was quite shocked to realize the domestic did not own a large wooden statue of her patron saint. Most of the mistresses' inquiries were about ethnic food. Several employers asked the domestic to make tortillas or chile, but the women were very hesitant about sharing food. All of the women felt the request for Mexican food was inappropriate, except when they considered the employer a friend. Even though the women engaged in conversations about Chicano culture, history, or social issues, inquiries frequently created tension. Consequently, such discussions were avoided as much as possible.

In past research, researchers assumed that employers transmitted cultural values and norms to the employee, providing a "bridge" to a middle class lifestyle. However, the women interviewed for this study strongly expressed the opposite view. They found that domestic skills did not transfer to any other setting, nor did they provide the legitimate "work experience" needed to move upwards in the formal sector. Often the domestics felt a sense of being trapped because they lacked suitable job experience, opportunities, and education. Mrs. Fernandez spoke of her limited alternatives in an assessment of her job skills:

> I'm not qualified to do much, you know. I've often thought about going back to school and getting some kind of training. I don't know what I would do if I would really have to quit housework because that wouldn't be a job to raise a family on if I had to. So I would have to go back and get some training in something (Age 35, 9 years' experience, mother of 4, eleventh grade education).

The two oldest women interveiwed (68 and 64 respectively) saw discrimination and racism limiting their job choices.

> There was a lot of discrimination, and Spanish people got just regular housework or laundry work. . . . There was so much discrimination that Spanish people couldn't get jobs outside of washing dishes — things like that (Mrs. Portillo, 30 years' experience, 68 years old, mother of two).

This study found the cultural exchange between domestic and employer to be much more diffuse than that described in research on domestics at the turn of the century (Katzman 1981) and in Third World countries (Smith 1971). However, I did find that material culture was frequently transmitted to the domestic who developed a need for particular appliances and products. Several women had acquired new appliances, such as microwave ovens, in the last few years. Some of the younger women had incorporated a "white middle class" decor and style of arranging furniture in their own homes. Many of the women acquired a taste for objects similar to those in the employer's home. However, it is difficult to attribute this interest solely to the work experience because of the substantial influence of the media. Younger women were more apt to incorporate new ways of doing things into their own homes. Although there was evidence of acculturation in the arrangement of furniture and wall decorations, certain traditional items remained, such as family pictures and religious art. I would argue that this readiness to incorporate material culture reflects class aspirations rather than assimilation to white American culture.

Cultural diffusion was not one way. Employers who turned over the control of the work process allowed workers to introduce new cleaning products and methods. A few of the older women became surrogate mothers to their employers and were called upon to discuss childrearing practices. The amount of cultural exchange was determined by the degree to which employers accepted domestics as experts in housekeeping.

Minimizing the Personal Cost of Being a Domestic

Many women found the stigma attached to domestic work painful. A few manifested embarassment and anger at being identified as a housecleaner. Other women were very defensive about their work and attempted to point out all the benefits associated with flexible work schedule and autonomy.

The women used several strategies for coping with the personal pain of being a domestic. They attempted to eliminate the stigma attached to the occupation by making a distinction between the positions of maid and housekeeper, defining the former as involving personal service. The younger women, in particular sought to redefine the job. Mrs. Fernandez noted the distinction between maid and housekeeper in the following story:

> They [the employer's children] started to introduce me to their friends as their maid. "This is our maid Angela." I would say, "I'm not your maid. I've come to clean your house, and a maid is someone who takes care of you and lives here or comes in everyday, and I come once a week and it is to take care of what you have messed up. I'm not your maid. I'm your housekeeper." (Age 35, 9 years' experience).

By identifyig themselves as professional housekeepers, the women emphasized their special skills and knowledge and situated their work among male-dominated jobs that are treated as semiskilled, such as carpet cleaning. This also served to define their relationships to their employers. Mrs. Montoya illustrated the relationship:

> I figure I'm not there to be their personal maid. I'm there to do their housecleaning — their upkeep of the house. Most of the women I work for are professionals, and so they feel it's not my job to run around behind them. Just to keep their house maintenance clean, and that's all they ask. (Age 33, 12 years' experience).

The women redefined their employers as clients, vendors, and customers. Defining themselves as professionals, these domestics no longer saw themselves as acting in the subordinate role of employee to the dominant role of employer. Without recognition of their authority, however, the domestics had to rely on mistresses' cooperation. This is similar to women's lack of authority in other female-dominated occupations such as nursing and teaching. (See Ritzer 1977 and chapters by Spencer and Corley and Mauksch in this volume.)

Another strategy women used to lessen the stigma of doing domestic work was to focus on the benefits to their families. By praising aspects of domestic service compatible with traditional mother and wife roles, the woman's social identity was shifted to family rather than work roles. Since the status of motherhood is much higher than that of domestic worker, identifying with the tradidional family role served to minimize the stigma attached to the work role. Again, this strategy was found particularly among younger and more educated women. Mrs. Montoya, a high school graduate and mother of two, stressed that domestic work was preferable to other jobs because it did not interfere with her role as a mother:

> I make my own hours so I can go to [school] programs when I'm needed. I go to conferences when I'm needed. When the kids are ill, I'm there. . . .It's one of the best jobs that I could find in my situation where I am home with my family before and after school. I'm always around.

The women were usually available to participate in school functions, and many played an active role in the community. The fact that these women identified primarily with traditional family roles is consistent with other research findings suggesting that jobs are not the central interest of workers' lives (Dublin 1956).

Women tended to deny that they were actually employed, as did their families. Many of the women remarked that their families did not consider them to be working outside the home; their employment was dismissed as "shadow work," the peculiarly nonwork status commonly given to housework (Oakley 1974; Illich 1982). Therefore, the women's families saw no reason to give them credit or to help out at home. A few husbands did not want their wives working and retaliated by becoming more demanding about housework, laundry, and meals. This attitude was particularly common in families where mothers worked part time. The women received little help from their husbands or their children in doing cooking, laundry, and housekeeping. Children occasionally helped with the housework, and retired husbands were described as sporadically cooking a meal, removing the laundry from the dryer, vacuuming the living room, or "telling the children what to do." Consequently, women working six- to seven-hour days, five days a week as domestics experienced the common "double day" syndrome known to many working mothers regardless of their occupation.

The women described their wages as providing "extras" not afforded by their husbands' incomes. The items listed as "extras" were: food, children's clothes, remodeling the house, savings, children's tuition, and payment of bills. Clearly, their contributions enhanced their family's subsistence and went beyond the stereotypical 'pin money.' The notion that their employment provided extras rather than subsistence for the family was part of these women's strategy for coping with the stigma of being a domestic worker. In essence, they maintained a social identity based on the family rather than on the work role. Since the status attached to being a mother and wife is much higher than that assigned to the domestic, women defined their work as adding to the fulfillment of their traditional female role.

DISCUSSION

Chicana domestic workers share experiences similar to those of other minority women. Although a few of those interviewed worked on a live-in basis prior to marriage, they only worked on a nonresidential basis after marriage. This is quite similar to the pattern found among Japanese-American women (Glenn 1981). Chicana domestic workers also experience domestic service as an "occupational ghetto" as have so many Japanese-American and black women in the United States. Minority women have not moved into the formal work sector as a consequence of their experience as domestics, but have continued to have few options. The present investigation begins to explain why domestic service does not constitute a "bridging occupation" for minority women.

The use of informal networks to obtain daywork as described by Chicana domestics is also found in the Japanese-American community; while community resources provide Japanese-American women with immediate employment as a domestic, the residential and social segregation also "tend to insulate members from information about other occupations" (Glenn 1981, 380). This method of job searching has likewise been documented for various other workers, including professionals (Reid 1972; Katz 1958; Caplow and McGee 1958). It follows that potential for social mobility is related to expanding resources within the community rather than to simple assimilation into another community's norms and values. I would argue that domestic service serves as a bridging occupation only when employers make their informal networks available to domestics. Research on minority women in domestic service indicates that employers do not share these informal networks; that is, domestics do not become "just one of the family." As a result, domestics experience social segregation and do not gain access to other occupations.

Analysis of the work histories collected from Chicana domestic workers shows that they found their options limited in low-paying, low-status, dead-end jobs. The women's choice of domestic service over another job (such as waitressing or farmwork) was most often based on the flexible schedule and potential for autonomy on the job. Selecting employers who worked outside the home and establishing verbal contracts were attempts to increase autonomy. The women also tried to modernize their occupation by redefining themselves as professional housecleaners. These strategies are all essentially individualistic. However, as unionization among housekeepers increases, these women will be able to pursue collective approaches to the struggle for better working conditions.

REFERENCES

Becker, H.S. 1952. "The career of the Chicago public schoolteacher," *American Journal of Sociology* 57:470.

Broom, L., and J.H. Smith. 1963. "Bridging occupations," *British Journal of Sociology* 14:321–34.

Caplow, T., and R. McGee. 1958. *The Academic Marketplace.* New York: Basic Books.

Chaplin, D. 1964. "Domestic service and the Negro," In *Blue Collar World*, edited by A.B. Shoistak and Wl. Gomberg, Englewood Cliffs, N.J.: Prentice-Hall. pp. 527–536.

Coley, S.M. 1981. "And Still I Rise: An Exploratory Study of Contemporary Black Private Household Workers." Ph.D. diss., Bryn Mawr College, Bryn Mawr, PA.

Dublin, R. 1956. "Industrial workers' world: A study of the central life interests of industrial workers," *Social Problems* 3:131–42.

Glenn, E.N. 1980. "The dialectics of wage work: Japanese-American women and domestic service, 1905–1940," *Feminist Studies* 6:432–71.

———. 1981. "Occupational ghettoization: Japanese-American women and domestic service, 1905–1970," *Ethnicity* 8:352–86.

———. 1986. *Issei, Nisei, War Bride: Three Generations of Japanese-American Women in Domestic Service.* Philadelphia: Temple University Press. University Press.

Illich, I. 1982. *Gender.* New York: Pantheon Books.

Katz, F.E. 1958. "Occupational contract network," *Social Forces* 41:52–5.

Katzman, D.H. 1981. *Seven Days a Week: Women and Domestic Service in Industrializing America.* New York: Oxford University Press, 1978.

Lerner, G. 1972. *Black Women in White America: A Documentary History.* New York: Pantheon Books.

McKinley, G.E. 1969. "The stranger in the gates: Employer reactions toward domestic servants in America, 1825–1875." Ph.D. Diss., Michigan State University, East Lansing.

Oakley, A. 1974. *The Sociology of Housework*. New York: Pantheon Books.

Reid, G. 1972. "Job search and the effectiveness of job-finding methods," *Industrial and Labor Relations Review* 25:479–95.

Ritzer, G. 1977. *Working Conflict and Change*. Englewood Cliffs, NJ: Prentice-Hall.

Rollins, J. 1985. *Between Women: Domestics and Their Employers*. Philadelphia: Temple University Press.

Romero, M. 1987. "Domestic service in the transition from rural to urban life: The case of La Chicana," *Women's Studies*, forthcoming.

Smith, M.L. 1971. "Institutionalized servitude: The female domestic servant in Lima, Peru." Ph.D. Diss., Indiana University, Bloomington.

CHAPTER 6

The Caretakers: Keeping the Area
Up and the Family Together

JANE C. HOOD*

PROLOGUE

July 1979

Millie Jones is a custodian. For three years she has worked nights on the first floor of a classroom building at Urban University (a fictitious name). Although she likes cleaning work, she took the public university job primarily because it paid more than she earned as a nurse's aide in a nursing home. Millie is a 48-year-old, divorced black woman who lives with five of her eight grown children (aged 16 to 25) and two grandchildren (aged two and five months). She has been working full time for the ten years since her youngest started school.

In addition to her 10:00 P.M. to 6:30 A.M. custodial job, Mrs. Jones works second shift Fridays and Saturdays at a nursing home. Urban University pays Millie Jones $5.33 an hour (plus a night differential of $0.20 cents an hour) and provides life and health insurance as well as sick leave. As a member of the American Federation of State, County and Municipal Employees, Mrs. Jones gets regular cost-of-living raises and has relatively high job security. Her other job pays just $3.33 an hour with no benefits, hardly any raises and minimal job security. On her two jobs, Mrs. Jones grosses $1063.40 a month. Although three of her sons work, she reports no regular contributions from them. If her daughters collect the AFDC payments for the two grandchildren, Mrs. Jones doesn't mention it.

---

*I am indebted to Arlene Kaplan Daniels for comments on an earlier draft of this paper.

93

When told that she and her fellow workers will be moved to day shift, Mrs. Jones thinks that day work will be better for her sleeping and eating habits and will make it easier for her to see her friends. "If you work at night, you ain't got no friends," she says. However, working first shift will make it harder to see her sister who works second shift, and most of all, working around all the students will make cleaning a lot harder. Working nights at Urban University, she has had plenty of time to do her work and no one to interfere with her. "You know what you have to do and there's no rush." When she finishes her work, she can sit down and rest in an empty student or faculty lounge. On days, not only will she have to work around crowds of students coming to and from classes, but she will also lose the night differential ($8.65 a week). To make up for the loss in pay, Mrs. Jones may have to increase the hours on her second job, and she won't be able to take care of her grandchildren or watch soap operas during the day.

Although Millie Jones thinks that the day shift will be better for her health, she and her coworkers resent management for making the change without consulting them. As she says, "They could have told us ladies. They wanted to change to save money, but they will be getting raises themselves."

November 1980

Millie Jones has been working first shift for a little over a year now. As she predicted, she is sleeping and eating better. However, she finds it harder to get her work done properly. She is more rushed because she must get into rooms and clean them quickly when they are not in use. Her supervisor is around more. He expects her to look busy even when she can't get into rooms that need cleaning. She can no longer rest at will after she has finished her work, and at break time lounge areas that were available to her at night are occupied. Millie says that she feels tired and worn out at the end of the day. Nonetheless, she goes home, cooks, washes clothes, serves dinner to her family, and then either watches TV or visits relatives before going to bed at 9:00 P.M. To get to work at 6:30 A.M., she must be up by 5:30 A.M. She is unable to care for her grandchildren which means that her 17-year-old daughter must arrange for childcare since she is still in school. To make up for the loss of the night differential, Mrs. Jones has doubled her hours at the second job and now earns $400 a month at that job, bringing her total monthly income to a little over $1200.

Mrs. Jones works hard at three jobs, and at each job she is a caretaker. On weekdays she takes care of her floor at Urban University where she must battle crowds of students to "keep her area up." On weekends she takes care of patients at the nursing home (cf. Diamond in this volume). Although the shift change prevents her from taking care of her grandchildren during the day, it has not stopped her from washing and cooking for them in the afternoons and evenings. Mrs. Jones is also a provider. As a provider, she has made sure that the elimination of the night differential from her paycheck has not caused hardship for her family. By adding hours at her low-paid nursing home job, Millie Jones has increased her total earnings, so that her family now finds it easier rather than harder to manage. Even though Millie is working harder at her main job and longer at her second job, she is feeling better overall. The energy gained by sleeping and eating better on the day shift appears to compensate for having to work harder and longer to support her family.

THE NIGHT-TO-DAY STUDY

Mrs. Jones's experience illustrates a complex web of life changes precipitated by the shift change at Urban University. Originally the mess created by faculty, staff, and students during the day was left for Millie Jones and her coworkers to clean up at night. This work might easily be labeled "dirty work" (cf. Hughes 1958, 49–53). However, even though Millie found night work lonely and exhausting, the sparsely populated night work environment afforded her autonomy and anonymity that were not possible during the day. As Melbin has observed, night work offers solitude, fewer social constraints and less persecution than day work can provide (1978, 9). Because cleaning up other people's trash is less demeaning when the people themselves are not around, night custodians are less likely than day workers to experience their jobs as "dirty work."

Because Millie was an AFSCME member, she earned higher wages and had more job security than she would have had in many other secondary labor market jobs.[1] Her union could do nothing, however, to prevent management from exercising its right to change her work schedule. Working days not only removed some of the pride from Mrs. Jones's work but also forced her to recognize her relationship to her household of five children and two grandchildren. Although Millie Jones was able to arrange her life so that, on balance, neither she nor her family suffeed from the shift change, the "simple" managerial desision to move the custodians to day shift had far from simple consequences for the work and family lives of Millie Jones and her coworkers. This paper describes the kaleidoscopic effects of that change in the lives of 20 female custodians and their male coworkers.

The Panel

Millie Jones was one of panel of 63 custodial workers interviewed in a longitudinal study of a shift change (1979–81).[2] One of 20 on the panel, she was in many ways typical of the group as a whole. Like Mrs. Jones, all but two of the women were black, and like her, half of them had high school education or above. Seven, including Millie, had previously worked in nursing as aides, assistants, or LPN's, and one had continued to get training to become an RN. Seven had done custodial work, including one who also had worked as a domestic; two had done clerical work; and four had done factory or other manual work before coming to Urban University. All but one lived with members of their nuclear or extended families, and every one of them had children or grandchildren nearby. Only two failed to mention childcare responsibilities in their interviews, and all of the women had strong ties to both nuclear and extended families.

Compared to the men in the study, the women were more likely to have had education beyond high school, more likely to be living with family members, and far more likely to have regular childrearing duties. Whereas most of the female workers were black, two-thirds of the male workers were white. Although both men and women felt that it was harder to get their work done during the day and reported feeling more rushed, the women were more likely than the men to say that working during the day was more taxing and that it was more difficult to take pride in their work. They were also more likely to have thought of getting a different job after being moved to day shift.

The Interviews

Baseline and follow-up interviews used interview schedules containing both open-ended questions, such as "How do you think your life will be affected by the shift change?," and closed-ended, forced-choice items, such as "Compared to working nights, how much easier or harder is it for you to get your work done (now that you are on days)?" The author conducted several of the interviews, but most were done by students trained and supervised by the author. The quantitative data were coded and analyzed by computer (see Hood 1984). This paper is based on the answers to open-ended questions, numerous marginal comments made by interviewers, field notes taken over the course of the study, and tape-recorded interviews done with union stewards and supervisors.

Because the Night-to-Day Study was conducted to document the effects of mandatory shift change, its scope is narrower than that of a study designed to chronicle the lives of female custodial workers. Instead of detailed, taped life-history interviews, we have bits and pieces of qualitative data that help us sketch a dotted outline of "the caretakers" but cannot really tell us how to paint the full portrait. The data collected, are sufficient, however, to explain: 1) how changing the timing of work can also change the nature of that work; 2) how low-status workers struggle to regain control of their work setting when that control is threatened; and 3) how gender-based differences in life circumstances and perspective make the consequences of a single event different for women than for men.

KEEPING THE AREA UP

To many sociologists, custodial work would appear to require few skills and to offer little if any intrinsic satisfaction. The occupation is ranked near the bottom of the National Opinion Research Center occupational prestige scale. Assigned an "eight," the job of janitor is lower than taxi driver and one rung higher than a bootblack (Montagna 1977, 34–35). Occupied by blacks, women, older workers, and workers justing entering the labor force, the job would probably be classified along with other jobs that offer low pay , no opportunity for advancement, and little job security as part of the secondary labor market. One would take such a job only if one could get nothing better.

However, work that occupies a low place on the occupational prestige scale is not necessarily unrewarding or demeaning. Cleaning one floor of an unoccupied public building is different from cleaning an occupied private building such as one's own house (housewives) or another's house (domestics) while others are around. Bad work in one setting can be transformed into good work in another. As Evelyn Nakano Glenn points out (elsewhere in this volume) domestic workers prefer cleaning unoccupied houses where they feel like their own bosses and, in some cases, even imagine that the houses belong to them. Furthermore, working for the state as a Building Maintenance Worker (BMW) I, II, or III is very different from working for either a single household or even a small private business. Custodians who work for the state often belong to AFSCME. Their pay, job security, and promotions are all governed by a union contract, and their locals may include both craft and clerical workers as well as custodians. Cost-of-living raises are the rule rather than the exception. Benefit packages are excellent, and after a six-month probationary period, job security is relatively high. Promotion takes place from within, allowing workers to move from BMW I to supervisory positions. The union protects workers from dismissal without just cause and will pursue grievances against both supervisors and clientele who treat workers unfairly. In addition, state workers are part of a large internal labor market within which they may move both vertically and horizontally. Given all of the above conditions, a public service custodial job might be considered part of the "*sub-primary*" rather than secondary sector of the labor market (*cf.* Edwards 1977, chap. 9).

For most of the workers, night work at Urban University was better work that they had had in the past. For women in particular, the job paid more than previous jobs as nursing assistants or private sector custodial workers and offered more job security than entry-level factory work. Opportunity for advancement was limited, but one could move three levels from Building Maintenance Worker I to Section Supervisor. When asked why they took their jobs, the female custodial workers said either that the job paid better than those they had previously held or that they had been unemployed for more than six months prior to starting their current jobs.

Extrinsic benefits, however, are not commonly thought to transform a demeaning, dirty job into "good work." Good work allows for autonomy and expression of oneself. Good work elevates and nurtures, and does not belittle or undermine a person. Good work allows one to take pride in accomplishments and to work independently most, if not all, of the time.

With few exceptions, the night custodians interviewed in 1979 described their work as good work by the above criteria. They liked the independence of working by themselves while everyone else was out of the building. They liked the freedom from supervision that allowed them to pace their own work and take breaks after finishing major tasks. As one woman put it, "You can get a lot of work done both at home and at work. You're not in anybody's way, and you're not always standing around saying 'excuse me.'" She could clean during the day at home while her five children were at work and school and clean at night on the job while faculty and students were at home.

At night the custodian "owns" the area for which she or he is responsible. As long as their areas pass inspection by the time they leave in the morning, and their supervisors hear few complaints from the daytime clientele, nighttime custodial workers can usually set their own pace and routine. They can vary the order in which they clean rooms or do daily tasks and make their own schedules for waxing floors. If the building is not occupied at night, they are free to work in any room at any time. They are also free to use facilities that belong by day to their clientele. They may cook their lunches in the office microwave oven, watch a late movie in the VIP lounge during their breaks, or take a short nap on the lobby sofa. They can also socialize with coworkers in comfortable surroundings that are public by day but theirs alone at night.

At Urban University, workers described strong proprietary feelings about "their" areas. One man said, for example, that he had been working in his area longer than he had lived in any apartment. His nighttime building therefore felt more like "home" than his daytime one. Several female workers complained of how difficult it was to inherit other workers' areas when they were transferred to other floors. If the area had not been "kept up like it should," one would have to "strip out" the floors and start over. It might take months to get a poorly kept floor "up to where it should be" (i.e., no waxed-over residues of dirt). And, female workers, in particular, complained that inherited areas were never as clean as they themselves would have kept them. Both male and female workers, however, made it clear that they had their own standards, and that they took pride in leaving their areas in good condition after a night's work.

When asked what they didn't like about their work, the third-shift custodial workers most often said "feeling tired all the time" and "not being able to get proper rest." Some complained that the work was routine and offered little challenge. Nonetheless, being able to decide the order of their tasks did allow workers to introduce variety.

THE WORK/FAMILY KALEIDOSCOPE

Working third shift gave workers more control over their work but had mixed effects on their personal lives. Childcare, housework, doctors' appointments, and bill paying were often easier to do during the day. However, if family members worked first shift, the third-shift worker saw them only in the evening. Since between 30 percent and 50 percent of all night workers take naps in the evening before going to work, many night workers don't see much of their families in the evening either. On weekends, night workers try to catch up on their sleep so that they will be ready to start work again on Sunday night. Although the night worker has the freedom to schedule sleep and other activities as she wishes during the day and evening, the cost of this freedom is a permanent state of exhaustion for all but the few who are truly "night people."[3]

Given the complex households run by most of the women in this study, the mandatory shift change forced them to reassemble their lives on several levels simultaneously. Like the pattern in a kaleidoscope, the arrangement of each of their lives was transformed by a single external alteration. In turn, the lives of their husbands, children, and grandchildren were also altered. The more complex the family network, the further the ripple effects of the pattern change extended.

Consider, for example, Mrs. Anna Williams, 58-year-old mother of eight children, age 17 to 37. In 1979, her household consisted of herself, her husband (age 58), a 17-year-old daughter, and an 8-year-old grandson. Three children and four grandchildren lived nearby. A granddaughter who was staying in a "home" because of a drug problem had had a baby the year before, and she was thinking of coming to live with the Williams' family with her baby in the future, which would mean that Anna Williams would have an infant as well as a young child to care for.[4]

While working night shift, Mrs. Williams got home at 7:00 A.M. She made breakfast for herself and her grandson and then saw him off to school. Between 8:00 A.M. and 11:00 A.M., she did laundry, shopped for groceries, and took care of bills. (She did not use a checking account and so paid bills in person, a practice common to most of the black workers.) In addition, she sometimes did extra work cleaning for other people during the day. Because Mrs. Williams slept from noon until 5:00, her grandson had to let himself in at 4:00 when he returned from school. He then had to stay in the house until Mrs. Williams got up. Mr. Williams worked at a construction job from 6:00 A.M. to 6:00 P.M., and their daughter, Joyce, worked until 4:00 P.M. at an insurance company. Consequently, no one was around to supervise the grandson until Mrs. Williams woke up (or the daughter came home). Anna Williams got up for an hour between 5:00 and 6:30 P.M., had something to eat, and saw her family briefly if they were home. Since Mr. Williams liked to play bingo and Joyce had meetings on Tuesday and Thursday evenings, the family rarely had evening meals together during the week. Instead, Mrs. Williams enlisted help with food preparation from her husband and daughter on weekends. Family members would then warm up food as needed during the week.

When asked how her family's schedule would be affected by the shift change, Mrs. Williams said that she would probably get up at 5:30 A.M., and that her daughter (who works variable hours) could see the grandson off to school. Otherwise, they would have to rely on outside childcare. She would be able to clean her own house in the afternoon after getting home at 3:30 P.M., but she didn't know when she would take care of business such as bills and doctors' appointments. Furthermore, she would have a hard time doing cleaning for others since her private clients would be at home in the evening and on the weekend. And if her granddaughter and great-grandchild came to live with her, she would have trouble caring for the baby. She did mention, however, that her 19-year-old daughter had said that she could care for the granddaughter's baby.

Given all of the above considerations, one can easily understand why Anna Williams was not in favor of the shift change when it was originally announced. In August 1979 she said that she would rather stay on third shift "for the time being" because she was able to do more for her family on that schedule. She made more money, had more time available during the day, and did not have to pay the $166 per year daytime parking fee at Urban University. If she worked days, she would lose the $450 night differential and would have to pay more for parking. However, Anna Williams ultimately decided that if she were moved to days, she would try it to see if she could adjust. After having worked for ten years as a domestic in Tennessee and another ten as a nursing assistant in the Midwest, she felt fortunate to have a state job at Urban University. At 58, with eight years of formal education, she did not anticipate finding another job that paid as well, even thought she said that she would "look into other things."

WORKING DAYS AT URBAN UNIVERSITY

Several of the other women described home situations as complicated as that of the Williams' household, and most thought that custodial work would be harder to do during the day. Nonetheless, nearly half the women (compared to just over a quarter of the men) favored the change to day shift. The reasons they gave were health and their family lives. A 40-year-old widowed mother of four school-aged children spoke of how hard it was to sleep during the day and of her fear of being out at night. The men who favored the change also mentioned family and social lives as among their reasons for wanting to go to day shift; but since 25 percent of the men lived alone (compared to only 10 percent of the women), fewer men were concerned about improving the fit between their own and other household members' schedules. Like the women, the men worried about whether they would be unable to finish their work while students and faculty were in the buildings. As one 35-year-old, white, married man complained:

> The students will get in the way of the cleaning and the bosses will complain. There will be more people bossing you around. They [the bosses] are basically stupid. They don't know how to clean correctly. They should have listened to the experienced custodians when we told them the job couldn't be done on days.

Although his wife worked first shift, this man expected to look for another third shift job rather than go on days.

Comments about custodians' powerlessness in their attempts to deal with management or about the weakness of the union were far more typical of the male custodians than of the women. A middle-aged black man complained that in making the shift change without consulting him or the other custodians, management had treated him "like a child" — and he added, "I ain't no white man's child." Whereas the men were insulted at not having been taken into account and at having been "pushed around" by management, the women spoke more often of the complex effects the shift change would have on their work and family lives. As Gilligan (1982) and Miller (1976) might have predicted, the males' objections focused on hierarchy, patterns of domination, and abstract principles of right and wrong, whereas the females' concerns were expressed in terms of networks, relationships, and ability to care for their areas and their families. This difference may help to explain the fact that men were far more likely than women to change their opinions about the shift change after it happened. Wounded pride heals, but a changed patterns of relationships with supervisors, clientele, and family has lasting effects.

After the change, 70 percent of the men as opposed to 48 percent of the women liked working days. Of the 32 men who were opposed to the change before, 23 decided afterwards that they liked the change or didn't care. Of the eight women who were opposed to the change beforehand, only two changed their minds later on. Another two who had liked the idea initially decided that they did not like it after the change. Although both men and women found the work harder to do during the day (71 percent of men; 86 percent of women), not being able to do their work properly affected the women more negatively than it did the men. Whereas men who had been opposed to the change said that they felt better on days because they were getting more sleep, the women more often said that they felt worse because of the tension of working around so many people. Women were more likely than men to report feeling rushed (62 percent vs. 38 percent) and to complain of pressure from supervisors and clientele.

In a tape recorded interview, Norma James, a union steward, explained why working days took all the pride out of her work:

JH: I'm interested in your own impression of how the change to first shift affected working conditions?

NJ: Very bad. Very bad. It takes all the respect of your work out. It's like we're not working, like we we're not doing anything. It looks the same from the time when I come in the morning, till I go home at night. . . . As soon as we do a floor, people walk on it, and it's right back to the way it was before. . . . And it doesn't show. And that hurts a person. That's not the same as a person who types all day and you can see your work. . . . It's just like we are not doing anything. It takes all the get-up out of it. . . . You don't see no finished job. You don't see nothing. All you see is what you know you did, but five minutes later it's just like nothing was ever done. . . . Now, when we leave, we leave it looking just like it did when we came in.

Later in the interview, Norma James explained why there was actually less work to do on the day shift than there had been on nights:

> You can't do it. You can't work with wall-to-wall people. People that know about cleaning can go through these buildings and they can see that the work is not being done properly and professionally, and we're professional people. I'm trained as a professional in my department, and you can't do professional work when you have people wall to wall. I can go out right now and clean up this spot (points to spot), and ten minutes later people will be walking all over it again. And they pay no attention to the signs. It's just like they're not there. You know if there's a chemical on the floor, you're going to try and watch for that person and say, "Hey, I got a sign that says 'Wet.'" These people don't hear you.

The personalization of day work carries with it both the danger of disempowerment by a higher-status clientele and the challenge of predicting and controlling clientele behavior. As Hughes points out, "People who do dirty work protect honorific self-conceptions from those who threaten to weaken them with disrespectful behavior" (1974, 280). Thus the meatcutter defines interactions with his customers as unwelcome interruptions from his "real work with meat" (Meara 1974, 275), and the apartment house janitor "reads" telltale garbage left around the trash bin to gain power over uncooperative tenants (Hughes 1958, 51; Gold 1952). Comments about how the workers really knew how to clean and "were trained as professionals," whereas the bosses were "stupid" and did not know how the job should be done, served as protective defenses against the frequent daytime assaults on the worker's pride.

Status discrepancies that contributed to injured pride were far more problematic during the day than they had been at night. At night workers were either alone or with their peers most of the time. One woman especially liked the fact that she could look as sloppy as she wanted to and did not have to have her hair done each day. A young white man didn't mind doing custodial work at night, but during the day, he was embarrassed when he saw college students who had graduated from his high school. Most important, workers had difficulty getting professors to do what was necessary and resented having professors and administrators tell them to do things that often were not even in their job descriptions. As one man put it, "Everyone is a custodian's boss." One woman described the situation this way:

> Any little move you make with some of these professors, it upsets them. This job is just not to be done during the day. It's like trying to clean a house with eight kids. . . . We have more bosses. Faculty and students tell you what to do. At home, I get home and slap my kids down for aggravating me.

A man described a conflict with a woman faculty member who insisted on exiting from the elevator at the place where he has waxed. When he asked her to get out at the floor above and walk down, she refused. Instead she walked right over his wax so that he had to redo it. To add insult to injury, she wouldn't talk to him for a month after that.

In order to get their higher-status clientele to do what they wanted them to, some workers employed "cultivating techniques." Cultivated relationships are often observed between a service person and his or her clientele (*cf.* Butler and Snizek 1976). In an article on milkmen and their customers, Bigus describes the cultivated relationship as one that is carried out to gain a reward. Although not limited to service relationships, cultivated relationships "are usually asymmetrical, with the less powerful party utilizing cultivating tactics to bring the relationship closer to a state of symmetry" (Bigus 1972, 131–32).

Successful cultivating techniques were described by a woman who had been a worker in 1979, but had become a supervisor since the shift change (the first black female supervisor and only the second female supervisor out of six section supervisors). When interviewed in April 1982, Carol Wright had been a supervisor for two months. She had worked third shift for six months before changing to first in August 1979. The worker-turned-supervisor spoke of how it was possible to overcome the crowding problem by scheduling cleaning with the building's occupants:

> We found out their schedules and we got used to them, finding out when the best time of day was for going in and cleaning up their office. Some didn't mind if the door was open, we'd clean and then come out. Some preferred that you didn't come in while they were there. Some, we'd clean while they were out to lunch break.

For Carol Wright and a minority of other workers (27 percent) having to plan and negotiate cleaning schedules was a challenge that made it easier rather than harder to take pride in their work on days. As Carol said, "It's more a creative-type work, not a routine cleaning offices." If having to work around wall-to-wall people wounded the pride of many workers, others were able to transform human obstacles into a clientele who could be managed. They then substituted pride in these managerial skills for pride in the once-clean floor.

In addition to access to rooms, cultivated relationships could also yield birthday and Christmas presents in exchange for special favors. Helping a faculty member move a file cabinet or watering plants while someone was on vacation could mean a ten-dollar tip or a fifth of Scotch. One supervisor claimed that the workers in his section "made out like bandits" at Christmas. However, unlike waitresses, taxi drivers, and milkmen, the custodians at Urban University used cultivation primarily in order to manage their work environment rather than as a means of gaining material awards.

When one-time requests of strangers and cultivated relationships with clientele did not suffice, workers sometimes used other strategies to protect their fresh wax from the intrusive footprints of unruly and disrespectful professors. One afternoon the author waited for an elevator for over fifteen minutes. As the crowd on the first floor grew, speculations circulated about what could be

keeping both elevators stuck on the fifth floor. Finally several of us began climb-
ing the stairs to the seventh and eighth floors. When we got to the fifth floor,
we peered around the corner and saw two young female custodians guarding
their drying floor while both elevators stood there, idle and open. They had
stopped the elevators to prevent anyone from stepping on their floors. This
"engineering solution" to their problem was far more effective than relying on
requests to professors. They also managed to bypass the status discrepancy problem: "If they walk on your floors, let them climb stairs."

KEEPING THE FAMILY TOGETHER ON DAY SHIFT

Although most workers found their work lives more stressful after the
change to days, home lives generally improved. Unlike the woman who was
so aggravated by faculty that she slapped her children around, most women
found that they had more rather than less patience with their children. Getting more and better sleep made the women less irritable. One woman said
that she enjoyed her children more because she was not as "mean"as she used
to be. For others, working days meant that they spent afternoons and evenings
with their families. They also had more time on weekends because they didn't
have to catch up on sleep. If husbands' schedules permitted, the couple did
more tasks together. Rather than shop alone during the day, the worker and
her husband would go shopping in the later afternoon or evening. Since the
women could no longer do housework during weekdays, some of them reported
getting more help from their families on the weekends. Three male workers commented that they helped their wives more now that they were together in the
evenings. Although women workers were still doing most of the housework
and childcare, some were able to get more help simply because other family
members were more likely to be around at the same time.

The Williams' family (described earlier) fit this pattern. After the shift
change, Anna Williams shopped with her husband, who had been laid off from
his construction job. The great-grandchild (but not the granddaughter) and
a daughter and unemployed son-in-law had moved in, and Anna was still caring for the grandson. Since she had begun working days, the whole family had
been having evening meals together at 4:45 P.M. After dinner Anna read, visited
with family and sometimes watched TV. She was in bed by 10:00 P.M. as she
had to get-up at 5:00 A.M. to get both children ready for the sitter. The daughter living with her uncle was unable to help in the mornings as she was in a
job-training program, but she did help Anna at other times. Anna's main problems on days were scheduling doctors' appointments and losing both the night
differential and the extra income she used to earn doing domestic work. Furthermore, as she had feared, day work at Urban University was indeed harder.
She had to rush to get ahead of the students in the morning. In spite of all
these problems, Anna Williams thought that the change in her work hours
had improved the overall quality of her life.

DISCUSSION AND CONCLUSIONS

This paper presents a diagonal "timeslice" in the lives of public service custodial workers. A mandatory shift change forced the workers to move from night to day work, and as it turned out, day work was an entirely different job from night work. Although men and women had many of the same reactions to the change, more women favored the change initially. Afterwards, men who had been opposed changed their minds, whereas women who objected to the shift change remained firm in their opposition. Before the change, men protested more vociferously to having the change imposed on them by management, while women more often allowed their objections to be tempered by the prospect of having a good night's sleep and increased time with their families. However, after the change, the women were more upset than the men when their own internal standards of work performance were violated by the new work conditions.

In contrast to sociologists' sterotypes of custodial work, unionized night work in public buildings is good work and may even be better than clerical work in a variety of ways. Day custodial work, however, is more like housework because one must clean and reclean, and one never sees the results of one's work. Day work is therefore less satisfying than night work unless one can shift one's focus to relationships with the clientele. Then, as with housework, job satisfaction is contingent on positive feedback from one's clientele (cf. Ferree 1975). The personalization of daytime custodial work, however, also creates status conflicts that can make day work far more demanding than night work.

Finally, especially for the women in the Night-to-Day-Study, night and day work cannot be compared without considering the entire "work/family role system" (Pleck 1977). Work is good work if it gives back more than it takes out. For half of the women, day work — even if harder and more demanding — gave back more energy than it took, allowing the women to enjoy their families and their leisure more than they had while working nights. For the others, the increased pressure on the job and the loss of work pride outweighed any gains made by being able to sleep nights and spend evenings with their families.

NOTES

1. Segmented labor market theorists distinguish among primary, subordinate-primary, and secondary labor market segments. Whereas the secondary market is seen as the domain of marginal workers such as service workers and low-level clerical workers with little job security and almost no chance for advancement, the subordinate-primary sector jobs offer some job security, stable employment, higher wages and established paths for advancement. They are distinguished from the secondary labor market largely by the presence of unions (Edwards 1977, 169–71).

2. Urban University announced in June 1979 that its 124 night custodians would begin working day shift on July 16. Baseline data, therefore, had to be gathered quickly. With the blessing of both the Facilities Department and the Union, we were able to conduct interviews on the job. By July 16, the researcher, her fiance, and four graduate students had interviewed 71 of the 124 workers. The department then decided to postpone the change and to move workers to day shift in three phases over a one-year period. We were therefore able to interview another 33 workers before the first group began working days on August 13. T1 interviews totaled 104, 84 percent of the night custodial worker population at Urban University. Of the remaining workers, 3 refused to be interviewed, and 17 were on vacation or sick leave or had mental or physical handicaps that made them difficult to interview. Thus, to the extent that the workers interviewed differ from the population as a whole, they include fewer older and handicapped workers.

Of the 104 workers interviewed in 1979, 76 were working at the university on first shift in August 1980. After an unsuccessful attempt to clean the busy library during the day, the 11 library custodians, with support from faculty and students, had won the right to return to night shift. Of the remaining 17, 3 were working second shift elsewhere at the university; 14 had quit, transferred out of the university, been fired or died. Thus, in 1980–81 we were able to interview 63 (83 percent) of the 76 who had made the change to day shift (T2). Of the remaining 13, 4 had not given permission for a follow-up at T1, 3 refused a second interview at T2, and 6 were not located by interviewers. Compared to the workers remaining in the panel, the 41 who dropped out included more men and whites, slightly more workers initially opposed to the change (62 percent vs. 53 percent), and more who planned to avoid working days by transferring to second shift, looking for another third-shift job, working days on another job, or retiring (32 percent vs. 8 percent).

Half the workers in the panel had 12 or more years of education. Their average age was 42. Two-thirds were male and 52 percent were black, 42 percent were married or living with someone at the time of the second interview, 34 percent were separated, widowed, or divorced, and 24 percent were single. In addition, 30 percent had regular childcare responsibilities for their own children or for grandchildren. The custodians were either: 1) older migrants from other jobs such as construction, machine tool work, or health care; 2) younger workers just entering the labor force; or 3) middle-aged and older workers who had done custodial work at Urban University or elsewhere most of their lives. Fifty-six percent had worked second or third shift in their previous jobs, and although only 3 workers said that they had taken their jobs at Urban University because it was night work, 37 percent said that they wanted to work nights at the time they took the job.

3. For a review of the shiftwork literature, see Hood and Milazzo, (1984).

4. Taking care of both the grandson and the infant great-granddaughter was defined as Anna Williams' responsibility even when the children's aunts

or mothers were around. Perhaps because the daughter and granddaughter were not defined as competent mothers, Mrs. Williams assumed the role of primary caretaker. (See Miller [elsewhere in this volume] on mothers of street walkers, and Stack [1974] on childcare patterns in a black female cooperative network.)

REFERENCES

Bigus, O.S. 1972. "The milkman and his customer: A cultivated relationship," *Urban Life and Culture* 1:131-65.

Butler, S., and W.E. Snizek. 1976. "The waitress-diner relationship: A multi-method approach to the study of subordinate influence," *Sociology of Work and Occupations* 3:2:209-222.

Edwards, R. 1977. *Contested Terrain; The Transformation of the Workplace in the Twentieth Century.* New York: Basic Books.

Ferree, M. 1975. "Working class jobs: Housework and paid work as sources of satisfaction," *Social Problems* 23:431-41.

Gilligan, C. 1982. *In a Different Voice.* Cambridge, MA: Harvard University Press.

Gold, R. 1952. "Janitors versus tenants: A status-income dilemma," *American Journal of Sociology* 57:486-93.

Hood, J.C. 1984. "When changing shifts means changing jobs: Quality of work-life for custodial workers on the day shift." Unpublished manuscript. University of Wisconsin-Milwaukee, Milwaukee, Wisconsin.

Hood, J.C., and N. Milazzo. 1984. "Shiftwork, stress and wellbeing," *Personal Administrator* 29:95-105.

Hughes, E.C. 1958. *Men and Their Work.* Glencoe, IL: The Free Press.

———. 1974. "Comments on 'Honor in dirty work,'" *Sociology of Work and Occupations* 1:284-87.

Meara, H. 1974. "Honor in dirty work: The case of American meat cutters and Turkish butchers," *Sociology of Work and Occupations* 1:259-83.

Melbin, M. 1978. "Night as frontier," *American Sociological Review* 43:3-22.

Miller, J.B. 1976. *Toward a New Psychology of Women.* Boston: Beacon.

Montagna, P. 1977. *Occupations and Society.* New York: Wiley.

Pleck, J.H. 1977. "The work-family role system," *Social Problems* 24:417-27.

Stack, C. 1974. *All Our Kin: Strategies for Survival in a Black Community.* New York: Harper and Row.

CHAPTER 7

"Some Peoples Calls It Crime:" Hustling, the Illegal Work of Underclass Women

ELEANOR M. MILLER

INTELLECTUAL CONTEXT: THE ADLER/SIMON THESIS

The "new female criminal" was discovered in 1975 with the publication of Freda Adler's *Sisters in Crime* and Rita James Simon's *Women and Crime*. Both works elaborate a theme that links increases in the criminality of women in the United States since the late 1960s to the contemporary "women's movement." Simon attributes a dramatic rise in crimes against property committed by women to an *objective* change in the circumstances of women made possible by the women's movement: recent increases in their labor force participation have given women unprecedented opportunities to commit white-collar crimes. Adler, on the other hand, attributes what she sees as a general increase in the criminality of women across all categories of crime to a *subjective* change: recent shifts in the sex-role attitudes and orientations of women make them more prone to a whole array of crimes. Both explanations have been shown to have serious flaws (for a more detailed discussion of these flaws than that below see Miller 1983).

The Simon thesis ignores evidence about the types of crime typically committed by women. The typical female offender is young, poor, and belongs to a minority. She has limited education and skills, is the mother of several children, and has been involved in prostitution or committed a petty property crime or a drug-related offense (Chapman 1980, 60). While she has, as Simon notes, been drawn into crimes of larceny, fraud, embezzlement, and forgery (U.S. General Accounting Office 1979, 17–18), these have *not* been crimes committed in the course of legitimate work. Rather, the larcenies of women tend to be counts of shoplifting; the crimes of fraud are instances of credit card fraud; the embezzlements are the more petty varieties; and the forgeries most often involve stolen personal checks. These are crimes, then, not of white-collar female employees, but rather of the unemployed, the poor. Even when women work, the jobs they have would not put them in positions to commit the crimes discussed by Simon. In recent years, women have for the most part taken jobs that have typically been "women's jobs." They are service workers, clerks, typists, salespeople, waitresses (U.S. Department of Commerce 1970; Gross 1968). Their jobs do not lend themselves to the commission of serious property crimes; this is even more true for the years when the first increases are noted (1966–1967) than it is today. Moreover, the greatest rise in property offenses among females seems to be concentrated among those women who, because of their youth, have little or no acquaintance with the world of work (Noblit and Burcart 1976).

The Adler thesis ignores the fact that the violent crime rate for women has remained relatively stable over time, that what has been increasing are the selected property crimes mentioned above (Steffensmeier 1980; Mukherjee and Fitzgerald 1981). If an attitudinal change were, indeed, responsible for the observed increases, one would expect increases across both crimes against property and crimes against persons. As already observed, this is not the case. In addition, changes in sex-role attitudes have been very gradual; most American women were not even exposed to the latest wave of the women's movement until the *end* of the 1960s or the early 1970s (Mason, Czajka and Arber 1976), and FBI data indicate 1966–1967 as the point at which the rates for selected property crimes begin and continue to increase.[1]

The larger study from which the material detailed below is taken (Miller 1986) was conceived and carried out against this intelletual backdrop. It challenges the arguments set forth by Simon and Adler. It is an attempt to understand the everyday lives and careers of female street hustlers who were living and engaging in illegal activities, especially prostitution, fraud, forgery, embezzlement, and larceny in Milwaukee, Wisconsin in 1979. It is based upon information gleaned from topical life-history interviews completed with 64 of these women during that year. One cannot assume that all of the women described in the 1976 national study cited above were street hustlers. However, for reasons that will become obvious below, it is probably safe to assume that most of them were. Moreover, the national trends in female criminality noted since the late 1960s are very much mirrored in the trends for Wisconsin female offenders among whom Milwaukee women are disproportionately represented (Bowker 1978, 7).

Obviously, research of the qualitative sort that will be described here cannot "test" macrolevel correlations of the type proposed by Adler and Simon. What it can do, however, is to offer descriptions and analyses of actual women of the kind being theorized about in the aggregate. Ideally, we should be able to at least recognize the individual in the picture painted of the whole. Depth studies of the individuals being aggregated should yield hypotheses crucial to bridging the gap between individual behavior and macrotrends by suggesting some of the mechanisms by which the one gets translated into the other. To this end, a portion of the 1979 study of Milwaukee's female street hustlers will be discussed here to begin to attempt to shed some light on the relationship between changes in the social and economic conditions of this city and recent increases in the hustling activities of its underclass females, but most importantly, to provide a detailed picture of just what those activities are, how they are organized, and how they are understood by those women who engage in them. It will be demonstrated that only when one frames these activities as illegal *work* rather than as crime can one understand them as those who engage in them do (See Miller, 1986 for a more detailed discussion of this argument). Moreover, only then does the impact of social and economic conditions — both nationally and locally — on increases in what others, quite accurately define as crime, become really clear.

THE SETTING

All of the fieldwork for this study of female street hustlers and the majority of the interviews on which it is based took place in Milwaukee, Wisconsin. At the time of the study, 1978-1979, the city had an estimated population of 637,317 (Wisconsin Department of Industry 1979, 1). Like many other northern cities of its kind, it is now in many ways a city in decline. Due to prolonged recession, the availability of cheaper, more easily disciplined labor elsewhere, foreign competition, and an outmoded physical and technical infrastructure, it has been plagued by "run-away shops." Thus, its large force of skilled and semi-skilled laborers have suffered from high levels of unemployment as, of course, have its unskilled workers and service workers.

A comparison of 1970 and 1980 census data lends support to a thesis about Milwaukee that originated in the 1960s: Milwaukee is very much two cities. Almost all outlying areas of the city show very low percentages for families below the poverty line in both 1970 and 1980. Conversely, all percentages on families with incomes below poverty increase as neighborhood location moves towards the center of the city. During this time the percentage of unemployed persons was increasing throughout the city. At any point in time, however, percents in predominantly black center-city neighborhoods were two or more times greater than the overall city percent (Palay 1984, not paginated).

The center city areas also have the highest levels of single female family heads. Moreover, data on single female family heads changed considerably between 1970 and 1980 as did other measures of economic well-being. In 1970, the city figure was 10.6 percent. By 1980 it had risen to 15.5 percent. Following national trends, more and more women were becoming heads of households, more of them and their children were falling into the ranks of the poor, and, in Milwaukee they constituted a larger and larger proportion of center city residents (Palay, 1984, unpaginated).

What appears, then, is a picture of a city highly segregated by race/ethnicity and income. In fact, what one sees is, indeed, two cities: a peripheral white city that has certainly fallen victim to the national recession and the erosion of the local economy but, despite that, remains relatively affluent and an increasingly poverty-ridden, predominantly minority inner city.

THE SAMPLE

The sample of female street hustlers for this study was gathered by starting "snowballs" rolling at four different locations: two halfway houses for female offenders, the Milwaukee House of Correction and a pre-release center for women who had served time in the state's correctional facility for female felons, Taycheedah. Women interviewed were asked to refer the investigator to other women who had been similarly engaged who might be willing to be investigated. By this method 84 women were contacted, 70 agreed to taped interviews, and 64 interviews were ultimately deemed usable and analyzed. About one-third of the 64 informants were institutionalized at the time of the interview. The remainder were actively hustling.

Of the women interviewed, 35 (55 percent) of the women were black, 24 (38 percent) were white, four (6 percent) were Hispanic and one (2 percent) was Native American. The mean age of the women was 23.38 years. The 64 women had 81 children among them, and 50 percent of the women had 5 or more siblings. At the time of the interview 72 percent of the women were single. When the last year of regular schooling is used to calculate means rather than including the schooling completed in correctional institutions, the mean number of years of schooling completed is 10.69. Including both part time and full time (licit) work, and work engaged in under Huber Law (work-release), the mean duration of longest "straight" employment for the entire sample was 7.83 months.

THE SOCIAL CONTEXT OF FEMALE STREET HUSTLING: DEVIANT STREET NETWORKS

Most street hustling is carried out in the context of deviant street networks.[2] By a deviant street network I mean a selection of individuals mobilized in relation to specific illicit ends. Such a network has fluid boundaries, may or may not have a real nucleus, and can be activated for relatively short or for extended periods of time. Network activity revolves around all sorts of clever "scams," but includes prostitution, petty larceny, forgery, credit card fraud, embezzlement, auto theft, drug traffic, burglary, and robbery. I would argue that only by becoming integrated into one or more deviant street networks can a street hustler "make a living by a hustle."[3] This is especially true for females, who are disadvantaged in terms of illegitimate opportunities in many of the same ways that they are disadvantaged with regard to legitimate opportunities.[4]

Network Structure and Functions

Generally speaking, the major function of deviant street networks is to facilitate street hustling as an income-producing strategy for those with whom one has historically engaged in such activity or those who have been identified as likely future partners in such endeavors. These networks often focus on a particular sort of street activity, such as dealing drugs, although they can be mobilized for other illegal pursuits as well. Through deviant street networks, information about opportunities to make money on a hustle and potential threats to one's ability to do so either by the authorities or nonnetwork hustlers is disseminated. They are especially important in helping one learn to tell whether or not a potential victim is a vice officer by hugging him in such a way as to detect "his piece" (gun), when a bust is "coming down," or when a chance to make "a piece of money" is about to present itself. In addition to being a source of information, deviant street networks may be a source of socio-emotional support, self-esteem, and courage. They are often also the locus of behavior that is exploitative, manipulative, and physically brutalizing.

In Milwaukee, there is an extensive set of deviant networks that are controlled predominantly by black males in their mid-to-late twenties and early thirties. These men are likely to have lengthy criminal records such that future encounters with the law would almost certainly result in extended prison terms. As a result, they attempt to confine themselves to criminal activity that is not easily detected. Their major source of continuous income derives from the hustling activity of women who turn their earnings over to them in exchange for affection, an allowance, the status of their company, and some measure of protection, even if it is simply permission to use the man's name as a "keepaway" [from me] for other predatory men. These men form loose alliances to control the women who work for them, to promote their own hustling endeavors, and to socialize.

Each man has two or three women working for him. These individuals together form a pseudo-family. The women refer to each other as "wives-in-law" and to the male for whom they hustle as "my man." To the degree that such men fear arrest and are successful in establishing such an arrangement, they are able to live "the fast life" with limited risk. Although these men may fit the stereotype of the "pimp" in appearance, lifestyle, and income-source, it is rare for them to procure "johns" for their women. Many of these women do work as prostitutes, but there is some diversity in their hustling activity. One woman I spoke with described a situation in which she worked primarily as a prostitute at the same time that one of her wives-in-law "busted paper" (forged) and the other "boosted" (shoplifted).

The descriptions provided by the women interviewed also indicate a dynamic rather than a static pattern of both deviant managers and deviant management. Males may begin their careers in deviant management over and over again as "men" in boyfriend/girlfriend sorts of arrangements wherein the male controls the female primarily in socioemotional ways, only later to approach the more business-like pimp type with the addition of one or two wives-in-law to work with their "bottom woman." What appears to occur in Milwaukee is a trend toward the pimp form as the deviant manager attempts to enlarge his stable. This trend is continually subverted, however, by police activity and by the demands for more personal relationships by the women.[5]

A common pattern over time is one in which one woman and her recently-released-from-prison lover start to generate an income based on her prostitution. At the same time, he begins hustling on his own, maybe selling a little "weed." He has become her man and, depending on her level of awareness and audience, she will acknowledge as much. With increased income and greater freedom from the risk of arrest and the hard work of streetwalking a possibility, the woman may be persuaded to take a wife-in-law. As a result, the first woman becomes bottom woman. This status entitles her to work less both on the street and at home because of the additional income and help with housework that may come with the other woman. It also may make her a manager in her own right, although one subordinate to the man. At a later stage, a second wife-in-law may be recruited. Usually these new wives-in-law are relatively new at street hustling because: 1) they are easier to control than more streetwise women; 2) such women can demand a higher price from johns than older hookers; and 3) the group is less likely to suffer a loss of income due to a lengthy prison term if she is arrested. Young runaways fit the bill nicely. From the man's point of view, this is a desirable arrangement because having more women enhances his prestige, increases his income, and reduces his risk and his work. In addition, he has probably obtained a new sexual partner in the deal.

His main problem, then, is one of social control. He especially needs to meet the sexual and socioemotional needs of his women without creating infighting and jealousy among them. Sometimes he may want to encourage a certain amount of discord among his women as a means of controlling them or at least to dissuade them from ganging up on him. If he is unsuccessful in achieving this delicate balance or is arrested, the pseudo-family dissolves. It may also break up due to the active intervention of one of the women. It is not uncommon for a jealous woman to put one of her wives-in-law in a position that leads to her arrest. Also, to the extent that a man's women know about their man's hustling activities, they have some power over him. Vice officers will often offer not to arrest a female street hustler in exchange for information about her man. Although a woman and her man may be together for quite some time, anywhere from a few months to several years, then, these pseudo-families are inherently unstable and are thus unlikely to survive for very long. When they dissolve, the women may become part of other pseudo-families or begin a one-to-one relationship with another man. Upon release from prison, a male may similarly attempt to hook up with one of his former women and be her man until he finds a suitable woman to be her wife-in-law. A female may also seek out her former man after release from jail or prison, pregnancy, illness, or an unsuccessful attempt to go straight or hustle alone. Then the cycle begins anew.

The desire for greater financial rewards and a more stable income, more prestige, less work, and fewer risks, then, prompts both men and women to form pseudo-families. Nonetheless, many of the women who come to the street are looking for caring relationships. What results is often a form of association that carries within itself the seeds of its own destruction. There are just too many ways in which the instrumental nature of the arrangement overrides the affectional aspirations of the women. Even the recruitment strategy employed by men sets them up for failure as pimps. Many of the women recruited are particularly vulnerable to males who project a caring, almost fatherly, demeanor because they are naive runaways or because they come from deeply troubled families. Men who recruit females using this fatherly ploy, however, are particularly vulnerable to being uncovered as exploiters at a later date. For these women the personal side of the relationship far outweighs the business side in importance. As a matter of fact, one of the most common reasons for a woman to leave a man is when some occurrence makes it obvious that the relationship, from his point of view, is entirely for business purposes. On such occasions, women would say: "He wasn't nothin' but a pimp."

WORKING

Recruitment to Street Hustling

Among female street hustlers in Milwaukee there are three analytically distinct, although occasionally intersecting, paths that lead to involvement in deviant street networks. The first is related to membership in a particular "domestic network."[6] The second stems from the vulnerable position young women find themselves in because they are runaways, and the third is the result of drug use.

The domestic network seems directly or indirectly responsible for the recruitment of black women who become involved in street hustling. Specifically, the reduced "boundedness" of domestic networks, as compared to the more nuclear family forms characteristic of the middle class, leave children more susceptible to recruitment to deviant street networks despite what are often heroic efforts on the part of parents or guardians to prevent this from occurring. This is especially the case when there is some degree of intersection between domestic networks and deviant street networks.

The route to involvement in deviant street networks taken by runaways or "pushouts" (those who left home because of physical or sexual abuse or were actually thrown out) seems to be available to young women with little regard for race, ethnicity, or social class. As mentioned above, these young women are prime targets for recruitment by men or bottom women to the position of wife-in-law.

The third route, that of drug use tends to be more often trod by whites and Hispanics than blacks. It may be simply that blacks are recruited at a younger age and are thus less likely to have an actual need for drugs motivate their participation in street hustling. Alternatively, the increased likelihood of Hispanics traveling this route may be explained by their greater access to hard drugs due to the fact that drugs often make their way to Milwaukee from (or via) Mexico. It may be hypothesized that the greater propensity of whites to be recruited by this route is due to the fact that the first route is even less available to them than it is to Hispanics given the more extended family form characteristic of Hispanics.[7] Moreover, at the same time, at least the whites in this sample may have had more money to spend on drugs than did most of the young black women interviewed.

The separate consideration of each route is not meant to suggest that in every case one can say without hestitation which particular path was taken. Theoretically, a young woman may have a highly crimogenic domestic network, be a habitual runaway, and be well on the road to becoming an addict all at the same time. A causally dominant route is usually discernable, however.

The phenomena described here that seem to be of especial importance are a set of structural conditions that account for a certain race effect. Black females participate in deviant street activity in Milwaukee to a degree that far surpasses the proportion of the city's at-risk female population they constitute. Although it is impossible to estimate what proportion of women 'on the hustle' in the city are black, my conservative guess would be that it is well over half. One possible reason for this is that black women have a greater number of avenues open to them that lead to the street than do white women, with Hispanic women located somewhere in between. Black women have access to all the routes available to other women with the addition of what seems to be a rather well-traveled route, the route directly via the domestic network. Hispanic women, it would appear, have available to them the route via running away open to white women. They are also more likely than whites to have the routes via drug use and domestic networks available to them, however.

Factors Affecting the Career of a Street Hustler

Once recruited to street life, there were several groups of factors that influenced the direction of a young woman's hustling career. The first group included her contacts with the criminal justice system, her fertility and general health, the effect of street life and age on her physical attractiveness, her drug use, and the hustling activities of the men with whom she was involved. Another set of factors included her relationship to her family/household of orientation post-recruitment and usually, not unrelatedly, the shifting arrangements for the care of any children she may have. Over time, many of these factors were, in turn, modified by the dynamics of the women's hustling itself. Thus, physical attractiveness, drug use, relationship to family/household of orientation, nature and frequency of contacts with the criminal justice system, fertility, and general health were all often influenced by the activities, relationships, events, behavior patterns, and psychological states peculiar to female street hustlers.

HUSTLING AND RELATIONSHIPS WITH FAMILY/HOUSEHOLD
OF ORIENTATION

Women whose departure from home was preceded by heated conflict with parents and/or guardians and pushouts were much less likely to sustain contact with primary caretakers from their families/households of orientation than women who were recruited directly through the interface of familial networks and deviant street networks. Even when primary caretakers were violently opposed to hustling as a career for their female charges and when the knowledge of initial hustling activity was verbally condemned or physically punished, the kin of women recruited directly via familial networks were likely to find some way of accommodating the young woman's new identity and the new behavior which accompanied it. An uneasy accommodation was also the response of primary caretakers of women whose recruitment occurred as a result of running away or drug use but who were indirectly recruited through the interface of familial networks and deviant street networks. The degree of periodic conflict surrounding the street activities of these women was greater than when women were recruited directly via familial networks. Of course, many of the latter parents and/or guardians had gone to great lengths to try to prevent recruitment. In fact, it was often the fear of just such an occurrence that was the impetus for the conflicts that preceded the young women's running away or problematic drug use in the first place. The fact that a well-known proscription had been violated was not easily forgotten.

No matter which route to the street was taken, women who had children before being recruited were more likely to sustain contact with their families/households of orientation than those who did not. In every instance, women from familial networks who had begun to hustle regularly and had children either arranged for a familial network member to care for the child(ren) or were forced by the members of their households as well as by the realities of their new lives to make such arrangements. In most cases, this arrangement was simply taken for granted. The caretaker was most often whoever had taken care of the woman herself, usually her mother or grandmother or, less frequently, another female relative or the mother or grandmother of the child's father. There seemed to be general agreement that such an arrangement was in the best interest of the child(ren). The young woman would then be expected to contribute to the support of the household in which her child(ren) resided, although it was usually anticipated that her contributions would be irregular both in terms of the frequency with which they were made and their amounts.

Young women who did not grow up in domestic networks were much more likely to have given any children born before their involvement in street life up for adoption. Some such children had been placed in foster homes at some point of contact with the criminal justice system. There were several instances, here, as well, however, where the child(ren) was (were) cared for by the father's family or the young woman's mother. These women were also much more likely to have married the fathers of their children than women from domestic networks. If the marriage had been dissolved and the father or his family took responsibility for the child(ren), this was likely to have been done with some degree of acrimony and as the result of a court battle. Such formal proceedings were rare among women from domestic networks. In effect, this sort of arrangement often meant that the young woman had no access or only limited access to her child(ren). It also meant that she had no claim to AFDC payments.[8]

Continued contact with domestic networks that interface with street networks provided a greater exposure to involvement in a variety of scams for some women. These are contacts with deviant street networks that may or may not overlap with the contacts with street networks the young woman no doubt already has. Supportive relationships with members of one's family/household of orientation may also have the countervailing effect of providing the young woman a refuge when, for one reason or another, she wants or needs temporarily to leave street life.

Because of the very good chance that the caretakers who are offering the young women emotional support are also caring for their children, these elder women are in a unique position to influence the hustling behavior of young female street hustlers. They have several options open to them which they can use as threats. They can seek custody of the child(ren) themselves, thus becoming the legitimate recipient of AFDC benefits for the children should they be deemed eligible. The psychological effect of the loss of custody on the young mother should also not be minimized. In addition, because they are in close contact with those women, often even when they are "on the run," these caretakers are in a position to inform the authorities of their whereabouts and activities should they decide it is in their interest, the interest of the child(ren) they are "keeping," or the interest of the young woman for them to do so. These sorts of options seem to be acted upon to "slow down" a woman who is perceived to be "moving too fast" in order to get her to make financial contributions to the support of the household and/or curb her drug use. Caretakers may also attempt to control their former female charges when they think they are in physical danger. Georgia describes her mother's efforts to curtail her drug use and hustling as follows:

At first I thought I was going into a nervous breakdown. And my mother, she got to talking about puttin' me out and gettin' me locked up. She said: "You get yourself together or we're going to have to put you away." And I went down to 105 pounds. I was really fading away, you know. And my mother said: "What about your kids? Don't you think they need a mother, too? Think about it."

Ultimately, these women can threaten to refuse to care for the child(ren) at all. Action on such a threat could immeasurably complicate the life of the young woman but, in fact, seems rarely to be taken unless the caretaker herself becomes unable to care for the child due to ill health, old age, etc. Particularly, for women who have developed drug dependencies, pressure of this sort may have the unintended consequence of forcing a woman more deeply into street life in an attempt to provide for her own needs as well as the needs of her household of orientation.

Young women who have been "cut loose" by their families/households either prior to recruitment, at recruitment, or later because they have become too much of an emotional and financial drain, become completely dependent on their own resourcefulness. Those who don't have children or have lost custody of their children have no claim on the welfare system through AFDC although they may still be able to qualify temporarily for the less desirable benefits available through General Assistance. In fact, this usually means that they become completely vulnerable to the men who control the streets and/or to their drug habits. If they have been forced to assume responsibility for their children, the physical and emotional abuse of these children is not unlikely even if they are placed in daycare or with a hired sitter for a good part of the day or evening. Children who remain in their mother's care while she continues to hustle, risk becoming part of the next generation of "pushouts." Another not uncommon occurrence is for these children to be placed in foster homes when their mothers are convicted of felonies and sent to Taycheedah for lengthy stays or come to the attention of social service agencies and are deemed unfit. Only women who are able to set up a scam where they are relatively safe from arrest and have some control over the conditions of their work have lives stable enough to care adequately for children themselves. Georgia describes trying to juggle childcare and the hassles of dealing with fellow deviant street network members:

> I had got accused . . . once you're known for getting money and you're around and somethin' come up missing, you're gonna get accused. And it was like four other women was in the house and my "man" and his brother. They said I took $550 that was under the mattress. So, I left the house that day. I was staying back by my grandmother. But, that potty chair and things was still mine, so I felt that it was still a part a my house, too, and my kids. So we goes over there and we spent the night. But I forgot to bring my little girl's clothes for school. So I left and got the clothes and came back. I took her to school and around lunchtime I brought her back. That's when my man and his brother . . . closed me off in the bedroom and started to beat me. I was flying around the room like somebody would take a ball and bounce it up against the wall. And I didn't know what was happenin' to my kids.

The only hustling activity that street women engage in that seems to be compatible with caring for small children is fairly high-level drug dealing. As the women say, however: "The 'man' holds the bag." It is not easy for women to achieve such positions in the drug trade, nor are they likely to occupy them for very long. Only rarely did women describe attempts to hustle as "outlaw women," completely independent of men. This usually occurred after they had been badly victimized by a man they really cared for. All who attempted solo hustling of this sort, did so only once. Only women who were relatively free of legal encumbrances or were new to the streets and didn't know any better, freely chose solo hustling. It was, then, a sort of stand for independence, for taking charge of one's life. Women said of such times: "I just decided nobody knows how to spend my money better than me." However, this was a phase destined to be short-lived. Men simply would not permit women to hustle in this fashion.

Hustling and Children

Generally speaking, female street hustlers did not involve their children in their work. In certain circumstances, most particularly in shoplifting and drug traffic, women described using children as "fronts." Drugs were secreted in baby clothes or diaper bags, and strollers were used as caches for boosted items. However, usually if children stayed with their mothers or were in her care at all, it was only intermittently. The tempo of hustling, the type of scam, the pattern of arrests and confinements, the extent of guilt feelings surrounding the issue of mothering, and the willingness of kin to take responsibility for children all influenced whether or not youngsters stayed with their mothers and for how long.

The inability or unwillingness of these women to care for their own children on a regular basis and their resultant felt inadequacies as mothers left them open to manipulation not only by the members of their own families/households, but also by the men who managed their hustling. It was common for a man who wanted a woman to work for him to buy presents for her children, to support them, and to participate to some extent in their care. Such arrangements were usually short-lived. The dynamics of hustling as well as the geographic mobility characteristic of those attempting to elude the authorities were certain to undermine these attempts at domesticity. Jealousies and other conflicts also developed when males who had fathered one or more of these children and who were sometimes also hustlers sought to visit their child(ren) or objected to these arrangements. When women had left men who had not posted bail for them or who had beaten them, they often used the one sure-fire technique for making contact with a former woman when such efforts would otherwise be rebuked: they would pretend to have information about a sick or injured child. Vice officers were also reportedly not above using such ploys to gain access to women.

Several women interviewed described situations in which they were "on the run" in the state or had run to another state to escape prosecution and returned home to see children on their birthdays or other special occasions or when they heard they were ill. This sort of behavior sometimes led to their arrest. Loretta describes one such instance:

> I was fightin' with a woman my man was goin' with that I didn't know. I
> pulled a knife out of the pouch in my bra. I remember cutting her . . . and
> I just panicked. And I's scared. So we run. I would write my people and send

them $25 in the mail. I would go away out somewhere and stick the letter and the money order in the mailbox so they wouldn't know where I'd be. We found out that my son had sickle-cell trait, that he had blood in his urine, a kidney infection. And at this time my son turned three. I went home, but that was a stupid idea because the police were watchin' my daddy's house to see if I would come there to see my son. That's how I finally got picked up.

Finally, there were women who said that the needs of their children motivated them to hustle when they would have preferred "straight" work, when they knew the risk of apprehension or street violence was high, or when to do so meant leaving the child(ren) alone or with someone they didn't trust.

Children, then, are often used to manipulate female street hustlers.[9] They are also sometimes a force motivating behavior that leads to risk-taking and arrest. Alternatively, children and/or children's caretakers may also be the cause of both temporary retreats from street life and less active participation in it. The women interviewed who had for the most part withdrawn from street life said that the knowledge that their children were growing to adulthood without knowing them very well or that they failed to understand the nature of their lives was a factor in their withdrawal. Active female street hustlers were also dismayed over such situations. They often spoke with feeling about the fact that their children called another woman, "momma." Given the dynamics of hustling and the lack of legitimate options available to them, however, it is unlikely that concern for children alone would motivate a permanent withdrawal from hustling for many of the women interviewed. This is most likely the case because of the ambiguous effect of children on a female street hustler's career. On the one hand, children are a moral force militating against involvement in street life, while on the other, they are responsibilities that promote it.

Hustling and Contacts with the Criminal Justice System

Female hustlers who had been working the streets of Milwaukee and other cities for several years were very likely to have accumulated so many arrests that some of them literally had difficulty keeping track of them all. Each arrest for prostitution and shoplifting (the two most frequent misdemeanors committed by fairly recent recruits to street life along with prostitution-related offenses such as disorderly conduct and vagrancy), usually resulted in probation and/or a fine. Very shortly, after starting to accummulate arrests, women were also being picked up for the nonpayment of those fines and having their probation revoked for various reasons including more criminal activity. As a result, it would not be unusual for a woman to be sitting in jail awaiting trial on a new charge, to be responsible for the payment of at least parts of fines, and, simultaneously, to be awaiting hearings for the violation of probation constituted by her new criminal activity. These hearings may, in turn, activate stayed or withheld sentences on old charges. If the woman has been "travelin'" at all, she may also have warrants outstanding or cases pending in other parts of the state or, indeed, in other states.

Whereas some of the female hustlers interviewed had a difficult time keeping track of their arrests, they had a remarkable ability to describe the intricacies of the sanctions imposed as a result of these arrests at any point in time. In terms of their work, it was the penalties that were important, not the arrests. They were the bottom-line, so to speak, for although the costs of street life were many and far-reaching for these women, fines and time were some of the more predictable of them. Surprisingly, legal fees were not usually problematic. Most of these women were automatically deemed indigent for the purposes of determining entitlement to legal assistance because of their status as welfare recipients. As a result they would be assigned a legal aide (public defender) for their defense or to represent them in revocation hearings. Most female street hustlers in Milwaukee pleaded guilty to the charges whatever they were and waived their right to a jury trial. To do otherwise would have increased the costs to them of doing business. If they couldn't make bail, there would be the direct cost of jail time before the trial. There would also be the indirect cost of foregone earnings while in jail. The women also believed, probably correctly, that their chances for leniency were better with most judges than they would have been with a jury and that juries would probably find them guilty in any event.

The experience of jail itself was one that was more painful for female street hustlers in Milwaukee than for male hustlers for several reasons. Men could call on other men for aid, whereas women were unlikely to be friendly enough with other women who were in a position to help them to ask for their assistance. This situation is at least in part the result of competition among women for men and of the fact that men deliberately undermine the networks of women so as to control them more effectively. In addition, the female hustlers interviewed usually had fewer personal financial resources to draw upon than their men. This made them dependent on others who, for various reasons, were often not dependable.

When women were detained, they frequently used their one phone call to inform whoever was in charge of their child(ren) to make the necessary arrangements. This call usually also served to inform their families/households of their need for assistance. If their kinspersons were willing and had the resources, they might come to their aid. Very often, however, a woman's call did not do double duty. If it was her man who normally bailed her out and her family/household members did not communicate with him or did not know how to get in touch with him, then the woman would sit in jail. In this case, she was not entitled to make a second phone call. Having responsibility for children, then could mean that she would spend more time in jail before having her case heard than a similarly situated male.

Another factor that made confinement especially difficult was that the local facilities in which street women were likely to be held were basically institutions for men. Because of their relatively small numbers, provisions for the health, education, drug rehabilitation, exercise, counseling, and worship of men were systematically denied women or were periodically unavailable. Women also reported being approached by males employed at these institutions with proposals for sexual services in exchange for certain privileges.

The pain of confinement was also increased due to the practice of routinely running checks on those proposed by the women as acceptable visitors or those visitors who just showed up at the appropriate time and place. Given that outstanding warrants are likely to be discovered during such checks, many of the people whose physical presence would comfort a confined woman came to visit only at some risk. Women generally enjoyed seeing their children when confined although some found such visits an embarrassment. Often those who might bring children could not or would not, however. Milwaukee women incarcerated in Taycheedah, for example are not terribly accessible by public transportation and the ride is almost a two-hour one. Even the House of Correction is some distance from Milwaukee. Thus, confinement can be a lonely ordeal.

For women who had been in the state facility for female juvenile delinquents (the former Oregon School for Girls), the conditions may not have been especially frightening, but they were to be avoided nonetheless. Since increasing contacts with the criminal justice system were likely to result in increasingly long periods of incarceration, women were likely to look for scams that carried with them less likelihood of arrest as they aged and scams that produced faster money. With age and the physical wear of street life, then, the costs of contacts with the criminal justice system increase and the chances of being rescued by men, infatuated tricks, or kinspersons decrease. For this reason, the tendency is for women to look for safer scams. The catch is that scams for which one is less likely to be arrested are also often those that carry heavier penalties.

Atlhough the time spent in jail or the House of Correction was often painful and to be avoided if possible, female street hustlers in Milwaukee generally looked upon it as an occupational hazard.[10] Apart from putting a halt to drug use or at least temporarily reducing it, the time spent in either of the two local facilities had little discernable deterrent or rehabilitative effect on the street women intermittently incarcerated there. What it did do was to make female street hustlers reconsider their methods. Exposure to similarly situated women led to greater sophistication with regard to criminal activity and greater wariness of men. The need for close personal relationships, however, as well as the need for protection meant that this wariness was only rarely translated into completely independent hustling. Although both facilities were sex-segregated, contact between sexes was frequent and women often met or learned of males who would become their future men in those institutions.

All this meant that the search for safer scams was accompanied by the search for really "good" "men" and/or scams that allowed a greater degree of independence and autonomy. For street women these desires often motivated efforts to become bottom women or to achieve a similar status *vis-a-vis* other female street hustlers so that one was one step removed from the risk of arrest, but still benefitted from the scams of those over whom one had authority.

One might, simultaneously, also engage in one's own scams with one's man. A really good man would share his hustles with his bottom woman; it was simply an indication of their mutual trust. These activities were apt to be more serious (and potentially more lucrative) than the prostitution, shoplifting, and petty frauds, forgeries, and drug deals committed by women newly recruited to street life. Women who were successful at achieving this desired status were eventually arrested on one or more felony charges. If convicted, their history of petty criminal activities combined with their most recent offense and usually resulted in a sentence of several years in Taycheedah.

Hustling and Drug Use, Fertility, and General Health

Drug dependency did not seem to motivate participation in street life for many of the women interviewed. The pattern of use was not simply one in which the woman began using intermittently, only to progress to daily use, become increasingly dependent, and perhaps, overdose. Rather the pattern that emerged was one of intermittent use both before and after the initiation of hustling, use that was sometimes heavy and sometimes light, that included different drugs at various times, and was sometimes of lengthy and sometimes of brief duration. Once on the streets, use was conditioned by patterns of arrest and confinement, income and competing demands on income, availability, psychological state, whim, and the tempo of street life generally.

One factor that seemed to have a very strong effect on problematic usage was relationships with addicted men who dealt. Women may have used drugs with their men only to have their use become problematic when their men's use became problematic or with his arrest or some other tragedy. The most frequent occasion for the step to really problematic use was the arrest, death, or disappearance of a man, or his rejection of them. Two responses to such an event were typical. On the one hand, females then had to provide for their own drug needs while suffering the psychological loss of someone upon whom they were dependent. In this instance, they were likely to hustle indiscriminantly and accumulate numerous arrests or an arrest on a serious charge. On the other hand, if they had been involved in their man's dealing and were regarded as good risks by his suppliers, his absence was the occasion for some of them to take over his business. None of this suggests that women who used drugs didn't have problems or that use didn't contribute to their continued hustling or arrests. It is simply to dispel the myth of the drug-crazed woman hungering for a fix as the typical street woman.

Clearly, drug use increases risk of arrest and can influence both type and frequency of hustling because it increases the need for fast money. Those women who do develop severe dependencies run the risk of ending up outside of deviant street networks completely because they get defined by other street people as trouble. They simply are not trustworthy enough to associate with.

Drug use is also associated with poor nutrition and poor health. All of the women who were heavy users had had hepatitis. It is likely that some of them have been exposed to AIDS. Drug-related ill health was just one of the many health-related reasons for female street hustlers to withdraw temporarily from street life. Other frequency cited ones were veneral disease, gastrointestinal disorders, penumonia, and complications of pregnancy.

Health-related reasons that were even more frequently mentioned as occasions for temporary withdrawal from street life than disease or pregnancy included the bruises, broken bones, cuts, and abrasions that were the result of the ever-present risk of violence on the streets. The beatings and sexual assaults female street hustlers received at the hands of their men, their dates, their wives-in-law, former women of their men, and other street people as well as the police were numerous and often brutal.

A complex set of factors, then, influence the shape and direction of a female street hustler's life during her most active working years, the period from her mid-to-late teens to her late twenties. Her relationships with kinspersons and men, contacts with the criminal justice system, fertility and general health, physical attractiveness, drug or alcohol use, and responsibility for children all have separate and interacting effects. Conversely, her involvement in illegal work has a feedback effect in that it may also influence some of the aforementioned characteristics and relationships.

WOMEN'S LIBERATION AND FEMALE STREET HUSTLING

My initial interest in the topic of female street hustlers was, as described at the outset of this paper, aroused by the arguments made by researchers who claimed that recent increases in the criminality of women were linked to the latest manifestation of the women's movement. Although the information of the women interviewed about the movement and their support for it varies quite predictably with their education, almost all are poorly educated and, thus, know very little about the movement. They neither share its assumptions about the nature of society and the current position of women in it nor support its strategies for change. They do believe women should receive equal pay for equal work and that women should be allowed to do "men's work" if they want to and are qualified, but they also believe that men and women are naturally designed and suited for different sorts of work, social roles, and statuses. My questions about the movement elicited some responses that were memorable. For example, there was: "The ERA? Isn't that a band that came to play at Taycheedah?" or "I like real feminist women like Raquel Welsh and Eva Gabor."

It became very clear to me that minority and non-minority women alike were much more likely to define their own personal problems in terms of racial prejudice and discrimination or general social inequality than in terms of sexual inequality. And, given the middle class nature of the women's movement, at least as it is most likely to reach the public through the news media, the question of their liberation just doesn't seem to be the first question one should ask when one attempts to speak of ameliorating the lives of female street hustlers.

CONCLUSION

Why Female Street Hustlers Do What They Do

If women's liberation does not motivate females to hustle, what does? From the point of view of the women interviewed, there are a variety of answers to that question. Some say for the excitement; others for the money; and still others seem to think that they, themselves, are innately evil, controlled by something beyond them. Very often they said: "The life just gets in your blood." When asked why a particular woman got involved in an especially dangerous and foolhardy undertaking or why women generally got involved in deviant street networks, however, they were unanimous in saying that it was because of some man. They rarely attributed their own involvement in street life to the influence of men, however. Rosemary described her situation as follows:

> I like the excitement. It's dangerous, I guess, but you meet different people. I just . . . relate to people better who are "in the life" . . . because . . . like a "square" girl, what do they talk about? Nothin'! "Oh, my boyfriend's this and that." I think it's boring. I like to talk about somethin' excitin', about . . . like money and how she went about gettin' the money. It's just a game. That's all it is. I realize it. It's not going to last forever. But, shit, I'm enjoyin' it while I'm doin' it.

On the other hand, Julie, a surly black woman with convictions for prostitution and shoplifting, was indignant at my questioning her motives. She came from a desperately poor home and when asked why she did what she did, she shot back angrily:

> For the money . . . because I needed it. Evidentally whatever it was I was doin' wasn't much from the start. I mean, you'd get out and figure, nothin' happened that time. I did it 'cause I had to. I mean 'cause my mother couldn't do it, and my daddy was a dog, and that's all I can say. So, when I look back, I say he was a dog because she couldn't make no money. She had too many babies. I just had to; I still do.

Among those who think that the street life is somehow "in their blood" or that something beyond their control somehow "makes them do what they do" is Yolanda. Her response to my query about whether or not she thought it likely that she'd get out of "the life" was:

> Yes, sometime I will . . . well, then, it's in my blood, too. But, if I was to have, um, someone special that didn't want me to be "in the life," and . . . well, maybe he wouldn't know that I was "in the life," you know? . . . If he was really good to me, I might take a crack at it [quitting].

What is being described here is a self-contained and, indeed, self-perpetuating world of illegal work. The only major force that eventually pushes some women out into the "straight" world is age. There is some evidence, however, that even women who appear at first glance to be rather well-integrated into the world of school and/or legitimate work, frequently keep one foot firmly planted in the fast life. It is in a very real sense more secure and familiar to them than the straight world is or may ever become.

The Link Between the Rise in Female Property Crime and Socio-Economic Change at the National and Local Levels

The female street hustlers interviewed included women who had just launched careers as street women as well as women who had been in the life for some years. They were similar in that they, and all the women who came between them in terms of length of time on the streets, were women who generally couldn't conceive of their lives without some element of illegal work.

First and foremost, these women generally have little education, almost no work experience, and few marketable skills. They are fully cognizant of the sorts of employment possibilities open to them. It is not that they are able to make more money on the streets than they would be able to make in the sorts of jobs they are most likely to land, however, that dissuades them from competing for legal work (in fact, after having been in Taycheedah Correctional Institution for Women, some of them have skills that are quite marketable). They are aware that most of the time their street earnings are meager, at least when they estimate exactly how much of it they themselves usually get to see. However, there is fast money to be made on the streets. If it is nothing else, it is exciting work. It even occasionally has a hint of glamour. Street hustlers, in their own way, have a degree of independence, excitement, and autonomy in their work that similarly qualified persons who labor in the world of legal work rarely enjoy. Moreover, they are frequently in situations where their physical attributes are paid homage to. This is, for them, a source of self-esteem. There aren't many others. Their choice of role models supports this view of what they consider desirable elements of a female's career; they overwhelmingly choose rather flashy female performers of color as persons they would like to emulate had they the opportunity. This is true across racial and ethnic categories.

The world of legal work simply cannot compete with the world of illegal work in their eyes, then, and over time they come to feel that they are women who either are driven to pursue their chosen career or that they are women who have unique qualities that make them especially suited for it. These sorts of beliefs sustain them in their commitment to street hustling even when they do work straight jobs. If they are temporarily out of work or frustrated with the nature of the work they are doing or with how long they have to work to accumulate a particular amount of money, they feel that they have and will always have the qualities that will allow them to survive on the streets should they need to.

Moreover, when they think of straight work, they are limited by their own sterotypical thinking about what work is appropriate for women versus men and by their lack of knowledge about how to get credentialed to do the sort of work that might compete in autonomy and excitement with the illegal work of the streets.[11]

Technically, almost every instance of hustling engaged in by female street hustlers is legally definable as a crime. Looked at from the point of view of the women, themselves, however, hustling is work that someone who hasn't shared their lives, who wasn't born into the households they were, who didn't grow up in the neighborhoods they did, who has never been as unremittingly poor as they would be but for hustling, has defined as in violation of the law. This is not to imply that they, themselves, don't in large measure, share those definitions. It is, however, to suggest that hustling for them is simple "illegal work" that underclass people often engage in just as upper class people spend their time doctoring and lawyering.[12] It is what many underclass people often do at one time or another to make ends meet; it is what these particular women do most of the time during this particular period of their lives for economic reasons as well as for reasons that stem only indirectly from economic deprivation.

It is, as was observed at the outset of this paper, impossible to test relationships between socioeconomic changes at the national and local levels and the phenomena described here. The data presented in this paper that detail the structure of the work of female street hustlers, its conditions and motivating forces, along with the description of the demographic and familial characteristics of these women is suggestive, however. On the most grounded level it makes sense to assume that if there is a link between the formation of domestic networks and sustained poverty, then conditions and policies that foster the latter will probably promote the former. Given that the data both nationally and locally highlight the differential impact of declining socioeconomic conditions on the welfare of young minority women, it also makes sense to suppose that if domestic networks do, indeed, leave these women more susceptible to recruitment to street hustling, then it is the socioeconomic conditions (rather than the women's movement) that should be examined as causative.

NOTES

1. Another interesting piece of evidence is Morris's study (1973) of coverage received by the women's movement in Los Angeles County. It reveals that neither of the two major newspapers there provided much information on the movment until after 1970.

2. The definition of a "deviant street network" I use here differs from that contained in the work of Cohen by that title (1980) in the following way. There it refers to "the relationships between patterns of visible street deviance, the police, and the wider ecological and social environment" and explicitly does not include "the personal social psychological interactions among participants of a particular street condition" (3). I do not mean to suggest the police officers

may not be part of deviant street networks, nor that I am unconcerned with the wider social and ecological environment. However, when I use the term, I intend to denote exactly that which Cohen excludes. Cohen's definition is completely appropriate for his analysis which is predominantly ecological. Given the more general work in the area of social networks and the broader scope of the work at hand, however, the usage employed here seems more appropriate for this work.

3. By using street jargon here I do not mean to imply that all female street hustlers "make a living" by doing what they do. Most of them have more than just themselves to support as they are also members of a domestic network or extended family household that includes children. Despite claims to the contrary, street life offers neither a secure nor a "good living." Women on the street usually are also receiving welfare and may be working a straight job. Moreover money must also be paid to a man for protection, emotional support, and often drugs and also to various agents of social control, including vice officers.

4. See Steffensmeier and Kokenda (1979), for example, for a discussion of the ideas of male thieves concerning the thieving capabilities of women and their trustworthiness as partners in crime.

5. Theoretically, the pure "pimp" form can only exist when the male has no reason to pretend that a personal relationship exists between him and each of the women who works for him or rarely risks having the true instrumental nature of the relationships revealed. The mere addition of new women undermines any semblance of individualized affection. This means that only males who can afford to maintain their own standard of living as successful "pimps" and reward their women handily as well are relieved of the burden of having to pretend to care for each woman. Financial success of this sort seems to be unachievable in a city like Milwaukee where the agents of social control are much more likely to be able to do their work effectively than they are in a larger city.

6. In employing the term "domestic network" here, I follow the usage of Carol Stack (1974). The domestic network is the characteristic familial form among underclass blacks. It is established as a result of reciprocal obligations that emerge from the swapping of goods and services over time. One may or may not be related by blood to the particular set of individuals with whom one has this sort of relationship. The constituency of a domestic network, then, is relatively fluid as compared to a middle class nuclear family form and may include members of several different households as well as individuals not so associated. The form itself is a response to sustained poverty and has become part of the culture of this group.

7. The argument implicit here and above is elaborated in Miller's *Street Woman* (1986). It is as follows. One important factor in explaining recruitment to deviant street networks is familial form. It is suggested that although the "domestic network" characteristic of underclass blacks and the extended family

households characteristic of underclass Hispanics are clear strengths as responses to sustained poverty, they are less effective, by their very structure, in protecting young female charges from recruitment to deviant street networks than are more bounded (and usually) smaller family forms. In fact, to the degree that their membership overlaps with that of deviant street networks, their structure may promote such recruitment. Thus, a continuum of sorts is being proposed in this regard with domestic networks on one end and more nuclear forms on the other. Extended forms are located somewhere between the two.

8. There is a clear racial/ethnic difference here. Whites simply seem not to have developed the pattern of childkeeping characteristic of poor minority members. Even where the mother of a white woman took care of her daughter's child(ren), the gesture was much more likely to be seen as an act of generosity than as an unquestioned matter of duty. Generally speaking, however, in these cases as in the cases of women whose families/households were embedded in domestic networks, women who had had children prior to becoming involved in hustling and who still had custody of those children were much more likely than those who did not to sustain contact with their families/households of orientation, albeit contact often fraught with tension.

9. Probation and parole officers also use the children of female offenders as leverage in shaping their behavior. In addition, state legislatures have recently attempted to write laws that have a similar effect. In California, for example, a woman who used heroin during her pregnancy many be charged with child abuse at the birth of the child.

10. Citizens' organizations have recently sprung up, particularly in areas adjacent to those employed by streetwalkers plying their trade, in an effort to discourage such activity and to prevent the harassment of neighborhood women not so engaged. Organizations such as SMASH (Stop Mashing and Sexual Harassment) have launched ambitious antiprostitution campaigns. Members of SMASH badger prostitutes and their customers by jotting down license numbers and vigorously rapping on car windows. They have asked police to enforce a seldomly used city ordinance dating from 1910 on mashing, which forbids accosting, insulting, or following a person of the opposite sex. Citations for mashing are intermittently issued. For the streetwalkers, themselves, this, too, is simply another (relatively minor) occupational hazard.

11. The view of hustling as "work" may go a long way in accounting for the reluctance of the underclass people Auletta (1982) studied to pursue training for straight jobs. In a very real sense, these people already have a set of job skills and a certain amount of work experience to the degree that they have been involved in hustling. Of course, hustling does have its price, but from the point of view of the underclass hustler, so does straight work.

12. See Valentine's excellent work (1978) for a detailed analysis of underclass hustling as work.

REFERENCES

Adler, F. 1975. *Sisters in Crime.* New York: McGraw-Hill.

Auletta, K. 1982. *The Under-Class.* New York: Random House.

Bowker, L.H. 1978. *Women, Crime, and the Criminal Justice System.* Lexington, MA: Lexington Books.

Chapman, J.R. 1980. *Economic Realities and the Female Offender.* Lexington, MA: Lexington Books.

Cohen, Bernard. 1980. *Deviant Street Networks: Prostitution in New York.* Lexington, MA: Lexington Books.

Gross, E. 1968. "Plus ca change . . . ? The sexual structure of occupations over time," *Social Problems* 16:198–208.

Mason, K.O., J.L. Czajka and S. Arber. 1976. "Change in U.S. women's sex-role attitudes, 1964–1974," *American Sociological Review* 41:573–96.

Miller, E.M. 1983. "A cross-cultural look at women and crime: An essay review," *Contemporary Crisis* 7:59–70.

Miller, E.M. 1986. *Street Women.* Philadelphia: Temple University Press.

Morris, Monica B. 1973. "The public definition of a social movement." *Sociology and Social Research* 57:526–534.

Mukherjee, S.K., and R.W. Fitzgerald. 1981. "The myth of rising female crime," In *Women and Crime,* edited by S.K. Mukherjee and J.A. Scutt. Sydney: George Allen & Unwin. pp. 127-66.

Noblit, G.W., and J.W. Burcart. 1976. "Women and crime: 1960–1970," *Social Science Quarterly* 56:650–57.

Palay, M.G. 1984. *Census Facts: Milwaukee Areas and Neighborhoods, 1970–1980 Statistics Compared.* Milwaukee: Division of Urban Outreach University of Wisconsin-Milwaukee and University of Wisconsin-Extension.

Simon, R.J. 1975. *Women and crime.* Lexington, MA: Lexington Books.

Stack, C.B. 1974. *All Our Kin: Strategies for Survival in a Black Community.* New York: Harper Colophon Books.

Steffensmeier, D.J. 1980. "Sex differences in patterns of adult crime, 1965–77: A review and assessment," *Soical Problems* 58:1080–1108.

Steffensmeier, D.J., and J. Kokenda. 1979. "The views of contemporary male thieves regarding patterns of female criminality." Paper presented at the annual meeting of the American Society of Criminology, Philadelphia, Pennsylvania.

U.S. Department of Commerce. Bureau of Census. *Historical Statistics of the United States, Colonial Times to 1970.* Vol. 1. Washington, DC: GAO.

U.S. General Accounting Office. 1979. *Female Offenders: Who are They and What are the Problems Confronting Them?* Washington, DC: GAO.

Valentine, B. 1978. *Hustling and Other Hard Work.* New York: Free Press.

Part III

PROFESSIONAL PRACTICE WITHOUT PROFESSIONAL POWER

CHAPTER 8

Registered Nurses, Gender, and Commitment

MARY C. CORLEY AND HANS O. MAUKSCH

Registered nurses have been the subject of much research on socialization, professionalism, autonomy, and job satisfaction. The study reported in this essay focuses on the infrequently examined concept of commitment. This orientation will be placed into the context of the nurse's work, her location in the system, and particularly, the identification of nursing with femaleness.

An understanding of the status, role, and function of nurses within the health care enterprise cannot be achieved without a sensitive and thorough acknowledgement that the social presence of the nurse is pervasively linked to the female gender. Not only are nurses statistically predominantly female, but the image and symbols associated with nursing are inextricably linked to female stereotypes and female status ascriptions. The status of nursing among professions, and the treatment of nurses and nursing in institutional and inter-occupational relationships can be directly related to the devaluing effect of the female gender. The socialization of young women who enter nursing includes experiences and messages which insert a reduction of status expectations into the socializing environment.

> The role of nursing in the health field is the epitome of women's roles in American society. Not accorded full professional status or an opportunity to obtain it the nurse is viewed as a working female who is not expected to make a life long commitment to her career. (Ashley 1976).

The above quotation suggests that commitment must be viewed in at least two perspectives. While, on one hand, the nurse, like other females, is assumed to have low career commitment, she's expected, on the other hand,

135

to have a naturally endowed commitment to provide service and to care for her patients. In both interpretations, the result has devaluing consequences. The commitment to the client shown by nurses is defined as fitting into a female stereotype and, thus, as a natural by-product of a female role. On the level of generalized conclusions, the suggestion will be made that a set of characteristics, which otherwise would earn applause and prestige, can be neutralized if not trivalized when identified with the presumed natural consequences of low status attributes. In fact, in our culture serving others is for losers; "it is low-level stuff" (Miller 1976, 60).

Although gender composition and gender based discriminatory prac- tices have experienced changes in the last fifteen years, nursing has largely re- mained a female (94 percent) occupation (U.S. Dept. of Labor 1977) with the increase of males being quite minimal (U.S. Dept. of Health and Human Ser- vices 1982). This pattern persists, although fewer women entered nursing dur- ing the 1970s in response to expanding opportunities for women in the labor force. According to Dunkelberger and Aadland (1984) more women in the 1970s appeared to reject stereotypical women's occupations such as nursing because they were considered "traditional" or "women's work."

The predominant place of employment for nurses is still the hospital. Although career opportunities have expanded and nurses do work in a wide variety of settings, two-thirds of the nursing labor force are employed by hos- pitals. The structure of hospital based nursing has been shown to have absorbed significant characteristics typically identified with female stereotypes: the physi- cian's handmaiden, the housewife-like management of the nursing unit on behalf of remote hospital administration, and the nurturant pallitative func- tions *vis a vis* the patient are all too frequently seen as naturally female than competence-based professional functions. (Mauksch 1973). The ambiguous and apparently subordinate place of the nurse in the hospital, coupled with the female identity have affected the literature on the professional status of the nurse. The part of human experience "assigned to women has been devalued and treated almost as if it did not exist or as only important enough for women to do" (Miller 1976, 74).

The very qualities which have been described as basic to the low valua- tion placed on the work of the nurse was used as a platform by two authors who established a claim for their profession in a prestige medical journal. Fagin and Diers (1983) describe nursing as a metaphor — for mothering, class strug- gle, equality, conscience, intimacy, and sexual license. Responding to these meta- phors requires that:

> . . . the answer . . . convey the feeling of satisfaction derived from the caring role; indifference to power for its own sake; the recognition that one is a doer who enjoys doing for and with others; but most of all, the pleasure associated with helping others from the position of a peer rather than from the assumed superordinate position of some other professions (117).

The Status of Nursing

The status of nursing has been a matter of considerable controversy. Much of the debate has concentrated on the question of whether nursing is or is not a profession. Some authors, particularly those who accept structural and functional autonomy as the dominant criteria, come to the conclusion that nursing does not quite have the ingredients which make a profession.

> By and large, every analyst with the possible exception of those in nursing agrees that insofar as the concept of professions has any definition at all, the nurse is not fully professional. Like many other occupations in and around medicine in the United States it is a would-be profession . . . (Freidson 1970).

An increasing number of students of occupations and professions are accepting the flawed nature of the very question which results frequently in the attribute of "the profession" being linked to politically acquired power and symbolic status. The extent to which the diminished autonomy of the nurse in the hospital network is a function of power, structure, and gender remain an inadequately explored issue.

For the line of inquiry pursued in this essay, the collection of essays edited by Etzioni (1969) as *The Semi-Professions* is of particular interest. The essays acknowledge an overt link between professional property and gender. Several of the chapters imply that an occupation composed of females cannot claim the status of a profession. This argument is made most explicitly in the chapter by Simpson and Simpson. Their claim that occupations identified as primarily female not only have difficulties being acknowledged as professions under current conditions but that this is likely to continue, demonstrates the depth with which the relationship between gender and status is viewed even by acknowledged scholars.

The social meaning of nursing and its management of prestige and power symbols are overshadowed by medicine and the public perception of a subordinate, supportive role. Obstacles to achieving professional recognition for practitioners of nursing include the partial dependence on physicians and the devaluation of the contribution nurses make to patient care (Muff 1982, 78). Hospital administrators viewing nursing from an economic and managerial perspective seek the least expensive and the most compliant worker. The deprofessionalizing effect of these images is again consistent with the low prestige of mother, housewife, and homemaker roles which elicit romantic, rather than status or economic rewards. Greer (1971) finds that "nurses are victimized by the essentialness of their work into accepting a shameful remuneration," and that this is an indictment of society "which is daring them to abandon the sick and dying, knowing that they will not do it" (136).

Discrimination against women has gradually decreased due to changes in federal law involving minorities and the efforts of the women's movement. Women, in general and in this case, nurses in particular, continue to show the consequences of being an oppressed group; among the internalized consequences are self-hatred among nurses (Roberts 1983). Divisiveness within nursing, fear of success, and inability to agree on what nursing is, represent major difficulties which have their roots in uncertainties of status.

Bullough (1978, 131) cites past tradition, the subordination of nurses, sex segregation, and the apprenticeship model in nursing education as sources of attitudes among present day nurses. These factors have long-term effects even when discrimination has receded. Historically, nursing education emphasized giving emotional support rather than diagnosing or treating the patient's present complaint. Part of the reason for this was to claim an independent niche for nurses, but it was also because nurses were felt to be more naturally maternal and expressive than physicians.

Commitment

After examining the data which emerged from a two-year study of nurse retention and nurse morale, and after recalling the nonverbal and informal communications which emanated from the interviews, the issue of commitment emerged as the theme best suited as a framework for this report. It was obvious that commitment did not provide a simple conceptual basis; it raised as many questions as it answered. Yet it provided a theme that permeated all information. It provided additional support to the complexity of the work and the function of the nurse. Commitment to the patient, to the institution, to the physician, and to career appeared at times as an alternative focus of orientation, at times as sources for strain and conflict, and at times as a syndrome of loyalties which were not experienced as competing.

Commitment to standards of professional practice, to knowledge, to the exercise of professional judgment and most importantly to the patients, provided a profoundly different orientation to work from the loyalty to the employing institution, to those in authority, or even to the profession itself. Tourtillot (1982) questions whether this commitment really exists among contemporary nurses.

In 1962, Vaillot reported on a study of commitment that was primarily philosophical in orientation. She explained that the socialization process by which nursing students became nurses was an existential experience moving from knowing to being. She identified a typology consisting of a utilizer-commited continuum. The utilizer rented herself to nursing whereas the committed became a nurse.

> The committed asks to be judged in terms of values to which she subscribes as a woman and a nurse . . . nursing is a means of self-expression. Consequently the work role never ends . . . It is life activity. It is a form of creative act, and the committed may have the urge to do nursing as the writer must write . . . (Vaillot 1962, 13).

The utilizer type of nurse is motivated in terms of goals meeting particular short-term needs. The work role is limited to actual time at work.

Vaillot referred to the typology which categorized the orientation of nurses as professionalizer, traditionalizer, or utilizer. These types were developed by Habenstein and Christ (1955).

> The professionalizer type of nurse focuses on the special modes of operation that must be evolved if the problem of healing is to be more adequately and intelligently met . . . The professionalizing nurse accepts the responsibility (of providing care to the sick) and for the services she promises to perform, in turn asks for special or exceptional treatment by society . . . professional prerogatives, one of which takes the form of organization of fellow-nurses into separate, prestigeful, and relatively autonomous groups. The traditionalizing nurse is characterized . . . by an alignment of her actions against those which have traditional legitimation. Her work is an extension of the healing arts long practiced in home and community . . . Her function within a pattern of complete and unquestioning deference to the doctor, is simply to bring into force all her nursing skills in the healing of the patient (41–42).

Given the currently needed kowledge base for practicing nurses the description by Haberstin and Christ is outdated in the 1980s. Yet there is some continuing validity to the concepts, although entry into nursing has become more complex. It clearly includes the requirement of a knowledge base for independent activity (Friss 1977, 28).

The purpose of the study reported in this paper was to learn about factors contributing to professional nurse job satisfaction. Six large medical centers, representing different geographic areas of the United States were chosen as study sites because they were experiencing high nurse turnover.* Pilot programs were to be put in place to address problems determined to be contributing to the nurse turnover by management following this input from the nurses. Small group interviews of nurses (staff and head nurses) were conducted by either one or both investigators. Groups included from three to fifteen nurses. Usually only one nurse from each work area was able to attend any one session. All participants were registered nurses (RN's). Although one investigator was employed by the organization, she was not employed at any of the sites where the interviews took place. The other investigator was a consultant to the project. Nurses were invited to attend one-hour sessions to discuss job satisfaction.

The open-ended questions included: What are the aspects of your job that produce satisfaction? What aspects contribute to your dissatisfaction? What recommendations would you make to improve nurse retention? The sessions were tape-recorded or responses were written down by the investigator. A total of 1,283 staff and head nurses participated in the sessions which were held in 1982 and again one year later after pilot programs had been implemented and in place a minimum of six months. A total of 87 small group sessions were conducted during the two years. No demographic data were collected on the nurses

---

*Annual turnover rates had ranged as high as 44 percent at one medical center and over 33 percent at the other five included in this study.

during these interviews. However, the similarity between their responses and our previous survey data led to the conclusion the two samples were similar. Quantitative data had been collected in early 1982 through a nationwide survey of a random sample of nurses from 172 medical centers including the six in this study and are reported elsewhere (Corley and Westerberg 1984).

The investigators were unsure of the effect of the group interview approach on nurses' willingness to be forthright. The results of this arrangement for data gathering were unexpectedly most favorable. The group served as a support for the nurses. They mutually reinforced the norms of the group, encouraging members to express their feelings about employment, work, and relationships. Nurses frequently nodded and/or voiced agreement with what was being said. Disagreements or individually held divergent views were accepted and explored. Because of their frustrations, they expressed need for support and responded eagerly to the support offered by the group interviews. The collective approach seemed to be just what was needed. The advantages of the interviews were that they provided anecdotal and descriptive data on how the nurses felt about their work and working conditions, enabling the investigators to add meaning and content to the distribution and properties of the data. Considering the complexity of the information sought and recognizing the emotional sensitivity of the issues explored, the investigators feel fully justified to have placed much emphasis on the qualitative component of the project methodology. While the survey data offer a sense of representativeness and while they offer confirming indications for the results yielded by the analysis of the interviews, the qualitative, in-depth exploring and listening provided a validity to the information gathered and a richness of meaning to the statements made which could not be replicated by structured instruments. The technique of group interviewing conveyed a sense of commitment which was generalized and incorporated into the the meaning of life and which was clearly different from commitment to specific tasks, behavior, and positions.

Nurses are employed by the centralized Department of Nursing Service. They work in geographically defined units called wards, usually housing 20 to 40 patients. They are responsible for carrying out nursing tasks, implementing physicians' orders, and administering organizational policies. One head nurse, a designated number of registered nurses, licensed practical nurses and nursing assistants comprise the nursing staff for each ward.

The workload for nurses tends to be unpredictable. Unusual patient behavior and acute changes in patient condition can create the need for more nursing time very quickly. The organization usually lacks a mechanism for addressing this unpredictable workload. Yet, understaffing and overload is a continuous theme of complaints expressed by nurses and even by nursing administrators. Notwithstanding the increasing complexity of treatments, procedures, and administrative and coordinating tasks, staffing of nursing units has essentially not reflected these additional demands.

It is significant that the issue of workload was primarily voiced as a factor which prevented nurses from offering patients the quality and quantity of

care which patients needed and deserved. Despite the fact that changes in patient care and medical treatment over the last year had led to overload and
understaffing, insistence on contractual claims for staffing had not yet become
a major theme. For patients with identical or comparable conditions, the chart
of 1986 is likely to contain four times as many medications and treatments as
was practicable 30 years ago. Greater knowledge and more recourses have translated into much more work for nurses per patient, yet staffing has not reflected
the dramatic growth of work demands.

In examining the interviews, it was evident that a number of analytic
approaches could be taken. As mentioned earlier, the issue of commitment suggested itself as fruitful, pervasive, and significant. The focus of commitment
included the institution, the profession, the quality and comprehensiveness
of their work assignments, and above all, the patient.

Patients were by far the most typical core concern when nurses spoke
of their sense of commitment, obligation, and motivation. A number of general
points deserved to be made since they will facilitate the linkage between the data
as reported and the theme of commitment.

> 1. It was evident that a pervasive, though not necessarily explicit, awareness
> of the level of commitment among nurses served as a basis and justification
> for neglect and reduced responsibility on the part of other hospital workers
> regardless of occupation. This is an interesting and an important phenomenon.
> Its implications helps to distinguish the highly motivating and stimulating
> consequence observed when commitment is shown by high-prestige, power-
> ful participants in the system from the absolving of commitment when shown
> by those whose special skills are devalued and who are seen as generalists who
> will absorb what does not get done by others.

> 2. As is true for other behaviors or characteristics associated with minority
> group status, commitment becomes romanticized rather than rewarded when
> associated with innate properties and natural tendencies imputed to that
> minority group. Rather than constituting a claim, commitment functions as
> confirmation of the already existing stereotype.

> 3. Because of the above two conditions, commitment exhibited by nurses not
> only reduces the pressure on others to fully complete their tasks and responsi-
> bilities but indeed, due to the predictable reliance on the nurse, the knowledge
> of the commitment among nurses absolves others, particularly those in posi-
> tions of power, from a sense of guilt or failure. Counting on the underdog
> to fill in the gaps is an interesting fringe benefit of status and power. Such
> conditions are embellished when it is possible to attach romantic notions to
> those who are being exploited and elevating the onus of their behavior by
> ascribing it to natural talents.

While the interview did not reveal, as can be expected, the entire dynamics of the prices paid for caring and absorbing, staff nurses and head nurses
consistently expressed a strong sense of frustration and feeling of powerlessness as they confronted problems and circumstances that they were unable to

solve or control. While there was little awareness that their own commitment was being exploited, they did feel strongly about an environment in which they saw others doing less than their own position or responsibility required.

Notwithstanding the reports of the many tasks which had to be performed although not part of the nurse's repertory, the main focus of frustration and dissatisfaction was the perceived inability to meet the goals of patient care and to perform sufficient nursing tasks to provide safe, adequate, and effective nursing care. Overwork was generally described as a condition keeping the nurse from caring adequately for her patients. Nurses described work environments with inadequate equipment, insufficient supplies, and inadequate staff; all this was couched in terms of concern for the quality of patient care.

Throughout the interviews, job satisfaction was linked with the opportunity to provide adequate patient care. Though benefits and salaries were important to all levels of nurses interviewed, the central focus of the meaning of the job and of being a nurse was linked to patient welfare.

Nurse as "Jill" of All Trades

A frequent target for comments were the support services which dealt with supplies, sanitation, and maintenance. Even the most frequently used supplies were often not available. Typically, full support services were staffed only from Monday through Friday and only during the day hours. Nursing which covers the needs of patient care seven days a week, around the clock were understandably frustrated by resources available for only fifty hours a week. Yet, contacts which the interviewers had with members of other departments and with administrators failed to yield a full understanding. The frequently expressed trust that nurses can always deal with the most adverse conditions because that is why they are nurses, had the peculiar ring of expecting the housewife to take care of that which, if she is not available, might call for a high-priced craftsperson.

The inadequacies reported during the interviews resulted in the very conditions which could have been predicted. Nurses undertook cleaning, fixing clogged commodes, washing beds prior to the admission of a new patient, borrowing and searching for equipment and supplies, and at times, sharing their food with patients. The interviewers did not have to rely only on the reports by nurses for these conditions. In several institutions they had ample opportunity to observe for themselves. Nurses felt that performing these tasks was the only available option for them since other action would jeopardize patients. Yet they were dissatisfied with this approach because it took time away from doing their own tasks of giving care to patients. Patient care time, already limited because of staff shortages and the volume of care required, was thus further compromised. They wanted to give optimal care, defined as quality and safe care, but found they could only give less than adequate care. For example:

> Lot of wasted time spent looking for something we needed because there is no one else to do it.

Nurses must be jack of all trades.

Nurses are there to pick up responsibility.

Supply is locked at 4:30 and you won't find it anyplace.

All the interview content which related to support services or to other technical functionaries in patient care showed little conflict about the priorities in the nurse's commitment. All these services were judged in terms of their contribution to patient care or in terms of their accomplishments as a way of supporting and facilitating the performance of nursing.

Quite different is the tenor of comments made about physicians and medical care. The theme of "dumping" tasks onto nursing was very prevalent in comments about the behavior of physicians, and concern about physicians' attitudes and relationships with patients were frequently encountered. However, the theme of commitment to medicine and loyalty to the physician was common and strongly felt. The traditional manifestations of the nurse's support of the physician was present although expressions of independence and assertiveness were quite frequent. At times, the conflict between simultaneously expressed attitudes was not felt or identified. Nevertheless, nurses feel themselves frequently caught between loyalty to the patient and the physician. At times critical comments about physicians, particularly about members of the house staff, were couched in terms as if it were the function of nurses to watch out for these doctors and to protect them as well as the patients. To what extent a change in gender alignment might profoundly alter such perceptions remains an open question.

The expressions of commitment to patients and to physicians are reminiscent of traditional female norms and expectations. Loyalty to the physician has been a theme in nursing and in nursing education since the day of Florence Nightingale. In earlier days, commitment to the patient was simply met by conscientious compliance with medical orders. The emergence of the distinction between commitment to the physician and a nursing-based commitment to nursing care is a reflection of the profound changes in the role of women during the last few decades.

Staff and Head Nurse Commitment to Patients

Nurses described a work environment characterized by difficulties obtaining supplies and equipment for patient care, by a nursing administration whose primary commitment was to the organization, by lack of recognition for their work, by too little nursing staff, by lack of power, and by the lack of commitment from others in the organization. Despite these impediments, the nurse's commitment to the patient was a major motivating factor for remaining with the organization. Commitment to the patient was evident in the following illustrative comments made by the nurses:

I am grateful for the opportunity to work in hospitals. Here we are giving the kind of nursing care that I have always wanted to give. Also, most of my fellow nurses are extremely cooperative. We have an excellent head nurse who is knowledgeable, fair, and sympathetic to each person's needs.

I enjoy my position and the challenge it represents, but it is very demanding physicially as well as in time. Because I am alone I can tolerate the demands but most nurses have other responsibilities and if you are to retain the best, there will have to be changes made to lighten the load.

Why have I stayed so long — surprisingly our patients receive good care despite the odds and somewhere there is another side to the rainbow.

Nurses described repeatedly the conflict they experience between the amount of hands-on care the patients need and the less desirable amount they can actually give. They frequently discussed nursing responsibilities in two categories: hands-on care and documentation in the clinical record and care plan. Ambivalence in feelings was evident on the importance of documentation. Some said, "We should be doing better care plans," or "Neglect of documentation — no time." Others said they had to make a choice, given the limited care they would give as a price for keeping records. They stated that the charting system was "archaic" characterized by "duplication" and that "according to JCAH (Joint Commission on Accredition of Hospitals), you did not do the nursing care unless you charted it."

Nurse Commitment Despite Obstacles

Nurses described behaviors reflecting commitment to patients despite obstructing circumstances. Nurses said there were "increasingly fewer hands to do the laying-on," and that they were told to prioritize care, difficult when everything was a priority. They found they had to work doubly hard to meet patients' care needs. They had major responsibilities on two levels: decisions about care and the actual provision of care because other disciplines left the hospital at 5:00 p.m.

Nurses' commitment to patient care was reflected in their frustration over not being able to provide the care the patient needed. The number of nurses hired was not based on the patient care needs. As a result, nurses felt uncomfortable leaving work because they knew everything had not been done. They often were physically exhausted while trying to provide safe care. Responsibility for the patients was felt to be a physical, professional, and moral burden:

Feel very uncomfortable when I leave knowing what didn't get done.

Too much work — dangerous, particularly evenings and nights (dangerous to patient safety).

Patients cannot speak for themselves (so the nurse had to do it).

Decisions are made without consideration of repercussions for patient (so the nurse had to look out for the patient).

In the interviews, nurses commented on their conflict in feelings of commitment. They perceived that the problems they encountered in their work environment reflected a lack of commitment to the patient on the part of the organization. Many nurses who felt strong commitment to the patient had a variety of responses affecting their commitment to the organization. Some stopped reporting problems because no solutions were provided in the past. Others reported profound physical and mental fatigue, a "tiredness" or boredom with patient care. Still others said they would resign or had resigned at the time of the interview. Those who had resigned said they would not return. Some nurses said they would not recruit their friends to work in the hospital: "I love nursing and especially psychiatric nursing but having no say over staffing — I don't plan to continue much longer."

DISCUSSION

What are the characteristics of staff and head nurse commitment? Their system of values (Becker 1960), reflected in what they consistently want, include the following factors: a) ability to provide care for the patient based on what they have defined as patient needs without interference from the physicians, the nursing hierarchy, or the patient's ability to pay; b) appreciation from the patient for nursing care provided; c) improvement in patient health or decline in discomfort as a result of the nurse's efforts; and d) recognition and rewards from the hospital system and its power and symbol wielders for the responsible care given.

The risks — or as Becker would define them, side-bets — involve the possibility of losing the professional license even if the system is at fault. Risks also include rejection by the patient and devaluation of the care received (this, too, may occur beyond the nurse's own sphere of control) and to be recipient of blame for errors or omissions in patient care. There are other side-bets; economic ones include employee benefits, particularly retirement provisions and mobility and leave policies. Emotional and personal risks appear intensively among the interviews. They relate to the strong need to feel that good, safe, adequate care has been given to patients. Greer (1971, 34) has said that the "most depressing phenomenon in the pattern of women's work is the plight of the nurses . . . The much vaunted emotional satisfactions of nursing have fallen foul of cuts in staffing. Nurses find that they have to do unskilled jobs like floorscrubbing because even domestic staff will not consent to be bullied the way they, the professionals, allow themselves to be."

Why is it that nurses do not try more radical approaches to resolve problems involving inadequate staffing and support services. Part of the reason why it has taken nurses so long to become militant is due to their discriminated position.

Feelings of powerlessness and fear of punishment can prevent people from challenging the status quo, and the fact that the fear is based upon former traditions and past punishments rather than present realities is often over-looked (Bullough 1978, 133).

Carmichael (1967) has referred to this as the submissive-aggression syn-drome, characterized by an inability of the oppressed person who feels aggressive to directly express it. The self-hatred and low self-esteem of the oppressed group create submissiveness when confronted by the figure in power. Brockner and Rubin (1985) refer to the entrapment that occurs in that people tend to stick with the status quo even when "rational analysis" would prescribe a change, brought about by the image persons have of their power "to make a decision."

Recently, nurses have joined labor unions in large numbers and met with management over a bargaining table. Others have taken on the role of whistle-blower at the expense of losing their positions. Frequently, the major issue has been over staffing levels. Some union contracts now include provisions for a nurse/patient ratio. Nurses have a "sense of their skill, are anything but passive and do resist oppressive conditions" (Sacks and Remy 1984, 9). On national and state levels, the American Nurses Association have political action groups which have become more influential in affecting the role of the nurse and the quality of health care made available to the population (Heide 1973, 824).

Our interviews of these nurses showed that they were satisfied with pro-viding patient care. Their commitment to the patients produced satisfaction. What they were dissatisfied with was the inability to accomplish what needed to be done for the patients. Nurses reported consensus on what commitment to the patient meant.

Numerous researchers have asserted that the nurse's formal education is underutilized on the job, and that because of this the nurse's reaction to the type of work to be performed is largely negative, and she is not committed to the organization (Alutto et al. 1971; Brief et al. 1980; and Kramer 1968; 1970). Our interview results led us to a more specified view. Nurses' commitment to the organization is contingent on the perceived commitment of the organiza-tion to the patient.

Commitment can take a variety of forms, organizational, professional, patient, colleague and self-commitment. Although the types of commitment are not mutually exclusive, the interview results showed that commitment to the patients was the major motivating factor for coming to work each day and staying on day after day. What makes the commitment to patients a problem to the nurse is the vast stores of knowledge she has acquired and continues to acquire making her aware of how much the patient needs. Not only must she provide basic comfort measures, she must also be alert to nursing actions required by changes in biochemical parameters or other pathophysiological changes and respond to the psychocultural needs of her client. Recognition and higher evaluation of nurses' vital work ("intense, emotionally connected cooperation and creativity necessary for human life and growth"), will benefit the personal integrity, and society will be healthier (Heide 1973, 259). Yet, as long as the functions performed by nurses are defined as "natural," nonspecific, and nonessential, the halo of dramatic conquest of disease will remain without competition and territorial encroachment. The very focus of work satisfaction which nurses identify as patient needs is used to devalue the professional and scientific properties of nursing and open nurses to the role of the institutional recipient of duties which others have rejected or shirked.

Beyond all these complexities, the nurse sees herself in an occupational and organizational position in which the freedom, power, and support needed to perform her functions is simply not accorded to her. Restrained within her own hierarchy, trivialized by the physician, taken for granted by administration and romanticized by the public, the nurse is excessively strained to be integrator and direct ministering agent of patient care. The rationally unjustifiable situation of nursing begins to make sense if compared with the expectations surrounding the housewife and mother. Listening to the aims and complaints of so many nurses, the investigators learned a lesson which begs for further exploration and which took shape in the form of the following summary statement:

> If you are powerless and you care, your caring will be taken for granted. If your caring can be explained as a result of natural tendencies, your caring will be taken for granted. If your caring leads you to absorb the unfinished work of others, more work will be dumped on you. If you complain and ask for relief, your request will be neglected at first and, subsequently will be interpreted as a failing of your natural endowment. However, if you persist in caring and learn to assess the restraints for what they are, you may discover your strength, get organized and discover the latent power which exists.

REFERENCES

Allutto, J., L.G. Hrebiniak, R.D. Alonso. 1971. "A study of differential socialization for members of one professional group," *Journal of Health and Social Behavior* 12:140–17.

Ashley, J. 1976. *Hospitals, Paternalism and the Role of the Nurse.* New York: Columbia University Press.

Becker, H.S. 1960. "Notes on the concept of commitment," *American Journal of Sociology* 66:32–40.

Brief, A.P., R.J. Aldag, M. Van Sell, N. Malone. 1980. "Anticipatory socialization and role stress among hospital nurses," *Journal of Health and Social Behavior* 20:161–64.

Brockner, J., J.Z. Rubin. 1985. *Entrapment in Escalating Conflicts: A Social Psychological Analysis.* New York: Springer Verlag.

Bullough, B. 1978. "Barriers to the nurse practitioner movement: Problems of women in a women's field," In *Organization of Health Workers and Labor Conflict* edited by S. Wolfe. Boston: Baywood Pub. Co. pp. 127–135.

Carmichael, S. 1967. *Black Power.* New York: Random House.

Corley, M., N. Westerberg. 1984. "Recruitment and retention of nurses in the Veterans Administration," Report submitted to the 98th Congress, Veterans Administration, Washington, D.C.

Dunkelberger, J.E., S.C. Aadland. 1984. "Expectation and attainment of nursing careers," *Nursing Research* 33:235–40.

Etzioni, A. 1969. *The Semi-Professions and Their Organization.* New York: Free Press.

Fagin, C., D. Diers. 1983. "Nursing as metaphor," *New England Journal of Medicine* 309. No. 2:116–17.

Friedson, E. 1970. *Profession of Medicine.* New York: Dodd, Mead & Co.

Friss, L. 1977. "What do nurses do?" *Journal of Nursing Administration* 7:24–28.

Greer, G. 1971. *The Female Eunuch.* New York: McGraw-Hill Book Co.

Habenstein, R.W., E.A. Christ. 1955. *Professionalizer, Traditionalizer, and Utilizer.* Columbia, Mo: University of Missouri Press.

Heide, W.S. 1973. "Nursing and women's liberation—a parallel," *American Journal of Nursing* 73:824–27.

Kramer, M. 1968. "Nurse role deprivation—a symptom of needed change," *Social Science and Medicine* 2:461–74.

Kramer, M. 1970. "Role conceptions of baccalauereate nurses and success in hospital nursing," *Nursing Research* 19:428–30.

Mauksch, H.O. 1973. "Ideology, interaction and patient care in hospitals," *Social Science and Medicine* 7:817–29.

Miller, J.B. 1976. *Toward a New Psychology of Women.* Boston: Beacon Pess.

Muff, J. 1982. "Why doesn't a smart girl like you go to medical school?" In *Socialization, Sexism and Stereotyping* edited by Janet Muff. St. Louis: The C.S. Mosby Co., 178–186.

Roberts, S.J. 1983. "Oppressed group behavior: implications for nursing," *Advances in Nursing Science* 3:21–30.

Sacks, K.B., D. Remy. 1984. *My Troubles are Going to Have Trouble With Me.* Rutgers, N.J.: Rutgers State University Press.

Simpson, R.L., I.H. Simpson. 1969. "Women and bureaucracy in the semi-professions." In *The Semi-Professions and Their Organization* edited by A. Etzioni. New York: The Free Press, 196–265.

Tourtillot, E.A. 1982. "Commitment—A lost characteristic?" New York: National League for Nursing (Pub. No. 23-1895).

U.S. Dept. of Health and Human Services. 1982. *The Registered Nursing Population*. HRS-P-OD-81–3. Revised, November.

U.S. Dept. of Labor. Bureau of Statistics. 1977. *U.S. Working Women: A Databook*. Washington, D.C.: Government Printing Office.

Vaillot, M.C. 1962. *Commitment to Nursing*. Philadelphia: Lippincott.

CHAPTER 9

Women Talking to Women:
Abortion Counselors and Genetic Counselors

BARBARA KATZ ROTHMAN AND MELINDA DETLEFS

INTRODUCTION

The past several decades have seen extraordinary changes in reproductive technology and ideology. One major change has been the legalization of abortion. A second, and related, change has been the development of techniques for prenatal diagnosis, which makes possible "selective abortions": abortions of fetuses with particular chromosomal or other anomalies. While the majority of Americans now support the availability of legal abortion, there is particularly strong support for abortion when the fetus is "defective". Abortion in general, and selective abortion in particular, raise fundamental ethical, social, and psychological issues. This paper takes a narrower view, looking at the new occupations that have developed in response to these technological and social changes.

The research reported here is drawn from two distinct but related data bases. One is the study of genetic counselors, conducted as part of a larger research project on the impact of prenatal diagnosis on women's experiences of pregnancy (Rothman 1986). It consists of interviews with 25 genetic counselors in a major metropolitan area in 1983. The second data base for this paper is a series of comparable interviews with 17 abortion counselors in the same metropolitan area in 1984 (Detlefs 1984). Both sets of interviews used a similar semistructured, open-ended format and covered the same or comparable areas. Barbara Katz Rothman was the primary investigator for the research on genetic counselors, and Melinda Detlefs, the primary investigator for the research on abortion counselors; Melinda Detlefs conducted the majority of the former and all of the latter interviews.

At first glance it would seem that both groups of counselors are doing fundamentally similar work: helping women to make decisions about terminating a pregnancy. Both are working in a medical setting, and both use women's relational skills to mediate between clients and institutions. Yet despite the obvious similarities, there are striking differences. While genetic counseling work has undergone a decline in status from being seen as "medical" work to being seen as "social" work, it still remains far more "professionalized" than abortion counseling. Abortion counseling has shifted from illegal political work — work highly valued by the networks and counterculture within which it was done, and strongly disdained by the society at large — to the more mundane work of easing women through legal and often profit-making clinics. Thus while the work itself in these two occupations may seem quite similar, the historical and social context renders it different and has strong effects on the ways women in the two occupations view themselves. Routes into — and out of — the two occupations are very different, reflecting the higher social status accorded genetic counseling. While a genetic counselor is likely to think of herself as "almost a doctor," today's abortion counselor more often calls her work "just a job."

Part I of this paper focuses on the genetic counselors, and Part II on the abortion counselors, but similar themes run through both sections. The emphasis is on the workers' evaluation of their work: what it means to them, and what they think it means to their clients, coworkers, and employing institutions. Both groups of counselors see themselves and their work as undervalued, particularly by the medical staffs and the institutions. Ironically, one of the effects of undervaluing the work has been that counselors are left alone with it — both groups actively enjoy their relative freedom from direct supervision. These two themes, the undervaluation of the work and the resulting "autonomy by default," are explored in Parts I and II.

Part III offers some explanation of the differences between the two occupations, linking the higher status of genetic counseling with its relation to eugenic values in American society, and abortion counseling's lower status with its connection to feminism. But more important than the differences are the similarities, and Part III concludes with a discussion of the similar role each occupation plays in its particular setting.

PART I: GENETIC COUNSELORS

In the early part of this century, genetic counseling openly and wholeheartedly embraced the eugenics movement, inlcuding its social reform mandate. The counseling was carried out by physicians, usually pediatricians, who advised parents of children born with birth defects (Sorenson, Swazey and Scotch 1981). Pediatricians worked with limited knowledge. They might be skillful enough to diagnose a condition, yet they could offer parents no more than an estimate, "usually quite tentative, of the likelihood of any future child being born with the same disease or disorder. An understanding of how the tragedy occurred often eluded not only the parents, but medical science as well" (Sorenson, Swazey, and Scotch 1981, 2).

The 1960s saw a breakthrough in prenatal diagnosis for genetic and other birth defects. One of the most important changes was the application of amniocentesis (the withdrawal of a small amount of the fluid surrounding the fetus in utero) for mid-pregnancy prenatal diagnosis. Examination of the amniotic fluid, which contains fetal cells and fetal products, can now provide definitive diagnosis of several hundered different disorders. The use of amniocentesis has increased dramatically in recent years and is now routine in pregnancies medically defined as "at risk" for genetic or other diagnosable fetal abnormalities. Because the incidence of Down's syndrome, a chromosomal disorder resulting in mental retardation as well as some physical problems, increases with maternal age, the "at risk" designation has come to include all pregnancies in which the mother is in her mid-thirties or beyond. Most of today's genetic counseling involves informing the "at risk" population of the availability of the test, interpreting test results, and helping prospective parents to make reproductive decisions.

Who are the people providing genetic counseling? Today's genetic counselors have a master of science degree in human genetics and counseling. They are usually employed by hospitals and work under physician supervision. Almost all are women, as are all 25 interviewed in this study. This represents a shift in the past decade. In a 1973 survey of people doing genetic counseling (Sorenson 1973), 80 percent were physicians, some with Ph.D.'s in addition to the M.D. degree; 11 percent were non-M.D. Ph.D.'s; only 9 percent were neither M.D.'s nor Ph.D.'s; and 74 percent were men. Most of the physicians were pediatricians whose genetic counseling grew out of the process of diagnosing genetic diseases and syndromes in babies and children, and then estimating recurrence probabilities for parents.

As the new reproductive technology developed, including amniocentesis, genetic counseling shifted from dealing primarily with the parents of children with genetic diseases, to dealing with reproductive decision making and risks *before* birth (prenatal counseling) — and the ties with pediatrics loosened. And as the counseling has become increasingly routine, the master's-level counselor has taken over most of the work. Individual physicians are no doubt doing a great deal of counseling about genetic diseases, but as a job title, "Genetic Counselor" has come to refer to a person with a master's degree in genetic counseling.

Genetic counseling services go beyond what the average obstetrician is willing or able to provide in prenatal care. People may need information obstetricians most often do not have: on the availability of state-funded schools for the retarded or disabled child, for example, if a family is considering continuing a pregnancy in which the fetus is diagnosed as having a particular disease or syndrome. But more fundamentally, counseling services fall outside the traditional doctor/patient relationship. In a study of which doctors do and which do not provide genetic counseling to their patient's, Rose Weitz elaborated this point:

Acceptance of [genetic counseling] requires a variety of departures from traditional medical practice. First, counseling depends not only on understanding patients' physical states but also on sensitivity to patients' emotional needs and problems. Medical training rarely encourages such skills, instead stressing affective neutrality. Second, [genetic counseling] primarliy consists of supplying knowledge to the patient, not of actively treating either "disease" or "diseased" gene. Traditional medical norms, on the other hand, orient physicians toward active intervention rather than disease prevention. Lastly, in the ideal [genetic counseling] situation, the client, not the physician makes the final decision. This contrasts sharply with traditional medical norms, which stress that good medical practice consists of professionals making expert judgements based on their own clinical judgement (1981, 208).

But for all of the differences between the role of the counselor and the role of the physician, a number of women go into genetic counseling precisely because it is the "next best thing" to a career in medicine. About half of the genetic counselors interviewed wore that ubiquitous symbol of medical authority, the white coat. There is no "laying on of hands" in genetic counseling; one talks and listens. The coat serves no obvious practical or protective purpose. When one counselor was asked about it — in a preinterview observation, the researcher mentioned that some counselors wore it and some not — she said how excited her father had been when he saw her at work, dressed in her white coat and badge. He said she was "almost a doctor." Medical school had been available for her brother, but not for her. Hers is a fairly common refrain among genetic counselors, wanting but not being able or willing to go through medical school:

> I always wanted to be a doctor. When I graduated from college, I knew I had to make a living because by fiance was to be in school for three more years, which destroyed my plans. I began teaching, had a child, knew I couldn't combine medical school with raising a child.

> It was the closest thing to medicine. I always wanted to be a doctor.

Indeed, one counselor interviewed was planning on leaving genetic counseling for medical school, and another said that most of her friends from genetic counseling training had already gone on to medical school.

For other counselors, the emphasis was on the "people orientation" of genetic counseling. "I like to work with people" was a commonly heard refrain.

> I was always interested in genetics, and it was a way to take genetics and combine it with human beings.

> Perfect balance — it was people-oriented, and I had decided not to go to medical school.

The rewards of genetic counseling were often expressed in terms reminiscent of the rewards of medicine. Counselors often used the expression "patient contact" to describe what they liked best about the job, sounding quite a bit like doctors, particularly obstetricians:

[What I like best is] helping people to have healthy children.

[I like] the rewards of giving the results. It's like you made the baby OK. You realize you're not God and you didn't, but it's a nice feeling.

In a weird kind of way, I made it possible for people to have children.

While some of the interpersonal rewards of genetic counseling may be like those of medicine, the similarities stop there. In terms of professional status, autonomy, and certainly salary, genetic counselors are in a very different position from that of physicians.

As described earlier, traditional medical norms make active intervention based on clinical judgement the ideal mode of practice. Within this medical value system, counseling ranks low as compared with, for example, skillfully puncturing the abdomen and uterus and withdrawing amniotic fluid. The latter technical/medical task is highly valued — and highly paid. Genetic counseling, on the other hand — talking to people and helping them to make life-changing decisions — gets turned over to lower-paid workers and is perceived as less important work. Thus one genetic counselor, in a published statement calling for the further use of non-M.D.'s as genetic counselors, said that using a nonphysician "saves money because it frees doctors' time for other tasks" and "spares him [sic] a repetitive and not very interesting task" (Powledge 1979).

This viewpoint is of course not unique to genetic counseling, but occurs in all areas of medicine and is often termed euphemistically a "team approach." The non-M.D. worker seeks professional recognition from and a peer relationship with the physicians on the team. The physicians may want the services of the non-M.D.'s, the "physician extenders" who save them from repetitive work, but they do not grant them equal status. Genetic counselors, like other health-related workers in this position (nurse-midwives, well-baby nurses, occupational therapists, and the like), are not likely to achieve full professional status. A more accurate description of their position is "semiprofessional" (Etzioni 1969). These semiprofessionals are all highly trained workers who, unlike physicians, do not have a substantial degree of control over their work. Instead, they function in a bureaucratic structure, answerable to both physicians and to program or hospital administrators.

It is no coincidence, then, that genetic counselors, like other semi-professionals in health care, are overwhelmingly women. As one of those interviewed said, "It's a classic women's occupation: low pay and no upward mobility." The history of the occupation drives the point home. The first genetic counseling program in the United States was the master's degree program established in 1969 at Sarah Lawrence College. The program began with a special orientation to women who wanted to return to school and the workforce after several years of homemaking. This special orientation no longer exists, and several other academic centers have joined Sarah Lawrence in providing master of science programs focusing on human genetics and counseling. Young people are entering the field — but they are almost all young *women*. Genetic counseling remains a "women's occupation," less valued and lower paid than the provision of technical-medical services.

While it seems that everybody in virtually every occupation complains about salary, genetic counselors are particularly troubled. One reported that she made less than her secretary. But it was not just salary that upset her:

> In the medical system hierarchy, the physician is at the top — no one else can reach administrative positions. You're limited as to where you can go and that's a fact of life.

The relationship to physicians was distressing to some but not all counselors. Asked how doctors treated them, some were satisfied, some not:

> I can't generalize. Some definitely respect what I have to say and my abilities, and some talk around me, over me — don't view me as a separate entity.

> A lot of the doctors treat you like nurses. And they treat nurses like subhumans.

The bulk of the counseling done by those genetic counselors interviewed was preamnio counseling: counseling pregnant women regarding the availablility of, and their choice to have or not to have, amniocentesis for prenatal diagnosis. Despite their semiprofessional status, most of the counselors seemed to have a great deal of freedom in how they handled these preamnio sessions, a kind of "autonomy by default." As long as the patient had signed the "informed consent" forms, providing proof that she was counseled, the physician did not seem to care what happened in the session. While the explicit purpose of genetic counseling is to help the client make educated decisions regarding reproduction and the available technology, genetic counselors serve the implicit function of protecting the physician and the hospital from malpractice suits. On the one hand, hospitals and physicians are spared the malpractice suits that may result if a genetically "defective" child is born — the new "wrongful life" suits. On the other hand, informed consent protects hospitals and physicians against the malpractice suits that may arise when there are complications from the amniocentesis procedure itself. The patient, having been counseled, is now on record as having given informed consent to the procedure — or the next best thing, an informed refusal. The responsibility for the outcome in many ways now shifts to the patient's shoulders. The record is what counts. Thus the forms are standardized, and the specific handling and content of the preamnio session is of little official or breaucratic concern.

For the counselors, this autonomy by default can represent an advantage of prenatal counseling over other health-related work. As one counselor said:

[I face] no interference, no doctor with a capital *D* giving a diagnosis, saying things which are anathema to the patient or to you in psychological terms, or in medical, genetic terms.

Other counselors said similar things, such as:

I have so much autonomy that I don't have to think about it, but I imagine that if I didn't have it, it would be of great concern to me.

Another counselor, who had been in the field for ten years working with individuals and families affected by genetic disease, as well as with prospective parents, said:

I'm not a physician, and I realize my limitations in that regard, but I think with literature search and with having seen enough of the genetic problems, most likely we could come up with a diagnosis as much as the physician. But basically, we can't work alone — working as a team is fine with me. At this stage and this age in life, autonomy is important. I don't need someone to run it out for me in terms of "now you do this" and "now you do that."

However it was experienced by these counselors individually, this is not true political autonomy for the profession, not true control of the profession over its own domain (Freidson 1970). In the larger structure, the counselors do not set the parameters of their work. That is, they do determine how they counsel, but not who. It is not up to the counselors to set the ages at which amnio is standardly offered, for example, or in other ways to define who is and who is not at risk, and therefore an appropriate candidate for counseling and amniocentesis. Limitations also arise at the interpersonal level, when situations move beyond the routine. Counselors may have to call the medical geneticist to get approval to do prenatal testing where indications are not routine — not advanced age, for example, but prior drug use. Similarly, in a postamniocentesis session, once the laboratory results have confirmed a fetal abnormality, the counselor is no longer alone but rather accompanied by one or more physicians — a medical geneticist and perhaps an obstetrician or pediatrician as well. In these sessions, the counselor most often has to defer to the physicians.

Thus the autonomy the counselors value so highly is truly an autonomy by default: theirs only when their work is considered of minimal importance. As the decisions to be made are seen to be of greater import, dominant professionals take control of the situation.

PART II: ABORTION COUNSELORS

We turn our attention now from the genetic counselors to the abortion counselors. Seventeen abortion counselors were interviewed; all but one were women. The educational range was from a high school degree to graduate train-

ing in psychology and a master's degree in social work. The counselors interviewed tended to be somewhat more highly educated than most abortion counselors: when entering a clinic or abortion service, the interviewer was most often
directed to a senior or more experienced counselor. In spite of this, it was striking that these abortion counselors viewed their work as a job, not a career.

Before the 1973 Supreme Court ruling making abortion legally available
"on demand," abortion counselors were abortion activists; they provided emotional support, help in decision making, referrals, and "coaching," since many
women seeking abortion had to undergo psychiatric evaluations to obtain
medical approval. These activists located and monitored abortion facilities. They
fought for legalization of abortion, even as they were working outside the law,
making referrals to illegal abortion services (Joffe 1978).

With legalization, the role of the abortion counselor changed dramatically. Two of the counselors we interviewed discussed the changes in the field
and the lack of political consciousness among newer counselors:

> Especially with younger women, I feel so dated. But the young women who
> are just coming out of college are not as concerned with the feminist move-
> ment, women's roles, and with a lot of the things I was very concerned about.
> There seems to be a big difference.

Another spoke almost longingly of how things were in the years before
she entered the field, when people were:

> . . . like adamant about it. And that's gone . . . after a while it's easy to start
> forgetting what's going on here and why you're doing it. . . . The awareness
> is gone, almost. At least here and a lot of places — now it's just shuffle, shuf-
> fle, shuffle, shuffle the people.

The most dramatic change we observed was that not all counselors identified themselves as "prochoice." Most of the counselors we interviewed had
not expressly sought out abortion work. They referred to "stumbling onto it,"
to being "in the right place at the right time," or getting involved "accidentally."
They came from a variety of backgrounds. About a third either became interested in the field while still in college, through peer counseling programs and
the like, or began abortion work straight after graduation. Another third had
either taken time out to raise a family or had worked in unrelated fields. The
remaining third came from associated areas, primarily from counseling rather
than from the health field. Although a handful had worked for physicians or
in hospitals, abortion work presented most of these women with their first experience working face-to-face with physicians in the medical world.

On the whole, there was "no real firm commitment" to doing abortion
work, as one counselor put it. While many counselors did come to the field
with some feminist orientation, the majority did not hold a political interest
in their work. In assessing the changes that have occurred in their work lives,

they tended to emphasize the personal rather than the political, suggesting a greater interest in "what abortion counseling can do for me" than in "what I can do for abortion work."

> I think of it in terms of my own growth, that it has changed for me because I've learned more.
>
> I find that I am more efficient and can do things faster and meet fewer obstacles.

Many of the counselors we spoke to were unhappy with their work in the abortion field and were planning to leave. In many cases, they were unprepared for the confrontation with political and moral issues their work thrust upon them. Disinclined to become politically active, they chose to remain passive participants in their work.

The relationship with the medical staff reinforced their attitude that their work was "just a job." It is difficult for counselors to gain acceptance within the medical hierarchy, where counseling and social work standardly rank low. Counselors must constantly prove their worthiness to the medical professionals at the abortion clinic:

> On interdisciplinary teams, usually the social worker is on the bottom of the totem pole. Basically people look down on the social worker — you can do all the dirty work, solve all the problems, but when it comes to . . . professional respect, I don't find it easily available to social workers.

The dominant profession has the power to confer status upon other workers. Physicians perceive their own role as the most valuable in the abortion process: other workers are seen as merely "helpers."

Their skills undervalued, abortion counselors, like genetic counselors receive low salaries. Surprisingly, of the counselors interviewed, some of those with the highest training, as well as those with little or no training, felt themselves fairly compensated. Both of these groups appeared to have lowered expectations. Yet most of the counselors thought their salaries inadequate for the work they performed, and some did express resentment:

> The only thing that we are resentful of is that the salaries are different — there is a different salary for the nurses and the counselors and it just seems to me that that says something about the worth of the employee. There's a clear-cut salary difference between nurses and counselors even though the educational level of the counselors is much higher.

The staff in abortion clinics work interdependently and function as a team. The underlying ideology holds that all team members work together toward a common goal. The clearest example of teamwork we found took place at an adolescent health center that offered abortions:

> We work as a team — the social work counselors, the gynecologists, and the
> nursing staff. We talk about things — what the needs are of the people, and
> how we can best respond to them, and how we best work with each other
> to help the adolescent or her boyfriend or family or whatever.

Not all teams function so well together, nor are all members accorded
the same value. One counselor had this to say regarding teamwork at her clinic:

> We are a health team, but again, my concern is that the counselors are not
> involved as much as they should be. I feel they should include the counselors
> more in the decision-making process, in administrative decisions.

Sometimes the poor treatment of patients by the medical staff makes the
counseling job more difficult and undermines team feelings. When asked if she
felt herself to be part of a health team offering abortion services, one counselor
responded: "On paper. I think that I'm the only one working for the patients,
and that is working against all of them."

So it is a strange "team," with members operating at the same time in
the same clinic with the same clients, yet not really spending time together.
Counselors are "front staff," and medical workers are "back staff."

> The back staff, being the medical team, they work pretty much together, and
> we work together. But it's hard for us to say, "Look, we need you to change
> this so we can do this," and vice versa. So there's a separation, but you can
> work with it in most cases.

Overall, counselors expressed satisfaction with their relations with
medical staff. In fact, several counselors extended the notion of team spirit to
include a family feeling. As one put it:

> We have a family sort of atmosphere. There is a lot of pressure, but in general
> there is a lot of time spent trying to feel like a community and not like we're
> separate camps.

But this counselor went on to talk about the constant effort it took to
develop and sustain good working relations among staff. With the back staff
completing one piece of work and the front another, it as easy for the team
to split into separate camps, especially when the two groups disagreed over treatment of clients. In teams such as these as in the family, mutual respect may
be present and interactions may be "friendly," but roles and expectations of
individual members are very different and often unequal.

The medical hierarchy, like the family, may not allow room for all
members to exercise their skills. Several of the abortion counselors felt that
they were underutilized, and that their autonomy was too limited. Asked about
work autonomy, two counselors gave the following, fairly typical replies:

It's important, but I don't have much of it here, in a way, just because I don't have the time I would need to do what I want. But no one is breathing down your back. Well, the doctors are, as far as having patients ready, but as far as what I do when I have the time, it is up to me.

Well, [autonomy is] important, but you cannot do that if you're working for a place that is primarily a business, and obviously we're here and it is a business, and that has to be taken into consideration.

As with the genetic counselors, to the degree that abortion counselors are granted autonomy, it may well be an "autonomy by default." One counselor expressed it in this way:

In some respect, because they don't take social services and counseling seriously, it really gives you an opportunity to create your own situations.

It is less direct supervision than time pressure that stops counselors from "creating their own situations," or working in their own style. A central feature of all of the clinics — nonprofit as well as for-profit — was the sense of rush. The omnipresent time constraints are inherent in the economics of the system. When asked what she liked least about abortion counseling, one counselor replied:

Probably the volume. There's too many people, and we have five counselors on staff for every abortion session, and yet I can see as many as twelve patients, and it's a continuing thing — back-to-back, because we're at the beginning of a funnel, and if we don't keep up a certain pace, then the medical-end situation gets bogged down, and everything gets bogged down. So there's a lot of pressure in terms of time.

Even in the public clinics we observed, the funding and revenue were limited and the counseling restricted by the exigencies of the appointments system. However, a few of the counselors explicitly held the "business" end of abortion clinics responsible for the limitation in their role:

I think the abortion business, which I'm in because this is a profit-oriented clinic, is just that: profit-oriented rather than women-oriented. So the emphasis is get as many cases as you can and the least amount of counseling time because only a certain amount of money is brought in.

I don't know if [a different sort of setting] would work from the business aspect, and no one is going to stay in business doing abortions unless they're making money. So it's a catch-22.

The profit incentive governs most medical services, not just abortion. Yet abortion is particularly vulnerable to abuse since demand exceeds supply in many areas. Public facilities do exist, but their fees remain on a par with the less expensive privately owned clinics. Often, cash only is accepted unless the patient qualifies for Medicaid. One counselor discussed the outcome for women "falling between the cracks" of the system.

> This is definitely a money-making business, and the orientation here is for the people who have invested to make their money . . . The real problem with me is when I see a woman come in and she falls between the cracks. She can't get public assistance, but yet it's really tough to come up with the $275 when you don't have any money. That's where it really hurts and gets difficult.

Clinics' profit orientation creates problems not only for women seeking abortions, but also for counselors who are saddled with the responsibility of bill collecting. Half of the counselors mentioned "cashiering" as part of the abortion process.

Under the circumstances — rushed, underpaid, and overworked; shuffling papers, bills, and people — the high rate of turnover among abortion counselors is hardly surprising.

PART III: COMPARISONS AND CONCLUDING THOUGHTS

Both the similarities and the differences in these two occupations can teach us something about the status of women in our society. Both of these, nearly exclusively *women's* occupations, are relatively new, dating in their present form back to the 1970s. Before that time, genetic counseling was done by physicians, and abortion counseling was largely underground.

Neither genetic counseling nor abortion counseling is the kind of occupation children tend to aspire to from childhood. Entry routes are often obscured and haphazard; people "fall into" these occupations. Genetic counseling, requiring a specific training program, has a more orderly entry, but it, too, is rarely selected as a first-choice occupation. Rather, it is seen as more accessible, and less demanding than medical school. Abortion counselors are even more likely to fall into the occupation, and without the commitment of an advanced specific degree, to fall back out again. Considering the advanced level of training required for the one, and often found in candidates for the other, neither job appears to offer a particularly appealing set of working conditions: much of the work is clerical and repetitive; status in the medical hierarchy is low; and salary is lower still.

What satisfactions are available come from two sources: from the relationship with clients and — closely related — form the relative autonomy of the counseling role. It is, for both groups of counselors, an autonomy by default. Within the medical system, the counseling work is not highly enough valued to be closely monitored: "no one watches over your shoulder." Counselors do what they think appropriate with clients; but the primary responsibility to the institution is in producing the requisite paperwork: history forms, consent forms, insurance forms, and more — shuffle, shuffle, shuffle. The "real" work of the clinics is what goes on in back, the technical-medical task of performing amniocenteses or abortions.

The major difference between these two occupations is the relatively higher social status of genetic counseling. While both genetic counseling and abortion counseling command relatively low status within medicine, and society as a whole, abortion counseling can claim even less status than genetic counseling. Genetic counseling makes claims of professional or "semi-professional" standing, pointing to entrance requirements such as advanced university-based training, licensing exams, and the like. Abortion counseling does not claim the status of a profession. Genetic counseling has much more of the cachet of medicine; to the outside world the genetic counselor is a medical professional, "almost a doctor." Abortion counseling, in contrast, is less valued, less admired work.

Wherein lies the difference? It is not in the nature of the work. While genetic counselors train in genetics, they do not establish the criteria under which they work. For prenatal diagnosis or preamniocentesis counseling, the work is crushingly routine from a genetics point of view. Rather, it is, we claim, the medicalization of selective abortion that raises the status of genetic counselors above that of abortion counselors, even though the work in both occupations is almost identical.

Both groups of counselors counsel women who are pregnant about the possibility of an abortion. What distinguishes the two is at least in part the way their work is perceived by society. Inasmuch as abortion performed to meet the needs of women is viewed with distaste by many, abortion counseling is often judged a form of "dirty work." In contrast, to the degree that selective abortion serves not women per se but eugenic principles — preventing the birth of disabled, retarded, or "defective" infants — that type of abortion gains status and acceptability, and so do the workers.

When a woman goes to an abortion counselor and says she cannot afford another child and therefore needs an abortion, that is perceived as abortion "on demand." When a woman's fetus is diagnosed as having, say, Down's syndrome, and the counselor encourages the woman to consider her family's economic situation as she decides whether to continue or terminate the pregnancy, that is perceived as a "therapeutic" abortion, or abortion for "medical indication."

The comparison of these two occupations suggests that the underlying eugenic values of American society raises the status of genetic counseling, while the underlying antifeminism of society lowers the status of abortion counseling geared entirely to the needs of the woman. And the relegation of both types of counseling to lower-paid women workers speaks to the devaluation of human services as compared with technical skills.

While the differences between the two occupations can be explained by their relation to dominant social values, the similarities arise from their essentially similar structuring within institutional settings. In both settings, women are used as mediators, doing the "people work" for the institution and for the technicians. While the "speedup" the counselors experience is reminiscent of any assembly-line work, part of what the counselor is doing is trying to help the client avoid feeling like she is in a factory. The counselor mediates between the industrial speedup and the human being who is being processed. Clients would presumably rebel against a genuinely autonomated assembly line. Rather than simply giving orders — sign on the dotted line; undress here; lie there; pay on your way out — the counselors are engaged in face-to-face interaction with clients, easing them through the clinic.

When the counselor does her work well, she gives the client the experience of being treated "as a person" — an interesting expression often used to contrast with "as a patient." And when the counselor does her work well, she may give herself the experience of autonomy, as she chooses how best to make the client feel that her needs have been met. Both clients and counselors may value this service, but it is not of primary value to the institution. In this sense, in doing her job well the counselor participates in her own, and her clients' exploitation. The point is most clearly illustrated in the profit-making clinics, where counselors are used only to the extent that their presence contributes to profit. But even in nonprofit settings, the institutional goals of processing as many clients as possible, of avoiding lawsuits, and of "freeing" high-paid technicians to work only on highly valued technical work, are best met by having some nurturant individual to mediate between the client and the institution.

Thus, in doing their jobs well, genetic counselors and abortion counselors, like teachers, nurses, and social workers, not only make things easier on their clients; they also help offset pressures to change the institutions for which they work.

REFERENCES

Detlefs, Melinda K. 1984. "Abortion counseling: A description of the current status of the occupation reported by seventeen abortion counselors in metropolitan New York," Master's thesis, City University of New York, Graduate School and University Center.

Etzioni, Amitai, ed. 1969. *The Semi-Professions and their Organization*. New York: Free Press.

Freidson, Eliot. 1970. *Professional Dominance: The Social Structure of Medical Care*. New York: Atherton.

Joffe, Carole. 1978. "What abortion counselors want from their clients," *Social Problems* 26:112–21.

Powledge, Tabitha. 1979. "Genetic counselors without doctorates," *Birth Defects: Original Article Series* 15:103–112.

Rothman, Barbara Katz. 1986. *The Tentative Pregnancy: Prenatal Diagnosis and the Future of Motherhood*. New York: Viking Press.

Sorenson, James R. 1973. "Counselors: A self portrait," *Genetic Counseling* 1:1.

Sorenson, James R., Judith Swazey and Norman Scotch. 1981 *Birth Defects* 17:191–192.

Weitz, Rose. 1981. "Barriers to acceptance of genetic counseling among primary care physicians," *Social Biology* 26:189–193.

CHAPTER 10

Public Schoolteaching:
A Suitable Job for a Woman?[1]

DEE ANN SPENCER

The work in this chapter is based on data gathered during a two-year field study supported by the National Institute of Education. To provide detailed descriptions of teachers' lives, I used research methods that focused on womens' day-to-day intimate experiences and therefore, chose a qualitative approach. Eight women of differing marital status, who taught different grade levels in different sized school districts from rural to urban, were observed at school and in their homes, were interviewed continually, and were asked to write diaries.[2] Also, comparative data were gathered from 42 other teachers.[3]

To the extent possible in a research relationship, the eight women I studied intensively shared their lives with me. We discussed and interacted with students, graded papers together, made bulletin boards, went to meetings, left school together, shopped for groceries, shared meals, and babysat. We went to family reunions, fished, traveled, attended the theater, and played piano duets — depending on the leisure activities each woman enjoyed.

THE DEPROFESSIONALIZATION OR PROLETARIANIZATION OF TEACHING: RESEARCHERS' PERSPECTIVES

From the academic's viewpoint, whether or not an occupation is considered a profession depends on the extent of control and autonomy of an individual in that occupation. According to Grimm (1978), professionalization is "the process by which an occupation claims and receives the legal autonomy to exercise a monopoly over the delivery of an important service" (p. 294). By this definition teaching and other female-dominated occupations such as library work, nursing, and social work, have not achieved professional status. Instead, they have been referred to as semiprofessions because they do not meet the standard definitions of a profession (Etzioni 1969).

Commitment

Some have asserted that teachers' lack of power, autonomy, and status is due to women's lack of consistent career patterns, their submissiveness to administrators, and their decision to put their families before jobs. Teaching has been assumed to be congruent with female socialization, as prestigious and monetarily rewarding work compared to other alternatives for women, as compatible with family life, and as work which allows women to be away from teaching for periods of time without loss of skills when they return (Geer 1968; Simpson and Simpson 1969; Lortie 1975). Some have blamed women teachers for acting unprofessionally. An example is described by Simpson and Simpson.

> In these ways a woman's family situation makes it improbable that she will develop a strong professional commitment, or . . . that she will be able to maintain it . . . [O]ne might surmise that an organization staffed mainly with such people would not have an atmosphere favorable to professionalism among its other employees (1969, 219).

Geer cites five characteristics of the teaching situation that account for lower commitment: 1) Unlike other occupations (scholars, artists, scientists) which create knowledge, or build upon past skills and knowledge, teaching requires the transmission of others' knowledge and skills. According to Geer, education students do not gain the kind of knowledge that "would make it a great waste if he [sic] did not spend his [sic] life in the classroom." 2) The teacher's clientele, students, are involuntarily present. Also, student's success is not seen as one teacher's success. Because students are children, with low status and are powerless in society, teachers have no opportunity to establish "useful and prestigious relationships in their daily work." 3) There is a lack of collegial relationships among teachers. Each teacher operates within the privacy of her own room to a small audience of children. 4) A teacher is not rewarded for achievement. There is little difference in the salaries of the least and most experienced teachers; there are no opportunities for promotion. 5) The length and frequency of vacations increases the possibility of "moonlighting," which can eventually conflict with commitment to teaching. Although I agree with these five points, I see them as evidence of the problems in broader societal structures which have defined womens' roles and in the organizational structures of schools which have diminished the status of the occupation, rather than as evidence of teachers' lack of commitment.

Historical evidence shows that the issue of commitment was never relevant in understanding why women stay in teaching. Based on the diaries and journals of women who taught, Hoffman (1981) shows that teachers began working because they needed to work and that the image of teachers as angels of mercy is inaccurate. She adds that women were not preoccupied with fears of being old maids but chose to work and enjoyed independence from married life. They worked to earn a paycheck and to gain satisfaction. Currently, it is not feasible to take time off or to only work part time; many families would not survive without the mother's paycheck, as evidenced by the fact that women teachers take very brief maternity leaves (Sweet and Jacobson 1983; Feiman-Nemser and Floden 1986). According to Feiman-Nemser and Floden (1986), many teachers express a strong commitment to teaching, while recognizing the devaluation of their work and wanting it to change.

It is difficult to accurately assess the woman teacher's commitment to her work, and in doing so one runs the risk of blaming the victim. Many social structures force women to quit work to have children or to choose teaching as a career when they may not be truly interested in it. This lack of choice is reflected in the comments of a 32-year-old married elementary teacher.

> My mother always told me, "Go back to school, get a degree in case you ever have to support yourself. A teacher would be good, or a nurse." I noticed that no one ever recommended that I be a brain surgeon in case I had to support myself.

To the extent women teachers do show lower commitment, the development of proletarianization may be a key factor.

Proletarianization

The concept of proletarianization has been used to explain the conditions under which a middle class occupation shifts to that of wage workers. To exemplify this process an analogy can be made between the historical development of clerical work and that of teaching. The basis for this analogy is found in the work of Glenn and Feldberg (1977), who trace clerical work from the nineteenth century, when the individual was visible and key to the successful operation of a business, to the highly bureaucratized organizational structure in which the individual has become depersonalized. Over the years, clerical work has shifted from white-collar to blue-collar and tasks have become externally structured and controlled as activities became manual rather than mental and jobs were simplified. Workers lost control over their tasks and had less contact with managers as the size of organizations grew and technology and organizational goals changed.

I would argue that teachers, like clerical workers, shifted in occupational status as the bureaucratic structure of schools grew. Before the turn of the century, and indeed, in some areas of the country for decades after that time, teachers could teach with few credentials, and as a result, as Warren (1985) explains, teaching was "careerless" because schools were in session infrequently and work, therefore, was sporadic and only part time. In fact, Clifford (1978) points out that persons could begin teaching at the age of 14 or 15 with no credentials, and even when normal schools were opened, teaching was selected by some because it was the least expensive kind of eduation. As the press for credentialism became widespread and mandatory, the conditions under which teachers worked did not reflect the increasing expectation for their pofessional behavior. Teaching, like other sex-segregated occupations, became devalued because it was "women's work." While their work became devalued, there was, concomitantly, a great demand for women teachers. The rapid expansion of schools necessitated a large pool of teachers and women were there to fill that need, not only because teaching was one of the few "suitable" jobs for a woman but also because men left teaching (Apple 1985). According to Apple (1985), the "cost opportunity" for men to stay in teaching was too great; certification requirements came into existence which men did not wish to fulfill and more lucrative opportunities arose for entering other work. Hiring women was considered "cost effective" for "cash poor," largely rural school districts (Warren 1985) because females were paid less than men, and therefore, by 1840, most teachers were women (Lightfoot 1978). By 1919, 86 percent of teachers were women — the largest percentage of women in teaching before or since that time (Shakeshaft 1981). Also since 1919 there has been a major change at the secondary school level, with males increasingly dominating that level.

With the expansion of schools has come increased specialization of teaching tasks. This, as with clerical workers, constricts teachers' options; choices are narrowed and control is limited. Apple (1985) explains that as a job becomes defined as "women's work" there is, at the same time, greater pressure to rationalize, and with it, increases in administrative control of teaching and curriculum. Or, in the author's words, "The job itself becomes different" (p. 462). Today, teachers have become subject to local, state, and federal requirements that specify expectations more so than ever before. Although accountability is not undesirable, the increased demands on teachers' time and energy has made teaching more mechanical and less creative or spontaneous.

Glenn and Feldberg explain that standardization of tasks makes it easier for managers to monitor work. The problem is that teachers, like clerical workers, become more vulnerable because they are open to constant inspection. This undermines their internal motivation and separates them from one another because it creates a competitive atmosphere rather than one of cooperation and independence. The simultaneous occurrence of isolationism and close inspection of work is explained by Apple (1985) as a process of intensification. Intensification, or increasing quantities of required work, links closely with the fact, mentioned in the previous paragraph, that teachers are subject to greater and greater demands for accountability. Intensification erodes the work of teachers, as evidenced in all aspects of their work — from not having time to go to the bathroom to mental work overload. As the details of completing increasingly segmented tasks (such as paper grading and writing reports) increase, it destroys leisure and self-direction. To participate in these activities takes time but when avoided, it increases isolationism. Apple continues to explain that as the reduction of quality of service to students — the main activity of teaching

— occurs, it is contradicted by the demands for quantity of performance or for technical tasks.

According to Glenn and Feldberg, managerial control in organizations was possible, in part, because managers were men and clerical workers were women. Males also occupy a disproportionate share of the elite positions in schools. Nearly all administrators are male, and, as pointed out by Grimm and Stern (1974), "when the administrative component of a female profession is itself expanding, the increasing demand for administrators will enhance the tendency of males to dominate the field" (p. 703). Lortie (1986) explains this historical process by showing how "arrangements for the exercise of authority" at the turn of the century reflected the condition of teaching. That is, because teachers were young, inexperienced, and had little training, a rationale developed which placed decision making in the hands of central administrators and board members — who were males. The low status of women reinforced the belief that administrators should be male. Male domination in administrative positions means a hierarchical-patriarchal arrangement in which decisions in schools are made by males and carried out by females — a situation comparable to clerical workers and managers. In both situations, relationships between those in control and the workers become strained and impersonal and contacts between them decrease.

Male managers also capitalize on the stereotype that women work to please others and are more sensitive and honest and less mercenary than men. Because "niceness" is stressed, orders given to women are disguised as personal requests that they find difficult to refuse. These same characteristics have been attributed to women teachers with the additional "ideology of 'true woman-hood' that emphasized woman's nurturant qualities and hence her suitability for teaching" (Shakeshaft 1981). Teachers then, like other women in female-dominated professions, have been linked to qualities of nurturance, caring, and socialization (Grimm 1978). Teaching, more than other female-dominated professions, came to be seen as an extension of mothering.

The result of viewing work as blue-collar rather than white-collar, continuing with Glenn and Feldberg's argument, is a downgrading of the work itself and a change in the workers' relationship to it. These changes removed the very features that attracted people to the work situation. Workers become less knowledgeable, less involved, less committed, and less able and willing to respond to variation. This phenomenon is evident in the fewer students who go into teaching and the high rates of dissatisfaction among experienced teachers. In clerical work and in teaching, this process is counterproductive because workers become alienated or "burned out." As loss of control over the work place becomes a significant feature of teachers' work, teaching becomes more similar to blue-collar work.

In summary, some have considered teaching a semi- or quasi-profession because of low pay and teachers' lack of control over their work place; the conditions under which teachers work have been described as more similar to those of blue-collar workers than to those of professionals. The ways in which the organizational structure of schools has developed over time, and the predominance of women in teaching, is regarded as having created and perpetuated these conditions.

These studies, including those concerned with commitment and those with proletarianization, are written from an academic point of view and perhaps reflect what has been described as the "perspective of a somewhat cold-eyed sociological observer looking from the outside" (Dreeben 1970 in Feiman-Nemser and Floden 1986, 505) because they make teachers the object of study rather than the subject (Hoffman 1981). As Traver (1986) points out, of the 35 chapters and 1,037 pages of *The Handbook of Research on Teaching, Third Edition* (Wittrock 1986), there is only one chapter which reviews attempts to understand teaching from the perspective of the teacher — Feiman-Nemser and Floden's, "The Cultures of Teaching."

As one study has shown, teachers' perceptions do not always concur with those of researchers. In her study of women elementary teachers, Biklen (1986) found that traditional sociological definitions of the concept of "career" are based on males' work patterns. Because men have been free from housework and child care they have been able to devote themselves (be committed) to careers. By this definition, women, who have put work secondary to their families, are not committed to a career. But in interviews with women teachers, she found that they regarded themselves as committed to teaching whether or not they had taken off to have children or only worked part time; they *thought* of themselves as teachers and planned to continue working. She calls for a reconceptualization of the meaning of the concept of career commitment to reflect women's perspectives.

I would suggest that while most studies of teachers, no matter how detailed, seem depersonalized and out of touch with the experiences of real teachers, one should keep in mind Feiman-Nemser and Floden's (1986) caution that we cannot rely totally on teachers' perceptions because they may glorify "teachers' beliefs simply because they are what teachers believe" (p. 507). The following section gives the teacher's view.

CONTRADICTIONS IN TEACHERS' PERCEPTIONS ABOUT TEACHING

Teachers' personal expectations and self-concepts do not always align with traditional expectations of them. Many studies of these contradictions have focused on teachers in their first year(s) of teaching, as they come to realize that their ideal of teaching is drastically different from the reality (Wright and Tuska 1968; Edgar and Warren 1969; Ryan *et al.* 1980). Evidence of disillusionment appears in the fact that as many as 15 percent of new graduates qualified to teach will not apply for teaching jobs. In 1981, 20 percent who were teaching were not doing so one year later (Feistritzer 1983). The following examples are disjunctures drawn from interviews with the 50 women teachers in my study.

1. Teaching as Respected Work versus Public Criticism of Teachers

Teachers choose teaching as a career because they believe it is respected work. But in the mass media, they have been accused of being illiterate and the cause of students' low scores on standardized tests. Teachers are disturbed by these reports and the knowledge that people in their communities were reading them. A 26 year old physical education teacher described the community's attitudes in the rural area where she taught.

> I don't know whether they [parents] just don't care or they figure, "Well, the school has been there for 60 years, it's going to be there another 60" . . . The townspeople are very biased. They all think their kids are right, regardless of what the situation is, and the teacher is the bad guy. Everything is the teacher's fault.

During the 19th century teachers lived with or "boarded" with community members and were integral and influential in community life (Clifford 1978), but today, teachers experience a loss in that prestige.

2. Teaching as a Profession versus Working Class Job Characteristics

Though teachers expect to have autonomy at work, they in fact have little choice about what, when, or where they teach; their classes are interrupted by announcements over intercom systems, and they have to engage in such demeaning tasks as monitoring bathrooms and performing janitorial duties in their classrooms. This problem is seen in the comments from a 30-year-old elementary school teacher.

> I think it [stress] is something that most people who are working, as either public employees or . . . with the public, feel when they are with people over whom they have no choice — like a waitress. People come in and she has to serve those people and has no control over who she wants in there. Teachers and public employees are in the same situation. The view from the classroom is that you have no control over the situation.

Also, teachers who are against unionization usually feel that way because they think it is unprofessional.

3. Teaching as a Helping Profession versus a Low Salary

Among the reasons teachers choose teaching as a career is that they want to "help" people, particularly children. They anticipate that rewards will be intrinsic and that pleasure will be derived simply from watching children learn. They find, however, that all children do not want to learn, all children are not desirable people with whom to work, and it is sometimes even dangerous to work with children. The following example provided by a 29-year-old single secondary teacher illustrates this point.

My students' lack of consideration and apathy adds to my anxiety and stress. Last week I had an unusual experience. One of my lovely students had made me a surprise in the form of a Chinese star (which is a form of a weapon) that is made of metal and filed off into very sharp points and edges. The star was placed above my head and so that when it was hit by a paper wad it would tumble down onto my head and hopefully inflict some damage. I was quite shocked at this malicious attempt to let me know that someone did not like having me around. . . . Instead of working on my master's degree, I should have gone to the police academy.

In addition to low intrinsic rewards, the reality of a low salary forces some teachers to live under extreme hardship as seen in the comments of a 29-year-old physical education teacher.

I mean I'm not living wildly or have big bills. You know if I was blowing money it would be one thing, but I'm not. I don't go anywhere or do anything. I go home to my mom's about once a month because that's all I can afford.

The lack of intrinsic rewards is not balanced or offset by extrinsic rewards. In general, the number of teachers who say they receive no extrinsic or intrinsic rewards increased significantly from 1964 to 1984 (Kottkamp, Provenzo and Cohn 1986). In my study, teachers had difficulty determining whether there are rewards at all in teaching.

4. Power over Classes versus Powerlessness in School Organizations

Classrooms are the social settings in which teachers hold the most powerful positions. Teachers are expected to gain and maintain control over students, and students are expected to comply with rules and obey their teachers. However, within the context of the school or school system as an organization, teachers take a subordinate role to administrators. Although administrators expect teachers to keep their classes under control, teachers are often treated in infantile ways. For example, a 52-year-old divorced teacher with three children explained,

To ask for help is to admit you're inadequate. You can't admit to being human if you want tenure. The response from the principal is, "Oh, you can't handle the child." It becomes a reflection of you — not the kid's problem.

Principals can assign teachers such duties as monitoring restrooms or detention rooms, can enter and observe classrooms without notifying teachers, and can schedule meetings without consulting teachers. In a few cases, principals go through teachers' desk drawers and grade their lesson plan books. Teachers, therefore, feel a contradiction between the expectation that they play a superordinate role with students and a subordinate role with administrators.

5. Desire for Autonomy versus Desire for Administrative Competence

Teachers want freedom to teach and control their classrooms without constraint or censorship but have to comply with stringent curriculum plans and guidelines. These detemine what they teach, how they teach, and when they teach. In open schools, or schools that were once open and have constructed thin folding walls, their autonomy is further constrained because teachers can see and hear what other teachers are saying and doing throughout the school day. However, teachers want to be relieved from certain kinds of decisions they define as administrative. Principals who do not carry out certain responsibilities, such as enforcing student discipline, are seen as ineffective and as burdening teachers with unnecessary work which takes time away from their teaching. However, teachers perceive that they receive less instructional help from principals now than they did 20 years ago (Kottkamp, Provenzo, and Cohn 1986). Teachers are uneasy about intrusions into their classrooms, though they would like some positive feedback. These sentiments are expressed by a 32-year-old married English teacher.

> I hate the observation process. I always feel insecure, nervous, and paranoid about the whole thing. I wish there were some other way to get evaluated. To base a teacher's performance on one visit to the classroom seems unfair. I'm not sure what a better solution would be. Perhaps more frequent and shorter informal visits — something like "How's everything going today?" or "What are you covering now?" "I just wanted to stop and say hello." I do think principals need to get a closer relationship with teachers. It doesn't have to be a buddy-buddy setup. But somehow, there needs to be more interaction. I haven't had a compliment (or a reprimand) all year.

6. Female Teachers versus Male Administrators

Despite the fact that research has shown that women are more effective than men in the principal role, males continue to fill administrative positions. Some reviewers have even concluded that hiring males has been detrimental to schools (Gross and Trask 1976 in Adkison 1981).

The inequitable patriarchal power relationships between teachers and principals affects the nature and frequency of interaction in schools. For example, women teachers feel constrained when interacting and negotiating with male principals so they tend to be passive and subservient when interacting with them. Contacts are often limited to formal settings, such as faculty meetings, infrequent classroom visitation by principals for the purpose of teacher evaluation, or teachers' requests for materials. Male teachers, however, have interactions on both a formal and informal basis; they play golf with their principals, or go hunting or fishing with them, or join them for an after-work drink.

At times, teachers encounter overt sexist remarks or sexual harassment (are kissed or pinched), as seen in the comments of a 37-year-old married home economics teacher.

> When I got into the carpool this morning, everyone was laughing. Mr. [the superintendent] had commented that I looked like Dolly [Parton] as I walked to the car. I asked if it was my long blonde hair. There was no comment (since my hair is short and brown) . . . that comment didn't set well with me and my whole day seemed off to a poor start. There was nothing to do but laugh it off, but I kept thinking what I could have done to give him the impression that I would even appreciate a comment like that. I took it as lack of respect for women. I would certainly not comment on the size of his testicles.

Even where principals have more collegial relations with women teachers, there is often a subtle undercurrent in which they refer to faculty as "the girls" or expect them to cook dishes for school gatherings.

7. Teaching as Specialized Work versus Teaching as Something Anyone Can Do

Teachers believe that their degree(s) and experience qualify them for specialized work, though others may not agree. Teachers' knowledge has been seen by many as "a mixture of idiosyncratic experience and personal synthesis" (Feiman-Nemser and Floden 1986, 512). This perception is based on the greater value our society places on scientific knowledge as compared to that which is utilized by teachers — practical and personal knowledge.

When teachers are dissatisfied or consider quitting teaching, they have difficulty assessing the uniqueness of their skills, as expressed in the comments of a 32-year-old single elementary teacher, who lamented, "My problem is I don't know what to do, but if there were something, I think I'd leave teaching today." They have difficulty seeing what they might do in another setting, often seeing their skills as limited to certain age groups. The fact that schools often hire substitute teachers who do not necessarily have certification to teach the grades or subjects they are asked to teach contributes to the notion that teaching is something anyone can do. Principals also contribute to this perception when they schedule teachers for classes for which they are not prepared — sometimes shortly before the beginning of a school year.

8. Teaching as Easy Work versus Exhaustion

Teachers contend with the common assumption that teaching is an easy job because the work days are short, vacations are long, and groups of children are easy to control. The reality is that teachers' work days often extend into the evenings, their summers are spent in school or working at other jobs, and control over children is demanding and exhausting. A 32-year-old married English teacher who often graded papers for 5 hours at a time described her feelings.

> I was tired when I got home from school. I'm tired of being tired. Tell me everybody gets tired and that it's just not me. Anyway, I put leftovers on the stove, we ate, and both of us fell asleep watching the local news. I always feel

better after a nap, but it's a vicious cycle. Now I'll probably stay up later than I should and then be tired tomorrow evening.

Paper grading and extracurricular duties take inordinate amounts of teachers' time outside the school day as do meetings, workshops, and parent conferences. The strain of standing all day, monitoring students' work and behaviors, and dealing with problems and disruptive behavior is draining and difficult. Unlike other workers, teachers often have no coffee breaks, lunch hours away from their work settings, or places to prop up their feet and complain.

9. Teaching as Hard Work versus "Rate Busting"

Teachers are committed to the work ethic. Not being prepared is unthinkable to most teachers and they are critical of colleagues who are unorganized, poorly prepared, or remiss in making classroom assignments. In fact, most teachers (90 percent) in my study came to school even when they were sick. As a 32-year-old elementary teacher who was married and had two children commented. "Teachers feel foolish to be home with a cold. It has to be catastrophic." However, teachers who work hard during the regular work day are critical of those who take work home, and those considered rate busters are puzzled by the others' negative reactions to them.

10. Isolation versus No Privacy

Teachers feel a sense of isolation from other adults. The most frequent question asked by teachers in my study was "Does anyone else feel like I do?" Teachers (particularly elementary school teachers) see other teachers only briefly and when they do, they rarely talk about instructional practices. Even in open schools where teachers in adjoining classroom areas see each other all day, they cannot talk because their total attention has to be on their classes. Despite this isolation, teachers have no moments of privacy when they can let down, relax, and rest because they are always before an audience of children. Teachers have to eat lunch under crowded conditions, sometimes with several hundred noisy children, and breaks in the day are filled with hall duty, playground duty, or bus duty. There is no place, including the restroom, to sit quietly by oneself. Some schools do not have separate restroom facilities for teachers, and in extreme cases, the restrooms do not have doors. This problem is illustrated in the comments of a 32-year-old secondary teacher who had lost self-control in front of her students.

> One of my students kept asking me why my eyes were red and then, "Why are you crying? Why are you crying?" All this attention got me started in earnest, and I had to leave the room. On my way into the restroom I ran into a teacher who asked what was wrong, and I just went ahead and told her the truth. Meanwhile, the inquisitive student had followed me to the restroom to find out what was wrong. All this was embarrassing!

11. Spontaneity versus Self-Control

Teachers are expected to be enthusiastic in their classes, exhibit warmth toward students, and motivate students by exhibiting a positive and dynamic example, but also to be in control. Too much noise or laughter by students is viewed by administrators or other teachers as a lack of control over classes. And loss of self-control is unforgivable. According to a 52-year-old divorced elementary teacher with three children, teachers think that because they are teachers they can handle everything. She described another teacher who had succumbed to the strains of her day and was "babbling" irrationally before her students. She went into the teacher's classroom, told her to leave, and calmly told the children she would read to them. When the teacher returned, she did not thank her and in fact, never spoke to her again. This woman interpreted the other teacher's reaction as understandable. To admit any sign of weakness is to admit failure; teachers are to be "paragons of virtue." She said it took her years to be able to break down and say, "This was a horrible day."

12. Being Well Liked versus Constraining Affection

Teachers who are well liked by students are given positive evaluations by administrators, because the teachers' popularity is seen as evidence of good rapport and is considered conducive to learning. Yet secondary teachers have to refrain from being overly friendly toward students and must limit displays of affection, particularly toward students of the opposite sex. Close friendships are not acceptable and overt displays of affection are judged by others as morally and ethically unacceptable behavior. A 24-year-old single business teacher had the problem of male students falling in love with her, which posed embarrassing and difficult problems for her.

> I have a terrible times with boys, senior boys, thinking and misinterpreting my friendship. It's happened four times and I've only been here two years. You know how embarrassing that is? "Well we hear you were dating so and so on the football team." Maybe he's my student aide or maybe he stayed after school to type three or four times. It's a crush, and I don't mean to sound like I'm anything special but it just happens.

13. Loving Children versus Unlovable Children

One of the reasons teachers cite for choosing teaching as a career is that they like (or love) children. The implication is that "children" means all children. Before graduation teachers thought of children as a nebulous mass of cherubic figures. However, teachers find that real children in real classrooms are not always lovable — or even likeable. This results in a serious contradiction because teachers cannot admit to not liking a student. To do so is an admission of failure or disloyalty to teaching. For women, particularly elementary teachers, the admission also reflects their failure as females — to admit to not liking a small child is "unwomanly."

THE RELATIONSHIP OF SCHOOL AND HOME
LIVES OF WOMEN TEACHERS

Examination of contradictions in teaching is only part of the life of a woman teacher. Historically, the *personal* lives of teachers were the concern of boards of education, who for decades placed rigid restrictions on teachers' moral behaviors, presumably to preserve their purity because they were dealing with children, which included prohibiting them from marrying and continuing to teach (unless their husbands were physically or mentally incapacitated — Woody 1929 in Shakeshaft 1981). Often teachers lived with families in the communities in which they taught (Clifford 1978). At the same time, people held peculiar notions about single teachers, as seen in the seminal work of Waller (1932), who described women teachers as "sex-starved spinsters" who come to grips with their lives as "maiden teachers" by giving male names to inanimate objects (". . . a car is John, an ashtray Mr. Johnson, a fountain-pen Mr. Wright . . ." p. 409).

The balancing act performed by today's women teachers between home and school is of a different nature. Married women could not teach in many school systems until after World War II, a factor distinguishing teaching from other female-dominated occupations. Also, the personal lives of teachers were more rigidly sanctioned. Today, by contrast, the home lives of teachers are virtually ignored.

In interviews with Vermont school teachers who taught between 1915 and 1950, Nelson (1982) found that teachers did not attempt to separate their home and school lives. For example, they brought their children to school because they had no satisfactory babysitting arrangements, and when they became pregnant, their own mothers or daughters substituted for them. The close interaction of the school and home life of these teachers resulted in their families cooperating more with housework. Thus, when they left teaching for a pregnancy or illness it was only for a brief period of time because they had a support network within their families and their schools. Problems that were easily resolved for Vermont teachers several decades ago, however, are a source of constant concern for teachers today.

The discrepancy between the ideal and real is most evident in the lives of teachers today in the impact their wages and working conditions have upon their lifestyles. This has always been a problem for women teachers, even a century ago, as seen in the comments of a woman who went West.

> One weary housewife-teacher noted in her diary, "Got breakfast done up the work then got ready for school . . . not very easy though to teach and keep house too (Myres 1982, 250).

Concerning today's teachers, I found that many teachers had a triple day of work. They taught all day, did most of the housework (including child-care), and then did more schoolwork such as grading papers. The seamless, overlapping quality of home and school was a particular problem for elementary teachers who had children, as they came home to the same kind of work they experienced at school. Talking only to small children during all ones' waking hours created a need to have adult interaction and conversation in order to be able to use more complex language structures, as well as expand their social lives beyond Smurfs and Care Bears. Yet married teachers with children rarely spent any of their time at home away from their families, because they felt guilty about leaving their children with babysitters. They said they would never stop working to stay home with their children but still worried that they were not being good mothers. This contradiction in societal and personal expectations for their behaviors as working women was particularly problematic when their own children were sick. But even when no such problems existed, teachers felt torn between school and home responsibilities. A 31-year-old English teacher who was married and had two children under age 4, never spent time outside school away from her children but still felt guilty about working.

> I hate to say it . . . I do feel a little guilty about not being the mother, staying at home, baking chocolate chip cookies for my children. But I think we're happier for the way it is. I would not be happy staying at home. If I stayed home all the time, I would be miserable, and I would make them miserable, and we would just all be miserable. This way we are all just real happy. Sounds terrible, doesn't it?

Single and divorced teachers had to cope with the realities of having only themselves to depend on — as expressed by a 39-year-old secondary teacher who had two children.

> I don't care how good a friend is, you hate to really lean on anybody too hard. It's pretty hard, but I feel like everybody's got their own problems. If you don't do those things, if you aren't objective, you're going to drive yourself nuts. And you end up getting depressed, and depression can be a real disabler. I can't afford to get depressed because there's not going to be anybody else who's going to feed the kids.

Although teachers would have liked to have been able to compartmentalize their school and home lives, they found it impossible. Instead, relationships in one facet of their lives were interrelated to relationships in other areas. Home and school events were ever-present realities, regardless of differing situational contexts. For example, marital choices, husbands' incomes and job locations, and the number of children in their families limited or broadened their alternatives for teaching jobs. Dissatisfaction with teaching influenced personal and marital relations, and personal problems influenced teaching effectiveness.

Also, teachers' salaries and working conditions affected their lifestyles and limited or broadened their choices for options or change. For instance, comparing two teachers who had similar characteristics (similar sized school districts, married to teachers, the same number of years of education — nearly completed master's degrees — and teaching experience of 10 years), differences in their teaching salaries made a critical difference in their lives.

Julie, who taught in the Midwest in an area where state expenditures on education were quite low, lived in a modular home in a rural wooded area with other modular homes and some trailers. She ate food grown in their garden and meat given them by in-laws or that her husband brought home from hunting and fishing expeditions. She did all the cooking and housework, and she and her husband spent their leisure time watching television, with relatives, or fishing; on rare occasions they saw a movie or ate at McDonald's.

Eleanor, on the other hand, lived in a two-story colonial-style home on a triple-sized lot with trees, a stream with a small bridge, and a large garden space. She and her husband shared cooking duties and enjoyed fixing gourmet meals. They went to concerts and the theater in their leisure time, traveled within and outside the country, and belonged to a wine-tasting group.

In summing up the difficulties of dealing with home and school, one teacher said

> I like teaching. I really enjoy it. I like my students and I feel like I'm a pretty good teacher, but it's hard. It's a hard life. I just say to myself, "What am I doing in this?"

SUMMARY AND CONCLUSIONS

In this paper both researchers' and teachers' views concerning the work of teaching have been discussed. From the viewpoint of many researchers or academics, teachers are thought to lack commitment to their work, perhaps because teaching has been deprofessionalized, becoming more similar to working-class jobs with regard to its depersonalized nature and limited autonomy. Therefore, teachers appear to feel less involved and more alienated or burned out.

From the viewpoint of teachers, the conditions under which they work create contradictions for them. These contradictions place them in double binds that are difficult to resolve. Because most teachers are women, these contradictions, combined with the working-class working conditions, place serious limitations on teachers' life-styles and home lives. A triple day of work is characteristic of most teachers' lives.

The study reported here, because qualitative techniques were used, is especially able to capture the viewpoint of the teachers, showing that they do *feel* the press of the processes of proletarianization and resultant intensification of work tasks, but still think of themselves as professionals. This conflict underlies many of the contradictions they experience. These findings should lead us to ask how we might reduce the extent of teachers' contradictory perspectives about their work and the resultant widespread dissatisfaction among them.

If we avoid labels such as "commitment," "professionalization," etc. and resist becoming victims of "Etzioni-itis" (Daniels 1985), what can we learn about women who teach that would affect the conditions under which they work? What can be done to attract good students into teaching and keep good teachers in the classroom? Always in the public eye, teachers are subject to criticism and plans for change and reform from many sources. Indeed, it often appears that everyone, outside the classroom that is, seems to know how teachers ought to teach. As expressed by Lortie:

> Meanwhile, the communication gap between researchers and practitioners is far from bridged. One major difficulty is that the interchange between the two groups is often viewed as one-way: research informs practice — period. With few exceptions, researchers do not ask teachers to identify important problems that require study, nor do they consult with teachers regarding alternative applications of particular findings. (1986, 575).

A good example of this communication gap is a recent report with far-reaching implications for educational reform — the Report on Teaching as a Profession developed by the Carnegie Forum on Education and the Economy (1986). The Forum recommended national certification of teachers, a national proficiency exam for teachers, a requirement of a master's degree for all teachers, and increases in salary as ways of recruiting more and better people into the field and keeping good or master teachers in schools. Three out of the four recommendations suggest that teachers be better trained and qualified, i.e., become better credentialed in the belief that this will restore public trust in them and what happens in schools, and ultimately, will gain status for teachers because they would be "professionalized."

This report raises some important questions. Why have past efforts to increase credentials not eliminated or reduced the supposed problems with teacher training? Why do we see continued negative perceptions about teachers' abilities, steadily increasing criticism? Apple (1983) has demonstrated that what these changes do is increase intensification of tasks, not qualifications. Teachers accept responsibility for all the tasks that are expected of them through intensification, and feel that the longer hours it takes for their work are evidence of greater professional status. Thus, Apple says, intensification "was misrecognized as a symbol of their increased *professionalism*" (p. 620).

If the Carnegie proposal follows the historical pattern of other such proposals to "professionalize" teaching, the efforts toward credentialing *will* be implemented by school districts, states, or at the national level. It is extremely doubtful, however, that suggestions concerning concomitant increases in pay will ever become reality. The effect will be that teachers will have greatly increased levels of intensification of work tasks and even fewer rewards.

If the teachers' perspective was considered, perhaps better strategies would be devised. For example, Lortie (1986) stresses that attention must be paid to those teachers already in the field. Experienced teachers play a major role in recruiting new teachers. Lortie asks, will "soured" teachers serve as good role models? Or will students who are better trained burn out quickly when they see they have few chances to "exercise" informed judgement beyond a narrow sphere" (p. 572)? He also recommends that to "professionalize" teaching, schools will have to decentralize how decisions are made. Teachers' involvement must be based on a belief that their efforts will bring status-related rewards and will also improve classroom conditions. Some control must be taken out of the hands of administrators and put back into the hands of teachers.

The voices of *women* teachers must especially be heard, not only because they are the majority of teachers, but because they deal with dual roles at school and at home. Descriptions of the effects of working conditions and pay on their lifestyles might help shape policy. Meanwhile, as long as there are teachers who live at subsistence levels, whose children qualify for free lunches, who never buy new clothes, who cannot leave home because they cannot afford a babysitter, who have never had a vacation, who must work at extra jobs to support their families, or must constantly deal with a triple day of work, efforts of reform will not match the reality of teachers' lives and ultimately, the quality of education will be seriously affected.

NOTES

1. Portions of this paper were adapted from *Contemporary Women Teachers: Balancing School and Home*. New York: Longman, Inc., 1986. All rights are reserved. The research reported in that book was made possible through a grant from the National Institute of Education (Contract NO. NIE-R-79-0008). The research reported does not, however, necessarily reflect the views of the agency. Portions of the paper also appeared in articles published by *The Elementary School Journal*, entitled "The home and school lives of women teachers," and "The home and school lives of women teachers: implications for staff development," (January 1984, 84:283–314).

I was fortunate to have the consultation of several valuable people throughout various stages of research and writing. Arlene Daniels, Peter M. Hall, Barbara Heyl, Sara Lightfoot, Caroline Persell, and Thomas L. Good all provided insightful comment, criticisms, and suggestions. Special gratitude goes to Hugh Mehan who followed the study from its inception to the completion of a book manuscript. He provided energizing, thought-provoking, supportive comments. And finally, thanks to Ursula Casanova, Project Officer at NIE, who was (and continues to be) consistently warm, supportive, and enthusiastic. She was a motivating force in a morass of data and bureaucratic paperwork and is a valued colleague.

2. Several considerations were taken into account in the selection process: teachers' geographic location; their willingness to share personal information about their lives on a long-term intensive basis; and their ability to

articulate feelings and recount events. Other selection criteria were related to conditions thought to affect teachers' home-school relationships: their marital status, the grade level they taught (elementary or secondary), and the size of the district in which they taught. They were individuals I had known as a teacher or observed as a researcher or who were recommended by others. The sample included four elementary school teachers and four secondary school teachers, who were classified in one of four marital categories: single, married without children, married with children, and divorced.

3. These teachers were chosen on the same bases as the case studies — marital status, level taught, and district size. They were contacted by telephone and asked if they would be willing to discuss their work and what they did outside school. All those contacted agreed to be interviewed. This sample included teachers in more than 60 schools, 30 school districts, and 6 states. The six states represent four regions of the country: the Midwest, Northeast, Southeast, and Southwest.

REFERENCES

Adkison, J.A. 1981. "Women in school administration: A review of the research," *Review of Education Research* 51(3):311–343.

Apple, M.W. 1983. "Work, gender, and teaching," *Teachers College Record* (Spring) 84:611–627.

———. "Teaching and "Women's Work": A comparative historical and ideological analysis," *Teachers College Record* (Spring) 86:455–473.

Biklen, S.K. 1986. "'I have always worked': Elementary schoolteaching as a career," *Phi Delta Kappan* (March) 67:504–508.

Carnegie Task Force on Teaching as a Profession. 1986. *A Nation Prepared: Teachers for the Twenty-First Century.* New York: Carnegie Forum on Education and The Economy.

Clifford, G.J. 1978. "Home and school in 19th century America: Some personal history reports from the U.S.," *History of Education Quarterly* 18:3–34.

Daniels, A.K. 1985. Comments at the conference on *Women and work: Integrating qualitative methods.* Wingspread Conference Center, Racine, Wisconsin, October.

Edgar, D.E. and R.L. Warren. 1969. "Power and autonomy in teacher socialization," *Sociology of Education* 42:386–399.

Etzioni, A. 1969. *The Semi-Professions and Their Organization: Teachers, Nurses, Social Workers.* New York: The Free Press.

Feiman-Nemser, S. and R.E. Flodern. 1986. "The cultures of teaching." In *The Handbook of Research on Teaching, Third Edition*, edited by M.C. Wittrock. New York: Macmillan, pp. 505–526.

Feistritzer Associates. 1983. *The American Teacher*. Feistritzer Publications.

Feistritzer, C.E. 1983. *The Condition of Teaching: A State by State Analysis*. Princeton, N.J.: The Carnegie Foundation for the Advancement of Teaching.

Geer, B. 1968. "Occupational commitment and the teaching profession," In *Institutions and the Person*, edited by H.S. Becker, B. Geer, D. Riesman, and R.S. Weiss. Chicago: Aldine, pp. 221–234.

Glenn, E.N. and Feldberg, R.L. 1977. "Degraded and deskilled: The proletarianization of clerical work," *Social Problems* 25(1):52–64.

Grant, W.V. and Eiden, L.J. 1982. *Digest of Education Statistics*. Washington, D.C.: Government Printing Office.

Grimm, J.W. 1978. "Women in female-dominated professions." In *Women Working*, edited by A.H. Stromberg and S. Harkess. Palo Alto, Calif: Mayfield, pp. 293–315.

Grimm, J.W. and Stern, R.N. 1974. "Sex roles and internal labor market structures: The "female" semi-professions," *Social Problems* 21(5):690–705.

Hoffman, M., Ed. 1981. *Women's "True" Profession*. Old Westbury, N.Y.: The Feminist Press.

Kottkamp, R.B., Provenzo, E.F. and M.M. Cohn. 1986. "Stability and change in a profession: Two decades of teacher attitudes, 1964-1984," *Phi Delta Kappan* (April) 67:559-567.

Lightfoot, S.L. 1978. *Worlds Apart*. New York: Basic Books

Lortie, D.S. 1975. *Schoolteacher: A Sociological Study*. Chicago: The University of Chicago Press.

Lortie, D.C. 1986. "Teacher status in Dade County: A case of structural strain?" *Phi Delta Kappan* (April) 67:568-575.

Myres, S.L. 1982. *Westering Women and the Frontier Experience, 1800–1915*. Albuquerque: University of New Mexico Press.

Nelson, M.K. 1982. "The intersection of home and work: Rural Vermont schoolteachers, 1915–1950," Paper presented at the annual meeting of the American Educational Research Association, New York, March 22.

Plisko, V.W. and Stern, J.D. 1985. "The condition of education, 1985 edition." *Statistical Reports, National Center for Education Statistics*. U.S. Government Printing Office, Washington, D.C.

Ryan, K., K. Newman, G. Mager, J. Applegate, T. Lasley, R. Flora, and J. Johnston. 1980. *Biting the Apple*. New York: Longman.

Shakeshaft, C. 1981. *Teaching Guide to Accompany Woman's 'True' Profession*. Old Westbury, N.Y.: The Feminist Press.

Simpson, R.L. and I.H. Simpson. 1969. "Women and Bureaucracy in the semi-professions," In *The Semi-Professions and Their Organization*, edited by Etzioni, A., New York: Free Press, pp. 196–265.

Sweet, J.A., and L.A. Jacobson. 1983. "Demographic aspects of the supply and demand for teachers," In *Handbook of Teaching and Policy*, edited by L.S. Shulman and G. Sykes, New York: Longman. pp. 192–213.

Traver, R. 1986. "Autobiography, feminism, and the study of teaching," Paper presented at the annual meetings of the American Educational Research Association, San Francisco, California, April 20.

U.S. News & World Report, "Teaching in trouble," 1986, (May 26), 52–57.

Waller, W. 1932. *The Sociology of Teaching*. New York: Wiley.

Wangberg, E.G., D.J. Metzger, and J.E. Levitov. 1982. "Working conditions and career options lead to female elementary teacher job dissatisfaction," *Journal of Teacher Education* 33(5):37–40.

Warren, D. 1985. "Learning from experience: History and teacher education," *Educational Researcher* 14:5–12.

Wittrock, M.C. (Ed.). 1986. *The Handbook of Research on Teaching, Third Edition*. New York: Macmillan.

Wright, B. & S. Tuska. 1968. "From dream to life in the psychology of becoming a teacher," *The School Review* 76:253–293.

CHAPTER 11

Women at the Top of Women's Fields: Social Work, Nursing, and Education

SHEILA K. COLLINS

In recent generations, a young girl's answer to the question, "What do you want to be when you grow up?," was likely to include mention of one of the so-called women's fields. After stating that she was going to be a mother, she would add "a teacher," "a nurse," or occasionally, "a social worker." Most people order off a menu, and the offerings for women in the world of paid work have been limited to roles and tasks consistent with those they perform in the home (Herzog 1982; Haskin 1982). As likely as women have been to select a women's field, they have been just as unlikely to state that they intended some-day to become the head of a hospital, director of an agency, or superintendent of a school district.

This chapter is about women whose careers have involved just such positions of responsibility in nursing, social work, and education. I conducted in-depth interviews with 30 women executives who occupied top management positions in 1980. The women were contacted at a time when much media coverage was being given to women entering male-dominated fields, and questions were being raised as to whether women would ever achieve top leadership positions in business and corporate industry.

I had gathered survey data on the career develoment of both top-and middle-level women administrators in nursing, social work, and education. As the responses to these questionnaires from a national stratified random sample were tabulated, many questions were being raised as well as answered.

In order to fill in the gaps and to develop a deeper understanding of the fabric of women administrators' work and family lives, I looked for interview candidates. Representatives from national professional organizations were asked to recommend women in top management regarded as outstanding by their peers. In selecting women to be interviewed, I was careful to include representatives from various geographic localities in the United States, from a diversity of ethnic backgrounds, and from different age groups. Interviews with women from social work and education were conducted in person — while jogging or over coffee; outside, in hotel rooms, or in conference lobbies. Interviews with nursing executives were held by phone, each conversation lasting about an hour and a half.

MEN'S AND WOMEN'S WORK LIVES

It is a relatively recent idea that women and men may work for the same reasons: to satisfy their need for survival, to experience pleasure, and to make a contribution (Astin 1984). Historically the career and work behavior of men and women has differed significantly due to sex-role socialization and the gender-based structures of opportunity.

Girls learn to value direct service to others (Astin 1984), while boys' games begin to prepare them to make their contribution in more diverse settings. Competitive games — avoided by young girls — teach boys to play with their enemies and to compete with their friends (Lever 1976).

The structure of opportunity reinforces socialization when both boys and girls see men occupying a large variety of jobs, while women are clustered in a few lower-paying, lower-status jobs. The sixty-cents-to-the-dollar ratio between men's and women's pay has not changed very much through the years in spite of women's increased education and labor force dedication (Lloyd and Niemi 1979).

As important as all these factors are to the structure of opportunity for women in women's fields, the fact that boys and girls, men and women, do not learn to work together may have the greatest impact. What is female is considered to be "less than," and that includes the activities women are likely to engage in most often, at home and in the workplace (Broverman et al. 1970).

Women's greater responsibility for childbirth, childrearing, and emotional and physical homecare accounts for the greater difference between the career behavior of women and men (Astin 1984). With little support for childcare and daycare on a national level, women's domestic responsibilities create discontinuities and interruptions in their work lives. These realities have led many women either to decide against marriage and/or having children or to select careers that allow for flexibility and interruption.

THE FEMALE FIELDS

Keeping in mind that contributing to the young, sick and elderly is the work of nursing, social work, and education and that women do this type of work, the low status of these fields should not be a surprise. A significant thread in the history and development of these fields has been the attempt to make legitimate not only the nurse, the teacher, or the social worker, but the work each performs as well. Each field approached this differently, perhaps tailoring strategies to the social and economic issues dominant at the time.

Education in colonial America was by and for men only, except for the dame schools in New England. Typically, these schools were held in the home of a woman who had the "rudiments of an education . . . [and] earn[ed] a pittance for herself by imparting to the children of her neighborhood her small store of learning" (Chubberly 1934, 125).

After the Civil War, many women entered college, and teaching became a woman's profession. By 1928, 85 percent of all elementary school teachers were women (Roser 1980), and as school administration grew, women began to obtain some of these positions. Though laws needed to be changed sometimes to enable women to act as school officers, in the early 1900s women were accepted as county superintendents, particularly in the western states (Woody 1929). Women's administrative leadership declined from 1929, when 55 percent of the elementary principals were women, to 1978, when women represented only 18 percent of elementary principals (Neidig 1980).

Nursing's roots grew from a sense of religious calling, and in feudal times noblewomen often ministered to the sick under the auspices of the church or a religious order of sisters (Pavey 1959). With the Reformation, hospital nursing declined, and thereafter most women engaged in nursing were untrained volunteers. Florence Nightingale's work in England during the Crimean War — since it was so highly publicized — had an especially large impact on the development of nursing in America. After the Civil War, nursing developed some military aspects, requiring that nurses obey superiors as a soldier his commander and wear uniforms as a symbol of discipline (Hoff 1911). The public saw the trained nurse as "a lady in the true sense of the word, one who would offer her life if need be . . . in her devotion to her calling" (Thomas 1901). Having attached itself to strong patriarchal systems like the church and the military, nursing was slow to respond to the first and second waves of the women's movement. Internal battles have raged over nursing's scientific and humanitarian roles and over the best ways to educate and train nurses in this century.

Another issue has been how nurses shaped their own profession. In this case, men have actually had a stronger impact; they have entered nursing in recent years, but in far fewer numbers than they have teaching and social work. However, they are overrepresented at the administrative level in relation to their numbers. Dominating medicine and hospital administration, men in nursing are in a position to shape the standards and practice of the profession (Stevens 1977; Lenininger 1979).

Social work is the youngest of the three groups, having grown out of women's pioneering contributions to social reform in the last century. Settlement house workers organized community services, and on behalf of immigrant groups became involved in political activities. In the early part of the century they fought for the abolition of child labor and for womens' suffrage, and they were behind the establishment of the Children's Bureau (Bolin 1973).

By 1920, social work required a college degree, and women made up 62 percent of the field. Men were more likely to advance to positions of leadership, but women continued to be the standard-bearers of theory and practice. By 1950, men were being actively recruited into the profession in order to counter its negative status and low pay. This was part of a larger effort to "defeminize" social work, to give the profession male characteristics and make it more scientific, rational, and administrative. By the middle 1960s, the prevailing division of labor in social work put women in direct service roles and men in planning, administration, and community organization (Chafetz 1972).

THE WOMEN ADMINISTRATORS

Ten women administrators were interviewed from each of the three fields. The women in education carried the title of superintendent if they were in a small school district, or assistant superintendent if from a large urban district. There was one black woman administrator in her thirties, and one Mexican American in her late forties among those interviewed. All of the educators were married; half of them had no children.

Nurses interviewed held titles such as vice-president for nursing or patient care, executive or medical center director, assistant or associate hospital administrator. Several of the nurses no longer considered themselves nurses since they had gotten additional degrees in hospital administration. None of the nursing administrators had children. Only three women had ever married, and of these, one had married for the first time that year in her late forties. Only one woman was in her late thirties; the rest were over forty.

The titles of the social workers varied more than those of the nurses and teachers, since social workers are employed in a greater variety of settings. Several women were directors of agencies or large social work departments in hospitals. One was dean of a school of social work while another was vice-president of a university. Half of the women had never had children, though several had been married at one time. Eight were over forty, and three of the women were black.

Motivation

Studies of men's career development have much to say about the importance of goal-setting and long-range planning. The women interviewed for the present study were asked if they had selected their careers in nursing, teaching, or social work at the outset. Most of the women did not perceive their career choices as clear decisions. They used expressions such as "It was an accident," "It selected me," or "It was the only choice when I was young." Sometimes they had had other aspirations; but coming up against closed doors, they chose a profession that was open to them. They made comments such as the following:

The depression meant it was difficult to get any job.

I backed into social work. I saw an ad in the Sunday paper, answered it, and later discovered it was a social work job.

My first idea was to be a math teacher. I took premed in college and drifted into nursing.

I was short of funds as a science major, and I met the director of the nursing program.

Father wanted me to be an engineer, but an accident in the lab meant that I went into sociology. Teaching was a salable skill.

When I was young, it was either teaching or nursing. I thought it was easier to do nursing.

In a few instances, the women mentioned role models who had influenced them saying: "My Girl Scout leader was also a minister's wife, and she told me about social work," or "I had an older friend who went into nursing."

An interest in helping people led many of the women to select a career in nurisng, teaching and social work, and the women made statements such as: "I was service-oriented from church, and I liked science," or "I was always interested in people, always for the underdog."

Many of the women saw their career advancement as a natural progression, not as the culmination of conscious planning. "The chief was out; I did her job" was a typical remark. Others saw their upward mobility as a response to financial need. "I was tired of being poor," said one; there was "no other way to go financially," said another.

The women identified recruitment as another path to advancement:

The faculty needed me, wanted me, and voted me in. (social worker)

Success led to graduate school. I was needed as an administrator, and encouraged and promoted from within. (nurse)

There were concerns at the hospital about equal employment opportunity. I was nominated and became a trainee. (nurse)

It wasn't my decision; I was just asked. (social worker)

Several nurses were more than a bit reluctant to say yes when recruited for administrative responsibility.

The supervisor asked me if I would go into administration. I thought about it for a year. I didn't feel qualified.

I fought it. If you have a degree, they want you in administration. I took it the third time it was offered.

Many social workers and educators mentioned becoming impatient with the way others managed things. Some admitted to ambitions to be in charge and to make things happen their way.

> I wanted to put into practice ideas I had. I was always rebellious in taking orders, and I knew I could do a better job than I observed being done. (educator)

> I always wanted to be in an executive-type position. I always saw that as where the action is! (educator)

> After fifteen years of teaching, I wanted another kind of challenge.

> I was goal-oriented by thirty. I wanted power. (social worker)

> I worked in child abuse and neglect. I was often feeling that I was being used by society as the only positive thing offered to those people and becoming an instrument of all that, and it depressed me. . . . I was also tired of being poor. I wanted to move into a decision-making, policy-making role. (social worker)

In summary, I found that the women in all three fields selected career areas by asessing both their own capabilities and the structure of opportunity. They knew people who were in women's fields, and they were offered opportunity there. Limitations placed on other aspirations, doors that were closed to them, played a big role in their choices to become social workers, nurses, and teachers as well.

In their movement into administration, the women offered different explanations for how it came about. Some, particularly the nurses, were reluctant to assume administrative roles when recruited to do so. Others found it too difficult to sit on their hands and watch others perform less capably than they. Still others admitted to an ambition to make things happen, to be in a position to change the way things were done in their organizations.

Rewards

When asked what were their greatest career rewards, the women spoke of their recent or immediate work situations. An overwhelming number of the rewards mentioned were intrinsic to their jobs. Only a couple of times was money mentioned, once as the "ability to do good things for my kids."

Most frequently the women seemed to be describing the pleasure of mastery and accomplishment as defined by Astin (1984). "Doing something that worked"; "knowing that what was right and good was done"; appreciating "the challenge of tough assignments"; "seeing projects completed" — these were among the rewards women singled out. One educator admitted that there was particular sweetness in having "achieved in spite of the professor who told me it would never happen."

In a 1966 study, Ginzberg defined four categories of motivating values that shaped the careers of educated women. A drive for autonomy and self-improvement such as that described by the women administrators would fit his *individualistic* type of career motivation. The drive to influence people and events, which Ginzberg called *influential*, was strongly evident in the women administrators' remarks about achievements building on their own strong belief systems. One educator mentioned seeing a program for children change under her leadership and helping women coaches get equal pay. Another woman found the power to hire and fire rewarding. Yet another liked being able to put policies in writing. Ginzberg's *communal* motivating value, which he defined as wanting to make a contribution to the larger community, was not present in the responses of women in the present study. They mentioned contributing to large systems, but these tended to be the hospital or school, the program or service being provided. For example, a nursing administrator took pride in the financial growth and quality of the hospital since she took charge. Finally, *supportive* motivating values were represented by such comments as [I enjoy] "seeing others I had helped accomplish things on their own." Some rewards deriving from personal relationships did not fit Ginzberg's supportive category. One educator took pleasure in the fact that everywhere she went she had friends. A social worker enjoyed teaching with friends and colleagues. A nurse mentioned enjoying patients, and another educator loved hearing from former students.

These comments seem to refer to what the women have received from people they initially were serving or helping — the rewards of reciprocity in their relationships. People to whom they have given have given back to them, and these gifts are a central part of their career rewards.

Career Costs

In sharp contrast to the intrinsic nature of the administrators' career rewards, most of the career costs they could name were extrinsic to their jobs. Far fewer costs were mentioned than rewards; one woman found it "hard . . . to think of the costs since I feel it was all worth it." The most frequently mentioned costs were in the women's personal, social, and family lives.

The women mentioned spending less time with their children than they might have wanted on occasion, and single, never-married women mentioned having less time for their parents and other relatives. Several women mentioned making a conscious decision not to marry or have children because of their careers. Other women postponed marriage until middle age, and one admitted that she hadn't had time to consider marriage again after being divorced for many years. If her work life were not so demanding, she mused, she might have considered getting married again. Another woman felt that she had not given enough time to her husband, while a woman who had been married 38 years recounted a close call. "We were several days from getting a divorce. He certainly got my attention."

One social worker, a mother with young children, said that she had found it therapeutic to make a list of the costs and benefits of her work: "I gave up having homemade cookies, and I gave up seeing my child take her first step, and I gave up seeing my son be the turkey in the school's Thanksgiving play."

The cost most frequently mentioned had to do with social life. Wanting more time for friends, or experienceing the loss of friends due to relocation, were among the costs cited. One educator said she missed "having women to go shopping with and do crazy things with." Some women felt there were "fewer friends the higher up you go;" they expressed a sense of isolation in their social lives, and regretted that they did not have enough time for hobbies.

There was one particularly dramatic example of the impact of social life on a career. A nurse who had relocated to a small community to become the director of a hospital, voluntarily stepped down from the position when she saw what she was up against. Business was often conducted on a golf course with community leaders — all men. This woman saw no way that she could do business under these circumstances without creating talk in the community.

Very few problems within the work itself were identified as career costs. Several women felt that the rewards they received from their top-level jobs were different from the rewards of direct service to others. One hospital administrator described it this way:

> The higher level I go, the more responsibility I obtain, the less overt satisfaction or reward you get. You have to develop a system where you reward yourself to keep motivated.

In contrast to the relative detachment shown by the above administrator, a social worker expressed feelings of great pain and personal loss at the downward turn of events in her hospital:

> In the place that I have been and worked . . . for twenty years . . . it *was* a first rate place. It grew and expanded and a lot of people got a lot of joy in being creative. . . . The last four years have been *hell*. Money has dried up, staff has been cut severely, programs have been slashed. The program has literally been dismantled piece by piece, and that is a painful process to watch.

Problems of Women in a Man's World

It is characteristic of successful people that they emphasize the positive aspects of a situation rather than the negative. Women in the present study did not volunteer much information about discrimination or sexism until they were asked to relate to other women's experiences. Since the top administration in all three fields is dominated by men (Kadushin 1976), I assumed that these women might have experienced some of the same difficulties as Astin's (1969) women doctorates. In Astin's study, the higher women went and the more dedicated to their careers they became, the more discrimination they encountered in hiring, salaries, promotions, and benefits.

Only two of the thirty women interviewed did not experience at least one of these difficulties, and most experienced three of four. A different salary structure for men and women was common practice in all three of the fields until a few years ago, probably as part of the so-called family wage system, which assumes that men are supporting a family and they therefore need more money than women. One nurse who had never been married told how she dealt with the system by being a part of it:

> Even with the facts before my eyes that should have told me that my logic was illogic, I used to pay men nurses differently — I'm sorry to say.

Reluctance to hire and promote women was also common. One hospital administrator saw this unequal treatment as consistent with attitudes "in the world" at the time, and with her own expectations as well:

> I was the fortunate one to be selected when I was. It never occurred to me to be upset about not being considered prior to that time.

Had this woman rejected the value system of her agency, she would have had to deal with the conflict between her own values and those of her colleagues.

Remnants of family wage ideology were still operating in one of the women's organizations, as seen in this example:

> The stupid things people say. Personnel calls and asks why I'm giving this person the job at this pay, because her husband is a lawyer.

When asked to describe how she handled this situation, the woman said her strategy was to "stay rational, talk it over" and "get angry later in the company of friends."

Prejudice against hiring a woman as a top administrator sometimes comes from the community. As a school superintendent, the woman administrator must deal with school committees made up of parents who are often biased against hiring a woman. One administrator found this to be a greater difficulty than that she had encountered earlier within her own school system. When asked to describe how she dealt with this situation, she replied: "There is little I can do. . . . Get through the situation with as much grace as I can, and then go and apply somewhere else."

Flexibility seemed to mark the women's use of strategies in dealing with discrimination. A social worker who noted that agencies promote males more rapidly than females described a number of responses that she used on different occasions. These included "screaming my head off, raling at the gods, involving colleagues who were also concerned, using my husband as a shoulder to cry on," and "having an overt temper tantrum."

Confrontation sometimes erupted, as in the following interaction between a nurse and a physician. According to the nurse, the doctor said: "You and your boss say you are an administrative person; but you are a nurse to me, and no nurse is going to tell me what to do." The nurse responded with the following:

> Let's sit down and talk. You seem to be reacting to some insecurities you might have because I am a woman in this authority [position] and my background as a nurse. I am concerned that this will affect patient care.

Another nurse implied one must be wise to know what strategy will work in which situation. "With one person, you come back again and again until you prove yourself. Someone else, you can come right on strong and sort of tell them off."

Making a niche for oneself is sometimes a strategy to cope with lack of opportunity. An educator described the career strategy she devised when she realized she had gone as far as the system would allow: "I learned to create opportunities for myself by writing grants, or working for myself during some periods as a consultant."

Many of the women felt that they had found their niche in the organizations where they currently worked. They were reluctant to move to another organization. As one nurse administrator put it:

> It is difficult to know all the ins and outs of what I might be getting into. I decided to stay where I know the politics of the system.

One black social worker described her strategy for dealing with other people's preconceptions about what women should and shouldn't do:

> I have felt some bias based on my being a woman, and some bias based on my being black. I have felt it. I have never made it my problem. That's my attitude.

Several women were quite articulate about differences they experienced in supervising men and women. An educator described it this way:

> It is hard to pull out what is related to what, but I find much more evasion from men, and it's evasion by just not doing something. Some less openness from men. More just not dealing with things and not saying it either.

A nurse depicted her impressions this way:

> Women tend to give the impression that they are more sensitive and perhaps take things more personally. Men seem to give the impression that they are more objective, not quite so sensitive. I've tried to be aware of these differences, not to do things to offend the women . . . not to expect the men to be as responsive.

Balancing Work and Family

Nearly all the women mentioned that balancing their career and family responsibilities was currently a concern or had been a concern in the past. A third of the women were single and had never married, and two-thirds had never had any children; yet most of the single women still faced family responsibilities for aging and ill parents, saying "It's a concern with elderly parents. I'm an only child," or "I am responsible for my parents and being a nurse I have always said that I would not institutionalize my parents. I will take care of them myself, even if it means leaving my job."

Those women who were mothers were concerned about balancing their career and family responsibilities, though more in the past, "when the children were small," or "when the children were going into their teens." There were only a few single women who had escaped this balancing act. As one single nurse put it, "By remaining single, I had made a decision not to have other responsibilities" (outside of work).

Being a wife can affect one's career life adversely, particularly when there are decisions about relocation. One woman gave up her own job to follow her husband when he found a new position in another city; no sooner had they arrived than the husband became ill. Another woman lost retirement benefits because she put her husband first. Having another income in the family initially seemed an advantage to one women who took a leave of absence from her job to complete her doctorate. She found she didn't like the effect on her marital relationship, however, of being supported by her husband. Her loss of independence and their differences of opinion over money made that a tough year.

A nursing director who was single herself said, "a wife has two full-time jobs. I don't know how they [her nursing staff] do it."

One woman summed up the difficulties: "Balancing career and family responsibilities is the most difficult thing a woman administrator has to deal with."

The women administrators were given a list from Hall's (1972) model of how women cope with conflict between their career and family responsibilities. The most frequently mentioned ways that women in the present study coped were hiring help with childcare and housework and prioritizing activities, eliminating the less important ones. Both of these strategies are just what Hall classified as "structural role redefinition." One social worker who worked a different shift from her husband described the effect of these coping strategies on her family.

> I don't eliminate much. I'm pretty greedy for life and pretty much work everything in. . . . My family works like crazy. . . . Ever since they were two or three they have dressed themselves, done their own laundry, made their own dinners, cleaned their own rooms, my husband too. We're pretty self-sufficient.

An educator — the mother of a large family — told of her strategies which included two examples of Hall's "reactive role behaviors" — changing one's work schedule and working harder.

> I'm a better parent. I'm not frustrated. I stayed home for seven years and got bored after ten A.M. When I was working on my master's, I did my reading from eleven P.M. to three A.M.

In summary, the mothers in this study relied on strategies that redefined their family roles. Hiring help and training their children to take responsibility meant that they didn't have to do it all. But many women had additional responsibilities for older family members who needed care. Staying single and having no children does not exempt women from the caretaker role. In fact, not having other family responsibilities may insure that the single woman will be responsible for eldercare in her family of origin, particularly if she is a member of a helping profession. As more people live longer, and as more women assume major responsibilities in the work field, this is certain to become a visible issue in families and in work organizations.

THE ROLE OF THE OBSERVER: A PERSONAL ACCOUNT

One of the fundamental tenets of modern science is that the observer affects that which is being studied. One way to deal with this problem is to include the observer as a part of what is being reported or analysed.

To the observing and interviewing of these women administrators I brought my own background and career experiences. Having been a teacher and a social worker, a mother, and the daughter of a nurse, I brought a deep respect for the fields in which these women had labored. I brought a strong belief in the importance of caring, at both personal and societal levels. Accustomed to the in-depth interviews of therapy sessions, I approached these women with the assumption that they had a great deal to offer. As media attention was focusing on women's movement toward leadership roles in male-dominated business organizations, I was interested in the experiences of women in fields where women had been employed for several generations. I was interested in their feelings about what had happened in their careers, and in the central values that sustained them. I believe that these women were honest with me, to the extent that they understood themselves and their surroundings.

I learned a great deal from them, so that even now I have vivid memories that are still full of meaning for me. My recollections, while revealing a great deal about what I needed to hear, also speak of the women and the power of the connections we made.

The social worker who watched a program she had developed be dismantled because of budget cuts — her pain was like that of a parent losing a child, or of a once rewarding marriage ending in divorce. All are caring costs, whether related to people or projects. Losing what we have invested in is painful.

The nursing administrator who stepped down from her high-level position when she realized community sexism would never let her do her job — she was matter-of-fact and easy-going about her decision, displaying a maturity that I have known few people to have developed.

The educator whose program became a national model, starting with just herself and growing to employ three hundred people — I recall vividly her sense of gratitude that she had been so fortunate.

The social worker whose career had been in academia — she told me with humor that she never let them forget how they treated her when they paid her less — colleagues are her family. Work is a set of relationships, and work environments are either toxic or enhancing, depending on the quality of those relationships.

The social worker who, without realizing it, became my supporter and cheerleader — she mentioned a motto that a friend had given her which she kept on her desk: "I want it, I've earned it, I deserve it, and I can do it!" The phrase had kept her going when she was doing a writing project like the one I was involved in at the time. Finding it there, my young son, without consultation with anyone, made three more copies and placed one on each wall of my small office. Perhaps because women have been told for so long that we can't or shouldn't do certain things, we need the encouragement of one another.

I memorized one woman's advice to women aspiring to be administrators:

1. Never accept the parameters that somebody might set.

2. Be incredibly competent (because women are pioneering).

3. Have a tremendous sense of belief in yourself.

4. Be understanding of the nature of the social context in which you aspire and have some understanding of and patience about what it means to threaten. That makes it possible to negotiate.

5. Use a conscious strategy to negotiate and be able to play differently in different situations.

And the black woman administrator who said about sexist and racist attitudes around her — "I have never made it *my* problem. That is my attitude!" I have retold this many times to my own students, and in a voice that emulates her incredible strength and resolution.

There are some other memories that are fainter and less encouraging. The hospital administrators who seem to have forgotten that they were nurses, their identification with their profession and with other women difficult to discern. In one instance, a woman told me that she doubted her experience could be applicable to other women since she had been in a convent for many years before assuming her top-level position. I remember feeling sad for her that she had lost so many connections in her life.

SUMMARY

From these interviews with top women administrators in women's fields it is clear that the women have maintained the female-socialized values of nurturance and of the importance of relationships. They have enjoyed the opportunity to influence their organizations and to make things happen. They have done this within a network of relationships — with colleagues, students, and patients — and these relationships have enriched their lives. In the terms of Carol Gilligan (1982), they have acted on a sensitivity to the needs of others and assumed responsibility for taking care. This is seen in their discussion of the search for balance between their work and family lives, even among women with no husbands or children of their own. To those women seem to fall the major responsibilities for aged parents and other relatives, at a time when their work responsibilities are most demanding.

These findings more than hint at the policy implication that, as a culture, we need to add more planning and resources to childcare and eldercare. As more women work and are employed in responsible positions such as these women administrators, the care of dependent persons will need to be assumed outside of each family unit.

With the increasing opportunities for contemporary women, these 30 women may be representatives of a vanishing breed. Their initial selections of the fields of nursing, social work, and education were made at a time when many other fields were closed to them. Their move into administration was, in their view, more a natural evolution than the result of long-range career planning.

Women coming up are more likely to have as their goal becoming a manager or administrator, and many are moving into business, law, and medicine. If women are able to progress upward in other fields and occupations, the helping fields will have to compete to attract bright, dedicated women. And these women will probably not rush to preside over organizations that have been decimated by societal indifference or antagonism to the caring function. It is time to ask the question, How much do we care about caring? And are we willing, as a society, to offer respect and a living wage to those who do it for us?

REFERENCES

Astin, H. 1969. *The Woman Doctorate in America.* New York: Russell Sage Foundation.

Astin, H. 1984. "The meaning of work in women's lives: A socio-psychological model of career choice and work behavior," *The Counseling Psychologist* 12:4, 117–16.

Bolin, W. 1973. *Feminism, Reform and Social Service: A History of Women in Social Work.* Minneapolis: Minnesota Resource Center for Social Work Education.

Broveman, I., D. Broverman, F. Clarkson, P. Rosencrantz, S. Vogel, 1970. "Sex role stereotyping and clinical judgements of mental health," *Journal of Consulting and Clinical Psychology* 34:1–7.

Chafetz, J. 1972. "Women in social work," *Social Work* 17:12–15.

Chubberly, E. 1934. *Public Education in the United States*. Boston: Houghton Mifflin.

Gilligan, C. 1982. *In a Different Voice*. Cambridge, MA: Harvard University Press.

Ginzberg, E. 1966. *Lifestyles of Educated Women*. New York: Columbia University Press.

Hall, D. 1972. "A model for coping with role conflict: The role behavior of college educated women," *Administrative Science Quarterly* 471-486.

Haskin, L. 1982. "Changing the assessment of sex-typed occupations." *Journal of Social Psychology* 117:271–84.

Herzog, A. 1982. "High school seniors' occupational plans and values: Trends in sex differences, 1976 through 1980," *Sociology of Education* 55:1–13.

Hoff, J. 1911. "The soldier nurse," *American Journal of Nursing* 11:342.

Kadushin, A. 1976. "Men in a women's profession," *Social Work* 21:440–47.

Lenininger, M. 1979. "Territoriality, power and creative leadership in administrative nursing contexts," *Nursing Dimensions* 33-42.

Lever, J. 1976. "Sex differences in the games children play," *Social Problems* 23:478–87.

Lloyd, C., and B. Niemi. 1979. *The Economics of Sex Differences*. New York: Columbia University Press.

Neidig, M. 1980. *The Other Half of the Talent Bank: Women Administrators*. Bethesda, MD. (Eric Document Reproduction Service No. Ed 181 600)

Pavey, A. 1959. *The Story of the Growth of Nursing as an Art, a Vocation and a Profession*. Philadelphia: Lippincott.

Roser, P. 1980. "Women fight old boys for school administrative jobs," *Learning* 3:31-4.

Stevens, B. 1977. "Education in nursing administration," *Supervisor Nurse* 19–23.

Thomas, D. 1901. "The ideal nurse," *Trained Nurse and Hospital Review* 261–265.

Woody, T. 1929. *A History of Women's Education in the United States*. Vol. II. New York: Science Press.

Part IV

MAKING IT IN
THE MALE WORLD

CHAPTER 12

Think Like a Man, Work Like a Dog, and Act Like a Lady: Occupational Dilemmas of Policewomen

SUSAN E. MARTIN

Throughout the occupational world, jobs are separated into "men's work" and "women's work" (Bridges 1982). Police work since its inception in 1829 has been dominated by men. Even after the acceptance of the first sworn woman officer in 1910, policewomen were limited to working with women, children, and typewriters for more than half a century (Milton 1972). Women only obtained the right to an equal opportunity in a law enforcement career with the passage of the 1972 Amendments to the Civil Rights Act of 1964. Since 1972 the number of policewomen has gradually increased so that by October 31, 1982 women made up 5.9 percent of the sworn officers nationwide (FBI 1983). Despite these advances, policewomen face a variety of barriers to full occupational integration.

This paper examines policing as an occupation and the problems that women face in entering the police world. It explores the nature of police work to illuminate the reasons for the traditional exclusion and continuing barriers to women on patrol, examines the particular problems of female officers on the job, and explores the ways policewomen have addressed these barriers in their effort to achieve a place in the police world.

THEORETICAL PERSPECTIVE

Understanding the barriers to full occupational integration faced by women in occupations from which they have traditionally been excluded requires examination of both *structural* characteristics of the occupation and the work organization in which they are employed and the ways that cultural mandates and behavioral norms related to gender shape interpersonal interaction in specific occupational contexts. Kanter's (1977) study of men and women employed in corporations suggests that occupational role incumbents' behavior is shaped by three key structural features of the organization and their position in it: the opportunity structure, the power structure, and relative numbers. These variables constrain and shape possibilities for action and press people to adapt to their situations.

Kanter observed that men and women behave differently in work organizations because men have more real power and greater opportunities for mobility. Both men and women, when placed in powerless and low mobility situations respond by lowering aspirations and developing different patterns of occupational behavior from those with greater power and opportunities. Blocked mobility leads to limited motivation which, in turn, sets in motion a downward cycle of deprivation and discouragement. Conversely, those with power and opportunities use these resources to gain allies and supporters and prove themselves, triggering an upward cycle of success. Although both cycles appear to be related to individual motivation, in fact, they arise in response to organizational factors.

Kanter also noted three perceptual phenomena associated with the presence of minority individuals when they are "tokens." First, tokens are highly visible, leading to performance pressures. Second, tokens polarize differences between themselves and dominants, resulting in greater boundary maintainence against the minorities. Third, dominants distort and stereotype tokens' characteristics.

Occupational behavior also is guided by an overarching set of culturally prescribed norms guiding sex role enactment. Norms of sex-appropriate behavior, however, may conflict with occupationally prescribed behaviors. For women in nontraditional occupations dilemmas arise when occupational norms call for "masculine" behavior and interaction with fellow workers as peers and equals but gender-related norms prescribe "feminine" behavior and interaction with men guided by asymmetrical norms (Goffman 1956, 1976). Thus, policewomen have to decide when and how to "act like a cop" and still "act like a lady" on the job.[1]

Because these gender-based norms affect men and women differently at work, it is necessary to distinguish between the effects of tokenism and sexism. Even when women workers have the skills, job savvy, and commitment to the job necessary for occupational success (Walshok 1981) and act like their male counterparts, they are harassed on the job, excluded from the informal cultural world of their fellow workers, and treated differently from others in the work environment (Acker and Van Houten 1974; Feldberg and Glenn 1979). Studies of men in traditionally female occupations find that the male tokens are not subject to the same amount or type of harassment or discrimination on the job as women in male occupations (Schreiber 1979; Fottler 1976;

Kadushin 1976; Zimmer 1986). Instead, men often have greater advancement opportunities than their female colleagues (Gripton 1974; Blankenship 1971; Gross and Trusk 1976).

Analyses of informal processes have only begun to identify the ways the norms governing interpersonal relations between men and women at work lead to different treatment for male and female tokens. What is clear, however, is that because of the asymmetry built into gender relations, tokenism has different effects on relations with dominants for male and female tokens (Goffman 1961; Spradley and Mann 1975). Differences in gender role expectations of men and women lead to contrasting opportunities for status attainment and the exercise of control over tokens' behavior. Thus the effects of tokenism, based on differentness, are not synonymous with those of sexism, in which one gender is valued more highly than the other.

In sum, to succeed in nontraditional occupations, women must overcome several barriers. Structural factors limit formal and informal opportunities to learn the job fully, get challenging assignments, gain experience in exercising authority, attain promotion, and obtain sponsors (who often are the key to further advancement). The characteristics of these structural barriers, in turn, are shaped by the nature of the occupation and the work organization, by the broader cultural norms related to dominant-minority relations, and by the ways that the specific norms related to gender affect the work.

METHODOLOGY

The data on policewomen presented in the paper are based on field research conducted in the Metropolitan Police Department of Washington, D.C. in 1975 and 1976. I joined the Police Reserve Corps, a police auxiliary unit of volunteers, received limited training, a uniform like that of sworn officers, and was assigned to one of the city's seven districts. As a reserve I could work whenever I wanted as a "helper" assigned to a one-officer car. After working three or four shifts per week for six months, I conducted semi-structured interviews with 28 policewomen and 27 policemen and eighteen male supervisors in the district. In addition, I spent many hours in conversation with a female detective (from another unit) who became my informant, attended several informal gatherings of policewomen which she held for my benefit, and interviewed several policewomen involved in implementing the department's policewomen on patrol program (for details see Martin 1980).[2]

POLICING IN AN OCCUPATIONAL PERSPECTIVE

Police Work

Police work can be classified in several ways. Police officers are blue-collar workers, with mediocre prestige working in the public service sector with professional aspirations but little recognition as a "profession."[3] However, these categories do not very accurately describe police work or explain why it has been traditionally reserved for men. Stewart and Cantor's (1974) approach is more helpful. They examined occupations in terms of autonomy, or the discretion held by the occupational groups and roles after other sources of control (*i.e.*, the culture, occupation, organization, and client) have operated. What makes policing unique and a "male" occupation is the fact that the police officer at the lowest level of the hierarchical organization has enormous discretionary decision-making authority over two of society's highest values — life and liberty.

Other aspects of police work also make it distinctive. Although the police perform a wide variety of tasks, their primary responsibilities involve maintenance of public order, enforcement of the law, and provision of a variety of services 24 hours a day.[4] Key common features across these diverse policing tasks are the potential for violence by clients and the need and power to use coercive means to enforce the officer's definition of the situation. As Bittner observed (1970, 39), "the police are nothing else than a mechanism for the distribution of situationally justified force in society." Their role as the representatives of the coercive potential of the state and legitimate users of force in everyday life helps explain certain attitudes and behavioral characteristics of the police that have been termed their "working personality" (Skolnick 1966) as well as the character of their work culture.

The police officer's "working personality" is shaped by the presence of danger and the potential for violence. These lead to a generalized suspiciousness and to isolation from the community. Authority contributes to the isolation by making officers "rule enforcers" that others avoid. Set apart from the public, which police officers often view as hostile, officers turn to their occupational community for support.

A prevailing "myth of policing," fostered by the media and the police themselves (Manning 1977), is that their work primarily involves "crime fighting" and the apprehension of criminals. In fact, only a small fraction of the officers' time is devoted to law enforcement (Reiss 1971; Wilson 1973). Nevertheless, crime fighting is visible, publicly valued, rewarded by the department and the informal occupational culture, and felt to be the most satisfying part of their work by most officers.

The reality of police work is far less glamorous. As the only 24-hour-a-day social service agency, the police perform a variety of services from assisting citizens locked out of their houses to taking the sick, drunk, and crazy to available treatment facilities. Officers also frequently are called upon to act as "peace officers" who maintain order among angry and upset citizens.

Discretion is built into police work. The law only abstractly defines events requiring police intervention and is simply one resource used by the police in dealing with disorder. Even when the law is clearly broken, the police are expected to use judgment rather than automatic full enforcement.

Discretion offers the potential for abuse. Consequently, since their inception, police departments have been structured as paramilitary organizations with a proliferation of rules, regulations, and efforts to supervise officers. Close, punitive control systems, in turn, have led officers to protect themselves from both an unpredictable public and their own officials through a cohesive, informal occupational community with its own stratification system and norms. These cultural norms of policing are: the rule of silence and use of silent treatment for offenders who "squeal" either in public or to supervisors; the requirement that an officer physically back up another officer or face rejection as a partner; the rule of maintaining respect for the police and use of ridicule to punish violators; and the belief that the ends justify the means in the apprehension of a felon (Westley 1970).

In response to the nature of the work and organizational pressures, a unique occupational subculture and singularly cohesive work group has evolved among patrol officers. The emphasis on danger, the potential for violence, and authority to use force if necessary isolate them from the community, and strengthen the bonds of group solidarity. These, in turn, heighten the barriers to informal acceptance for anyone who is perceived as not trustworthy or unable to conform to group norms.[5] The culture also serves to obscure the fact that the day-to-day reality of police work does not evolve around crime fighting or demand extensive physical skills, but involves emotional and intellectual labor and requires interpersonal skills.

The Police Culture and Policemen's Opposition to Female Officers

The policemen's opposition to female officers is based on concerns about the disruptive effect of women on the division of labor, the work norms, the work group's solidarity, and on the sexist ideology that undergirds their definition of the work as "men's work" and their identity as masculine men. The use of women on patrol implies either that the men's unique asset, their physical superiority, is irrelevant (as it is on most assignments) or that the man working with a policewoman will be at a disadvantage in a physical confrontation he would not face working with a male partner. The possibility that policewomen may reduce the likelihood of a physical confrontation or act appropriately by protecting their male partners is no comfort because it undermines both the male and female sex role stereotypes that permeate the officers' perceptual world. Women are not "supposed" to fight or control other male citizens. Moreover, being "defended" by a woman is regarded as an affront to a policeman's manhood.

Women also pose a threat to work group solidarity by penetrating the emotional masks men wear, inhibiting their use of "raunchy" language, posing the spectre of sexual intimacy between partners, and fostering competition among the men and thus a competing set of loyalties.

In exploring the threat women pose to male officers Hunt (1984, 294) notes that the policemen's culture is a "symbolic universe permeated by gender meanings and that this symbolic structure is preponderant over other factors which explain the behavior of police." Men, and by association things masculine, are perceived as existing in the "dirty" public domain; women, and by association femininity, represent the "clean world of the home, untainted, and for that reason, untrustworthy. Success in policing rests on negotiation of masculine symbols and rejection of attitudes and behaviors associated with the feminine domain. Thus sexism is not simply a matter of sex role learning but organizationally crucial to policing and the occupational identity of individual policewomen (Hunt 1985, 15).

In sum, policewomen appear to make the policeman's work more dangerous but less rewarding; threaten to disrupt the prevalent norms, group solidarity, and social status of the occupation; and challenge the policemen's symbolic universe which is based on the meanings of masculinity and femininity and their individual and social identity within it.

BARRIERS TO POLICEWOMEN'S OCCUPATIONAL INTEGRATION

Structural Barriers: Equality versus Equity

Unlike entrants to the professions who are socialized through an extensive educational process and who are committed to their occupation when they enter the job, the entrance requirements for police are low; skills and commitment to police work are acquired through brief formal training at the academy and in the early months of street experience. Departmental policies have an important impact on that experience although formally they have tended to be "sex blind." However, what is sex neutral on its face has put the burden of change on the women. By treating them the same as the male recruits, departments have failed to recognize and confront sex-differentiated patterns, the few irreducible (biological) differences between the sexes, and the women's handicaps stemming from men's attitudes and departmental policies.

The women entered policing at a disadvantage. Few expected to be police officers or went through an extensive anticipatory socialization process in which they vicariously rehearsed police roles. Unlike many of the men in my sample, none of the women had been in the military or had had firearms training. Few had played team sports that involved physical contact and imbued the spirit of the team player.

At the training academy civilian patterns and perceptions are broken down and replaced with the goals and perspectives of the police organization including an emphasis on social solidarity among officers (Harris 1973). The training fostered inequality in several ways. Emphasis on meeting physical fitness standards that do not have to be maintained beyond the academy magnifies the importance of the physical differences between the sexes. Informal coddling of women by some physical education instructors who were protective or unable to deal with some women's manipulative efforts to evade the standards also had several negative effects on all the women. It allowed some women to move to the next stage of recruit training not fully prepared. It fostered the expectation of those women that they could get along by being "different" rather than learning the lessons of group loyalty and "suffering in silence" necessary for acceptance as an officer. And it undermined the confidence of male officers in all policewomen and divided the female officers. As one woman noted:

> Some women tried to be treated differently in p.t. That pissed me off because it reflected on me. I tried to keep up with the men . . . The other women are angry at me because they wanted an excuse for not trying and didn't want any woman to excel because they'd lose their excuse.

At the same time, the training failed to focus on or develop interpersonal skills necessary to do the job well. These skills are often more highly developed in women than men, but women were deprived of a job-relevant training opportunity in which they were likely to excel. Consequently, the new policewomen enter male turf on male terms with little recognition of the problems they would face or the interpersonal strengths they could bring to the job.[6] The early months on the street are very important since it is then that the reputation that follows an officer through a career is formed. Opportunities for learning and gaining self confidence have a multiplier effect because once established, habits and reputations are difficult to change. Self-confidence grows with mastery of policing skills and positive feedback on performance. An officer who does not have or take opportunities to develop street patrol skills because of limited assignments, instruction, or overprotection is likely to act hesitantly. Such officers are viewed not only as incompetent but as threats to others' safety. Others do not want to let them handle situations, thereby perpetuating the cycle of incompetence.

The women officers faced several disadvantages when they first went out on the street. As teenagers many had been sheltered from street life. On the average they were smaller and not as strong as the male rookies. They had to overcome the openly hostile attitudes of some of their trainers, supervisors, and partners as well as a dual standard of evaluation. Since they were visible tokens, they faced performance pressures as representatives of their group. One woman summed up the pressures she faced as follows:

> If you're a man and a police officer, it's accepted that you can do the job. . . . But if you're a woman, everybody's watching to see how brave you are, how commanding you can be, and how well you can take charge of a situation. You have to prove to the citizens that you're a police officer when you take over a scene and you have to do twice as much to prove to your partner and official that you can handle the job.

Since the timidity of some policewomen and the protectiveness of many men in making assignments and working with female partners were not consciously reversed, many women did not have opportunities to learn to act with decisiveness and confidence. Consequently a self-fulfilling prophecy became a reality. These women sought to manipulate others' expectations of them rather than altering their own behavior. How this process occurred was described by an experienced female supervisor:

> A woman comes to a male sergeant after he's given her an assignment and . . . cries. (Usually he'll) give in to her . . . Men are not conditioned or trained to say, "You have to do it." Most officials I've spoken to admit that if a woman came to them and said she was scared of an assignment, they could not make her go . . . Some of the men fear sending a woman out because they think, "Suppose she gets hurt, am I to blame?" The men feel guilty.

One issue where the department has had to face women's "differentness" has both substantive and symbolic significance: pregnancy policy. This issue illustrates the dilemma of equal versus equitable treatment and the ways that a policy without discriminatory intent can differentially affect male and female officers. Since only women can get pregnant, treating pregnancy just like other "health" related matters may put a substantial burden on women officers or on the department.

Unlike many other occupations, the danger of a physical confrontation on the street (and departmental liability for any harmful consequences to a pregnancy) has resulted in a policy of removing pregnant women from patrol. If there are only a few women on patrol, their reassignment for several months and absence for several more months has little impact. As the number of female officers (most of whom are in their childbearing years) increases, however, large numbers of pregnancies cause deployment problems and the appearance of unfairness to male officers.

How pregnancy policy raised the equity versus equality issue was illustrated by the D.C. department's changing policies on this matter. To save money, it abolished light duty status for all officers except pregnant women in the summer of 1975. This led to a lawsuit that resulted in abolition of light duty for pregnant women as well several months later. On becoming pregnant a woman was to be put on extended administative leave until after her delivery but was prohibited from accepting any other full-time employment during the nearly one year she was on leave. The women protested and light duty was subsequently restored for all officers unable to perform street duties for more than five days. The department's vacillating pregnancy policy left a residue of anger among both male and female officers.

Cultural Mandate and Interactional Barriers

> Social interaction is the battlefield where the daily war between the sexes is fought. It is here that women are constantly reminded where their "place" is and here that they are put back in their place, should they venture out. Thus social interaction is the most common means of social control employed against women (Henley and Freeman 1975, 391).

Policewomen face interactional dilemmas because as police officers they are expected to behave with other police officers according to the norms governing relations among peers; as women they are expected to adhere to norms governing male-female relationships. The former role-set calls for symmetrical interactions among status equals; the latter for asymmetrical relations between superordinates (male) and subordinates (female). Thus, in addition to dilemmas as "tokens," policewomen must cope with norms that put them at a disadvantage in male-female interaction in the workplace.

A major interactional mechanism for controlling women is men's language. Policewomen are constantly kept in their "place" by the men's refusal to refer to them as "women." Instead they are called "ladies" or "girls." These terms suggest that women should be protected from the dirty and violent aspects of the world of policing. However this view makes women untrustworthy as officers. Alternatively, women are called "lesbians," "broads," "bitches," or "whores," when they are accepted as streetwise persons belonging in the public world but implicitly are viewed as lacking the qualities associated with femininity.

Cursing and "raunchy" language also create dilemmas. Traditional expectations define "men's language" as not fit for women's ears. Many men are uncomfortable cursing in front of policewomen but resent the inhibition on their expressiveness caused by women's presence. Similarly, when women curse men become offended and withdraw the deference they give to "ladies." If the women act like ladies and avoid cursing, however, they give up the means to make emphatic statements and their words are taken less seriously.

The frequent sexual jokes or gossip about the women remind them that they are desired sexual objects, visible outsiders, and feared competitors. In turn, this joking makes many of the women, concerned about even the appearance of impropriety, avoid interactions that might be viewed as having a sexual connotation. They maintain their moral reputation, but sacrifice the opportunity to build the close interpersonal relationships necessary for sponsorship and protection.

Sex role stereotyping enables men to cast women into the roles reflected in their linguistic categories. At the same time, men cast themselves into counter-roles with semisexual bases that neutralize the threat women pose and simultaneously attempt to control them (Hunt 1985). These stereotypic roles limit women's behavioral options and have a negative impact on the women's work. Women either get pressed into the seductress, maiden, mother, or pet roles or get labeled lesbians or bitches (Kanter 1977). The former are deprofessionalized, protected from occupational demands, excluded from opportunities to develop occupational skills, and criticized for failing to fulfill their duties as officers. The latter are permitted to remain in the policeman's informal world but their dangerous qualities are neutralized by defeminization and pejorative categorization.[7]

Relating to Citizens

Police officers face recurrent uncertainties in relating to citizens who often seek to disrupt interaction and disavow the identity officers ascribe to them. Officers cannot depend on citizens to accept police definitions of the situation and must deal with denials, accounts, and efforts to activate irrelevant statuses. Activation of other statuses may occur because even when a person is enacting a focal role as officer or as complainant or suspect, the demands related to more diffuse ascribed age, sex, and race statuses remain in effect, modulating role performance (Goffman 1961). While the assymmetrical status norm dictates that in general deference flows upward to the police officer who has higher status than most citizens encountered (Sykes and Clark 1975), lower "irrelevant" status characteristics of an officer may lead to a reversal of the flow. Although all officers occasionally face such deference reversals, such situations continually threaten interactions for policewomen who must find ways to turn them to their advantage, minimize their occurrence, and limit their effects on the officer's control of the situation.

In examining the activation of the sex status of the officer and citizen, there are four possible status combinations: male police officers with male and female citizens and policewomen with male and female citizens. Each combination of statuses has different sets of expectations and management problems.

As officers, policemen have status superiority over male citizens who are obligated to defer and comply. As men, however, male citizens and policemen are status equals. Activation of sex status by either implies a reduction in social distance. Generally this pattern is to the citizen's advantage since it says in effect, "act like a man (*i.e.*, control yourself) and I won't have to exert my authority as an officer to control you." It also benefits the officer since it maintains the necessity to use force. Thus it is a tool that can be used effectively in some situations by policemen. In other interactions, however, activation of participants' sex status may be regarded by the policeman as a denial of deference due to him. When policemen rely too heavily on their formal authority or reject a male citizen's effort to be treated "as a man" the result is a "duel of manhood" which has a high probability of a physical or verbal confrontation that might well have been avoided.

Policemen have double status superiority over female citizens and generally face fewer problems in such encounters. They often initiate activation of female status to gain compliance by asserting "act like a lady and I'll treat you like one," and by extending courtesies and exemptions appropriate for her sex status. If this strategy works, the officer has gained control while enhancing his sense of manly generosity. If it fails, he can apply a show of force.

Interactions between policewomen and male citizens are problematic because the normative prescriptions and others' expectations are sometimes in direct conflict. By virtue of their office, policewomen expect deference to their position from citizens; by virtue of their female status they are subordinates of men. Policewomen are usually given deference, in part because it does not challenge a male citizen's manhood if he gives in and goes along whereas fighting a woman may cause a man a loss of status. However, the man's deference is revocable, particularly if the policewoman acts "unladylike" in fulfilling her occupational role obligations. Since they often are at a physical disadvantage, female officers may have to rely on the deference of males as a control strategy although most asserted that they do not do so and consciously minimize rather than activate their female status except in clearly nonthreatening instances.

In instances when men do seek to activate the female status of police-women, the latter must find ways to manage while maintaining control. Women may have to cope with frequent snickers and comments and occasional sexual remarks and invitations. Usually policewomen overlook them, rationalizing by "thinking of the source" or respond with a cold, stony stare. Others make such remarks as, "You wouldn't say that to a male officer, would you?" which generally get the point across. A variety of verbal and nonverbal cues involv-ing use of the voice, appearance, facial expression, and body postures also con-vey the message that despite their small stature the policewoman is to be taken seriously. Learning to emit these messages, however, requires breaking long-standing habits such as smiling and other ingratiating behaviors which often are unconscious. Instead policewomen learn literally to "stand up to people." Those women that do not learn to give such cues are more likely both to find their authority challenged and to have to "back off," losing control of situations when this occurs.

In dealing with female citizens, policewomen get both greater coopera-tion and more "hassles" than male officers. While their common female status implies a reduction of social distance, it revokes the special consideration given to female citizens by policemen, and for this reason, may arouse the female citizen's anger at not being able to flirt or cry her way out of a situation. Women also are more willing to fight female officers than male officers. Conversely, policewomen often are viewed as more sympathetic and so are able to gain the cooperation of female citizens, particularly victims, who refuse to talk to male officers.

Effective officers of both sexes appeal to "sex appropriate behavior" on the part of citizens as well as respect for the officer's authority to gain citizen cooperation. They use citizen's expectations and values to their advantage, draw-ing on mutually shared statuses to diminish social distance; invoke the parent child complex (Goffman 1976) to increase their informal authority and con-trol; and only draw on the authority of their office to increase their different "assets" and diminish their "liabilities" as officers when necessary. The way gender operates, however, differs according to the "irrelevant" statuses of the officer and citizen in their interaction.

Ineffective officers, on the other hand, either too rigidly rely on their formal authority or cannot transcend the limitations on their behavior posed by adherence to traditional sex role norms. For female officers this limitation means they fail to use the authority of their office, relying instead on deference to them as women. If this strategy fails, they cannot act effectively.

POLICEWOMEN'S ROLE DILEMMAS AND CHOICES

Policewomen seeking full acceptance into their occupation face a number of dilemmas growing from normative conflicts, the men's opposition to their presence, and their efforts to cast women into stereotypic sex role categories. In managing on the job relations and defining their work identities, police-women adopt one of several strategies. The principal choices are between two polar patterns of behavior variously labeled "defeminized" and "deprofessional-ized" (Hochschild 1975), and overachievement and accommodation (Walshok 1981).

The defeminized woman seeks to overcome barriers to being treated as a peer and professional by doing more than is expected of men and of other women. The deprofessionalized woman accommodates to men's pressures to behave according to sex role norms by acting as a junior partner in exchange for exemptions appropriate for a "lady" on the job and by avoiding participa-tion in the informal peer group's activities. Those who choose the defemin-ized option I term "*police*women"; those adopting the deprofessionalized op-tion I call "police*women*" although, in fact, most women fall between these poles of the continuum in defining their own occupational identities (Martin 1978).

*Police*women view their female status as irrelevant to the job. They em-phasize their "professionalism" and strong adherence to police norms and values including assertiveness, the willingness to use violence, the rule of silence, and physical support of a partner. They strive to achieve a high number of arrests, derive work satisfaction principally from law enforcement activities, and have made clear they do not want to be "overprotected" by male officers. They are comfortable on street patrol and may aspire to become detectives or be pro-moted. They tolerate as a "fact of life" that policewomen must try harder, with-stand harassment, and gain recognition as officers by being "exceptions." They seek acceptance as an officer who more than fulfills the occupational norms rather than personal acceptance on the basis of their likability. Even when they believe that their assignments and other aspects of males' behavior reflect sex discrimination, they remain silent, proving they can "take it" or individually confront the harasser. The *police*women are critical of many of the female of-ficers whom they term "feeble" or "mediocres" who seek special treatment, "have a crybaby attitude" and "just sit and bitch." Thus *police*women adhere to an individualistic model of occupational success through overachievement.

*Police*women do not feel that their feminine identity is threatened by their job. Off duty they behave in "feminine" ways and on the job comfortably blend "masculine" assertiveness with interpersonal skills to gain control of situations. Nevertheless, although they are accepted as officers, they frequently are stereo-typed by their male coworkers as "dykes" and "whores" and often are excluded (or excuse themselves) from the policemen's informal social world, thereby limiting their access to information and informal influence.

Police*women* are not comfortable on street patrol or with the task of con-trolling citizens' behavior. They are concerned about their own physical limitations, fearful of injury, and view street patrol as a threat to their femininity which is important on the job as well as off. They acquiesce to the stereotypic roles of mother, sister, seductress, and pet; resent constant tests of their competence and loyalty; resist pressures to perform; and either refuse to exert extra effort or try but cannot prove themselves to be exceptional officers. Some seek and enjoy men's protection and their treatment as "ladies"; others seem helpless to alter their situation. In general they resent the double standard of treatment which they regard as discrimination and have been more likely than *police*women to turn to Policewomen in Action, a policewomen's organization established by the department, to have their grievances heard. Police*women*, too, generally avoid informal social interaction with the men since it threatens their desexualized status. They do not desire promotion (it involves commanding men which makes them uncomfortable) but rather seek administrative, clerical or community services assignments or hope to leave policing in the near future.

Are the two polar types — defeminized or deprofessionalized women, *police*women or police*women* — the only options available for women in nontraditional occupations? Hunt (1985) asserts that the *police*women and police*women* continuum implies a static and closed world in which the women accept the limited stereotypic role choices open to them. She points to the emergence of a role transcender, the "real woman cop" who combines the masculine attributes of the "street cop" and the feminine attributes of the "moral woman" thereby forcing a change in the policemen's perceptual world. Zimmer (1986), too, developed a typology that included women prison guards in the "inventive" role.

Role transcenders may well be emerging although the *police*woman role option allows for (and may even demand) creative blending of occupational and sex role expectations at the individual level. Indeed, many of the *police*women, like Hunt's "real women cops" challenged the men's stereotypes and may have altered their perceptual world.[8] Nevertheless, these women, regardless of label, no less than other female officers, faced dilemmas and handicaps not encountered by male officers.

CONCLUSION

Four levels of social control — the society and culture, occupation, organization, and client — create dilemmas for women seeking to enter the male dominated occupation of policing. These dilemmas affect the ways the policewomen cope with the stresses of performing their occupational role. Because cultural norms and behavioral expectations for women conflict with situationally appropriate behavior, policewomen must find ways to manage the conflict and mesh their occupational and sex roles. In addition, they face structural problems as newcomers present in only token numbers in an organization which offer them limited power and mobility opportunities. The nature of police work, the paramilitary structure of the formal organization, the importance of the informal occupational culture, and departmental training and assignment policies each contribute to policewomen's difficulties. Thus cultural factors that shape the attitudes and behaviors of supervisors, colleagues, and clients interact with and operate through structural features of the occupation and the specific working conditions within the organizational context.

The women are treated as women by male coworkers and so must adopt strategies to cope with the strains of their work situation. One group, labeled *police*women, react by overachievement, invisibility, and staunch adherence to the informal occupational rules in order to prove themselves exceptions. Successful as officers, they pay a price in terms of performance pressure and social isolation. Police*women*, on the other hand, adapt to the stereotypic roles into which they are cast and lower their occupational aspirations. They are accepted as persons but tend to fail as patrol officers.

To what extent are the problems of policewomen unique? Women in many nontraditional occupations face variations of the structural problems related to limited power, opportunities for mobility, and numbers. They also are subjected to cultural mandates and conflicts regarding "femininity." What makes policing uniquely difficult for women officers are two characteristics of the job that make it "men's work": the authority vested in the officer to enforce the law and the right to physically control others when they violate the law. The combination of social authority and the occasional use of physical force produces a "double whammy" that increases the occupational resistence to women's incursion. The barriers to women in law and medicine have been substantially reduced in the past decade as the stereotypes on which they rested were undermined. But the "irreducible differences" between men and women — their physical differences and the qualities associated with them — remain a factor in policing. Because women are physically smaller and weaker than men, and thereby are believed to convey less authority, they continue at a disadvantage in policing that is at once real and symbolic.

Despite these formidable barriers, however, the outlook for women in policing is not entirely bleak. Changes have occurred and these can be accelerated by departmental policies as well as by cultural changes. Short term factors permitting optimism are the gradual increase in the numbers and successful role performance of policewomen, increasing signs of acceptance of policewomen by younger officers and citizens, and the availability of policewomen as real and media role models for young girls and women to emulate. Longer term signs pointing toward greater opportunities for policewomen are changes adopted by some police departments that have facilitated women's acquisition of occupational skills, changes in sex role norms, and changes in patrol work that make it less incompatible with the newly emerging female role.

One apparently successful approach is temporary sex segregation in training and initial assignments. In several instances where the women were trained separately or assigned to work alone or together, and could not manipulate, compete with, or rely on men, they acquired the skills necessary to perform well. For example, the New Jersey State Police, faced with a sex discrimination suit and a 100 percent attrition rate for women in the preceding academy class, created a one time all-women class. While attrition remained high, the experience proved valuable in pinpointing the variety of problems that affected the women (*e.g.*, injuries from wearing ankle-high sneakers, difficulties with exercises requiring upper body strength) and ways to overcome them (*e.g.*, low-top shoes, special exercises, and more emphasis on judo and karate for the women, as well as in service training for academy instructors) (Patterson 1980).

There is also limited evidence that assignment of women to work alone, as partners, or in groups facilitates the development of their occupational skills. In Washington, D.C., 23 policewomen were assigned to a plainclothes detail as part of a "crackdown" on prostitution. The commanding officer of that operation reported that the operation benefitted the women who . . . "discovered they could work together, demonstrated they could be self-reliant, utilize their own judgment, and make their own decisions." It also helped them gain the respect of their male counterparts who were "impressed with the many strengths displayed by the women" (Martin 1980, 132). Hunt also observed (personal communication) that because men and women were not permitted to ride together in the department she studied, the women who worked alone or in pairs, developed independence. Although the department did not mean to aid the women, in fact, "it made them better cops because they could not fall back on old patterns and depend on men to protect them."

To address the continuing problems of policewomen, departments must move beyond the policy of absolute equality. They should adopt special training elements designed to address women's needs and in-service training programs for instructors and supervisors to enable them to address both their difficulty in dealing with women who seek to be "coddled" and their higher performance standards.

Merton (1957) observed that social structures change as cultural mandates change. These, in turn, respond to frequent occurrences of patterned conflict. The growing number of women in nontraditional occupations and the conflicts that this produces suggest that changes in sex role norms will continue and accelerate. As this occurs, some of the conflicts that policewomen face are likely to ease.

Finally, continued modification of the patrol officer's role is likely to benefit policewomen. Police work encompasses a continuum of activities ranging from control to support. Traditionally, emphasis was on the former. Public demand for better police service and an end to "police brutality" and departmental efforts to professionalize the police and bridge the gap betwen the police and the community have resulted in great pressure on officers to incorporate both control and support elements. The result is a wider role repertoire demanded of patrol officers and the need to act in ways that are stereotypically masculine *and* stereotypically feminine.

In conclusion, the barriers to policewomen are built into both formal and informal work structures and into culturally mandated patterns governing male-female interaction in the job. These make it difficult to achieve true equality for women officers. Although change appears to be underway at a slow and uncertain pace, policewomen remain outsiders faced with a dilemma not encountered by policemen: how simultaneously to think like a man, work like a dog, and act like a lady.

NOTES

1. To make the matter more complex, Goffman (1961) observed that even when an individual enacts a focal role, such as surgeon or police officer, diffuse age and sex roles remain in effect. Because a man in the role of surgeon "must act at times during surgery like a male" (Goffman 1961, 139), questions arise about how he allots his time and action between roles. For a woman in the role of surgeon (or police officer), the allocation dilemma arises, with the additional question: does the occupational role require that she act like a man or act like a woman, (since male and female sex role performances call for different types of behavior)? What is the effect of her ascribed female status on the female surgeon's achieved occupational one?

2. Although the research was initiated a decade ago, several factors suggest that the findings are still valid. First, while studying an elite 60 officer "career criminal" unit in 1983, I observed that all the eight women in the unit faced at least occasional harassment as women. Several bounced from squad to squad until one sergeant accepted them as full working members and taught them undercover techniques. Second, other recent studies of policewomen (Hunt 1984 and 1985) and women prison guards (Jurik 1985; Zimmer 1986) support my findings.

3. The police ranked 54th among 90 occupations in 1961 (Reiss 1961, 54–7).

4. Banton (1964) distinguished between "law officers" and "peace officers." Bittner (1967) wrote about "law enforcement" and "peace keeping" tasks on skid row. Wilson (1973) diffrentiated between maintenance of order and enforcement of the law. For other discussions of the conflicts among the various facets of the police role see Skolnick (1966), Rubinstein (1974), Rumbaut and Bittner (1979), and Sykes and Brent (1983).

5. To promote group solidarity and the selection of trustworthy coworkers, police entrance requirements and recruitment mechanisms for many years informally assured a homogeneous group of officers. Persons who did not "fit" on the basis of their race or sex, as well as those missing the "mark of affinity" related to the candidate's conception of masculinity (Gray 1975), were screened out. These mechanisms have been undermined by antidiscrimination laws.

6. Even in departments that place greater emphasis on social relations skills, however, the informal view that they are not part of "real" police work limits women trainees' ability to raise their status.

7. Hunt (1985) observed that the seductress is regarded as "whore" and included her in the defeminized group. She also noted that women cast into the maiden, mother and sister or pet roles are not only deprofessionalized but desexualized as well due to the incest taboo associated with these roles.

8. For example see Ann (Martin 1980, chapter 1).

REFERENCES

Acker, J. and D. Van Houten. 1974. "Differential recruitment and control: The sex structuring of organizations," *Administrative Science Quarterly* 19:152–63.

Banton, M. 1964. *Policemen in the Community*. New York: Basic Books.

Bittner, E. 1967. " The police on skid row: A study in peacekeeping," *American Sociological Review* 32:699–715.

———. 1970. *The Functions of Police in Modern Society*. Chevy Chase, MD: National Institute of Mental Health.

Blankenship W.C. 1971. "Head libarians: How many men? How many women?" In *The Professional Woman*, edited by A. Theodore, Cambridge, MA: Schenkman, pp. 93–102.

Bridges, W.P. 1982. "The sexual segregation of occupations: Theories of labor stratification in industry," *American Journal of Sociology* 88:270–95.

Edwards, A. 1943. *Comprehensive Occupational Statistics for the United States, 1870–1940*. Washington, DC: U.S. Government Printing Office.

Feldberg, R. and E.N. Glenn. 1979. "Male and female: Job versus gender models in the sociology of work," *Social Problems* 26:524–38.

Fottler, M.P. 1976. "Attitudes of female nurses toward the male nurse: A study of occupational segregation," *Journal of Health and Social Behavior* 17:98–110.

Goffman, E. 1956. "The nature of deference and demeanor." *American Anthropologist* 58:473–502.

———. 1961. *Encounters*. Indianapolis, IN: Bobbs-Merrill.

———. 1976. "Gender Displays," *Studies in the anthropology of visual communication* 3.

Gray, T. 1975. "Selecting for a police subculture," In *Police in America*. edited by J. Skolnick and T. Gray, Boston: Little Brown, pp. 46–56.

Gripton, J. 1974. "Sexism in social work: Male takeover of a female profession," *The Social Worker* 42:78–89.

Gross, N. and A. Trusk. 1976. *The Sex Factor and the Management of Schools.* New York: Wiley.

Harris, R. 1973. *The Police Academy: An Inside View.* New York: Wiley.

Henley, N. and J. Freeman. 1975. "The Sexual Politics of Interpersonal Behavior," In *Women: A Feminist Perspective.* edited by J. Freeman, Palo Alto, CA: Mayfield, pp. 391–401.

Hochschild, A. 1975. "Making it: Marginality and obstacles to minority consciousness," *Annals of the New York Academy of Science* 208:79–82.

Hunt, J. 1984. "Development of rapport through the negotiation of gender in field work among police," *Human Organization* 43:283–96.

————. 1985. "The logic of sexism among police," Unpublished revision of manuscript presented at the annual meeting of the American Society of Criminology, November 1984 in Cincinnati, Ohio.

Jurik, N. 1985. "An officer and a lady: Organizational barriers to women working as correctional officers in men's prisons," *Social Problems* 32:275–88.

Kadushin, C. 1976. "Men in a women's profession," *Social Work* 21:440–47.

Kanter, R. 1977. *Men and Women of the Corporation.* New York: Basic Books.

Krause, E. 1971. *The Sociology of Occupations.* Boston: Little Brown.

Manning, P. 1977. *Police Work: The Social Organization of Policing.* Cambridge, MA: MIT Press.

Martin, S.E. 1978. "Sexual politics in the workplace: The interactional world of policewomen," *Symbolic Interaction* 1:44–60.

————. 1980. *"Breaking and Entering": Policewomen on Patrol.* Berkeley, CA: University of California Press.

Merton, R.K. 1957. *Social Theory and Social Structure.* Glencoe, IL: Free Press.

Milton, C. 1972. *Women in Policing.* Washington: Police Foundation.

Morris, R.T. and R.J. Murphy. 1959. "The situs dimension in occupational structure," *American Sociological Review* 24:231–39.

Pavalko, R. 1971. *The Sociology of Occupations and Professions.* Itasca, IL.: F.E. Peacock.

Patterson, M.J. 1980. "Training tailored for women," *Police Magazine* 3:22–9.

Reiss, A. 1961. *Occupational and Social Status.* New York: Free Press.

————. 1971. *The Police and the Public.* New Haven: Yale University Press.

Rubinstein, J. 1974. *City Police.* New York: Ballantine Books.

Rumbaut, R. and E. Bittner. 1979. "Changing conceptions of the police role: A sociological view," In *Crime and Justice: An Annual Review of Research.* edited by N. Morris and M. Tonry, Chicago: University of Chicago Press, pp. 239–288.

Schreiber, C. 1979. *Men and Women in Transitional Occupations.* Cambridge, MA: MIT Press.

Skolnick, J. 1966. *Justice Without Trial.* New York: Wiley.

Spradley, J.P. and B. Mann. 1975. *The Cocktail Waitress: Women's Work in a Man's World.* New York: Wiley.

Stewart, P. and M. Cantor, eds. 1974. *Varieties of Work Experience.* Cambridge, MA: Schenkman.

Sykes, R. and B. Breit. 1983. *Policing: A Social Behaviorist Perspective.* New Brunswick: Rutgers University Press.

Sykes, R. and J. Clark. 1975. "A theory of deference exchange in police-civilian encounters," *American Journal of Sociology* 81:584–600.

United States Federal Bureau of Investigation. 1983. *Uniform Crime Report— 1982.* Washington, DC: U.S. Government Printing Office.

Walshok, M.L. 1981. *Blue Collar Women.* Garden City, NY: Anchor.

Westley, W. 1970. *Violence and the Police.* Cambridge, MA: MIT Press.

Wilson, J.Q. 1973. *Varieties of Police Behavior.* New York: Atheneum.

Zimmer, L. 1986. *Women Guarding Men: A Study of Female Guards who Work in Prisons for Men.* Chicago: University of Chicago Press.

CHAPTER 13

Women Working for Women:
The Manager and Her Secretary

ANNE STATHAM

INTRODUCTION

I began this study looking at women managers. I was not long into it before I discovered the important role secretaries play in the life of any manager, particularly the woman manager. Because their work is so inextricably linked, it became increasingly difficult to think or talk about one and not the other. To capitalize on this discovery, I began interviewing both manager and secretary. As I continued to explore the nature of the relationships formed between these two groups of women and to notice the similarities and contrasts in their work demands, I became increasingly convinced that the manager's and the secretary's story are appropriately told together.

Women's Relationships in the Workplace

The secretary and the manager are often found working together in the same offices, collaborating on the same projects. Yet their roles are obviously quite different. Or are they?

In some ways the two types of jobs *are* very different. Managers are those "in charge"; they comprise nearly 23 percent (22.7 percent) of the labor force and the majority (86.1 percent) are men. Secretaries are those who "serve"; they comprise 17.3 percent of the labor force and the majority (77.1 percent) are women (U.S. Commerce Department. Bureau of the Census 1980). These differences aside, however, both are responsible for seeing that the work gets done, that information flows in an effective manner, and that the work of others is organized and coordinated. Recent studies of office workers indicate that secretaries actually do more managing than has previously been acknowledged (Glenn and Feldberg 1984).

Other similarities exist. Both jobs are fairly formal in their organization, with fixed work settings and hours. The secretaries in this study worked relatively fixed schedules, as did the managers, though they sometimes worked extra hours on special projects. Secretaries tend to have less autonomy than managers, though both usually work for people who exert some control over their work activities. The most obvious *difference* between them is in their prestige and authority — though again even this difference may not necessarily be great. A certain secretary (for example, the secretary to the president) may exert a great deal of power and be held in high esteem. In general, then, the line separating manager from secretary is fluid, particularly when both actors are female. The way the relationship is managed becomes quite interesting, especially as managers are increasingly likely to be women.

Past research makes it difficult to predict how women managers and their secretaries will relate to each other. On the one hand, women managers might be expected to form close working relationships with their secretaries, given women's presumed tendency to be more people-oriented (*cf*. Rossi 1972). Much evidence suggests that women's relationships with each other are more personal and self-revealing than the relationships men form with each other (Rubin 1985; Rubin 1983; Caldwell and Peplau 1982). However, men are also known to self-disclose to women (Komarovsky 1976), and further, forming close relationships may not be the essential ingredient for effective management. The "feeling rules" (Hochschild 1983) of the workplace often dictate that personal feelings be left out of decisions, that participants carefully monitor their responses to form the most instrumental, segmented relationships possible with coworkers. In that case, the tendency to form personal relationships may actually interfere with the woman manager's job performance.

Another body of research suggests instead that women have very hostile relationships with one another in the workplace. For example, Harriman (1985, 128) asserts that the "petty, childish bickering often associated with female behavior [in the workplace] . . . may result from the similarity between women . . . [that] exacerbates the feeling children generally have that their parents can read their minds" or from transferring the hostility between mother and daughter to workplace relationships. There is no empirical support for these assertions, yet they appear frequently in the literature. There is evidence that as a general rule, women prefer not to work for other women (Ferber, Huber, and Spitze 1979; Kanter 1977). However, Kanter (1977) and Harriman (1985) both suggest that these feelings may reflect the woman manager's relative lack of power as much as interaction problems. After all, secretaries usually take their status and prestige directly from their bosses. Additionally, some research suggests that women come to feel more positively about working for women after the *experience* of having done so (Harriman 1985; Ferber, Huber, and Spitze 1979).

A New Approach

This study examines the relationships formed between women managers and their secretaries. An interactionist perspective is taken, with the focus on the process rather than the structure of the relationship. Status differences are not presumed but are taken as variable. As with most relationships, this one arises from a process of establishing contracts based on personal reciprocity between the actors (Brain 1976) within the structure that exists. The methodology I have chosen allows me to examine indicators of that process.

I have taken a woman's culture approach, and in doing so, do not accept as given previous negative perceptions of women managers but allow for alternative realities to emerge. Women's ability to manage other women is a critical factor in determining women's overall ability to manage effectively. Aside from the common perception that women cannot manage other women, there is the more general assumption that women managers are "less successful" than their male counterparts (Brown 1979; Dubno 1984; Massengill and DiMarco 1979; Grant 1983) because of individual inadequacies (Deaux 1979; Wood and Greenfield 1976; Moses and Boehm 1975; Rosen and Jerdee 1978; Hennig and Jardim 1977) and structural barriers (Cann 1984; West 1982; Harlan and Weiss 1981; Riger and Gilligan 1980; Kanter 1977). These studies point to differences between men and women managers in situations where women perform poorly. No one has systematically considered the possibility that women bring *strengths* to management positions. The behavior of women managers, if not conforming to "male models," may be judged inadequate. However, their new approaches may represent strengths not heretofore appreciated in academic or work circles. Assessments of their performance may fail to take this into account. Hence, this study is concerned with delineating the differences between women and men in management, particularly with regard to the relationships with secretaries, and with exploring the implications of those differences. Perhaps women *do* relate differently to their secretaries, but in ways that enhance work performance.

METHOD

The information for this study comes from 22 female and 18 male managers and their secretaries interviewed in three settings: a manufacturing firm, a technical institute, and a financial institution. These settings were expected to offer a range along the continuum of cultural acceptance of the women as manager, with the manufacturing firm being the least accepting and the financial institution the most. As all interviews were done in the work settings, I had many opportunities to observe work behaviors and to become friendly with other staff (*e.g.*, receptionists and security guards), who were able to give me additional information about the settings. All of this information plus the interview material itself, confirmed my expectations about the cultural support for the women managers: the three settings varied along this continuum as expected — though in all three settings, women experienced very definite barriers for promotion. (See Statham 1986 for an elaboration.)

I obtained the sample by using informal contacts in the settings for initial interviews and then asking these individuals to give me names and numbers of others with whom I might talk. In this process, I made special efforts to: 1) cover all areas in the organizations; 2) talk with all of the highest-level women managers; and 3) talk with men at comparable levels. I was successful in talking with all of the highest-level women in the three settings and in obtaining a sample of men at comparable management levels. This is not the case with many previous studies comparing men and women managers; the men are often at much higher levels, confounding many of the results. After completing each interview with a manager, I asked if I could talk with his or her secretary about the possibility of doing an interview. None of the managers refused and only one secretary did. All of the secretaries in this study were women; there were 32 secretaries in all, since several of the managers I talked with shared a single secretary. Their levels were very similar across the three organizations. They were unionized in the technical institute, though many publicly wondered if the union was helpful or effective. Working conditions seemed to be similar in all three settings, perhaps because the National Labor Relations Board regulated the working conditions of the secretaries who were not unionized. I did not find differences in secretaries' reactions to men and women managers to be related to their different job levels. Hence, this variable is not used in the analysis.

The interviews lasted from 45 to 90 minutes. Respondents answered 10 broad questions, beginning with "Tell me about your job," and proceeding to questions about things liked or disliked about the job, future plans, family/work conflict, perceived sex differences between men and women at work, and preferences for working with either sex. All interviews were tape-recorded and fully transcribed; they were analyzed using the constant comparative method described by Glaser and Strauss (1967).

FINDINGS

Similarities in Job Demands

The secretary and manager faced similar dilemmas in their work. Both gave me long (and exhausting) lists of all of the things they had to do in response to the general question "Tell me about your job." Managers said such things as:

> I supervise ten programs . . . accounting and accounting check programs, clerk typist, secretarial science, court and conference reporting . . . cosmetology . . . radio broadcasting, banking and finance . . . word processing and word processing specialist, and I have 30 full-time instructors . . . and average 50 to 75 part-time instructors in any one semester.

For many, these lists were actively growing, particularly in firms where personnel cutbacks had occurred. Said one of these women, ". . . it's like you have a job and they just take another piece of clay and stick it to it . . ."

And secretaries offered job descriptions such as the following:

> I do dealer development work, maintain logs, maintain maps where our dealers are. The contracts come in, terminations . . . master list. . . . I maintain the personal records . . . when it's their proper review time, all the paperwork is done . . . If they need special sign-up cards, all the paper work is done.

For both manager and secretary, time management was a critical problem; it was an essential and often difficult job requirement. Demands on their time often seemed overwhelming. For managers, time management problems resulted from input from above or below. Supervisors typically caused problems by interjecting new demands. For instance, one manager complained about

> . . . getting time lines from four different people. That's difficult to cope with. . . . I can do one thing very well, but I can't do ten things very well . . . and when I say, "If I do this, I can't do that," my boss just says, "You'll have to do it tomorrow." That's 72 hours of work!

This leads to the second type of time problem — managing demands from below. Current advice on effective management (Josefowitz 1985) says the manager must free him or herself from daily tasks to allow ample time for planning. A common complaint from both sexes in this study was that they had too little time for planning. A male manager said, "I should be doing 80 percent planning and 20 doing, and instead it's the other way around." Another, who eventually *did* leave this job, complained of " . . . fighting fires in the trenches all the time . . . with no chance for thoughtful planning." And a woman manager found pressure from both sides, lamenting, "I would suspect that others as well as myself aren't given the leisure to make decisions in a rational manner. We make them out of desperation."

Planning was seen as a premium activity, one essential for good management but made difficult by external demands. Either supervisors would intervene with new demands or capable subordinates would not be available for the delegation of "fire-fighting" tasks.

While conflicting and overwhelming time demands were common and troubling for the managers (both male and female), they were endemic for the secretaries, whose jobs demanded that they complete tasks assigned or requested by several others. This required the organizing and prioritizing of these tasks and seeking additional help if needed. Miscalculations could be devastating, for the secretary as well as the manager.

Some secretaries found the time pressure very disconcerting.

> There are times when it is very overwhelming. I find myself losing grasp of what I have to do and I just have to sit down and think, "Now, what it is

I have to do? What is it I would like to do? What it is I want to do?" And then I constantly have to keep prioritizing the situation, otherwise I lose control of what I am doing and feel very uncomfortable, and I don't like that feeling of not being able to keep control.

Three factors were especially likely to create time management problems for secretaries: multiple supervisors; open access to others (*i.e.*, serving as a receptionist in *addition* to other regular duties); and the telephone. Frequent phone interruptions were singled out as a particular burden:

It is a very big adjustment on this job. I'm on the phone constantly. . . . It cut into my concentration a lot because I'd be right in the middle of something very, very important . . . I had to discipline myself to remember that the phone is important always, no matter what I was working on . . . I had to learn to sort my thoughts, to be able to handle people diplomatically and give them all the information, and still get back to what I was doing and not make mistakes.

In sum, both secretary and manager found themselves managing a vast array of demands. For managers, complexity tended to come in the form of multiple *levels* of demands (being caught in the middle), while for secretaries multiple *sources* of demands were the most troublesome feature.

Their Views of Each Other

Despite the similarities of their work demands, managers and secretaries perceived their situations to be very different. They saw themselves as motivated by different things. Most of the women managers I interviewed had made a conscious choice to enter management, and even those who did not now enjoyed their positions. They were attracted by the prestige and rewards inherent in their jobs. Most of them talked about "most disliked" previous jobs as lacking challenge (being boring) and being physically exhausting (factory work, shoe selling, waitressing, etc.). In terms of "rising to the top," they perceived strict limits on how far they could go ("I've come about as far as a woman can come in this company," several women said), and all of my respondents shared clear perceptions about where those limits were (the point to which women had thus far risen). Only one of the women with whom I talked aspired to become president of her organization, while the men — confident of their ability to "rise to the top" — more often aspired to do so.

The secretaries less often felt that the importance of their work was recognized by others, though several identified quite strongly with their professional role and took pride in their training and abilities. A number of them belonged to professional secretarial organizations and were very conscious of their need for skill upgrading; one or two even planned to seek certification by a particular secretarial organization. They were most often motivated, however, by the ease of finding employment and the fit of job requirements with their skills. For some, secretarial training had seemed their "only option" when they were in high school, and some regretted that other options had not been presented to them.

While several secretaries aspired to become managers, on the whole there was the feeling that by being a secretary one could avoid many of the stresses of the corporate world. Said one secretary, of her overworked woman manager, "I wouldn't do what she does, not if you paid me a million dollars. I like being able to leave at 4:30 and not feel I should be staying."

The majority expressed the belief that women managers had to work "twice as hard" as men. One of them said: "They [men] can get away with dumping their work onto someone else and walking out the door . . . Women can't."

Likewise, women managers expressed a desire to distance themselves from the secretarial role. Several had moved up from secretarial positions, especially those in the manufacturing firm. Said one, after working through an adjustment to a newly created job, "I would never go back to the secretarial ranks again." She felt she had "grown beyond that."

Another woman in the same firm noted that she was very careful in her friendships with secretaries to "not become associated with them at work," so as to preserve her managerial image. And another woman who had been promoted from a secretarial position but was later forced by a personnel cutback to assume some of her former duties fought this reversal bitterly, and sometimes refused to cooperate. (She was eventually laid off, her position supposedly "eliminated.")

The secretaries were not anxious to enter into the foray that they saw their women managers engulfed in; stress and hard work were their primary reasons. The women managers, in turn, were anxious to preserve their status differential. So how did these distancing techniques affect the ability of managers and secretaries to work together and the types of relationships they formed?

Their Relationships

Given the literature suggesting that women do not work well together, I was unprepared for the nearly unanimous positive acclaim the secretaries gave their women managers. Only one of these secretaries described her manager in the harsh terms found so often in the literature, and this secretary worked for a second woman manager whom she really appreciated. Several of the secretaries admitted to having misgivings before working for these women, but now a majority wondered if they could "ever go back to working for men again," and all but one of them now felt women were *not* difficult to work for.

Consideration and appreciation. Both the secretaries and the women managers themselves felt that women managers established better relationships with their subordinates. The managers were seen, first of all, as being more considerate. One woman manager said "I tried not to make them do things (*i.e.*, make coffee) that I wouldn't want to do myself." And several secretaries made remarks such as the following:

> I think women are much more respectful of their secretaries, more sensitive to them, appreciate more the things they do. Just simple things like saying thank you for tasks that are completed. So many men just say good morning and good night to their secretaries and that's about it. I've watched a lot of these men interacting with their secretaries and thought, "I don't think I could ever work for him!"

> She is a very people-oriented manager . . . If she sees you working feverishly on a project . . . and the clock is ticking and she has a few minutes . . . she will sit down right with you and start working . . . She cares if you get your vacation in, time off. She is very appreciative of the things you do for her. . . . I don't think I've had a man boss that was quite as good as her in that respect.

And it seems the consideration went both ways.

> I'm very protective of_____. So many people need to see her. I try to screen and answer questions if I can. I play an administrative function. And she's very sppportive of me and very sensitive to my moods. She can tell when I'm having a bad day when no one else can. And I can with her, too. I get even more protective on those days.

These secretaries also believed their managers appreciated and respected their skills and capabilities more than men. Some managers made comments along these lines:

> Women have come up through the ranks, have been there, so have more confidence in their subordinates and delegate more responsibility to them. Men see their secretaries as there to answer the phone for them and open their mail, and that's pretty much it.

The secretaries concurred:

> Most men think every girl who sits at a desk with a typewriter is a secretary. Women don't. Also, they don't understand what a secretary really is. Women understand the responsibility that comes with being a secretary.

> I prefer working with women. They are more respectful of me and my opinions.

Some of these comments suggest that "coming up from the secretarial ranks" is necessary for their appreciation. However, only three of the managers described as considerate and appreciative had ever been secretaries, and one of the secretaries allowed that "women's empathetic nature" may be just as important.

> Men don't work up from the bottom, so they don't understand our position very well. Women, even if they don't work up from the bottom, seem to have the empathy to understand.

Contrast these comments with that of a man supervisor, complaining about all the paperwork involved in his job: "Sometimes I could be a secretary and do the work I do."

While most of the men who discussed secretaries did not make such disparaging remarks (with most of the men the subject never came up), their remarks suggested that they saw secretaries as "helpmates," often taking over functions they disliked. "I really need a good secretary to take care of me. They take the air of responsibility off your mind, organizing yourself," said one manager who recently lost his secretary to budget cuts. And a secretary said of her boss: "I don't think he knows what I'm doing half the time. Once he gets it off his mind, he forgets about it."

Another secretary gave even more compelling evidence that secretaries were not taken seriously by male managers; she told of an occasion when she wanted to hire a male clerk and was told by a superior, "We want to see some women around here; we want to see legs."

The men's secretaries usually offered different positive remarks about their superiors than did the women's secretaries; they described them as "relaxed and easy to work for" or "amazing in their intelligence and energy." One secretary did describe her boss as considerate and understanding; another said her boss gave her "positive reinforcement"; and yet another called her boss a "pussy cat," despite his own self-description as "having a temper." However, these comments were much less frequent and elaborate than those made about women managers, and eight out of thirteen complained that their bosses were disorganized and depended on them to "hold them together." One of these women said of her manager:

> He isn't over expressive as far as he would like to show his gratitude for a job that you've done well . . . but he shows it in other ways . . . your performance appraisal . . . He may even say a nice comment to someone else . . . [about] the nice job you do.

Several other secretaries felt their bosses had come to "trust" them, as shown by the responsibilities they had given them. Again, however, the men managers rarely said as much to their secretaries.

Bringing them along. Women managers were not only seen as more considerate and appreciative but also as more supportive of the secretary as an individual with a career path of her own. The literature on this topic suggests that secretaries are seen as extensions or helpmates of their bosses, and that they can progress only if their bosses progress (Kanter 1977). Since the literature deals mostly with male bosses and their secretaries, the situation may be very different with the woman boss, particularly if she makes an effort to encourage her secretary to progress on her own. And these data suggest that she does.

The women managers I interviewed encouraged their secretaries in several ways. Some simply talked to their secretaries about their futures, often helping them to plan for it.

_____gives me lots of responsibility, more than other secretaries here who have been here much longer, and she has been telling her boss what a good job I'm going. I'm just thrilled. She told me that if I tell her what I want to do, she'll work to see that a position would be there for me when I'm ready for it. It's so wonderful to have a boss who looks out for you like that.

My boss has encouraged me to think about my career, going to school. She's talked with me about it a lot. She's the one who got me thinking about it.

Others encouraged the secretary's career growth by incorporating tasks "beyond the scope of secretary" into their daily routines. These tasks fostered autonomous career growth in two ways: 1) by preparing the secretaries for a specific job, or 2) by challenging them to perform at levels they might never have attempted otherwise.

Working for_____, I did things I've always wanted to do and never really had a chance to do before. She asked me what I liked and I told her writing, and she gave me lots of responsibilities like that. I got to use my interests, and now I notice things I never really did before. . . . My new boss doesn't even seem to notice me. I had broken my engagement several weeks before he even knew I had been engaged!

I was her secretary, but more than that. We were like a team, filling in where the other was weak. I felt I really found my niche working for her. It really broke my heart when they laid me off. I thought I would follow in her footsteps.

She trusts me. . . . She doesn't question what I do. She has confidence . . . that makes you feel good. I worked for the man that sat in here prior . . . and that was just a bad experience . . . He never let you do anything; he only told you what he wanted you to know. . . . I enjoy doing [these things] because she gives you credit. . . . Like with this book . . . she stepped out and she doesn't even look at it anymore.

One secretary simply found that her personal growth accelerated when she began working for women bosses. "I love my job and the ladies I work with. I feel I've found myself after all this time."

The situations described by the secretaries to the men were *very* different. Some were given responsibility — some even used similar words ("I'm more like his assistant"; "We're like a team") — but there were crucial differences. For one thing, these secretaries frequently reported being delegated responsibility for tasks they felt they did not have the authority to perform — for instance, managing their supervisor's subordinates. The result was not pleasure and challenge for the secretary but inordinate "hassles" as the secretary often felt "caught" between a demanding boss and a resentful subordinate. One of the secretaries talked about this explicitly.

I'm like on an equal level with another office worker . . . then my supervisor would put me in the position . . . of I have to correct her or him . . . I'm not real comfortable with that . . . If there was a position as lead secretary

. . . then it [would] be my responsibility . . . But when I'm . . . on the same level, I would feel maybe they would resent my telling them what to do or criticizing them. . . . . I really don't know why he feels I should do this kind of thing . . . I tell him I don't feel I should do that.

Another secretary noted the reaction of female professionals, in particular, when she went to them with criticisms her boss should perhaps have delivered.

They tend to take it personally and can't deal with that. . . . They can't take it constructively . . . Instead, you're attacking me and I get defensive and close off everything that you are saying to me.

Further, this secretary felt she was not being compensated for her work.

I don't get the acknowledgment with the responsibility . . . I really run the office . . . I'm not getting the recognition . . . for doing all this work, and I'm not getting it monetarily either because my check doesn't reflect it any more than some of the other secretaries who are not busy that many months of the year.

Several secretaries described the "diplomacy" necessary to persuade their boss's recalcitrant subordinates to deliver.

He and I run the department and I am accessible to the [subordinates] in the department. I let him know what's going on; I also tell them what he wants to be done and follow up on it . . . but it really comes from him . . . I do put a little pressure on them, but I do try to be businesslike . . . When something really has to get done . . . I am very straightforward . . . It does happen sometimes you have to go along with what they say.

But were these secretaries being given responsibility? One secretary thought not. "I don't think he gives me responsibility; I think he depends on me a lot." She was also expected to push subordinates to "deliver":

Sometimes, I have to guess what my boss is going to say, and based on that I'll give decisions to people . . . He tells someone to do something, and I'm the one that's got to be sure the thing gets done . . . One of our [officers] in particular struggles . . . in making deadlines. And I have to very nicely push without becoming a pain in the ass . . . If I can't get anywhere . . . I just take it back to_____ and say, "This is what you wanted done, and I'm not getting anywhere with it," and then he goes and raises hell.

Still another woman felt uncomfortable supervising — "I don't like telling people what to do . . . I feel like I don't want people to resent me because I'm shoving work on them . . ." — but she often found herself doing so:

This person, I don't know if you've visited him or not . . . He always has a "Why?" . . . A lot of things he can't see, but there are the procedures that

have to be followed . . . I'm sure because I am not on his level, he is above
me, he would rather talk to my boss, but when he has no choice, he has to
come to me.

Men managers were also less likely to delegate a task on the basis of its
benefit to the secretary (expanding her career horizon) than they were to delegate tasks they disliked doing.

He doesn't like the detail . . . He doesn't want to see all that little itty-bitty
stuff . . . He wants to know about it, but he doesn't want to do it, so he delegates
it to me, to the managers . . .

One secretary described the large volume of paperwork she did (sometimes things other supervisors in this organization did), while her supervisor
said:

It can be a paperwork nightmare, and I guess if there's any frustration that
I have with my job, it is the amount of paperwork that is involved . . .

Some of the men managers talked about their dislike for organizing, saying
they relied on their secretaries for this. The secretaries concurred.

I try to keep my boss on time and . . . organized . . . haul him out of one
meeting to get to another on time and make sure all the materials are ready
as he's flying out the door . . . and setting up appointments.

One secretary described a boss who had promised to give her more responsibility, but had so far not delivered. "He just hasn't had the time to sit
down and do it," she said.

Among all of these secretaries to men, there was only one case where
the manager was attempting to upgrade his secretary's position to be "more
administrative," and this man was close to retirement. Another manager
talked about a secretary he had helped to get such a promotion, but his view
was that,

. . . now, she regrets it . . . It's boring there . . . She misses being here, knowing so much about what's going on. And it will be hard on her marriage.

Helping secretaries develop their own careers did not seem to be of much
importance to these men managers.

Management Style: Orientation to Image, People, Autonomy, and Tasks

I have described elsewhere (Statham 1987) the two different management
models used by the men and women interviewed for this study. The men used
what I call an *image-engrossed, autonomy-invested* style. They talked more about

the importance of their work for the organization than they did about actually doing the work. They were also more likely to stress giving autonomy to subordinates rather than investing in their development. Hence, their approach to delegation was very different. The men said it was important to "give people the flexibility to do their jobs," or "assume the job is getting done unless I get complaints." For them, good management entailed *not* being involved in what their subordinates were doing. The basic strategy was to:

> . . . hire people with personalities that fit your needs and let them go . . . They'll work like crazy . . .

> . . . hire people who take pride in their work . . . and get out of their way.
> . . . Back off and let them do it.

> . . . search for good people and stay out of their way. And be certain they know what's expected.

Other men expressed it differently, but the upshot — minimal interference — was the same. The reasons given for the strategy sometimes involved the development of the individual: "If you don't give people that freedom . . . then they are not growing . . . If you are going to move forward, you have got to let people take risks."

But more often the reasons were job-related: "The more you interfere, the less gets done," or "I realize you can't hold people responsible if you make the decisions."

People are often more motivated if they feel they have a stake in the task. But one said what I suspect was really on the minds of many managers: "I want them to become less dependent on me, so I can become more independent."

Another man said that his "objective is to get through work in four hour days. That's really what I'd like to do."

The women used what I call a *task-engrossed, person-invested* style. Their focus was on getting the task done and investing in the development of others partly to that end. They were more likely to delegate and then provide follow-up.

> I delegate and make them very accountable for what they're doing, but I guess the people-side of me says, "Make sure you see them once in a while; know what they're doing."

Their secretaries appreciated that the women managers would ". . . follow up without making you feel that she's checking up on you . . . She's an *excellent* delegator." In doing so, tasks were more readily accomplished.

> She gives you an opportunity to expand . . . it's really neat the way she does it, because she applies the pressure, but she does it in such a way that you want to do it. You think, "Oh, how am I ever going to get this accomplished?" Then, after it's done, you look back and think, "I really did do that," and she has the confidence in you to make you want to do it.

The men and women definitely disapproved of each other's styles. For example, one secretary commented about the manner in which her male boss granted autonomy:

> I think I would be a little bit harder on them than he is. . . . I would definitely want to know certain things and would not take any type of bumbling excuse. If I'm trying to get a hold of somebody, you know, and I can't, I want to know why and where you are.

The men were apprehensive about the women's approach as well.

> _____ would get on the phone, and instead of spending a minute . . . she would spend two minutes. She knew everybody's wife or husband's name; she knew if they had kids and sometimes the kids' names . . . She was not placing her priorities in the right place. She was here to do a job . . . You can't go out to lunch with them and get chummy with them and then come back at 1:00 and say "Okay, you've got to do this job," and chew them out . . .

This man was clearly making an evaluation of the woman's capacity to perform, as was another who noted that differences in "how women relate to others . . . [being] more sensitive . . . can affect their performance . . . make them less willing to confront the problem and solve it."

Women often perceived the autonomy men gave them as "neglect." One woman talked about a manager who ". . . set me in an office across the street, . . . game me a stack of files, and said, "This is your job. Do it." I was totally frustrated; I had no guidance . . ."

This particular manager allowed that "eventually, it clicked," but it was a painful experience, and she was not using the autonomy-invested approach with her own subordinates. By two accounts (those of a secretary and manager subordinate), she used a very person-invested approach.

Management by Women: Investment in People and Tasks

In contrast to prevailing perceptions of women managers, the women in this study were *not* perceived as being *primarily* people-oriented. Their dedication and commitment to accomplishing the *tasks* were thought to be equally important. The secretaries perceived that the women did more work than the men. "Women strive to get the job done immediately. Men look to see who they can get to do the job for them." Men can get away with dumping their work onto someone else and walking out the door.

Women's "detail orientation," often portrayed as a negative trait, was viewed positively by the secretaries.

> Women are the motivators and organizers, the ones with the organization and energy to come up with new ideas and carry it through, and prioritize.

A man doesn't understand that it's all the little problems underneath the big ones that causes all the problems. A woman does.

The women managers agreed.

Woman carry a project through a little better; they can see other alternatives. Men have ideas but don't always implement support areas or details that have to go with it. That way they need others to bounce their ideas off of.

An important point here is that the women's people orientation was seen as a way of accomplishing the task. Hence, orientation to tasks and to people may not be as distinct as is commonly assumed in the literature on management — at least not for women managers. The women managers in this study more often used participative management techniques, albeit only partly for altrustic reasons: "I try to be as considerate as possible of the staff, to work around their needs," said one manager. And another, "I was a counselor once . . . and I knew how it felt, like, not to be contacted and not to be part of the decision making."

Women managers also used the techniques of participatory management to avoid challenges from their subordinates and to proceed with the task at hand, "If everyone's part of the decision, they feel more like carrying it out" or, "I get a lot of input from the staff . . . and by the time we make decisions, they accept it and I don't have a lot of problems with them."

Women who did not use this technique most often reported being challenged. For instance, one woman said she "preferred" participative decision-making but often felt one did "not have the time . . . maybe a year . . . to bring everyone up to a certain level of understanding," and so she would "not put people through the exercise," but would often make decisions herself. She reported something men who "decided on their own" did not experience: challenges that involved lengthy interactions and negotiations with subordinates, often ending with ultimatums.

I gave her some alternatives and asked her to decide, with a deadline . . . She could move to another job . . . or a number of other things. But that group was moving.

Seen from one perspective as a person-invested approach, the women managers' tendency to delegate large and rewarding tasks to their secretaries may also be seen as facilitating task accomplishment. Turning over entire tasks may free the managers to focus more fully on others.

In general, women managers believed personalized attention made their subordinates more effective and productive, "I feel that if my people are happy, they are going to do a better job for me, and they do."

DISCUSSION

This study shows differences between men and women managers that call into question the conventional wisdom on management styles. First, these findings contradict the common notion that women do not work well together (Harriman 1985; Ferber, Huber, and Spitze 1979; Kanter 1977). The women managers and secretaries interviewed for this study, with one exception, all enjoyed working together. Their professional relationships were mutually reinforcing, each recognizing the other's contributions and career needs. The relationships formed with men, while satisfying in their own right, seemed to involve the secretary in more traditional "helpmate" activities. Certainly, traditional sex-role definitions enter into these tendencies; women managers are apparently freer to form relationships beyond the traditional boss-secretary type.

This difference in relationships can be seen within a broader context of sex differences in management style. The women managers generally exhibited a person-invested style. Yet, in contrast to prevailing assumptions in the literature, they seemed to be equally task-oriented. In fact, their people orientation or person investment was often directly used to facilitate task accomplishment. This finding calls for a drastic rethinking of the distinction often made in the management literature between task and people orientations (cf. Stogdill 1974; White and Lippitt 1968; Fiedler 1967). Perhaps we should develop new typologies that allow us to emphasize both dimensions equally.

Other ways of distinguishing among managers are suggested by these findings, especially by the distinction outlined earlier between the task-engrossed, person-invested style of the men. Kanter (1983) suggests that organizations that encourage managers to preserve their limited base of traditional control and status will be less successful in adapting to the new demands of our world economy than those that encourage power sharing and emphasize outcome. It would be reasonable to conclude, based on the observations reported here, that women's management style could be a critical factor in helping us move from less productive, segmented organizations to the more adaptive, successful, change-supportive organizations acclaimed by Kanter.

The differences between the men and women managers are relevant for yet another reason. The fact that such pervasive differences emerged suggests the existence of alternative management models among men and women. Each appreciated their own sex-specific approach and disliked the other. These attitudes are especially critical for women managers, who are largely supervised and evaluated by men. To the extent that women are expected to focus on their own power in the workplace and provide autonomy to subordinates, they will be systematically judged inadequate. Yet women may not be managing *inadequately*; they may simply be doing so *differently*. The existence of these alternative approaches may represent a strength not a weakness, a fact that must be recognized in the literature and by those doing the evaluating. Otherwise, important contributions women can make to the art of managing will be needlessly lost.

REFERENCES

Brain, Robert. 1976. *Friends and Lovers*. New York: Basic Books.

Brown, Linda Keller. 1979. "Women and business management," *Signs: Journal of Women in Culture and Society* 5:267–88.

Caldwell, Mayta and Letitia Peplau. 1982. "Sex differences in same sex friendships," *Sex Roles* 8:721–32.

Cann, Carlton H. 1984. "Women, organization and power: Structural and individual perspectives,"*Women and Work Conference: Selected Papers*. Arlington: University of Texas at Arlington.

Deaux, Kay. 1979. "Self evaluations of male and female managers," *Sex Roles* 5:571–80.

Dubno, Peter. 1984. "Management attitudes toward women executives: A longitudinal approach." Working paper #83–95. New York University Graduate School of Business Administration, College of Business and Public Administration.

Ferber, Mariane, Joan Huber, and Glenna Spitze. 1979. "Preference for men as bosses and professionals," *Social Forces* 58:466–76.

Fiedler, Fred E. 1967. *A Theory of Leadership Effectiveness*. New York: McGraw-Hill.

Gilligan, Carol. 1982. *In a Different Voice*. Cambridge, MA: Harvard University Press.

Glaser, Barney G., and Anselm L. Strauss. 1967. *The Discovery of Grounded Theory: Strategies for Qualitative Research*. New York: Aldine Publishing Company.

Glenn, Evelyn, and Roslyn Feldberg. 1984. "Clerical work: The female occupation." In *Women: A Feminist Perspective*, 3rd ed., ed. Jo Freeman, pp. 316–336. Palo Alto, CA: Mayfield.

Grant, Linda. 1983. "Peer expectations about outstanding competencies of men and women medical students," *Sociology of Health and Illness* 5:42–61.

Harlan, Anne, and Carol Weiss. 1981. *Moving Up: Women in Managerial Career Ladders*. Wellesley College Center for Research on Women, Working Paper no. 86. Wellesley, MA.

Harriman, Ann. 1985. *Women/Men Management*. New York: Praeger.

Hennig, Margaret, and Anne Jardim. 1977. *The Managerial Women*. New York: Pocket Books.

Hochschild, Arlie Russell. 1983. *The Managed Heart: Commercialization of Human Feelings*. Berkeley: University of California Press.

Josefowitz, Nataska. 1985. *You're the Boss!* New York: Warner Books.

Kanter, Rosabeth Moss. 1977. *Men and Women of the Corporation.* New York: Basic Books.

————. 1983. *The Change Masters: Innovation for Productivity in the American Corporation.* New York: Simon and Schuster.

Komarovsky, Mirra. 1976. *Dilemmas of Masculinity: A Study of College Youth.* New York: Norton.

Massingill, Douglas, and Nicholas DiMarco. 1979. "Sex-role stereotypes and requisite management characteristics: A current replication," *Sex Roles* 5:561–70.

Moses, Joseph, and Virginia Boehm. 1975. "Relationship of assessment-center performance to management process of women," *Journal of Applied Psychology* 60:527–29.

Riger, Stephanie, and Pat Gilligan. 1980. "Women in management: An exploration of competing paradigms," *American Psychologist* 35:902–10.

Rosen, Benson, and Thomas Jerdee. 1978. "Perceived sex differences in managerially relevant characteristics," *Sex Roles* 4:837–43.

Rossi, Alice. 1972. "Women in science: Why so few?" In *Toward a Sociology of Women,* ed. Constantina Safilios-Rothchild, pp. 141–153. Lexington, MA: Xerox.

Rubin, Lillian. 1983. *Intimate Strangers.* New York: Harper and Row Publishers.

————. 1985. *Just Friends: The Role of Friendship in Our Lives.* New York: Harper and Row.

Statham, Anne. 1986. "Gender and management styles: Findings and implications." Paper presented at the annual meeting of the American Sociological Association, New York, August.

Statham, Anne. 1987. "The gender model revisited: Differences in management styles between men and women." *Sex Roles: A Journal for Research,* forthcoming.

Stogdill, R.M. 1974. *Handbook of Leadership: A Survey of Theory and Research.* New York: Free Press.

U.S. Commerce Dept. Bureau of the Census. 1980. United States summary. Chap. C, Part 1 of *Characteristics of the Population.* Vol. 1 of Census Population. Washington, DC: Bureau of the Census.

West, Candace. 1982. "Why can't a woman be more like a man?" *Work and Occupations* 9:5–29.

White, R., and R. Lippitt. 1968. "Leader behavior and member reaction in three "social climates."" In *Group Dynamics: Research and Theory*, D. Cartwright and A. Zander 3rd ed., pp. 318–335. New York: Harper and Row.

Wood, Marion, and Susan Greenfield. 1976. "Women managers and fear of success: A study in the field," *Sex Roles* 2:375–87.

CHAPTER 14

Women in Direct Sales: A Comparison of Mary Kay and Amway Sales Workers

MAUREEN CONNELLY AND PATRICIA RHOTON

Women who work in direct sales do not get involved as a result of a life-long dream to enter that field. Their entry could be explained more readily by the concept of "occupational drift" than "occupational choice." Working in direct sales is a "choice" heavily influenced by the fact that this is an occupation requiring little or no preparation or experience, no or few geographical restrictions, and in most cases a minimum amount of financial investment. Some contact with a direct sales organization seems to be almost a universal experience among adult American women — be it coerced participation in a neighbor's Tupperware party or merely occasional purchases from a local "Avon lady." For a significant number of women, however, this casual involvement leads to some formal affiliation. According to the Direct Selling Association (1984) the sales forces of these companies encompass approximately five million individuals, 80 percent of whom are women working part time. The social science literature has directed scant attention to this phenomenon. Given the number of women estimated to be involved in this activity (four million), part time direct sales work is clearly an important area of study.

This paper looks at the experiences of women in direct sales, particularly women involved in two major sales organizations — Mary Kay Cosmetics and Amway Corporation. These two corporations were selected because their organizations and day to day operations seem to reflect differences between a "masculine" and "feminine" work culture. These differences appear in the structural aspects of these organizations as well as in the motivation for women's involvement. Analysis is based on participant observation of these organizations and their activities over a three-year period and a series of in-depth inter-

245

views with a sample of 20 women who had participated or were currently involved in Mary Kay or Amway.

RELEVANT LITERATURE

The sociology literature has devoted little attention to the direct sales
phenomenon. (See Green and D'Aiuts 1977, Taylor 1978 for the few existing
studies.) Most discussions have appeared in business pubications (e.g. Bage 1980,
Coburn 1982, Koil 1981). The literature on similar occupations, for example,
on self-employment, does not provide useful insights, particularly regarding
women. This literature deals with the specific nature of self-employment; i.e.,
the characteristics of those who attempt to start their own businesses or the
characteristics of those successful and nonsuccessful in their self-employment
ventures (Daum 1984). Most of this research concentrates on men, limiting its
relevance for women in direct sales. Other works in this area have either looked
at the nature of direct sales organizations in general while concentrating on
Tupperware specifically (Peven 1968) or looked at women historically in the more
structured setting of retail sales in department stores (Benson 1983).

Sex differences in occupations have been neglected partly because of a
reluctance in the social sciences to explore general sex differences, given the
political impact of this scholarly work. The first major wave of social science
research concerned with differences coincided with the rebirth of the women's
movement in the 1960s. Research during that wave seemed either to downplay
the existence of sex differences (see Maccoby and Jacklin 1974), or to argue for
the socialized basis for observed differences. This wave of research aimed at
distinguishing between biological sex, which for the most part are unalterable,
and gender or sex roles, which are variable, socialized and therefore alterable.

Friedan's "second stage of the women's movement" (Friedan 1981) appears to parallel a comparable second stage of research and writing emerging
in the 1980s. Exemplified in the work of Gilligan (1982), this research reexamines
issues of sex differences. Rather than denying that any differences exist, it af-
firms a distinct women's culture, a distinct female experience. It deemphasizes
questions of causality and argues for the legitimization of sex differences and
the valuation of the distinctly feminine.

METHODOLOGICAL APPROACH

Information on the two direct sales organizations under consideration
here has been gathered in a number of ways. Participant observation with the
Amway organization, the organization studied more extensively, included attendance at rallies or group meetings (24 within a 12 month period), reading
Amway motivational literature, listening to tapes on a weekly basis and becoming involved in numerous discussions with Amway distributors. For comparative

purposes, contact was also established with Mary Kay consultants. This contact consisted of attendance at Mary Kay parties, training meetings and regional gatherings.

During the summer of 1985, more formal interviews were undertaken. Twenty women (ten from each organization) were interviewed. Snow ball sampling procedures were used to generate interviews in Columbus, Ohio and Frostburg, Maryland (*i.e.*, initial contacts were asked to provide names of two other potential interviewees). The instrument used was an open-ended questionnaire focusing on aspects of the women's motivation for participation; satisfaction and problems encountered; information detailing her life cycle stage and standard demographic data. Interviews were conducted in the women's home using tape recorders. Although written notes were made during the taping, the interviews were later transcribed for more detailed analysis. The discussions and analysis that follow incorporate responses from these interviews as well as material from the participant observations.

TWO MAJOR DIRECT SALES ORGANIZATIONS

Direct selling can be seen as "the marketing of products or services directly to a consumer, on a one-to-one or small group (party plan) basis" (July 1985: 1). Companies such as Shaklee, Avon, Tupperware, Fuller Brush, Home Interiors, Amway and Mary Kay are examples of direct sales organizations currently operating in the United States and in some cases internationally. Mary Kay and Amway were chosen because of a number of similarities between the two. Both were formed by charismatic leaders who remain intimately involved in the current operation of the organization. Both are appropriately classified as multilevel marketing organizations in which the individual entrepreneur is both wholesaler and retailer. Both require that the worker engage in selling the corporation's products and recruiting other "salespersons." Both distribute products that are readily available locally considerably cheaper. Although the product lines carried by these two organizations are very different, both distribute products that are at the upper end of the scale in terms of price and quality. Mary Kay has a number of different products all related in some way to skin care or makeup. Amway started out with a single line of soaps, but now has a wide range of products such as water treatment systems, vitamins, safety equipment, satellite disks and a "personal shopper's catalog" similar but smaller than Sears' or J.C. Penney's.

Certain work is basic to all direct sales organizations — selling the company's products and recruiting others to do the same. Yet numerous and important differences exist between these two organizations. First, aspects of the reward system vary. Amway emphasizes cash incentives for both sales and recruitment. Successful movement up the Amway distributor ranks results in a increasing profit percentage. While this system exists as well in Mary Kay Cosmetics, emphasis is placed on nontransferable goods-in-kind as rewards.

Success in Mary Kay is motivated by incentives of furs, jewelry, and cars which the company gives to successful consultants.

Structural links between the individual and the corporation also differ. Amway emphasizes a rigid hierarchical structure, and a distributor's link to the corporation is mediated by various levels. Bookkeeping on product sales and distribution of profit checks and other routine aspects of Amway "work" are routed through the upline sponsors or downline recruits. Distributors are counseled to be cognizant of the hierarchical structure even in disclosing their personal frustrations as Amway Distributors. Frustrations and complaints are never to be shared with subordinates downline; rather, the distributor is instructed to take problems upline and to share successes downline. The first direct contact the individual has with the corporation beyond filing the initial application does not occur until the person reaches the status of direct distributor — a position obtained with monthly sales of $7,000 plus and achieved by relatively few in the distributor ranks. In contrast, consultants in Mary Kay have a more direct and unmediated link to the corporation. Admittedly, a hierarchical structure exists in Mary Kay. Subordinate to each consultant are those they have recruited — termed "offspring." Yet routine aspects of the work, such as orders, are not routed through the hierarchical structure but carried out by each individual consultant, who is directly linked to the company.

While both organizations strongly support the ideal of the traditional family, the two differ in the way that a woman functions within the organizational structure. Women working in Amway are most often involved initially by their spouse. A traditional division of labor exists and is perpetuated within the Amway family, with the wife performing the secretarial and bookkeeping functions in the home while the husband goes out and shows the plan and sponsors new recruits. The value system emphasizes achievement and success as traditionally defined by how much money an individual is making. In contrast, Mary Kay seems to reflect a uniquely feminine work experience. Spouses of consultants have peripheral involvement in their wives' work. There is also a great deal of emphasis placed on nurturance and support, which coexists and even dominates the emphasis on success.

GETTING INVOLVED IN DIRECT SALES

Reasons for engaging in direct sales are varied. Women often seek this essentially part time employment for its convenience. They can make extra money, perform most of their work at home, structure the work day and fit the work into the confines of their existing life and its associated constraints.

The route to involvement varies in the two organizations. Mary Kay consultants make their own choice to become involved. Although they may have been encouraged to participate by family or friends, particularly if these are Mary Kay consultants, their decisions have not been precipitated by their husbands. In contrast, in Amway the husband in the family is usually the first person approached as a potential recruit.

The Amway woman is more often than not unmotivated to participate. She usually does not share her husband's vision of immediate and dramatic financial success. Rather, she often anticipates the extra work of their involvement — the products that need to be transported and the paperwork that needs to be completed and transmitted. When women are motivated initially to join Amway, it is often for reasons other than the expected financial gain. For example, the wife may see this work as a way of improving the family's and the couple's relationship. She thinks she can become involved in her husband's work in a way not possible in his traditional job. Amway can be seen as a way of improving her relationship with her husband, as something they can "share together."

Additional motivators for participation are evident in the company's suggestions for appealing to potential recruits. Amway emphasizes the "democratic" nature of participation: no individual can buy into the Amway corporation — movement up the hierarchy must be earned. Furthermore, Amway equalizes traditional social class advantages: formal education is not a prerequisite for success. Anyone can be successful so long as they follow the plan and work hard. Mary Kay stresses the concept of flextime; young mothers can stay home with their children during the day and schedule their parties at night, while mothers with older children can schedule their parties during the day and be home when the children return from school.

THE WORK OF DIRECT SALES

Some physical labor is involved in the selling of both organizations' products, but the two companies vary in the amount of physical labor required. This difference is related not only to the type of product sold but also to the organization's procedures for distributing products and processing paperwork. Physical labor is more intense in the Amway organization: the product comes in larger quantities and larger containers, and distributors must pick up their orders at the home of the upline distributor. The order is broken down as downline distributors arrive to pick up their portions of the consolidated order, and this pattern is repeated until the product is delivered to a consumer. Within Amway "families," a standard pattern of division of labor exists in which these tasks are relegated to the wife. Mary Kay has a more "refined" approach to product distribution: orders are smaller in bulk and are delivered by UPS to each consultants' home. The physical labor consists of unloading the smaller size boxes and taking them to individual customers.

The distribution of the products is, however, only a minor aspect of the labor involved in selling. Getting people to use the products encompasses emotional and mental labor and impression management. Both companies purposefully socialize their workers for these various activities. In Mary Kay consultants are instructed to offer potential customers a "free facial" as a vehicle for introducing the product line. These facials can be performed on an individual basis or in a group party setting. Regardless of the setting, the facials are carefully structured — consultants are trained to introduce each product in a precise and standard fashion. Once a product has been purchased consultants are advised in ways to maintain contact with the consumer and encourage continued consumption. For example, they are advised to send each customer a birthday card and to allow the person a product discount as a birthday present.

The selling of Mary Kay products is couched in a nurturance ideology. At meetings for current and potential consultants, the altruistic nature of their work is often emphasized. Selling Mary Kay is defined as important work since "you are helping other women become more beautiful."

In discussing the work of selling in the Amway organization, it is important to distinguish between the official company position and that articulated by various 'groups' within the Amway organization. The term "group" refers to large organizational structures which have emerged around key people within the organization. Technically, all direct distributors have their own groups as soon as they sponsor someone. Their group consists of persons they have sponsored directly and the people that their recruits have sponsored. While all distributors can have their own groups, some are considerably more active than others. An indication of the size and the prominence of a particular direct distributor and the resultant group is whether or not the group is referred to by that direct distributor's name.

The official position of the Amway Company regarding selling and recruitment is quite similar to that of Mary Kay. Distributors are to perform two major tasks, selling products and recruiting other members into the organization. Furthermore, distributors are encouraged to sell their products by demonstrating the product's use. As with Mary Kay, the person is instructed to do so using a structured presentation, either before individual potential customers or groups of customers.

Some of the more prominent groups within the Amway organization, however, deemphasize selling to customers. Rather they suggest that Amway work consists of merely recruiting other families who will consume approximately $100.00 worth of Amway products per month. Instead of selling products the recruit only has to sell the idea of selling the idea.

Furthermore, Amway distributors are encouraged to become the ultimate Amway consumers: members of some groups are encouraged to purge themselves of all "poison products" from their homes — i.e., those not available through Amway. Distributors often point with pride to their attire reassuring their potential recruits that all items on their body are available from the Amway catalog. "If Amway doesn't sell it you don't need it." Sponsoring or recruiting other members is the second major task in multilevel direct sales organizations. All such organizations encourage their members to recruit other members, and they provide monetary incentives for doing so. In each organization, the sponsor receives a proportion of the sales generated by recruits. Amway and

Mary Kay differ, however, in some important aspects of this recruitment.

The two organizations seem to differ in how sponsorship relates to the hierarchical structure of the sales force. Lineage and hierarchy appear to be reinforced in the Amway organization. "Downline" and "upline" are omnipresent in the Amway vocabulary. The organization reinforces this hierarchy in its incentive operation: if the recruit's immediate sponsor should drop out of the organization, their percentage of the recruit's sales goes to that sponsor's sponsor. No similar mechanism exists in Mary Kay; there, when a consultant drops out of the company, the 3 percent portion of recruit's sales reverts to the parent organization.

In Mary Kay, a nurturance theme seems to be reflected in sponsorship and the language used to describe aspects of it. Individuals sponsored are called "offspring" — a marked contrast to the term "downline" used in Amway. Should a Mary Kay consultant be geographically distant from her sponsor, the emotional support and training provided by this relationship can be acquired from a surrogate. In such a situation, the "offspring" gets "adopted" by a consultant working in the same geographic area. This geographically proximate consultant receives no monetary compensation for "adopting." However, a strong norm encourages her to provide the same services and support to her adopted offspring as to her own offspring, whose sales she directly profits from. This policy is in marked contrast to the Amway procedure, in which reliance is put solely on the upline person. Regardless of geographic distance, the sponsor is required to perform the training and motivational function. This expectation applies even to the mechanics of the product distribution. A distributor, for example, even at a great geographic distance, must still channel their downline's orders, if necessary, mailing the products down line. The Amway organization has a mechanism for switching groups, but the procedure is formal in nature and rarely used. A distributor can switch to a geographically proximate group only with the agreement of all parties involved. Since this switch will result in the termination of the original sponsor's percentage of the recruit's sales, there is little incentive for the sponsor to agree to this arrangement.

Furthermore, the members in the two organizations differ in their emphasis on the sponsorship function and, seemingly, their degree of comfort with this activity. We have seen that in some Amway groups, sponsorship is presented as the only work involved in participation and as work entailing very little labor. Although the Amway corporation itself repeatedly warns against using this "chain letter" approach in the presentation of the plan the strength and regularity of such warnings are evidence of the frequency of such patterns.

At Mary Kay meetings, sponsorship is down-played. Recruiting other women is mentioned, yet the fact that a person financially profits from such activity is not emphasized. A number of women we interviewed talked of sponsorship as the "least attractive" aspect of their experience. One individual has been working as a Mary Kay consultant for four years. Throughout the interview, she outgoingly discussed how Mary Kay "changed her life." Yet, when talking of recruitment of others she became uncomfortable, shy, hesitant and said "I guess I need to work on that . . . but I don't know . . . somehow I don't feel right asking other people to join," and was unable to articulate why she was uncomfortable recruiting others. She has four "offspring," and talked at length of the satisfaction she got working with them — and yet, she hesitated to recruit and viewed herself as "needing to work on this." In hearing women like her talk of recruitment, we felt their hesitancy was tied to unarticulated issues of exploitation, and somehow recruiting others and financially profiting from their recruits' work seemed unnatural and not quite right.

A final aspect of sponsorship is what could be termed the secondary market aspect of this activity. Both Mary Kay and Amway make a multitude of training and facilitating products available to the recruit. The products range from motivational tapes and books to a computer designed for the direct sales home office. These products, designed to enhance the recruit's success as a direct sales worker, are consumed by the sales force, and they need them solely because of their involvement in Mary Kay and Amway. The two companies differ in the extensiveness of this secondary market and its relationship to the sponsorship activity.

Mary Kay's secondary market products are fewer in number and are purchased directly from the parent company. An Amway distributor is exposed to a much larger array of motivational products and these are often retailed by the distributor's group as well as by the company. Certain Amway groups produce and market their own motivational materials. For example, one such group distributes for purchase by its downline a motivational "book of the month," "tape of the week," and "rally of the quarter." The upline in this group profits then not only from their downline's sales of Amway products, but also from the downline's consumption of the motivational aids.

IMPRESSION MANAGEMENT

Impression management occurs throughout both of these organizations. Each encourages conformity to an organizational dress code coupled with a positive attitude and outlook on life. Subtly, each seems to justify these behavioral and attitudinal presentations of self in light of other aspects of the organization's ideology.

Mary Kay stresses that the well-groomed woman never leaves her house without being "made up." "Looking Good and Feeling Great" is a term used by various consultants to summarize this norm. In her autobiography, the organization's founder, Mary Kay, articulates the justifications for and functions of this activity. Positing a link between outward experience and emotional state, she writes "A tremendous change comes over a woman when she's looking good and knows it. A woman's psychology is such that when she looks attractive, she becomes more confident" (Ash 1981, 129). Cultivation of a consultant's grooming is then encouraged not merely as a vehicle for advertising the company's products, but as a technique for promoting the growth of the women involved. Like the dissonance theorists, Mary Kay posits the need to change behavior first, with the idea that internal changes will automatically follow. She describes, for example, a consultant who initially struggled with her sales. The woman was encouraged to buy a new dress and then almost immediately increased her sales. "The secret was that at long last she was confident that she looked good. And, with her new self confidence, she was able to project more enthusiasm and conviction in her presentation" (Ash 1981, 130).

A similar justification is given for the organization's emphasis on a positive outlook. "Mary Kay Enthusiasm" and the idea "You Can Do It" are keynotes in the presentation of self. Again the emphasis is on the ramifications these ideas have for the women involved. "For me, the most meaningful thing about the growth of Mary Kay Cosmetics has been seeing so many women achieve. All of us here thrive on helping instill in other women the 'You can do it' spirit. So many women just don't know how great they really are. They come to us all vogue on the outside and vague on the inside. It's so rewarding to watch them develop and grow" (Ash 1981, 8). Thus impression management in Mary Kay is tied to personal growth as well as being a tool for the sale of the products.

Amway also has a dress code for its distributors. Men are expected to wear suits and ties; women are expected to wear dresses, heels and makeup. Sports jackets on men and pants on women are viewed as not adequately conveying the Amway image — one of a professional albeit an at-home entrepreneur. Concurrent with this code of dress, distributors are expected to convey a positive and enthusiastic attitude when dealing with the world. Uplines, for example, will coach recruits on the appropriate response to the inquiry "How are things going?" Amway distributors are instructed to respond with a "Great, never been better" and to do so with conviction and enthusiasm. In some of the Amway interviews, the women involved expressed their initial discomfort with this policy. One distributor described her distrust and perception of it as being "phony." "It's not normal to be that 'up' all the time." Distributors are instructed never to reveal their doubts and concerns to those below them in the organization, "Never say anything negative downline." Rather, if feeling less than enthusiastic and great, the recruit is to bring these concerns upline.

DIVISION OF WORK TIME WITHIN DIRECT SALES

For most of the women interviewed, work in direct sales organizations is essentially a part time activity. Asking them to articulate how they divided their time, for example, how many hours they devoted to attending rallies and meetings, seemed a fruitless activity. They were often stunned by this question, would struggle with it for a while and then would almost lament "I can't really say . . . That's so difficult to answer."

There are a number of explanations for this difficulty. Often, the total amount of time devoted to the direct sales organization fluctuated during their phases of involvement. "Are you talking about the time I spend now or when I first joined or when I was most into Amway?," one woman asked. Furthermore, one of the prime motivators these women often had for being involved in direct sales is the very irregularity of the time allocation and the possibility of their controlling their own allocation. In contrast to traditional nine-to-five jobs, direct sales can be "fitted" into the day and other rhythms of life. One successful Mary Kay distributor, for example, varies her schedule seasonally. A golf enthusiast, she works more than full time during the colder months of the year. During the summer, she takes a vacation from Mary Kay. Other distributors and consultants "fit" their work into the demands of their family life and other employment if they are already in an employment situation. The Mary Kay organization specifically states that Mary Kay work should be subordinate to family demands — "God first, family second, career third" (Ash 1981, 56). In discussing her own experience with other direct sales work, Ash writes:

> ... One of the nicest things about my flexible hours was that I could always be home to give my tender loving care if one of the children was ill. There was very little I ever let interfere with my work — except my family. Employers need to understand that these are a woman's priorities. I've seen women with nine-to-five jobs come to work when they had a very sick child at home. In my opinion, their employers would have been better off to tell them to stay at home and take care of the child. There's no way a mother can keep her mind on her work when she's worried about a sick child (1981, 60).

THE PLEASURES OF DIRECT SALES

Motivation for seeking particular employment is related to, but not synonomous with, the pleasures of the work. Often when selecting a type of work, motivation comes from the anticipated pleasures of the work, from what the person discerns as its pleasures. At times, however, the pleasures of work are emergent phenomena — almost unexpected by-products of the employment. In our interviews, we asked for both the reasons for choosing direct sales as well as what the interviewee saw as "the most attractive aspects" of her work. Often, the women interviewed linked these two. They referred back to their motivation when addressing the pleasures. Yet at times, the question regarding pleasures elicited very different information. One woman, for example, talked of the impact Mary Kay work has on her children. Since becoming involved in direct sales, she sees her family as being affected by the company's "You Can Do It!" philosophy. Thus, she described her children as becoming more positive, confident and enthusiastic as a result of her work.

Not only was a range of pleasures articulated, but they often differed from those articulated by the organizations. The Amway organization, for example, in its motivational tapes and rallies, emphasizes the pleasure of new found wealth. A typical plan presentation found in some Amway groups starts by asking the potential recruits to fantasize their dream home or vacation. Commenting on the gestalt of an Amway rally, 60 Minutes concluded "What they are really selling is — the hope of getting rich beyond your wildest dreams" (1983, 2). Some of the Amway women interviewed mentioned that this idea of making "easy money" was one of their initial reasons for getting involved. Those who dropped out of Amway often linked their dissatisfaction to their failure to achieve this dream of unlimited and easy wealth. Most of the women detailed pleasures often not addressed by the Amway organization. For example, they met friends through the rallies and meetings, they got to spend some time traveling with their husbands without their children, or they came in contact with a group of people who "looked together." Interestingly, one theme promoted by sponsors and at rallies was never mentioned by the women we interviewed. Amway is often touted as a means of getting free from the clock — the successful distributor gets to "throw the alarm clock out," often in the midst of a celebration specifically for that purpose. Yet, none of the women interviewed mentioned this, even those who have worked or were working in more traditional and time structured employment. Perhaps this is a pleasure or a theme more suited to the male Amway recruits. Perhaps women, particularly those encumbered by the demands of child care, cannot fathom a life in which work-related demands are ever entirely restricted to certain times of the day.

Mary Kay similarly attempts to attract with a vision of material success. Furs, jewelry, and the ultimate, a pink Cadillac, are pleasures to be reaped by the successful consultants. Some of the women interviewed mentioned that working for Mary Kay resulted in "things I'd probably never buy for myself." However, the theme most addressed in the interviews was the flexibility they had with respect to the time afforded by their work — "I can fit Mary Kay in."

THE PROBLEMS IN DIRECT SALES

In a similar vein, in our interviews, we asked the women to articulate the "least attractive aspects" of their work. As one might expect, more problems were addressed by those who had aborted or curtailed their involvement prior to our interviews. Former Amway women seemed more bitter in their discussions. They often saw the problems they experienced as externally caused and linked to some deception by sponsors and the Amway corporation. One woman, for example, focused on the effort involved to be successful. She initiated involvement, thinking that it would entail very little time, and dropped out when she realized "more time was needed." Others complained that they discovered that they weren't making enough money. When their dream for unlimited wealth was not realized, they became disenchanted with the work.

In our Mary Kay interviews, the women more often talked of their own personal problems in executing the work. A number discussed their problems recruiting, their reluctance to approach friends or family, or their fears and anxieties regarding "cold bookings" (approaching complete strangers).

These problems seem to be both intrinsic and extrinsic to the work per se. Sales and recruitment by their very nature entail some imposition upon others. Mary Kay women, as previously stated, often addressed this and their difficulty in doing so. When asked to speculate on what types of people are more successful in direct sales, they often described people who were more aggressive than they. Amway complaints often were extrinsic to the work per se — the previously discussed discrepancy between their promised "easy money" and the reality of their commission checks.

Our analysis also suggests that there are problems in the rules and roles of the organization. Within the direct sales normative structure, a paradox exists. The worker is viewed as free, an independent, at-home entrepreneur. Yet within both organizations, workers experience extensive normative constraints. Codes of dress and set routines for presentation of products and recruitment of other members are restrictions on one's freedom. Although these structures can aid in making the transition into sales, they also limit the worker's options.

A model of the perfect family unit is fostered by some of the more successful Amway groups. Their rallies and tapes presented the specialization of functions within the family unit as a requisite for success. The husband in such a family functioned in the public arena — charged with the tasks of presenting the plan and recruiting others. The wife in such a family functioned in the background. Ever supportive, she performed the "clerical" aspects of the work — did the bookkeeping, and moved the products through the various distributor channels. Although it was agreed that singles can do it too, the suggested route to success consistently portrayed this ideal family unit.

In Mary Kay, this traditional division of labor does not exist. This organization recruits women, not family units. Although at the yearly meetings there are some activities for Mary Kay husbands, the organization has minimal expectations regarding their actual participation. At best, the husband is expected to be emotionally supportive of his wife's work. He may babysit the children while she does facials and encourage her involvement, but rarely does he participate in the work itself.

SOLVING THE PROBLEMS IN DIRECT SALES

A variety of coping mechanisms exist for solving the problems extrinsic and intrinsic to this work. Getting out or "sneaking out" of the organization appears to be the dominant solution used by individuals as a response to problems. Becoming involved in direct sales, in contrast to other forms of work, often entails minimal investment from the individual. One does not undergo a formal education as training for this work, and setting up the business can be done with a minimal monetary investment. Ergo, when confronted by problems, a relatively easy solution exists in getting out — deciding to no longer be a direct sales worker. Mechling, for example, estimates that three out of four Amway sales distributors quit after the first year (1980, 462). This was the strategy used by almost half of the women we interviewed. Some severed their ties to the organization. Some "snuck out," maintaining a nominal affiliation, but viewing themselves as no longer "working" in direct sales. One woman, for example, described herself as now merely being "a good customer." She maintains her official affiliation as an option for her retirement years.

Criticism of direct sales organizations often focuses on former members who have large inventories which cannot be returned to the company. This is a function of inventory loading — a practice in which the direct sales entrepreneur is coerced into purchasing large quantities of products in order to qualify for certain incentives. A recent court case in California (Barlett versus Patterson, *et al.*) addressed such an occurrence. The plaintiffs charged that their Amway upline coerced them into purchasing over $50,000 in products to qualify for the status of "direct distributor" (Juth 1985, 16). None of the women we interviewed had this experience.

Aside from this coping mechanism, our interviewees did not directly address the issue of their coping strategies. However, we thought that coping mechanisms were reflected in their discussions. Lack of success, for example, is often coped with in one of two ways. Some women blamed the parent organization and deemed themselves as having been misled when they were originally recruited. Some of the elements that seemed most attractive in the beginning were ultimately blamed for failure. Workers are afforded unlimited flexibility in the amount of time devoted to their work, yet this flexibility and the fact that the worker determines it seems to relieve the organization from responsibility for individual failure. Success is often, even by the workers, equated with effort. If the recruit is not doing well — not making the fortune one had come to anticipate — failure to do so is often attributed to not putting in enough time. Such internalization of responsibility and blame seems to be reflected in their analyses regarding success. They seem to believe that if only they had been more aggressive or invested more effort they might have realized their dream.

CONFLICTS BETWEEN DIRECT SALES AND OTHER ASPECTS OF THE WOMAN'S LIFE

Our interviews and observations suggest that in contrast to other types of work, direct sales is less likely to create problems in other spheres. By its very nature, this work can be fit into one's existing life demands and constraints. In fact, given the ideology of both Mary Kay and Amway — that family is important — women in direct sales were unlikely to say that they experienced conflicting role demands. Women in Mary Kay, for example, often quote the organization's prioritization — God first, family second, Mary Kay third — when asked to address this issue. They often described how legitimate it is in Mary Kay to cite family obligations as a reason for not doing some Mary Kay work.

A few of the women we interviewed described some conflict with their extended family and friends. These conflicts revolved not around the issue of competing demands but rather around the perceived legitimacy of their work. Thus, they described their family as being critical of the direct sales organization and not supportive of their work. One respondent said she would never forget what her mother said when she got into Mary Kay, "You have a college degree and you're peddling lipstick!" Such conflicts seemed to be dealt with by avoidance. The women talked of avoiding the issue — not mentioning the organization and their involvement when interacting with these individuals.

THE REALITIES OF DIRECT SALES FROM AN ECONOMIC STANDPOINT

While prescribed recruitment material tells the recruiter to stress the positive aspect of self-employment, it has little to say about the start-up costs involved in establishing such a business. Costs involved in purchasing special telephone equipment such as an answering machine or a device to record phone conversations can be considerable. Even if the recruit decides to start out with just the basics, not investing in office and storage equipment, there are still numerous items as product handouts, samples, customer gifts, and supplemental literature. All of these items are designed to bring the products to potential purchaser's attention and to keep the products in their minds. However the cost of these items has to be taken out of whatever profit is made by the individual doing the direct selling.

Money is made in two ways in a direct sales organization. First the difference between what the worker pays for the product and what the worker sells the product for is profit; however, this amount is affected by a number of factors. Each organization has built-in incentives to increase the volume of products sold so the more product that the individual purchases from the company the less the products cost. This practice can have serious consequences for the recruits of an individual who is trying to build volume quickly since they may encourage their recruits to purchase a large inventory irrespective of the recruit's ability to sell.

Purchased inventory can be an incentive to a recruit in the sense that the large amounts of money tied up in inventory can certainly motivate one to do some selling. However, if the recruit decides that he or she no longer wants to be involved in the organization it may be awkward to return the products. Some women seem to feel that it is easier to withdraw from the organization if they do not try to return the products they have purchased. In some cases this is because the products have some use to the individual — some can be used by the household, some can be given away as gifts or some can be sold either at cost or at a loss. Others are left with larger quantities of products that they cannot use or feel comfortable trying to sell. Since both organizations have a very liberal return policy it seems that the reason individuals end up with large unsold inventories of goods is not the actual difficulties of returning the goods but the difficulty of facing their sponsor and announcing their intention to quit. In order to avoid this, it becomes easier to keep the inventory and so avoid any confrontation.

In both organizations there is a financial advantage to be gained in a situation in which the sponsor has a number of recruits who make regular sales to a small group of individuals. This advantage occurs because the recruit who sells the item to a customer absorbs the cost of the sale and yet may make only a 3 percent or 6 percent bonus or profit on the transaction because their overall volume is below a certain level. If the sponsor has enough volume to be at a higher profit level then the difference in profit percentage goes to the sponsor, rewarding the sponsor for the time, energy, and money spent on training and motivating recruits.

From the company's perspective there are a number of advantages in using this type of sales personnel. First, the company invests absolutely no money in the salesperson until that individual has risen far enough in the organization to have already made a firm commitment to the company itself. If the individual does not make any sales, the company is under no obligation to give any money to the salesperson. Nor does the company have to worry about such costly and/or time-consuming items as pension plans, social security taxes, unemployment compensation, workman's compensation or health plans. This is different from a situation where the salesperson works on a draw until their sales are high enough to work for straight commission.

Also, each recruit provides his or her own warehouse space, office, office help, supplies, typewriters, phones, file cabinets, shelving and photocopying equipment. They purchase the forms needed to do the paperwork that the company requires, from the company itself. In actuality these companies have two related lines, one involving the sale of the actual products and a secondary business of selling sales and motivational support material to the salesperson. This material can be used either to make the sales process easier or more professional or keep the level of interest and effort high.

NONECONOMIC RETURNS FROM PARTICIPATION IN DIRECT SALES

The heart of the direct sales organization is the distribution system. This system itself has many advantages for the distributor. Its basic appeal lies in the ready made support network of individuals who are not going to make any money unless the new recruit succeeds in selling the product at some level. Unless the person sponsored either buys the product for their own use or sells the product to others, no money changes hands. Thus sponsors will make a concerted effort to help their recruits to the very best of their ability. In many cases the training period is a pleasant time of constructive dreaming of what if, of goal setting, meeting new people, sharing new experiences, and in some cases traveling to new places.

This participation in direct sales can also precipitate a change with respect to the women's entry or reentry into other parts of the labor force. One woman who is a makeup and wardrobe consultant became involved in Mary Kay as a side to her existing business. Others found outside jobs when they realized that they were not making enough money through their sales work. Some went into direct sales when they could not find a job they wanted in their geographic area. The most successful Mary Kay woman interviewed had left a job that she had begun to dislike intensely.

CONCLUSIONS: DIRECT SALES AND A FEMALE WORK CULTURE

The primary analysis of direct sales presented here suggests a number of themes related to larger issues relevant to women and work: integration of work and family, a distinct female work culture or experience, and exploitation of women workers.

Traditionally women more than men confront the need to balance work with family or home responsibility. Women who are employed outside the home often do a "double day." While these women allocate fewer hours daily or weekly to household responsibility than do full time homemakers, they spend more time on these tasks than do their spouses. Blumstein and Schwartz, for example, conclude from their study of American couples, "working women . . . still do the vast bulk of [housework]" (1983, 145). Furthermore, they see women interweaving their work and family concerns; wives allow their relationships to affect their jobs and their jobs to affect their relationships (1983, 155). For example, when women select their place of employment they often use criteria that reflect their family responsibility. They choose a particular job because it is convenient to the house, daycare, or their children's school.

Direct sales work then seems almost ideally suited to the interweaving of work and family. The ideology of direct sales companies often espouses consideration of family concerns and, if anything, allows family responsibility to override work. The flexible hours of direct sales pragmatically facilitate this balancing of work and family.

The idea that women have a distinct culture, a mode of experiencing, that distinguishes them from men is the thesis advocated by Gilligan (1982) and others. Gilligan suggests that relationships are primary considerations for women, that female solutions to moral problems, for example, tend to emphasize the ethics of care, human attachment, and the resolution of conflict through communication and cooperation. That this distinct culture might be reflected in the world of work seems plausible and seems to integrate numerous findings and speculations regarding women and their work (see Statham, chapter 13, this volume). The low status of the teaching, nursing, and social work professions which women have historically dominated, all emphasize nurturance and helping.

The idea of a distinctive female work culture and perhaps a distinctive female work experience have been present throughout our analysis. It is our thesis that Mary Kay is different from Amway in some important ways, and that these differences reflect a female work culture. A number of aspects of Mary Kay work seem to echo this culture: the theme of nurturance; the less rigid hierarchical structure; the ambivalence regarding exploitation; and the nature of the reward system.

Nurturance, caring for others, appears as a dominant theme in Mary Kay work. The work itself is touted as nurturing — "You are helping other women become more beautiful." Caring for and helping others was mentioned or alluded to so frequently that an uninformed observer might have concluded that the usual Mary Kay meeting was a meeting for social workers or others in the "helping" professions. Not only is nurturance emphasized in the relationship with customers, it also permeates the organizational's internal relationships. The terminology of "offspring" and "adopters" symbolically conveys a maternal and nurturing relationship, particularly when these terms are compared to their Amway equivalent, "downline." That adopting exists as a viable alternative to overcome problems of geographical distance likewise suggests the importance of support within the organization.

The nurturing aspect of the company's founder is also emphasized. A highlight of the yearly meeting in Dallas is the invitation to Mary Kay's home. During this visit to her residence, consultants are given cookies that she has baked herself in her own kitchen.

Similarly, this theme of nurturance is reinforced by the lack of hierarchical structure in Mary Kay. Amway emphasizes one's posistion within a hierarchical chain of command even in the routine work of placing orders. In contrast, Mary Kay emphasizes a closer link between each consultant and the parent organization. Meetings are held on the basis of geographic proximity rather than a chain of command.

Perhaps here our analysis is on more tentative and speculative ground, but we think that exploitation of others is less acceptable within the Mary Kay world. As we have seen, a number of the Mary Kay consultants talked about their hesitancy in recruiting others. While they realized that this activity was important and necessary for success, they experienced difficulty doing so. Consistently, they were unable to articulate the reasons surrounding this difficulty. At times, they merely said it "didn't feel right" to them. Given that some of these women are quite comfortable with other aspects of their direct sales work — meeting customers and giving facials to groups of strangers, we thought that their hesitancy reflected something other than their self-perceived lack of aggression.

Finally, the nature of the reward structure in Mary Kay seems more compatible with a traditional female experience. Rewards and incentives in the organization often are in the form of nontransferable goods. Cash incentives exist, but these are not emphasized to the extent that they are in Amway. Meetings do not symbolically display the checks received by successful consultants. Reference is made to money, how much one can earn in Mary Kay, but such references are more fleeting and veiled. Rather, the incentives and rewards touted are the luxury items "given" away by Mary Kay. The bumble bee pins, furs, jewelry, and cars are often the motivators — the "prizes" received for performance. Thus, working for Mary Kay seems to reinforce the wage structure of a traditional homemaker role.

In contrast the typical scenario presented on Amway motivational tapes illustrates a far different sequence of events. There the enthusiastic husband brings his reluctant and often antagonistic wife into the "family" of Amway work. Although the husband's motivation is not the focus of concern in this paper, the prominent place given to money in the motivational literature suggests that for them the freedom of choice afforded by the money that will be made is a large part of the attraction. The promise is access to the good life — luxurious housing, expensive cars, and exotic vacations — all while freed from the constraints of traditional employment. Furthermore, this work allows for the participation of the spouse in the earning process without interfering with her primary function as homemaker.

Direct sales in general, whether performed by females or males, is a grey area in the labor force. As a means of making money, there seems to be a wide range of success. Only three of the women involved made enough money in direct sales to consider it the equivalent of a full time source of income, yet the majority of the women interviewed on the whole were more positive about their experiences than we expected that they would be. In the majority of the interviews, the women or household either lost money or made very little in terms of what they had expected to make originally. Yet in most cases they either continued to use the products or continued to sell the products to friends, relatives and neighbors even though they were not making a large amount of money by doing so. Most of them focused on the growth that they had experienced on a personal level. Their experiences had resulted in their feeling better about their lives, their spouses, or themselves. Even the women who expressed some bitterness (always those involved in Amway, never those involved in Mary Kay) found more positive than negative things to say about their experiences. It may be that in direct sales organizations the product is only a vehicle for the social interaction that takes place, and the financial losses that occur are not very important in terms of what the participants perceive themselves to have gained. As one respondent said, "It's the women in it, they are very good people."

REFERENCES

Ash, M.K. 1981. *Mary Kay*. New York: Barnes and Noble Books.

Benson, S.P. 1983. "The customers ain't God': The work culture of department-store saleswomen, 1890–1940," In *Working Class America: Essays on Labor, Community, and American Society*, edited by M.H. Frisch and D.J. Walkowitz, Urbana, Illinois: University of Illinois Press.

Bage, T.J. 1980. "Selling to farmers," *Advertising Age* 51 (November): S4–S5.

Blumstein, P. and P. Schwartz. 1983. *American Couples*. New York: William Morrow.

Coburn, M.F. 1982. "Direct's sleeker sell," *Advertising Age* 53 (March 1): M18.

Daum, M. 1984. *Correlates and Consequences of Salaried and Self-Employment in Middle and Late-Life.*" Brookdale Center on Aging: New York.

Freidan, B. 1981. *The Second Stage*. New York: Summit.

Galginaitis, C. 1980. "What do farmers think?" *Advertising Age* 51 (November 24): 55–57.

Galluccio, N. and A. Lappen. 1979. "Avon calling . . . with acquisition still on her mind,' *Forbes* 123 (April 16): 142–45.

Gilligan, C. 1982. *In a Different Voice*. Cambridge, Massachusetts: Harvard University.

Green, J. and F. D'Aiuto. 1977. "A case study of economic distribution via social networks," *Human Organization* 36 (Fall): 309–15.

Koil, M. 1981. "Racing the competition," *Advertising Age* 52 (May 4): S14–S15.

Jobin, J. 1982. "Direct sales," *Women's Day* 45 (May 18): 20–25, 143.

Juth, C. 1985. "Structural factors creating and maintaining illegal and deviant behavior in direct sales organization: A case study of Amway Corporation." Paper presented at the 80th Annual Meeting of the American Sociological Association, August 26–30, Washington, D.C.

McElena, J.K. 1978. "Motivate distributors by tickling competitive nerve!" *Advertising Age* 49 (October 16):2–6.

Maccoby, C. and N. Jacklin. 1974. *The Psychology of Sex Differences*. Stanford, California: Stanford University Press.

Maxa, R. 1977. *Dare to be Great*. New York: William Morrow.

Mechling, T. 1980. "Patriotism, capitalism and positive thinking," *Commonweal* 29 (August 29):459–62.

Peven, D.E. 1968. "The use of religious revival technique to indoctrinate persons: The home-party sales organization," *Sociological Quarterly* 9 (Winter): 97–106.

Richmond, E. 1975. "On the road to riches," *Harpers Magazine* 250 (February): 12.

Rubin, L. 1983. *Intimate Strangers*. New York: Harper and Row.

Rudnitsky, H. 1981. "The flight of the bumblebee." *Forbes* 127 (June 22): 104–06.

Taylor, R. 1978. "Marilyn's friends and Rita's customers: A study of party-selling as play and work," *The Sociological Review* 26 (August): 573–94.

60 Minutes. 1983. "Soap and Hope." Volume XV, Number 17 as broadcast over the CBS Television Network Sunday, January 9, 7:30–8:30 EST:2–7.

Wedemyer, D. 1975. "There's a tupperware party starting every 10 seconds . . . " *Ms.* 4 (August): 71-4, 82-5.

CHAPTER 15

Invisible Amidst the Glitter: Hispanic Women in the Southern California Electronics Industry

M. PATRICIA FERNANDEZ KELLY AND ANNA M. GARCIA

INTRODUCTION[1]

Electronics has been portrayed as an industry upon which economic re-vitalization in the West depends. Computer technology, developed in the 1950s and refined over the next three decades, transformed the daily experience of millions of people ushering in an era based on cybernetics. Moreover, in its application to manufacturing, electronics has spawned popular visions of a world made wholesome by the availability of intelligent machines capable of replacing dehumanizing manual labor. As with all popular images, this one captures elements of our evolving reality. Nevertheless, there is more to this story than computers and robots taking over factory work.

The significance of the electronics industry lies, in fact in its embodiment of new tendencies in the structural relations between employers and workers. The internationalization of investments, exportation of jobs to less developed countries (LDCs), extremely low rates of unionization, and the combination of automation in advanced industrial powers with labor-intensive operations abroad, are all central features of contemporary electronics production [2] (Portes and Walton, 1982).

Domestically, as well as internationally, electronics firms account for one of the most vigorous employment rates of any sector over the last two decades. From 1967 to 1980 electronics component employment in the United States grew at 2.4 percent a year. From 1980 to the most recent 1983 figures, there was an additional 2.3 percent increase. (Glasmeier, Hall, and Markusen, 1983; Bradshaw, 1987). Perhaps more significantly, over 85 percent in this industry's work force is composed of women, the majority of whom are young and single.

265

More than three million women are currently employed, directly or indirectly, in electronics manufacturing in less developed countries (United Nations Industrial Development Organization, 1981). More than a million work in the United States.

Electronics firms in the United States originally hired local, white women who left their jobs after relatively short periods of employment, either to get married or to devote attention to their families. More recently, the number of minority workers has increased. Asian and Hispanic women workers in electronics plants in California, New York and Florida are but three examples of this trend. Over 100,000 Hispanic women are employed in electronics production in Southern California alone.

Our purpose in this chapter is to examine an aspect of the changing relations between capital and labor in the context of recent transformations in the electronics industry by emphasizing the role that women, especially Hispanic women, have in the production process. As an illustration we discuss the case of Southern California where one of the largest concentrations of electronics firms now exist.

HIGH-TECH AND WOMEN'S WORK: THE SOUTHERN CALIFORNIA CASE

Under the term Southern California we include three counties: Los Angeles, Orange, and San Diego comprising 9,121 square miles, that is 5.7 percent of the total area of the state. Although proportionally small, 48 percent of the state's population lives in this southern portion. One of the area's unique characteristics is its proximity to Mexico. The San Diego-Tijuana border is the busiest in the world in terms of the movement of commodities, information, and labor. Historically, Southern California has been an agricultural emporium linked to the employment of immigrants first from Asia and, for the last thirty years, from Mexico. In recent times, manufacturing, defense, and aerospace have accounted for a a significant proportion of the area's economy[3]

Prosperity has distinguished California for many years. However, during the recession of the late 1970s and early 1980s, many companies closed down manufacturing facilities of various kinds and laid off thousands of workers. It is estimated that between 16,000 and 30,000 jobs were directly lost to plant closings in Los Angeles in 1980.[4] The vacuum created by these losses has been filled, to a large extent, by openings in high tech industries. Nonetheless, the majority of jobs in that sector require little or no skill. Electronics assemblers are among the lowest paid industrial workers in the U.S., earning hourly wages barely above the minimum. For many blue-collar workers, the consequence of this transition has been a shrinking of employment alternatives, income and security. Yet, the same factors are having an impact upon the reorganization of labor markets in California and upon the demand for immigrant workers. According to Morales (1984):

> Los Angeles has the distinction of absorbing new immigrants from Asia and Latin America the way New York once accepted Europeans. With a population of more than 7.4 million and a labor force of over 3.5 million, Los Angeles County is thought to contain between 400,000 and 1.1 million undocumented persons . . . At least half of the undocumented persons come from Mexico.

With slight modifications, the same remarks can be extended to Orange and San Diego Counties.

During the late 1960s, Southern California made significant gains as a center for the production of high-tech goods. In 1968 there were fewer than 30 electronics firms in Los Angeles, 12 in Orange and 20 in San Diego; by 1975 these areas had 120, 40, and 80 firms respectively. Toward the end of 1984, according to the California Employment Development Department there were 486, 326, and 132 electronics components and accessories firms in Los Angeles, Orange, and San Diego Counties. It is commonly believed that Santa Clara (Silicon Valley) is home to the largest number of electronics firms in the state. Actually, it is within the boundaries of Los Angeles County that the largest number of electronics companies in the nation are located (Castell, 1985). As Table I shows, the most recent growth spurt is occurring in Orange County.

Other than the proximity to markets and research centers, producers are seeking benefits derived from the presence of large, affordable labor pools, com-

Table I
Top High Tech Plant Locations
1972–1977

Rank	Area	New Plant
1	Anaheim, California	464
2	Los Angeles, California	367
3	San Jose, California	339
4	Dallas, Texas	276
5	Chicago, Illinois	224
6	Houston, Texas	204
7	Boston, Massachusetts	191
8	Minneapolis, Minnesota	158
9	San Francisco, California	151
10	Detroit, Michigan	145
11	Denver, Colorado	139
12	San Diego, California	123

Source: Institute of Urban and Regional Development, University of California, Berkeley.
Note: The differences between rankings of total employment and number of new high-tech plants partly result from the size of new facilities. San Diego had larger plants than other areas which, frequently, had smaller, spin-off plants.

paratively low wage and unionization rates, and access to cheap land and improved transportation. These are all variables explaining the decentralization of manufacturing on an intraregional scale evidenced, for example, in the movement of electronics firms from Northern to Southern California. Indeed, the same factors explain the decentralization of manufacturing on a world scale that has characterized production over the last 20 years. It is not surprising, therefore, that governments throughout the U.S. are devising incentive packages stressing the advantages of their own locations and courting investments in high-tech.

Such packages are strikingly similar in letter and spirit to "holiday programs" offered by LDCs trying to attract foreign capital for export manufacturing. Southern California is no exception to this trend. Advertisements and public affairs literature mention a good climate, the proximity to Mexico, and

Table II
Total Persons and Spanish Origin Persons
by Type of Spanish Origin: 1980

| | Spanish Origin | | | | |
Total Persons	Total	Mexican	Puerto Rican	Cuban	Other
California					
23,557,902	4,544,331	3,637,466	93,038	61,004	752,823
Percentage	19.2	15.4	0.4	0.3	3.2
Orange Co.					
1,932,702	285,722	228,665	5,903	5,166	45,988
Percentage	14.8	11.3	0.3	0.3	2.4
Los Angeles Co.					
7,477,503	2,065,503	1,643,150	36,928	46,363	339,062
Percentage	27.6	22.0	0.5	0.6	4.5
San Diego Co.					
1,861,846	274,530	227,195	5,484	1,531	40,320
Percentage	14.7	12.2	0.3	0.1	2.2
Southern CA (3 counties)					
11,272,051	2,625,755	2,099,010	48,315	53,060	425,370
Percentage	23.3	18.6	0.4	0.4	3.8
.48					

Source: Census of Population 1980, U.S. Department of Commerce, Supplementary Report: Persons of Spanish Origin by state.

the availability of large numbers of trained and trainable workers in that area as positive features from the vantage point of the investor. Many of those workers are immigrants or native citizens of Mexican ancestry.

The importance of Hispanics in general, and of Hispanic women in particular, for contemporary industry is substantiated by aggregate data. A comparison of the 1970 and 1980 Census of Population shows that while all other ethnic groups in the U.S. have lost their relative share of employment in the manufacturing sector, Hispanics have maintained or increased their share. According to the 1980 Census, Hispanics form 19.2 percent of the total population of California and 23.3 percent of all people living in the southern part of the state (see Table II). Spanish-origin persons in Los Angeles, Orange, and San Diego Counties represent 20.5 percent of the total labor force in the area. Yet, they have an average labor force participation rate of 68.6 percent (see Table III) with almost half employed in the manufacturing sector.

Southern California, where the majority of Hispanic women are of Mexican descent, provides a good example of the labor force participation rate of minority women. The total female labor force in that area is 1,164,553 persons. In Table IV we include comparative information about the rate of employment of women belonging to different ethnic groups. As may be seen, the employment rate of Hispanic women in Southern California is relatively high. Almost 53 percent of all Hispanic women in Los Angeles County are gainfully employed. The equivalent figures for Orange and San Diego Counties are 58.5 and 49.2 percent respectively. Perhaps more significant is the observation, also derived from the Population Census, that approximately 35 percent of all women employed in manufacturing in the United States are Hispanic.

These findings run counter to the widespread notion that Hispanic women's incorporation into the labor force is not significant, and that when present it is isolated in the services sector. Moreover, our ethnographic research suggests that Hispanic women's participation in wage employment has been underestimated given biases present in conventional aggregate compilations.[5] Many recent immigrants and female heads of household may be found in the informal economy, doing piece work at home or temporarily employed in small fly-by-night operations. Nevertheless, even available data suggest that the gainful employment of Hispanic women has increased concomitantly with the shift from basic manufacturing to services and with the rise of electronics production. The recent industrial development of Southern California is a case in point.

It is relatively simple to show the importance of Hispanic women's participation in manufacturing and their steady presence in the labor force. It is more difficult to assess their position as part of the electronics industry. The main obstacle lies in selecting appropriate occupational categories. In Table V we present information, provided by the California Employment Development Department, on occupations relevant to electronics manufacture in three counties under consideration. The presence of minorities in the large occupational category "operators, fabricators, and laborers" is striking. Fully 67 percent of

Table III

Labor Force Status by Sex 1980

	Total	White not Hispanic	Black not Hispanic	Native American Not Hispanic	Asian Not Hispanic	Remaining Races Not Hispanic	Hispanics All Races
ORANGE COUNTY							
Total Labor Force	1,028,597	827,057	13,130	7,029	42,698	1,582	137,101
Labor Force Participation Rate	70.0	69.6	79.0	72.3	67.4	67.1	73.0
Male Labor Force	597,631	476,569	7,886	3,959	24,058	1,017	84,142
Labor Force Participation Rate	83.2	82.8	86.7	84.1	78.3	80.8	86.5
Female Labor Force	430,966	350,488	5,244	3,070	18,640	565	52,959
Labor Force Participation Rate	57.4	57.1	69.6	61.2	57.1	51.5	58.5
LOS ANGELES COUNTY							
Total Labor Force	3,705,516	2,136,488	403,416	21,008	226,755	9,644	908,185
Labor Force Participaiton Rate	65.8	65.5	62.0	65.9	68.0	64.0	67.6
Male Labor Force	2,119,718	1,221,662	206,313	11,465	124,126	5,751	550,401
Labor Force Participation Rate	78.2	78.0	69.6	78.1	77.2	74.4	82.7

Female Labor Force	1,585,798	914,826	197,103	9,543	102,649	3,893	357,784
Labor Force Participation Rate	54.2	53.9	55.7	55.5	59.9	53.1	52.7
SAN DIEGO COUNTY							
Total Labor Force	931,995	712,722	51,847	6,676	39,893	1,590	119,267
Labor Force Participation Rate	65.0	64.3	71.4	66.3	65.8	62.2	66.3
Male Labor Force	571,930	436,936	33,061	4,311	21,075	974	75,573
Labor Force Participation Rate	78.4	77.5	81.7	80.1	76.2	73.2	82.9
Female Labor Force	360,065	275,786	18,786	2,365	18,818	616	43,694
Labor Force Participation Rate	51.1	50.6	58.4	50.4	57.0	50.3	49.2
Total Labor Force							
Three Counties	5,666,108	3,676,267	468,393	34,713	309,346	12,816	1,164,553

Source: Summary tape file No. 4 from the 1980 Census, U.S. Department of Labor and State of California Employment Development Department.

Table IV

Female Workers 16 Years or over in Selected Occupations
By Race/Ethnicity In Southern California

Occupation	Total No.	White Not Hisp.	Black Not Hisp.	Hisp. All	Asian Not Hisp.	Native American Not Hisp.	Other Races	Total Minorities
Operators, fabricators, and laborers	25,679	83,765	19,149	126,558	19,675	1,536	729	167,737
% of total:		.33	.08	.51	.08	.01	.00	.67
Machine operators, assemblers and inspectors	190,214	56,369	13,166	101,870	17,135	1,044	568	133,826
% of total:		.30	.07	.54	.09	.01	.00	.70
Metal working, and plastic working machine operators	5,878	2,511	402	2,687	230	47	0	3,367
% of total:		.43	.07	.46	.04	.01	0	.57
Metal and plastic machine operators	8,654	2,535	901	4,922	317	24	21	6,118
% of total:		.29	.10	.57	.04	.00	.00	.71
Machine operators assorted materials	45,536	14,662	2,867	25,443	2,151	257	143	30,860
% of total:		.32	.06	.56	.05	.01	.00	.68
Fabricators, assemblers and hand-working occupations	106,132	39,090	8,699	49,881	7,507	608	251	67,031
% of total:		.37	.08	.47	.07	.01	.00	.63

Source: 1980 Census Data.

the work force in that category belongs to a minority group. Of those, 51 percent are Hispanic females. Table VI contains a summary of similar findings for all of Southern California.

The significance of Hispanic women's participation in the electronics industry may also be gleaned through the observation of discrete occupations. For example, in the category of "machine operators, assemblers and inspectors," minority women constitute 70 percent of workers. Hispanic women form 76 percent of that number. Finally, under "metal and plastic machine operator," the total minority population is 71 percent of the work force. Hispanic women comprise almost 80 percent of that figure.

In sum, while empirical data accurately portraying the participation of Hispanic women in various kinds of electronics manufacturing is only now being collected, our most recent findings indicate that their participation in industry in general, and in electronics in particular, is more significant than usually acknowledged. Testimonies from managers make clear that the availability of a large pool of Hispanic female workers is one of the factors contributing to the location of electronics firms in Southern California.

A VIEW FROM BELOW[6]

Early in 1983, when Fermina Calero turned 24 years old, inflation along Mexico's Northern border reached above 100 percent. For three years and a half, the young woman had been working as an *operadora* in a *maquiladora*,[7] the subsidary of a semiconductors firm based in the U.S. Southwest. Her job consisted of the delicate process of bonding. Soldering minute filaments of gold to nodes neatly marked on printed circuits required precision, speed, and steady gazing through the lens of a microscope. Fermina liked the gadgets around her. They made her feel as if she were inside a laboratory. A lab technician or a secretary was what she had longed to be while growing up as a maid or a clerk in small dilapidated shops. This at least, thought Fermina, was a real job. Some progress has been made since she had left her home town in Jalisco and arrived with her family in Tijuana more than a decade before.

At first she had gone to school but soon it became clear that a household formed by three younger children and a sickly mother could not depend upon the wages of her father, an unskilled construction worker. As an eldest child, it was her turn to find a job. She followed the path of thousands of other young women seeking a livelihood in the interstices of an underdeveloped economy.

By sheer historical coincidence, Fermina was living in Tijuana at the same time that a new form of export-led industrialization was spawning factories in border cities. This made it possible for her to find a job in a sector that favored primarily the employment of women. By the end of 1982 there were approximately 112 *maquiladoras* in Tijuana dedicated to the assembly of electronics

Table V

Civilian Labor Force 16 Years and over by Race/Ethnicity in Selected Occupations
Southern California

Occupation	Total No.	% White Not Hisp.	% Black Not Hisp.	% Hisp. All Races	% Asian Not Hisp.	% Native American Not Hisp.	% Other Races Not Hisp.	% Total Minority	
Operators, Fabricators, and Laborers:									
	185,627	26.22	9.11	56.90	6.86	.54	.33	73.77	Los Angeles County
	40,223	53.03	1.51	36.19	8.20	.90	.14	46.96	Orange County
	25,679	53.60	6.35	24.84	14.19	.67	.31	46.39	San Diego County
Total:	251,529	48,671	16,911	105,622				136,937	Los Angeles County
		21,330		14,557				18,888	Orange County
		13,763		6,379				11,912	San Diego County
Total:		83,764		126,558				167,737	
								.66	
Machine Operators, Assemblers and Inspectors									
	141,810	23.36	8.13	59.96	7.69	.49	.34	76.63	Los Angeles County
	30,329	48.41	1.69	39.38	9.57	.81	.10	51.58	Orange County
	18,075	47.36	6.22	27.09	18.41	.57	.31	52.63	San Diego County
Total:	190,214			85,029				108,669	Los Angeles County
				11,944				15,694	Orange County
				4,897				9,513	San Diego County
Total:				.54				.70	

1) Hispanic females (all races) = 75.45% of total minority females.

1) Hispanic females (all races) = 76.37% of total minority females.

Machine operators, assorted materials

33,810	25.97	7.38	62.23	3.49	.53	74.02	.37	Los Angeles County
7,855	47.89	1.28	44.59	5.49	.56	52.10	.16	Orange County
3,871	54.76	7.00	23.27	13.94	.87	45.23	.12	San Diego County
Total: 45,536	8,780		21,039			25,026		Los Angeles County
			3,503			4,092		Orange County
			901			1,751		San Diego County
			Total: 25,443			30,869		
			.56			.68		

1) Hispanic females (all races) = 82.42% of total minority females.

Metalworking and Plastic Working Machine Operators

4,403	38.22	7.63	49.94	3.27	.93	61.77	.00	Los Angeles County
912	53.39	.54	37.93	7.45	.65	46.60	.00	Orange County
563	60.59	10.83	25.39	3.19		.00		San Diego County
Total: 5,878	1,683		2,119			2,720		Los Angeles County
	487		346			425		Orange Conunty
	341		142			222		San Diego
Total: 2,511			2,687			3,367		
.43			.46			.57		

1) Hispanic females (all races) = 79.8% of total minority females.

Table VI

Summary: Civilian Labor Force 16 Years and over in Selected Occupations by Race/Ethnicity Southern California

	White Not Hisp.	Black Not Hisp.	Hispanic All	Asian Not Hisp.	Nat. Am. Not Hisp.	Other Minor.	Total
Total No.							
Operators, Fabricators, Laborers:							
256,790	83,756	19,149	126,558	19,675	1,536	729	167,737
%	.33	.08	.51	.08	.01	.00	.67
Machine Operators, Assemblers and Inspectors:							
190,214	56,369	13,166	101,870	17,135	1,044	568	13,826
%	.30	.07	.54	.09	.01	.00	.70
Metal Working and Plastic Working Machine Operators:							
5,878	2,511	402	2,687	230	47	0	3,367
%	.30	.07	.54	.09	.01	.00	.57
Metal and Plastic Machine Operators:							
8,654	2,535	901	4,922	317	24	21	6,118
%	.29	.10	.57	.04	.00	.00	.71
Machine Operators, Assorted Materials:							
45,536	14,662	2,867	25,443	2,151	257	143	30,869
%	.32	.06	.56	.05	.01	.00	.68
Fabricators, Assemblers and Hand Working Occupations:							
106,132	39,090	8,699	49,881	7,507	608	251	67,031
%	.37	.08	.47	.07	.01	.00	.63

Source: 1980 Census Data.

products, clothing and other light commodities. During her three years of work at the factory, Fermina earned 65 cents an hour on the average; slightly over $31 dollars for a 48 hour week. Small as the wage had been, it had contributed substantially to the well-being of her whole family.

But large events can transform the life of small people. Toward the end of 1982 and in the following months, successive currency devaluations threw into havoc many local economies. Inflation skyrocketted to unprecedented heights transforming the costs and benefits of low-wage industrial employment. At the same time that employers noticed curious labor shortages along the border, working women had to resort to new calculations and alternatives. Reflectively, Fermina told me:

> It was a better job than most in Tijuana for someone like myself, but money kept shrinking and living kept getting more expensive. There was no future, no chance for improvement. So I made a decision. I was thinking about my family when I crossed the border and went to live with my aunt and uncle in Encinitas.

Since the fall of 1983, the young woman had stayed with relatives in North County, an area adjacent to San Diego where she had soon found a job at Nova-Tech, a small but expanding company competing in the production of personal computers.

Periodically, Fermina wrote and wired money to her mother but because she had arrived in the U.S. illegally, she didn't dare go back to Tijuana to visit. At Nova-Tech, there were hundreds of people from Mexico or of Mexican ancestry. A few had been born in the United States. Some were commuters, that is, they lived in Mexico but travelled daily across the border to work. Many were undocumented immigrants. This was true as much for the maintenance man as for the assemblers who were predominantly female.

Once, since Fermina had been working at Nova-Tech, the plant had been raided by the *Migra*.[8] Almost 50 people had been herded into light green vehicles and taken to deportation stations. Frightened, she had taken refuge in a supplies closet for over half an hour, until the sound of voices and footsteps had subsided. There had been no further consequence but she did not forget the feelings that overwhelmed her in the darkness: "I came to this country to work hard," she said, "but now I live torn between duty and shame."

Aside from the danger of deportation, life was passing quietly for Fermina as 1984 came to an end. She was earning almost $5 an hour for a forty hour week and she frequently worked overtime. She contributed $200 a month to her aunt's household, and $350 to her family in Tijuana. The rest was barely enough for transportation, meals at work, and personal expenses. Fermina, who liked children, enjoyed living with her five cousins. She hoped to have a family of her own some day.

THE VIEW FROM ABOVE

Nova-Tech is a family-owned company founded in the early 1950s. The firm produced digital voltimeters and oscilloscopes until 1982, with sales averaging $3 million per year. In March of 1982, the company expanded to include the production of a small and versatile computer which had been successfully exhibited in a San Francisco show. It was during that time that new workers were actively recruited. Notices calling for assemblers appeared in local newspapers and classified ads leaflets. We called, in English, to inquire about openings and were told that all positions had been filled. Moments later we called again, in Spanish, and were told to come and file an application. The company had a conscious policy targetting groups perceived as the most desirable. Mr. Carmichael, the company's general manager saw good reasons for this:

> The personal computer market is very competitive. Companies rise and fall in a matter of months. We have a good product but we can only stay alive by producing efficiently and selling at a competitive price . . . American workers are spoiled by wealth and prosperity; unions have priced them out of the market. Foreign workers, whether Viet Namese or Mexican, are driven by the same forces that led our ancestors to succeed. They are reliable, they work hard, they don't make trouble, they are what a pioneer industry like ours needs . . . We considered opening a plant in Mexico but here we are closer to U.S. markets and we don't have to deal with foreign red tape. The workers are the same; they don't care about borders, all they care about is finding a job and feeding their families.

By June 1982, Nova-Tech was shipping 100 of its portable computers every month, and by December the amount had risen to 5,000 units. The value of the shipments reached $22 million. Earnings soared by about 1,000 percent. By late 1983, when Fermina Calero joined the company, Nova-Tech was employing almost 700 workers and was said to rank fourth among personal computer makers. Reported sales were $75.2 million. Profits reached $12.9 million. During 1984, Mr. Camichael appeared secure in the ability of the company to compete in the personal computer market: "Our manufacturing and labor expenses are a third to half that of others," he claimed.

On November 7, 1984, eyewitnesses vividly described the arrival and entrance of some 17 Immigration and Naturalization Service vehicles and officers at Nova-Tech's facility. INS agents closed off all possible exits, initiated an inquiry, and boarded undocumented Mexican workers into vans. Some 50 individuals, most of them women, were taken from the facility. It was said that a few workers had avoided deportation by hiding in closets. This was not the first time the plant had been raided.

GENDER AND THE NEW ECONOMY:
THE CRITICAL ISSUES

The experiences outlined above — a small but innovative company fighting for survival in a highly competitive market; a young Mexican woman working illegally in a growing electronics firm — are not isolated examples. Census and ethnographic data suggest that over 100,000 Hispanic women, many of them undocumented immigrants, may be working in electronics production in Southern California. This phenomenon is worthy of scholarly attention for several reasons.

First, although it might appear paradoxical to some, electronics (the harbinger of progress in advanced technology) is predominantly an employer of unskilled and semiskilled workers, many of whom are minority women. To a large extent, employment policies in electronics manufacturing reflect national trends. Labor Department (1983) forecasts show that the largest number of jobs over the next decade will be created in low paying occupations in services and, to some extent, in direct production of nondurable and durable goods.[11] While skilled and professional employment will grow significantly during the same period, the largest demand will be for unskilled and semiskilled workers. Electronics manufacture alone will have required 50 times more janitors than engineers by the end of the century. More than 70 percent of all workers in the same industry will have been involved in direct production and assembly.

Second, the ethnographic accounts offered above show a circuit linking two types of international migration: one involves massive transfers of capital from advanced industrial countries to underdeveloped and developing areas where the cost of labor is six to thirteen times lower, and where host governments are bound to keep labor disturbances at bay. A related type of migration is that formed by the growing number of individuals flowing from underdeveloped and developed areas to advanced industrial countries in search of employment. Saskia Sassen Koob (1985) has discussed at length the case of depressed sites such as the New York Metropolitan Area where capital flight during the 1970s created new conditions for the redeployment of resources and the employment of recently arrived immigrants in competitive industries.[9]

In Southern California, Florida and, to some extent Texas, the situation is somewhat different. There, the presence of large pools of older established immigrants and native citizens of Hispanic ancestry, as well as the expanding numbers of new arrivals from Latin America, the Caribbean and Southeast Asia are creating attractive conditions for certain types of production. Perhaps one of the most interesting aspects about manufacturing in Southern California is that it often combines the employment of immigrants, domestically, with the relocation of production facilities to areas of the world where those immigrants tend to come from. This circuit does not necessarily involve a casual relationship. However, it does evidence a strategy through which employers seek to reduce the economic and political costs of production both in their native countries and abroad.

Third, the fact that the electronics industry is largely an employer of women cannot be taken lightly. In this respect the industry mirrors national trends characterized by the unprecedented incorporation of married and unmarried females into the labor force. By 1985, women in the United States had surpassed the number of men in the formal sector of employment for the first time in that country's history. One of our tasks, as scholars, is to investigate the meaning of this event by refining our understanding of gender relations as they affect the contemporary exchanges between capital and labor. Trying to unveil the riddles of female employment can lead to a better understanding of the conditions under which, and reasons why various segments of the working class are found allocated to different types of service delivery and commodity production.

In a recent essay, historian Joan Scott (1987) points to two aspects of gender. On the one hand, this concept denotes a process of differentiation among individuals based upon perceived sexual traits. While gender depends upon the dichotomous distinction male/female, it should not be equated with sex, a biological concept. Rather, gender is an *historical* category which has evolved into sanctioned roles and acceptable behaviors for men and women. For this reason gender, together with class and ethnicity, is an indispensable term for explaining the social division of labor.

On the other hand, gender is also a constitutive element in collective exchanges through which relations of power are expressed. A voluminous literature published over the last 15 years has exposed the factors leading to women's subordination in modern and ancient societies. At the core of the argument on women's subordination lies the contradiction between productive and reproductive functions exacerbated under industrial capitalism by the separation between domestic and work spheres, between the private world of nurturance and the public realm of competitive labor.

Women's confinement to the household, which followed major historical events such as the struggle for the family wage and the advent of protective legislation, further accentuated dependency on male providers. At the same time, the proper roles of the sexes became strongly attached to the fictive separation between production and reproduction. All along, since then, women have stepped out of their socially imposed boundaries in order to support themselves and their families. But, all along, they have done so engulfed in a cloud of public ambivalence and tension. The tension issues from the objective need to reconcile domestic and wage-earning requirements. The ambivalence stems from the widespread cultural understanding that women are supplementary wage earners and that their primary role is to be fulfilled at home. Both aspects combine to render women vulnerable in the labor market. The same vulnerability and nebulous structural position make them suitable for certain types of employment, mainly in low-wage, unskilled and semiskilled jobs. It is against this backdrop that the demand for female labor in contemporary industry should be examined.

Elsewhere (Fernandez Kelly 1983; 1985) I have discussed the historical moments in which women have been massively incorporated into the labor force under industrial capitalism. Although women have always been wage earners, there are three periods over the last two centuries and a half when they have flooded the labor market. The first period coincided with the advent of industrial capitalism, a time of flux characterized by limited availability of capital for investment, changing technology and emerging consumer markets. The second period paralleled World War II (and, to some extent World War I) when the involvement of men in armed confrontation made it necessary for women to replace them in factories and offices. As several writers and at least one documentary have shown, such an incorporation was achieved in part by stretching the ideological boundaries in the definition of women's role and equating factory operations to domestic tasks (Milkman, 1980).

We are the witnesses to and participants of a third moment in which women are massively represented in the labor force. Again, this is a time of profound changes. The internationalization of capital investments, the application of revolutionary technologies, and changes in the balance of power between employers and workers have deeply altered the conditions for profitable production. Thus, the evidence seems to indicate that women's massive incorporation into the labor force is often linked to processes of economic and political restructuring. Furthermore, women's large presence in the labor market signals changes in the nature of wage employment and in the relationship between employees and investors. The case of the electronics industry is a case in point.

The reasons behind the widespread hiring of women in electronics firms throughout the world have been examined by several authors since the mid-1970s (Nash and Fernandez Kelly, 1983). Industrial promoters, public officials, and some academic researchers have agreed that the jobs offered by that industry require keen eyesight, manual dexterity and "a liking for minute handiwork." Indeed, these characteristics are commonly found among women. However, a focus on them alone does not allow for a satisfactory explanation of low wages linked to women's employment, or of the wage differentials that have historically characterized men and women's jobs. Beneath the deceptively obvious statements lies a complicated political reality joining women's culture, the survival needs of domestic units, and the personnel requirements of companies. Frequently, women are hired because they are bearers of highly replaceable, tractable, and unexpensive labor. This is especially true for minority and immigrant women.

RECENT CHANGES IN ELECTRONICS PRODUCTION: A PROFILE

Virtually from its inception, electronics production has been organized internationally with major firms assembling abroad or establishing partnerships with companies in other countries. Within three years of the development of the silicon chip in 1959, Fairchild initiated the production of integrated circuits in Hong Kong. Other firms soon followed a similar path opening factories in South Korea and Taiwan, and confirming the economic rationality of transferring assembly operations to geographical locations offering advantages such as tax exemptions, abundant labor supplies, and comparatively low wages.

Accelerated improvements in technology, volatile consumer product markets, and fierce competition (bearing some similarity to that which characterized the advent of the industrial revolution) created the need to further reduce production costs. During the early 1970s Singapore, Malaysia, the Philippines, and the U.S.-Mexico Border with its *Maquiladora* program joined the stream as favored locations for Export Processing Zones specializing in the assembly of electronics products for sale in the world market. Between 1965 and 1975 the number of Export Processing Zones in Latin America and Asia grew from a few to more than 120. At present there are hundreds more.[10]

The late 1970s paralleled rising demand for even smaller computer components with greater capacity for storage and transmission of information. This brought about the "Very Large Scale Integration" (VLSI) period characterized by the downfall of certain types of production and the invention of new products. The manufacture of personal computers and video games, for example, underwent profound changes as demand declined and inventories swelled. Companies which had startled observers with the inventiveness of their products and the sudden wealth of their founders, disappeared overnight. Others, like Nova-Tech, fought for survival.

At the same time, fifth generation computer components revolutionized highly specialized fields in defense, medicine, genetic engineering and communications. The advent of VLSI production transformed the requirements for competitive manufacture and limited the potential for firms' geographical mobility. Because of their miniscule size and growing capacity, the most advanced electronics components are extremely sensitive to contaminants, particularly those transmitted by human handling. Their manufacture requires massive investments in automation and sophisticated wafer processing, design and testing. It also requires high levels of quality control and customized assembly often linked to the demands of specialized markets. These are conditions not easily achieved in most LDCs.

Thus, there is a virtual bifurcation of the electronics manufacturing with one segment catering to large consumer markets and another one fulfilling the demands of unique buyers. The first segment bears some resemblance to industries such as garment production where fierce competition, changing tastes, and inbred obsolescence go hand in hand with limited capital investments, rapidly changing markets, and low levels of quality control. The second segment is rapidly becoming a capital-intensive industry in its own right. By one estimate, the total investment in Research and Development (R&D), plant and equipment necessary for a firm to compete in the production of 256K random access memory chips is between $150 and $200 million. This compares with an average of approximately $14,000 to start a simple printed circuits operation (Scott, No Date).

This most recent stage in the growth of electronics is producing unexpected adjustments. While the number of facilities in overseas locations will continue to grow over the next decade, forecasts indicate that they will be directed to the production of relatively simple integrated circuits requiring large amounts of intensive manual labor and comparatively less sophisticated technology. This ensures further expansion in the number of Export Processing Zones in Asia and Latin America. Since the enactment of the Caribbean Basin Initiative by the U.S. Congress in the early 1980s, a new frontier in export processing was opened in the Western hemisphere.

Nonetheless, the share of overseas electronics production is decreasing in relation to Very Large Scale Integration facilities in the United States which are making new gains (Siegel, 1984; O'Connor, 1983). Domestically, this process is associated with relocation policies stirred by the proximity to markets, the availability of low-cost labor pools, the access to R&D centers and incentives granted to industrial production. Thus, between 1981 and 1984 almost 25,000 simple component assembly jobs in Northern California disappeared as many companies originally located in Silicon Valley relocated to Southern California, Miami, and Austin.

To note the growing bifurcation in electronics production is a precondition for explaining different labor requirements as well as the concentration of various types of facilities in different geographical areas. However, we should also note that there are connections between the two sectors. These connections are often established through direct subcontracting or through arrangements tying together complementary types of production. In this respect, electronics reflects another widespread characteristic of contemporary industrial activity: the reliance on subcontracting as part of a strategy to diversify risks and lower production costs. Subcontracting creates links between advanced sectors and producers of simple components. The same process is giving rise to an informal (or underground) sector in electronics production. Workers, differentiated by ethnicity, gender and class, are found in the various strata bound by the subcontracting chain.

AN ILLUSTRATION

Megatek is a multimillion dollar interest operating as a directly owned subsidiary of American Inter Com and specializing in the production of interactive graphic computer terminals. It is located in an area significantly known as The Golden Triangle in La Jolla, San Diego County. Its facility covers a surface of approximately 4,000 square feet in a sprawling industrial park which combines precisely trimmed lawns with angular buildings fashioned in metal, glossy paint, and reflective glass. Impressive proportions match abstract decors, neutral, yet vaguely intimidating. To enter Megatek is to enter a temple of advanced technology, a confirmation of popular visions of the future.

Mr. Wyatt has been a Chief Executive Officer at Megatek for several years. He occupies an office whose most striking feature is a framed poster showing outer space contraptions and the refrain "Star Wars: The Next Frontier." This allusion to the Strategic Defense Initiative, vehemently promoted by the Reagan Administration, is more than a casual ornament. More than 50 percent of Megatek's production is defense-related. The rest finds its way into the cutting edge of scientific research and mass communications.

Graphic computer terminals are used for modelling and depicting the behavior, potentials and actual appearance of three-dimensional structures no matter how complex or small. From the cockpit of a missile to the orbital movement of electrons, all are possible spheres of application for this singular product. Its creation requires large investments in Research and Development. Thus, at Megatek more than half of three hundred employees are engineers and computer programmers. They are, by and large, young, affluent and male. Their job is to create languages, functions, and unique features suited to specialized requirements.

Admittedly, Megatek is a factory of sorts, but the raw materials are bits of information; the components are finished machines operating in harmony and yielding startling results. Only the testing department bears a slim resemblance to the factory of the recent past. Thirty workers, most of them women in live-colored uniforms, sit along tables intently looking at screens and through microscopes. Their appearance is mixed; some are Caucasian, others are Chicano, still others are Asian.

Megatek is the largest company operating within the Lehrman Industrial Park. It was correctly anticipated that its presence would cause the creation of other related operations. One of them is Data Wave, a firm that specializes in the production of software and which caters almost exclusively to Megatek's complex needs. Entry level salaries at Data Wave start at $30,000 a year. As part of a package of additional benefits, employees have access to a pagoda-like restaurant, swimming pool, tennis courts, jogging track, and fully equipped exercise room. Strolling behind the bamboo stalks and luscious vegetation that surround this quiet haven, one is tempted to ask whether the company also provides cosmetic surgery to its employees. It does not, most of the time.

Because of the nature of their production, Megatek and Data Wave are not directly involved in the assembly of electronics components. For that purpose they rely on several small companies located in Kearny Mesa, about 15 miles away from Lehrman Park, where a significant concentration of similar firms exists. One of them, Qual-tron, is owned by a former Megatek employee. His company specializes in different kinds of integrated circuits, produced under contract for some five regular clients and a varying number of occasional customers.

Given its position in the pecking order of electronics production, Qual-tron must have flexibility. That is one of the reasons why the majority of its

80 workers are Mexican women. When demand goes up, openings are announced by word of mouth and temporary workers are hired among the neighbors and relatives of the core personnel. When demand goes down, they are dismissed perfunctorily.

Qual-tron is a firm caught between the pressure of cheap overseas production and the threat of a rapidly changing technology. Its competitive edge depends on the ability to adapt. The owner is clear in that respect: "We can't fight the low wages paid in Asia or in Mexico; but we can offer a better product faster. Because we are close to our customers, we can have a slim advantage, we can make things easier for them."

The firm's versatility often means living on the margins of legality. A recent inspection by a field enforcement officer from the Wage and Hours Division (Department of Industrial Relations) revealed that workers at Qual-tron are often paid in cash for overtime, and at the regular rate of $4.50 instead of the time-and-a-half wage required by law. When activity peaks, some employees are allowed to take batches of components to their own homes where they are processed at piece rate. Rates can be as low as 7¢ per unit and 75 percent of firms in Kearny Mesa make regular or intermittent use of home workers; many of them are Mexican immigrants and Indo Chinese refugees. Maribel Guzman who has worked at Qual-tron for two years thinks home work is a good idea:

> I'm always looking for ways to earn a little more. My husband is a mechanic and we have two children. Since we came to California, I have worked in all sorts of jobs. But with a family to look after, and the cost of childcare being what it is, I can use the extra money. Sometimes, my neighbor helps and I give her part of what I get. She can't leave home because she has a baby and doesn't speak a word of English, but she too needs the money.

The extent to which home work in electronics is performed by Mexican immigrants is hard to assess given its highly elusive nature. However, informed observers in Los Angeles, Orange, and San Diego Counties believe it is common at the lower end of the industrial hierarchy, that is, where immigrants and refugees are most likely to be found. According to a Wage and Hours Enforcement Officer in San Diego:

> Such practices are all over. Home work in electronics is legal in the State of California. The problem arises from the way home work takes place. For example, employers don't ask how many individuals take part in the actual assembly; records are not kept on the hours worked . . . A Mexican or a Viet Namese can take home a thousand coils for wiring one evening, and put every close neighbor and family member to work, and return the next day to the plant, and only one standard piece rate fee is paid. It is very difficult to control that kind of thing; it's not even worth our time trying to wipe it out. When there are people eager to work for pennies, you can expect that kind of thing to happen.

The preceding examples suggest that the consolidation of a Southern California electronics emporium is occurring on the basis of more than the presence of highly advanced R&D facilities, universities, and design centers. One of the most attractive features in the area is the large labor pool formed by minorities, particularly Hispanic women. Their participation in manufacturing may have been underestimated by scholars, but not by entrepreneurs.

CONCLUSIONS

What, then, is to be made of high-tech industries said to be the embodiment of a second industrial revolution in the United States? Contrary to generalized expectations, comparatively few of the openings provided by these new firms will happen in fields such as engineering. The majority of the openings will be for assemblers and other direct production workers.

The same forces that led to the transfer of production to overseas locations and the establishment of Export Processing Zones in less developed countries are now transforming regions within the United States into attractive locations for high-tech manufacturing. In the same vein, electronics production involves a particular labor/capital circuit consisting of outward investments in offshore manufacture and new international labor flows into domestic areas where highly advanced forms of production are taking place. Florida, Texas and Southern California, among others, are competing for high-tech industries on this basis. Our research shows that Hispanic workers, many of them women and immigrants, are playing a decisive role in this development.

The meaning of these labor recruitment strategies is still unclear. On the one hand, it could be argued that the electronics industry is providing vital employment to minorities and to unskilled and semiskilled workers. On the other hand, it is possible that the growing employment of Hispanics (especially recent immigrants, refugees, and undocumented workers) reflects deteriorating conditions for labor as a whole. Past research has consistently shown that immigrants, especially undocumented workers, tend to have a vulnerable position in the labor market. The same is true of unskilled and semiskilled women. Yet, these are precisely the kinds of workers favored by these new industries.

What ultimately matters is whether workers in electronics manufacture can make similar gains to those made by past generations employed in traditional industries. Some factors mitigate against that possibility. For example, overseas production and the geographical decentralization of assembly operation have weakened U.S. workers' chances for unionization. From the beginning, electronics companies have been characterized by high rates of turnover, low wages and few opportunities for occupational advancement. They have been, in addition, notoriously resistant to organizing drives. The most advanced producers in the electronics industry overtly express their distaste for workers' organizations and unions as factors considered deleterious to business.

In spite of this, some observers point out that electronics is a young industry still adjusting to market conditions. They note that older sectors like auto and steel experienced early phases during which competition and underdeveloped markets fostered extremely low wages, job insecurity, and bad working conditions. With the passage of time, the same industries expanded, affording benefits to their employees. Something similar, they claim, can happen in electronics.

Whatever the outcome, the present structure of electronics production bears little resemblance to the image of a "post-industrial society" where the benefits of advanced technology should render class conflict superfluous and manual work a thing of the past. It is high time that we divide fantasy from reality.

NOTES

1. Unless otherwise specified, the information contained in this article was collected as part of A Collaborative Study of Hispanic Women in Garment and Electronics Industries, sponsored by the Ford and Tinker Foundations between 1983 and 1986. Special thanks are due to Ms. Patricia Biggers, Dr. Bill Diaz and Mr. Herny Ramos for their personal encouragement, and to Ms. Lisa Portes for her editorial suggestions.

2. For a comprehensive view of internationalization in garment and electronics production see Frobel, Heinrichs, and Kreye, 1979.

3. For studies related to the working experience of Hispanic women see Alclay, 1984; DeLay, 1983; Guhleman and Tienda, No Date; Gurak and Kritz, 1982; Haug, 1983; Safa, 1981; Tienda, 1983.

4. For an overview of factors leading to plant closings in the United States see Bluestone and Harrison, 1981.

5. For recent findings regarding the growth of the informal sector or underground economy in the United States see Portes and Sassen Koob, 1987. For a discussion of informalization in garment production in California and Florida see Fernandez Kelly and Garcia, 1986.

6. The names of firms and individuals in the following ethnographic accounts have been altered for reasons of confidentiality. However, the situations are real.

7. *Operadora* is a widespread term used along the border to designate assemblies and other types of direct production workers. A *maquiladora* is a factory operating as a directly owned subsidiary or subcontracted affiliate of a multinational corporation (generally based in the United States). Incentives granted to *maquiladora* operations by the Mexican government originally included a) Amendments to the Customs Code allowing for the temporary

288   PATRICIA FERNANDEZ KELLY AND ANNA M. GARCIA

entrance of foreign machinery, components, and materials, b) Waiving of foreign
investment provisions permitting up to 100 percent foreign control over industrial investments; and c) The purchase or lease of Mexican land for industrial
purposes for up to 99 years through trusts entered with national banks. These
and other stimuli originally applied to a 12.5 mile border belt. Since 1972 they
have been extended to the rest of the country with the exception of three highly
industrialized areas: Mexico City, Guadalajara, and Monterrey.

8. A term commonly used to designate the Immigration and Naturalization Service.

9. See also Bonilla, 1984.

10. For a succint history of the electronics industry see Siegel, 1984.

REFERENCES

Alclay, R. 1984. "Hispanic Women in the United States: Family and Work Relations." *Migration Today* Vol. 12 (3).

Baca, R. and B. Dexter. No Date. "Mexican undocumented women workers
in Los Angeles: A research note," in *Female Immigrants to the United States:
Caribbean, Latin American, and African Experiences.* eds. D. Mortimer and
R. Bryce-Laporte. Washington, D.C.: Smithsonian Institution.

Bluestone, B. and B. Harrison. 1981. *The Deindustrialization of America.* New
York: The Free Alliance.

Bonilla, F. 1984 *Labor Migration and Capitalism: The Puerto Rican Experience.*
New York: History Task Force for Puerto Rican History.

Bradshaw, T.K. and M. Freeman. 1984. "The Future of the electronics Industry
in California Communities," Institute of Governmental Studies, University of California.

Castell, M. 1985. "Towards the informational city, high technology economic
change and spatial structure: some exploratory hypotheses," Working
Paper No. 430, University of California at Berkeley, Institute of Urban
and Regional Development.

DeLey, M. 1983. "The work experience of undocumented Mexican women,"
International Migration Review eds. M. LaPorte and B. LaPorte. Washington, D.C.: Smithsonian Institution.

Fernandez Kelly, M.P. 1983. *For We Are Sold, I and My People: Women and Industry in Mexico's Frontier.* Albany: State University of New York Press.

———. 1985. "Contemporary production and the new international division
of labor," in *The Americas in the New International Division of Labor.* ed.
Steve Sanderson. New York: Holmes and Meier.

Fernandez Kelly, M.P. and Anna M. Garcia. 1986. "The Making of an Underground Economy: Hispanic Women, Home Work, and the Advanced Capitalist State." *Urban Anthropology* Vol. 14(1–3).

Frobel, F., J. Heinrichs, and O. Kreye. 1979. *The New International Division of Labor.* New York: Cambridge University Press.

Gershuny. J.I. 1979. "The informal economy: its role in industrial society," *Futures* 11:3–16.

Glassmeier, A., A.R. Markusen and P. Hall. 1983. Defining High Technology Industries. Working Paper No. 407. University of California at Berkeley: Institute of Urban and Regional Development.

Guhleman, P. and M. Tienda. No Date. "A socio-economic profile of Hispanic-American female workers: perspectives on labor force participation and earnings," CD Working Paper 81–7. University of Wisconsin-Madison.

Gurak, D. and M. Kritz. 1982. "Hispanic workers in the garment and restaurant industries in Los Angeles County," Working Papers in U.S.-Mexican Studies, No. 12. university of California, San Diego.

Haug, M. 1983. "Miami's garment industry and its workers," in *Research on the Sociology of Women.* Greenwich: JAI Press.

Milkman, R. 1980. "Organizing the Sexual Division of Labor: Historical Perspectives on 'Women's Work' and the American Labor Movement," *Socialist Review,* 10 (Jan.-Feb.), 95–150.

Morales, R. 1984. "Transnational Labor: Undocumented Workers in the Los Angeles Automobile Industry." *International Migration Review.* 17 4: 570–596.

Nash, J. and M.P. Fernandez Kelly. 1983. *Women, Men and the New International Division of Labor.* Albany: State University of New York Press.

O'Connor, D. "Changing patterns of international production in the semiconductor industry: the role of transnational corporations," Presented to Conference on Microelecronics in Transition, University of California at Santa Cruz, May 12–15.

Portes, A. and S. Sassen Koob. 1987. "Making it underground," *American Journal of Sociology,* forthcoming.

Portes, A. and J. Walton. 1982. *Labor, Class, and the International System.* New York: Aberdeen Press.

Safa, H.I. 191. "The differential incorporation of Hispanic women in the U.S. labor force," in *Female Immigrants to the United States: Caribbean, Latin American, and African Experiences.* eds. D. Mortimer and R. Bryce-Laporte. Washington, D.C.: Smithsonian Institution.

Sassen Koob, S. 1985. "Growth and informalization at the core: the case of New York City," in *The Urban Informal Sector: Recent Trends in Research and Theory*. Conference Proceedings. Department of Sociology, The John Hopkins University, Baltimore.

Scott, A.J. "Industrial Organization and the Logic of Intra-Metropolitan Location: A Case Study of the Printed Circuits Industry in the Greater Los Angeles Region. Department of Geography. University of California.

Scott, J. 1987. "Is the concept of gender useful to historians?" *Historical Review*, forthcoming.

Siegel, L. 1984. "Delicate bonds: the semiconductor industry," Mountain View, California: Pacific Studies Center.

Tienda, M. 1983. "Market characteristics and Hispanic earnings: a comparison of natives and immigrants," *Social Problems* 31:59–72.

United Nations Industrial Development Organization. 1981. "Export processing zones in less developed countries," Working Paper No. 167.

United States Department of Labor, Bureau of Labor Statistics. 1983. "Employment forecasts of the eighties," Washington, D.C.

Part V

WHAT DOES IT ALL MEAN?

CHAPTER 16

Policy Implications:
The Worth of Women's Work

RUTH NEEDLEMAN AND ANNE NELSON

The close examination of women's work lives presented in the preceding chapters demonstrates the tremendous energy, creativity, persistence, and skill of America's working women. Forced to accept the most tedious jobs, they devise ways of asserting their autonomy, as well as their originality and personal pride in labor. Pressed by the constraints of job demands, women improve performance by skillfully managing the social relations surrounding the physical task. This is particularly true where there is an asymmetry in power. "The lower-status person," Glenn writes in Chapter Four, "has to be attuned to the feeling and needs of the higher-status person" (p. 68). We saw this to be true for women in hospitals and schools, as well as for domestic workers.

At the same time, these chapters highlight the degree to which women's work experiences are tied to their home and family responsibilities and are bound by gender stereotypes. Discrimination forces women into stressful, low paying occupations. Above all, the authors document the degree to which society undervalues the contributions of women in their work.

IMPORTANCE OF QUALITATIVE RESEARCH FOR POLICYMAKERS

Qualitative research opens a window on aspects of women's work lives usually missed by more quantitative approaches. In particular, this research explores the complex and critical relations between a woman's work and her home life. Further, it demonstrates the need to analyze employment and wage factors in relation to the entire life experience of workers, male as well as female.

The impact of a shift change on janitorial workers, as tracked by Hood in this volume, demonstrates how critical this home/work/family relationship is.

Traditionally, sociologists have assumed that women's work behavior is gender based but that men's is not; they have viewed family and parenting as female issues alone. As a result, most studies of male employees have ignored the worker's life outside the job and viewed women, in contrast, largely in terms of marriage and childbearing. The studies in this collection document the more recent findings of sociologists like Feldberg and Glenn (1982) who show that women's workplace behavior, like men's, is affected by job-related factors as well as by family roles and responsibilities. In each chapter, the authors examine the multiple influences on women's work behavior, and demonstrate the short-comings of labor policies and laws that regulate such a limited portion of the work force and protect or provide for such a small percentage of workers' overall needs.

THE NATURE OF WOMEN'S WORK

These multidimensional portraits of women at work accurately convey the nature of most women's work experience. Like the domestics, secretaries, nurses, and teachers discussed in this book, most women work in jobs considered traditionally female. More than half (55 percent) are employed in clerical or service occupations, according to Department of Labor statistics (U.S. Dept. of Labor, Women's Bureau 1983, 51). In fact, the ten leading jobs for women are secretary, cashier, bookkeeper, registered nurse, waitress, elementary school teacher, nurse's aide, sales worker or supervisor, and typist (U.S. Dept. of Labor, Women's Bureau 1985, 3).

Women's work very often includes service to others, whether to a patient, an employer, or the public, and generally parallels the kinds of tasks women are expected to do because of their gender. Caring and caretaking are an integral part of many female occupations. As Collins points out in her chapter, "Most people order off a menu, and the offerings for women in the world of paid work have been limited, at a fixed price, to roles and tasks consistent with those performed by women in the home" (p. 187).

It is, unfortunately, this gender-based characteristic of women's work that exacerbates the exploitation of female labor. Because many tasks in traditionally female occupations are considered "natural" for women — an extension of their gender role — they are not classified as skilled work, and often are not classified as work at all. Romero discusses how domestic workers sometimes receive little support at home because their performance of housework is not perceived by other family members as a job. Nurses find that their work-related skills are also overlooked or dismissed. "Palliative functions vis a vis the patient," according to Corley and Mauksch, "are too frequently seen as natural, female, rather than competence-based professional functions (p. 136).

If women perform certain work "naturally" with no special training or skill, then women's work could conceivably be handled by anyone. This seems to be the conclusion many employers draw. Spencer points out, for example, how teaching has been denigrated by the use of untrained and unprepared substitutes. "The fact that the schools often hire substitute teachers who do not necessarily have certification to teach the grades or subjects they are asked to teach," she writes, "contributes to the notion that teaching is something anyone can do" (p. 176). Views such as these contribute to the undervalued status of women's occupations in the labor market.

Women's ability to manage social relations is rarely if ever acknowledged as a skill. Even though this talent seems to have a direct and positive effect on productivity, as with managers or nurse's aides (Statham and Diamond), it, too, is discouraged and devalued. It is often seen as "natural" for women, hence not part of the job, certainly not something to be rewarded.

As a result, women's work is overloaded, undervalued, and often invisible when it comes to compensation. Contributions women bring to jobs are taken for granted; superiors will rely on their skill but rarely pay them for it. One reason there is a significant wage gap between average male and female earnings is because women are not compensated for much of the work they perform.

Another equally important feature of most female occupations is their subordinate position within a given field. There is no clearer example than that of the medical profession. Nurse's aides, nurses, social workers, abortion and genetic counselors, even female hospital administrators are held accountable to a male structure of authority. As Corley and Mauksch explain, physicians dominate the hospital hierarchy and control the major areas of policy decision making. Collins describes how one female hospital administator resigned because the male-determined patterns of conducting business (at the golf course) would have subjected her to unacceptable value judgments. There is, in fact, no occupation or profession described in these pages in which a woman holds the authority to determine overall work conditions and institutional priorities.

The rest of this chapter will examine the exploitative nature of women's work and suggest policy alternatives. The discussion focuses on four subject areas: occupational segregation, wage discrimination, family needs, and social protections.

Clearly, major shifts in policy are needed to eliminate occupational segregation, reduce wage discrimination, and accommodate family needs. The fact is that current trends in policy and legislation reflect an antifamily bias, a lack of genuine concern for children and parenting, and a contempt for jobs involving caring and caretaking. To overcome these values and attitudes, there must be a coordinated effort involving women workers themselves, labor and women's organizations, academic researchers, and policy makers.

OCCUPATIONAL SEGREGATION

As indicated above, women are concentrated overwhelmingly in service and clerical occupations and have made surprisingly small inroads into traditional male areas. Despite a growing body of evidence to the contrary, male free-market economists still argue that women prefer and choose these occupations because they are easier, more convenient, and more suitable to the double responsibilities so many working mothers bear.

Our studies provide important insights into the job selection process as it exists in the real world. Today's female worker still finds herself sidetracked by closed job markets and restrictive family demands. Most of the women whose stories we have read ended up in their occupations by necessity or default, not by preference. "I backed into social work," admitted one woman (Collins, p. 191). "I took pre-med in college and drifted into nursing," explained another (Collins, p. 191). "Teaching was a back-up" for a third. Secetaries expressed a similar sentiment; they spoke of "falling into their jobs," waiting for a better chance (Statham).

A majority of the female administrators interviewed found themselves drafted into these higher-status positions or pressured into them by poverty or circumstance. In some cases, they were already doing the work (Collins). Chicano women forced by financial problems to re-enter the work force after marrying and having a family could find little other than household work (Romero). Domestic work, Glenn indicates, is an "economic ghetto for women of color" (p. 57).

That women choose certain occupations because of the difficulties in balancing home, childcare, and work responsibilities reflects the absence of opportunity not the exercise of choice. As Collins emphasizes, "The career and work behavior of men and women begins to look very different due to sex-role socialization and the different structure of opportunity" (p. 188). The attraction of household work and direct sales, for example, is the flexibility in scheduling these occupations offer; women can work around family demands (Glenn; Romero; Connelly and Rhoton). Clearly, greater availability of childcare and after-school programs, or the extension of business hours, would *enable* women to consider other occupations.

Efforts of women to break into nontraditional areas are discouraged or blocked in a variety of ways. Again, these studies help us to identify obstacles and to appreciate the resistance women often confront in a male-dominated job. The experience of policewomen, while perhaps extreme because of the strong, physical, male culture involved, targets the most common problems. These begin with entry level requirements, initial training, and assignments (Martin). Physical strength and size are emphasized over any other job prerequisites, even to the exclusion of other skills equally critical to the job and more easily acquired by women. "The culture [of police]," Martin explains, "serves to obscure the fact that the day-to-day reality of police work does not revolve around crime fighting or demand extensive physical skills, but involves emotional and intellectual labor and requires interpersonal skills" (p. 209).

Success in the field also requires integration into social patterns of behavior that are male determined. For policewomen, it may mean barroom discussions or late-night card games; for managers and administrators, it may mean barroom discussions or golf. There are striking similarities between the obstacles faced by policewomen and those that thwart the efforts of female managers and administrators. Managers, too, run up against male-biased training programs and evaluation standards. Like female police, female managers and administrators are judged by their ability to perform like men and are rarely permitted to demonstrate the effectiveness of different approaches (Statham; Collins).

Not only are women discouraged from entering traditionally male jobs but the traditionally female jobs are characterized by the absence of career ladders. There is no progression from nurse to physician, from secretary to manager, from electronics assembly worker to electrician, or, for that matter, from nurse's aide to nurse. Blocked mobility, Martin points out, leads to limited motivation (p. 206). But the victim is often charged with the crime, as in the case where women are prevented from advancing along a career ladder and are then blamed for a lack of career commitment.

Occupational segregation is perpetuated by inadequate training, education, career ladders, and promotional opportunities. Improved educational opportunities are essential if women are to move out of traditional job areas. These opportunities should be designed to compensate for the late stage at which many women begin careers because of family responsibilities. An expansion of special apprenticeship programs and professional training for women can also help prepare them to overcome barriers and cope with male resistance. If women are to take advantage of existing programs, greater financial support is needed. There are few financial aid programs designed for women who may have to attend on a part time basis and who may need childcare and financial support for the family while in school. Opportunities must range from obtaining high school equivalency diplomas to advanced vocational training and college degree work. The rapidly changing nature of work requires programs strong in basic reading, writing, and analytical skills to give the worker greater self-confidence, flexibility, and adaptability. Also, training should not track women into low-paying, traditionally female job areas.

Training may also have to provide separate programs for women workers, for the reasons Martin so effectively lays out. Studies have shown that women are less assertive and participate less in mixed groups, and may not develop the necessary leadership skills in situations where men assume controlling roles.[1] In addition, training for nontraditional jobs, especially where physical strength is important, should reflect the special needs of women workers and should facilitate their entry, not by lowering standards but by providing a more rigorous and appropriate curriculum.

Finally, training programs for the professions should credit women workers with skills they have already acquired. For example, nurses or genetic counselors who wish to move up in the medical profession should not have to go through the same training as a college graduate with no hospital or health care work experience. Alternative career ladders need to be built into fields, so that women can apply their past experience and knowledge to obtain more challenging and responsible positions.

Entry level jobs and requirements should be redesigned so they do not exclude women. Also, job descriptions and evaluation procedures should acknowledge the kinds of work women do perform and reward them for the skills they demonstrate. This upgrading of women's occupations would help them secure promotions; it would also lessen the stigma attached to their jobs, thereby attracting more men into these fields. Without efforts to integrate traditionally female as well as male occupations, labor market segregation will persist.

DISCRIMINATORY WAGE SYSTEMS

Women still earn on the average sixty-four cents on each dollar paid to men; even where women work in the same occupations as men, their income falls significantly below that of their male peers. Among sales workers, for example, women earn only 51 percent of men's salaries (U.S. Dept. of Labor, Women's Bureau 1983, 93). Connelly and Rhoton's comparative study of Amway and Mary Kay sales provides some insight into that wage differential. Women make up 50 percent of all workers in the $3,000 to $15,000 income range, but less than 3 percent of those earning $50,000 and over (U.S. Dept. of Labor, Women's Bureau 1983, 83; Needleman 1986).

As Diamond so aptly writes, "The wage created poverty" (p. 41). The wage is the minimum wage, which applies to many traditionally female occupations and which accounts for the large number of female-headed households living in poverty. Over 25 percent of families maintained by *working* women are poor; only 5 percent of families with an employed adult male can claim poverty status (Women's Economic Agenda Working Group 1985, 13). What's more, the Bureau of Labor Statistics job projections for 1995 show the following occupations as those most likely to generate more jobs; nurse's aides and orderlies, sales clerks, cashiers, waitresses, and janitors (Women's Economic Agenda Working Group 1985, 14). Longstanding wage discrimination in women's occupations threatens now to undercut the standard of living for a growing number of American workers.

Poverty wage scales force women to increase their already burdensome workload. One of the women janitors in Hood's study routinely moonlighted two days a week in a nursing home and chose the night shift in order to receive a shift differential in wages. When she was forced to work days, she doubled her hours at the nursing home (p. 94). Diamond's research also indicates that moonlighting and overtime are necessary practices among nursing home workers. Many teachers also moonlight during the school year.

Sex-based wage discrimination is bound up with the undervaluation of women's work. Historically it was argued that women's income was not essential to the support of a family, and therefore women's wages could be lower than men's. Employees proceeded to set separate wage scales for their female employees. Eventually, employers displaced male workers with females as a means of lowering wages. Secretarial work, teaching, and genetic counseling are examples of professions that became female-dominated, and then dead-end and low-paid; as a consequence, they lost status.

Many of these chapters recount the frustrations and disappointments of female workers whose pride in their occupation is undermined by their low wages and eroded by society's underevaluation of their work. Often job descriptions, where they exist, do not list the kinds of responsibilities and tasks expected of a female worker — whether a secretary or a nurse.

Studies of job evaluation systems have confirmed a male bias. Points are awarded for different skills, responsibilities, and work environments.[2] Heavy lifting counts for points, but not repeating lifting of small objects. Also, nurses and nurse's aides are not compensated for the lifting and turning of patients. Full-body motion receives credit but not repeated motions involving only arms, hands, and wrists; secretaries and electronics workers are on the losing end here. In other cases, employers practice old-fashioned double standards in evaluating certain skills. AT&T placed great importance on contact with the public when it set salaries for its management personnel, but did not even acknowledge it as a factor in evaluating telephone operators until challenged by the union (Steinberg 1984, 2).

A number of the preceding chapters provide examples of discriminatory job evaluation. "Secretaries," Statham stresses, "actually do more managing than has previously been acknowledged" (p. 226). Nurses take primary responsibility for a patient's life and health, since it is the nurse who works nights and weekend shifts and oversees the patient on a day-to-day basis. Yet this reality is rarely reflected in a nurse's paycheck. The skill of managing social relations is especially likely to go unrecognized though it is often of critical importance in the workplace. Diamond shows that were it not for the unrecognized and surreptitious caring for nursing home residents by aides, schedules could not be met. Statham's findings suggest that secretaries whose female managers are supportive of their career goals and respectful of their skills are more productive. The other side of management skills is demonstrated by women in subordinate positions who learn to handle the moods and manipulations of their superiors. Household workers, as both Glenn and Romero point out, learn to avoid doing added work as "personal favors" or based on appeals to friendship. Secretaries, nurses, and counselors also must learn this skill or be taken advantage of to perform a myriad of "gender-natural" tasks. The ability to manage relationships effectively should be valued highly in the marketplace and paid accordingly, but instead this talent is discounted or discouraged.

Collins raises the central question in her chapter when she asks: "How much do we care about caring, and are we willing, as a society, to offer respect and a living wage to those who do it for us" (p. 200)? Not only must caring and caretaking be rewarded in the labor market, but the millions of women engaged in home and childcare work should also receive compensation. Women's work in general should be valued for its contribution and paid accordingly. Many pay-equity efforts have moved us in this direction, but legislation is needed to secure job evaluation studies in the private sector and to eliminate discrimination in the public sector.

Women in nontraditional occupations face wage discrimination in part because they are measured by standards established by the male incumbents. A female manager will be evaluated on her ability to manage like a man, and as a result may be denied an increase or a promotion (Statham). Collins observes that "a different salary structure for men and women was common in all three fields" of administration, teaching, nursing, and social work (pp. 194-195).

Other factors contribute to the low wage levels of women workers as well.[3] As Kelly and Garcia show, industries mainly employing women, like electronics and garment, have been severely affected by international markets and competition. Cheap, unprotected, and unorganized labor overseas — usually female labor — has driven down wage levels in this country for many workers. In addition, the occupation in which most women work are the least unionized and protected. Organized female workers earn on the average 30 percent more than unorganized workers. Increased unionization would boost wage scales.

Minimum wage laws set a standard that maintains many women and their families in poverty. The minimum should enable a worker to live decently on one job and should not become the standard wage for female workers. At the same time, measures are needed to improve enforcement of fair labor standards, from wages to overtime. Homework, piecework, and service work of various kinds are rarely monitored; existing legislation should be extended to cover all workers, including undocumented workers.

FAMILY NEEDS

The chapters in this collection also show problems in the areas of family and health. These problems will continue to grow with the expansion of the service sector where the majority of women work. A particular problem in this area is that of family-work conflicts.

Work and family intrude on each other. Women — the family generalists, parents of last resort for most crises and of first resort for everyday cleaning, cooking, and caring — have developed skills throughout their lives to serve family needs. Those skills are among the ones carried into the workplace. When women work, their responsibilities at home are lightened relatively little by other family members. When the husband of Anna Williams was laid off, there was no suggestion that he should assume any household responsibilities beyond accompanying his wife on shopping expeditions (Hood). She was left with bills to pay in person and doctors' appointments to schedule, although by this point she was working the day shift and had no time to make these arrangements. Amway and Mary Kay salespeople fit their work around their household schedules. Care of children and saving of husbands' dignity were extremely important to the Chicano and Japanese-American housekeepers, described by Romero and Glenn. Jobs were shaped to meet family demands. Little thought was given to seeking, learning, and achieving support from outside. While part time household work is one method for integrating work into family life, both part time and full time jobs carry burdens.

Hood reports on the "complex households run by most of the women," households of husbands, children, and grandchildren. Older children helped out. Parents took care of the basic food, shelter, and clothing needs, but were not around for sizable chunks of home time. Relatives and friends in the neighborhood performed sitting services. Spencer refers to the women teachers "soured" by the conflict between roles at school and at home. She goes on to say, ". . . as long as there are teachers who . . . must constantly deal with a triple day of work . . . the quality of education will be seriously affected" (p. 183).

Given the low wages of the women studied, out-of-home childcare services were not possible. In 1985, most parents paid about $3,000 per child per year for such care, with the range being from $1,500 to $10,000 a year. The median annual earnings for part time women workers who work 52 weeks and for full time women workers ($5,000 and $13,000 respectively in 1982) could not cover these charges (Conference Board, 1985). Federal and state support for childcare services has been cut back radically in the last few years, and the difficulty of paying for childcare has turned many women to part time work. Because they wish to give their children care, these mothers take a 50 percent or greater cut in their own earnings.

Public policies that would make quality childcare available around-the-clock for shift workers — infant to school age for young children, and after school for older children — would go a long way toward ending the cycle typical for children who grow up in poverty, a cycle that includes poor health, a shorter life, and dim educational prospects. Other childcare alternatives are industry-sponsored off-site and on-site centers, labor union-sponsored centers, voucher or vendor systems that cover the costs of care for employees, and community-based family providers in the neighborhood. All of these services need to provide for the growth, education, and well-being of the children, safeguarding today's families and increasing the odds for stability and success for tomorrow's young workers.

Few women described in these studies had maternity coverage. Indeed, the majority of all working women in this country do not have any coverage — one indication of our shamefully weak family-support system. There is no federal maternity leave policy; instead, pregnant women are guaranteed the same fringe benefits given to disabled workers. Maternity leave is customarily established or negotiated from employer to employer with differing results, if it is provided at all. When provided, it usually covers six to ten weeks of leave, typically at about half pay. Every other industrial country has a statutory ma-

ternity policy providing the essential benefits to working women. These countries provide both paid and unpaid leave periods. Paid leave may be at full wages
but more often is a proportion of full pay. Extended leaves — the right of a
woman to return to work up to a year after the birth of a child at the same
pay level — would help to cover the costs of childbearing. Guaranteed light
duty when necessary during pregnancy is another need usually not met in the
workplace.

Especially in the absence of childcare services, childbearing often involves
work interruptions to care for sickness or other childhood needs. Personal time
or parental time, paid in full or in part, can help parents cope with emergency
interruptions. Flextime arrangements enable parents to work and accommodate
children's schedules. Both parental/personal leave and flextime are provided
by many large employers. The women in this study were, for the most part,
not covered by these formal provisions.

Work intruded on the family in very personal ways for the women we
studied. They expressed feelings of exhaustion, short tempers when they arrived home, depression. "Understaffing and overload is a continuous theme
of complaints expressed by nurses and even by nursing administrators," write
Corley and Mauksch (p. 140). "Some . . . reported profound fatigue, a 'tiredness'
or boredom with patient care." One nurse said, "I love nursing . . . but I don't
plan to continue much longer," and another described her profession as "just
physically and mentally exhausting and draining" (p. 145). Theoretically lov-
ing children, teachers found they had to stretch a lot to handle the unlikable
child. Diamond describes how nursing assistants, aware of the fragility of the
older women in the nursing home and trying to help patients hold fast to their
identity, found they often could not cope with both job and patient needs.
Stress was high for the women on whom we focused. Even the genetic and
abortion counselors who had switched from intimate counseling to "shuffle,
shuffle, shuffle the people" were under stress; in their case, the stress was
bureaucratic (Rothman and Detlefs). The pace at which these women worked,
often in isolation, give them little chance for common activity or rest.

Surely, we know how to alter those conditions. American labor has a
long history of resisting speedups and lobbying for rest times and rest places.
Legislation and the enforcement and organization of preunion caucuses or union
representation can help humanize the workplace. In their absence, family and
home life both suffer.

SOCIAL PROTECTIONS

A rearrangement of social protections is underway in this country. Some
protections have never been provided in a uniform way — health insurance,
for example. Some have applied to some workers but not to all; farm work,
domestic service, and government work are often excluded. Pensions are generally nonexistent outside large corporate structures or civil service retirement

systems. Only 20 percent of all older women receive any pension, and for most of these women, Social Security is the only entitlement that applies (U.S. Commerce Department, 1980).

Women who have earned low wages all their lives will receive low retirement benefits. Permanent part time workers receive the same benefits full time workers receive, prorated to the number of hours worked, if they have worked a thousand hours in a single year (roughly twenty hours per week). But sick leave, holiday pay, paid vacation, medical and other insurance, company benefits, and membership in retirement plans are generally denied temporary employees or irregular part-timers.

The growth of the part time, temporary workforce is one aspect of the changed economic forces now operating. Part-timers were more than 17 percent of the workforce in 1985 — 19 million people, two-thirds of whom were women (Nardone, 1986). Not all wanted to be part time employees; 5.6 million part-timers would have rather worked full time. Low wages, few benefits, and no tenure claims make part-timers a cost benefit to financially pressed employers. But they almost certainly will lead to a greater demand for public health and welfare services.

For household workers — many of whom work part time, while others, as described by Glenn, "[pieced] together a 40 or 48 hour week out of a combination of full and half-day jobs" (p. 59) — there are no benefits other than Social Security. And that retirement benefit is unsubstantial because part time employment depresses lifetime earnings and because pay problems arise for these workers "not so much from starting pay, as from the lack of raises" (p. 64). Low lifetime earnings provide little Social Security protection. Glenn speaks of the long work lives of the women she studied, many working well into their seventies.

Other protections, such the Child Nutrition, Medicaid, and Food Stamp programs, have been discontinued or reduced. Eligibility requirements for these benefits have been tightened and regulations often changed. For many, especially for immigrant women — the Japanese and Chicano household workers described by Glenn and Romero and the Hispanic factory workers studied by Kelly and Garcia — it can be difficult to gain access to the necessary information and to achieve the accuracy required in completing and filing applications.

Lack of union membership is also a problem. Health, retirement, and other protective benefits are often negotiated for union members. Yet the great majority of working women do not belong to a union. Of the women studied here, only the janitors belonged to a union. The high-technology employers in southern California researched by Kelly and Garcia actively resisted organizing campaigns, "overtly express[ing] their distaste for workers' organizations and unions as deleterious to business practices" (p. 286). Office workers expressed professional aloofness to collective activity (Statham).

The heavy demands of work and family hamper women in their efforts to educate themselves about what protections are or could be available to them. Ways are needed to bring these ill-used workers together. Information on health insurance and childcare, probably the two most important protections that could be supplied, might provide a springboard for concerted efforts to improve women's economic and social status.

WOMEN'S RESPONSES TO WORKPLACE PROBLEMS

The great strength of women on the bottom rungs of the work ladder lies in their numbers. Although opposition to the system was present among these women, on the whole they accommodated themselves to it for lack of opportunity to make changes. Part of the feeling of having little chance to make change is caused by the racial and ethnic discrimination that pervades the lives of black women and those who do not speak our language. Part of it lies in fear of reprisal. Corley and Mauksch ask, "Why is it that nurses do not try more radical approaches to resolve problems involving inadequate staffing and support services" (p. 145)? In response, the authors quote Bullogh (1978) who says, "Feelings of powerlessness and fear of punishment can prevent people from challenging the status quo," even when the fear is not based on reality.

Contributors to this volume have given us a story of powerless people who strive to maintain their own definitions of themselves and of their work in contradiction to the definitions of those for whom they work. Glenn's study points to an underlying theme for those in the caretaking occupations: the judgments held by others are not congruent with the reality of the work. The Japanese-Americans Glenn describes suffered wounds to their self-esteem from being domestic workers — a particularly embarrassing occupation in their culture — but their self-esteem did not suffer from *doing* the work. In the doing, "they [revealed] considerable pride." They respected the work and found autonomy and dignity in a setting designed to rob them of these.

Autonomy — power over one's time and activities — is often achieved by default and by forms of resistance. Autonomy by default may be gained by working unseen. Nursing assistants in Diamond's study, when not watched, performed extra services and kindnesses. Janitors told Hood that much about the night shift was better than the day shift: they had plenty of time to do their work, no one interfered with them or showed disrespect, and they could see the results of their work. Secretaries, though overwhelmed by the time pressure, considered that they were avoiding the stresses felt by their women managers: "I wouldn't do what she does, not if you paid me a million dollars. I like being able to leave at 4:30 and not feel I should be staying" (Statham, p. 231). Autonomy was possible for policewomen while they worked with the public outside the male-dominated, hostile station. Housekeepers tried to work when the employer was not at home. Genetic and abortion counselors, although overworked and bureaucratized, considered that one favorable aspect of their job was that most of the time they were left alone to do it.

Women in every occupation described here tried to prevent the downgrading of their work. They were inventive in finding ways to control the quality of their work and the order in which it was done. They protested lack of equipment, allocation of insufficient time to do the work properly, and the rigidity of bureaucratic regulation and forms. Self-determination was the workers' goal, but since that was also the goal of supervisors, open resistance was shunned in favor of tactics such as the claiming of certain space as their own. This resistance permitted employees to retain a sense of pride in what they did and a sense of humanity toward others — clients, coworkers, managers.

Most of the working women studied here had a high commitment to their work. They wanted to do it properly, and in the absence of the resources to do so — time, equipment, assistance from other departments — they overloaded themselves. This overload and determination were sources of pride and self-respect. They also served as rebukes to higher-status groups who showed less commitment. But overload, a form of partial resistance, also made these women objects of exploitation. Take the nurses, for example, who were constantly shortchanged on support services, supplies, and maintenance because the unfinished work of others was "dumped" on them.

The forms of protest described in these pages range from coping and overworking to gaining control and quitting. That these are all individual rather than collective ways of responding is attributable to the considerable isolation of the women studied.

What is wanted and needed are new policies, something more than the bravery of resistance reported here. Effectuating new policies, however, calls for collective action. From a collective spirit, courageous spokespersons can emerge and become heroines to their group. Labor history is studded with the rise of rank-and-file members to leadership, the transformation of workers from assemblers to policymakers. Protests about work conditions and pay can lead to more than accommodation. The movement from individual to collective consciousness is empowering. From it can come human control over the work human beings do.

NOTES

1. For a discussion of the importance of special training programs for women workers, see Needleman 1987; Broverman, Vogel, Broverson, Carlson and Rosenkranz 1972; Izraeli 1984; Lockheed and Hall 1976; and Megargee 1969.

2. For a discussion of job evaluation procedures and problems of bias, see the articles in Remick 1984, Part 2.

3. It is important to note that leading economists have found "less than half of the gross earnings differentials can be accounted for by such human capital factors as education, training, experience, and skill requirements". (Marshall 1983, 18). More than half the wage gap can, therefore, be attributed to sex discrimination in the labor force.

REFERENCES

Broverman, Inge, Susan R. Vogel, Donald Broverson, Frank E. Carlson and Paul S. Rosenkranz. 1972. "Sex-role stereotypes: A current appraisal," *Journal of Social Issues* 28:59–78.

Bullough, B. 1978. "Barriers to the nurse practitioner movement: Problems of women in a women's field." In *Organization of Health Workers and Labor Conflict*. ed. S. Wolfe. Boston: Baywoud Publishing Company.

Conference Board. 1985. "Corporate financial assistance for childcare," *The Conference Board 1985 Study*. New York: New York.

Feldberg, Roslyn L. and Evelyn Nakano Glenn. 1982. "Male and female: Job versus gender models in the sociology of work," in *Women and Work*, ed. Rachel Kahn-Hut, Arlene Kaplan Daniels and Richard Colvard. New York: Oxford University Press.

Izraeli, Dafna. 1984. "The attitudinal effects of gender mix in union committee," *Industrial and Labor Relations Review* 37:212–221.

Lockheed, Marlaine, and Katherine Patterson Hall. "Conceptualizing sex as a status characteristic: Applications to leadership training strategies," *Journal of Social Issues* 32:111–124.

Marshall, Ray. 1983. *Women and Work in the 1980's: A Perspective on Basic Trends Affecting Women's Jobs and Job Opportunities*. Washington, DC: Women's Research and Education Institute of the Congressional Caucus for Women's Issues.

Megargee, Edwin. 1969. "Influence of sex roles on the manifestation of leadership," *Journal of Applied Psychology* 53:377–382.

Nardone, Thomas. 1986. "Part-time workers: Who are they?" *Monthly Labor Review* 109:13–19.

Needleman, Ruth. 1986. "A world in transition: Women and economic change," *Labor Studies Journal* 10:207–228.

——. 1986. "Women in unions: Current issues," In *Women Workers: Past, Present and Future*. ed. Michael Moskow, Karen Kozeira, and Lucretia Dewey. Washington, DC: Industrial Relations Research Association.

Remick, Helen. 1984. "Technical issues in job evaluation," In *Comparable Worth and Wage Discrimination: Technical Possibilities and Political Realities* ed. Helen Remick. Philadelphia: Temple University Press.

Steinberg, Ronnie J. 1984. "A want of harmony: Perspective in wage discrimination and comparable worth," In *Comparable Worth and Wage Discrimination: Technical Possibilities and Political Realities*. ed. Helen Remick, Philadelphia: Temple University Press.

U.S. Commerce Department, Bureau of the Census. 1980. Census population Volume I. *Characteristics of the Population*. United States Summary. Washington, DC.

U.S. Dept. of Labor. Women's Bureau. 1983. *Time of Change: 1983 Handbook on Workers* Washington, DC: Government Printing Office.

———. Women's Bureau. 1985. *Women's Bureau: Meeting the Challenges of the 80's*. Washington, DC: Government Printing Office.

Women's Economic Agenda Working Group. 1985. *A National Agenda for Change: Toward Economic Justice for Women*. Washington, DC: Institute for Policy Studies.

CHAPTER 17

The Qualitative Approach to the Study of Women's Work: Different Method/ Different Knowledge

ELEANOR M. MILLER, HANS O. MAUKSCH, ANNE STATHAM

The primary goal of the project, the conference, and this anthology was to shed such light on women's work so that concepts and unifying factors could be identified. The enterprise sought to identify categories of work and to examine how women do whatever their work might be. Emerging early in the development of the project was the recognition that the studies which seemed relevant to these goals employed qualitative methodology. It seemed that the relationship between qualitative methodologies and the inquiry into women and work demanded special attention. In this chapter the attributes of qualitative methodologies are examined as an exploration of the unique contribution of this methodology to concrete studies of women's experience and to the larger task of carving out a sociology for women (Smith 1974, 1981).

The editors of this volume started with the premise that sociological inquiry is suitably pursued with the help of a wide variety of methodologies and that the all too frequent and all too glib jousting between presumed believers in quantitative or qualitative approaches is scientifically not warranted. It is pervasively damaging to the actual richness of choice available to the sociologist. The key issues are the establishment of a meaningful and scholarly relationship between the research questions asked, the conceptual framework chosen, and the methodology employed as three factors which will influence the nature, thrust, and scientific properties of the answers obtained. The range of the much debated options of research approaches can be viewed in several ways. Certainly, quantification leans toward an emphasis on reliability while the search for meaning and process, which is characteristic of qualitative research, places greater emphasis on validity as part of the ever vexing efforts to maximize both of these goals in any research endeavor.

While the structure, distribution and relationship of factors are dimensions which quantitative approaches can effectively explore, the primary thrust of qualitative methodology is on meaning and process. Qualitative methodologies can be seen as systematized exercises in role taking and in the formulation of experiences and interactions. In a somewhat oversimplified way one can say that concern with prediction is a theme strongly identified with quantitative research approaches while *verstehen* is the form of knowledge emphasized by qualitative techniques. Rather than fueling disputes among sociologists, reciprocal benefits and the power of triangulated knowledge should be a source of pride in the choices available within the sociological repertoire.

We would argue that there are numerous ways in which the studies contained in this volume provide insights valuable on conceptual, theory construction, and policy levels, insights that directly result from their having been conducted using qualitative methodologies. Furthermore, we would argue that these insights would have eluded researchers pondering the various sorts of data deemed earmarked for quantitative analysis. More importantly, we hold that the active role of women in the social construction of a work reality that is uniquely theirs would have remained beyond the grasp of those adhering to a deductive, positivistic perspective.

This is not to contend that quantitative methodologies have no place in the study of women's work or that the tools of those methodologies have not been demonstrated to be very powerful in refining concepts, describing experience, constructing theory, and grounding policy. We do not contend that quantitative data have not been used in an effort to ameliorate the conditions or raise the status and compensation of women's work. We emphasize, however, that different sorts of knowledge are produced by qualitative methodologies than by quantitative ones and we focus attention on some of the epistemological strengths of the qualitative approaches. Our goal is an heuristic one, then, that demands a certain momentary neglect of the contributions and strengths of positivistic approaches.

It is not difficult to demonstrate that, historically, studies in the sociology of work defined completely out of existence much of the labor of women because it was done in the home and did not give rise to a wage at a time when the advance of capital and the concomitant need to control workers and centralize the work process had institutionalized these elements as essential to the nature of modern work. In addition, labor that seemed to be but an extension of women's nurturant essence was also defined as a normative part of the gender role, and thus, as not exemplifying the voluntaristic and energy-expending elements that were thought to characterize work. In short, work was what men did and even if women occupied wage-producing roles in the world of work, these roles were still thought of as partaking less of the essential nature of work than did the labor of men.

Thus, the world view by which the exploitation and devaluation of women's labor both in the home and outside of it was seen as both just and natural came to characterize the sociological study of work in general and what passed for the study of the work of women, to the degree that it was studied. In short, it became a legitimizing and objectivating umbrella by which one piece of reality was transformed into the stuff of scientific knowledge and another piece was somehow deemed unreal, nonexistent.

How one accounts for the production of such a biased and truncated reality, whether, for example, from the standpoint of classicist theorists Marx (1983) or Simmel (1984) or the contemporary theorists Berger and Luckmann (1967) or Schur (1984), is unimportant for our purposes. Although the mechanics of the process and the neutrality or ill-will of those whose experience is reflected in that which is seen as real and worthy of study may be debated, that the process occurs is, we would argue, not debatable. Reality is produced, objectivated, and incorporated into the common sense notions that form the basis of what gets transformed into scientific knowledge without regard or with little regard for the experiences of powerless groups whether those groups are defined by their sex, their age, their color, or a number of other master traits that make them deviant simply by their possession.

Qualitative methodologies bring into central focus the points of view of those being studied and their active participation in constructing worlds that are sometimes quite different from the worlds they are thought to live in by those in power. They make problematic the relationship between these worlds and the world of the dominant. Rather than assuming that the world view and scientific knowledge of the dominant group is the only reality, qualitative methodologies, then, lay the basis for challenges to the monopoly on reality construction and scientific knowledge production of the powerful. To the degree that those who employ them approach in their application what the methods promise, qualitative methodologies are revolutionary by their very nature. The definition of reality of the dominant group is thus called into question and its status as but one among many competing realities is revealed. At the same time, the realities of the powerless are given a certain legitimacy and the function of the former in the exploitation and devaluation of the latter becomes apparent.

One important point that follows from the above does not come through in the papers, although it was discussed at the preceeding conference. It is the widespread stand either directly taken or implied in all sorts or arenas within the social sciences that qualitative methodologies are not truly scientific, that they are ad hoc, value-loaded, ideological, too subject to researcher bias. This all too pervasive labelling is based on misconceptions and on selective identification of presumed purity. Any research project, whether totally number-dependent or completely narrative in composition, is fundamentally molded by the assumptions and theory which are basic to the study and by the questions which in their peculiar form and phrasing influence the answers which can be obtained. It would be false to argue that qualitative research is value neutral or devoid of ideology; rather it is important to acknowledge that there is an inherent value component to every methodology. Assumptions about human behavior and the nature of social systems are just as much an integral part of quantitative approaches as they are of qualitative ones. It can even be asserted that the inherent bias which favors the power perspective of society may well be an unintended, but, nevertheless, crucial by-product of the very nature of quantitative analysis. This kind of methodology is skewed towards central tendencies, categories, and probabilistic relationships.

Qualitative approaches favor and give weight to subjective experiences, phenomena associated with those who, for whatever reason, do not conform to the patterns produced by mass data. The assumption that the manipulation of numbers is rigorous but that qualitative data are tainted and imprecise are unfortunately the result of the application of a selective, positivistic bias to a model of data gathering in which all the rules of rigor can be applied to the ferreting out of the meaning, context, and continuity of human experience. The challenges offered by insights only attainable by qualitative methodologies confront positivistic knowledge on at least two related levels. The engagement occurs at the microlevel of the everyday lives of the people being studied, and at the macrolevel of the imposition of the world view of a dominant group on the lived reality of a less powerful one. It is to an attempt to document the ways in which the studies at hand give rise to the kind of insight into the lived labor of women that we now turn.

METHODOLOGY-LINKED INSIGHTS

One of the most important contributions to the sociology of work and occupations that qualitative methodologies can make, one that is of special import in studies of the labor of powerless groups, is to reveal the full scope of what is actually done as an integral part of the job, both as the world of paid work views it and as the women themselves define it. This contribution will, we think, become more and more obvious if qualitative studies play a substantive role in defining the context within which the comparable worth debates that are already being waged in the courts as well as in scholarly circles continue to take place. Efforts to preserve a certain regard for the human element that the product being produced must contain in order for a woman to feel some level of satisfaction and pride about what she does may also be an important part of women's labor. There are those dimensions of paid work that are complicated and enlarged by the fact that women's paid work, whether in the market place or in the illicit world of an informal economy, and their unpaid work in the home, are often inextricably intertwined. Although these are factors which affect the amount, quality and conditions of women's work every day, usually to their detriment, it is ironic that they also often account for its lack of value in a market that is organized by the dictates of patriarchy and capitalism. In short, there is an element of double jeopardy.

Examples of the hidden nature of much of women's abound in the studies included in this volume. Glenn's account of the work lives of women domestics illustrates very well many of the points made. There is the effort on the part of the domestic to prevent her employer from engaging in a speedup, so to speak, by adding more and more tasks the more adept she gets at accomplishing the agreed-upon ones. There are the psychological costs of having to repeat tasks already completed because members of the household continue to dirty what she has cleaned or mess what she has made orderly. There are the insulting tests of loyalty and honesty that Glenn describes domestics being put to and the efforts of domestics to control the conditions of work so as to produce a level of cleanliness and order about which they can be proud while having simultaneously to do their work in a way their employer thinks she has the right to define for this professional. On top of that the domestic must often accomplish her tasks under the watchful eye of her employer as well as under the feet of the employer and her household members. Why does she put up with this work? Certainly, the fact that she has few marketable skills plays a major role here, but more important than that is the fact that this work allows her to combine family responsibilities with paid work. Moreover, it is work that brings in a wage, but because of its very nature, it is not a threat to those who feel that women should not work outside the home. As a matter of fact, Romero points out that some family members of domestics do not see the work of women domestics as work at all. The Corley-Mauksch study of nurses underscores the double-edged sword of the biological elements within the assumed nature of all women's work, but especially that work which is seen as most consistent with women's gender role. Women often do an incredible amount of emotional work, from relationship management to actual caring activities of a sentimental and affective sort. In fact, it is often just this element that provides women with a good deal of the satisfaction they derive from their work and it is this element that often attracts them to one line of work rather than another. However, this is precisely the facet of her labor that perhaps best explains the low value of women's work both in terms of money and prestige. Moreover, because it draws on commitments to widely-held values that undergird gender norms, it is often effectively used to manipulate women in the workplace and extract unpaid work from them. Corley and Mauksch give the example of the nurse who is expected informally to work without compensation beyond her usual shift. The goad that is used to elicit this behavior is the ideology that a dedicated, professional nurse (woman) would automatically feel obliged to perform this service: it is not only unprofessional if she does not, it is unnatural if she should not want to. Ironically, although this part of the job accounts at least partially for its low status, the control the organization exerts over its clientele is only possible because of the emotional/relational work that is being done by these women workers. This observation applies whether they are seeking abortions or genetic counseling as described by Detlefs and Rothman or temporarily being helped to survive as are the elderly women Diamond views as working at being residents/patients. In fact, a human and humanizing response is thus, as Diamond so very well states, coopted and becomes but a part of the business of producing other units of activity that may be commodified and turned into capital.

Relatively high status women workers, including the managers described by Statham, the teachers described by Spencer, and the women in positions of authority in social work, nursing, and education described by Collins, as well as women in rather lowly positions, such as the street hustlers in Miller's article, the assembly workers studied by Fernandez-Kelly and Garcia, and the custodians studied by Hood, all demonstrate ways in which the unpaid work of the homemaker complicates and constrains paid work. For example, childcare concerns may simply operate as a kind of background noise, accompanying the need to decide about the frozen meat one has tossed on the table before leaving the house. In other situations, household responsibilities loom large and impossibly complicate the lives of women workers. Miller, for example, describes a female street hustler who has returned to a house she has been living in with her "man" and "wives-in-law" to retrieve a potty chair, after having gone to a relative's home to fetch her daughter's clothes for school. This last errand, however, is one which, she feels, draws her back into street life, when her goal is to leave it and, in fact, leads to her being brutally beaten.

Finally, there are those elements of the job that entail great physical and psychological costs for women that, in turn, make them literally unemployable for the remainder of their lives. The injury to the eyesight of assembly plant workers documented by Fernandez-Kelly and Garcia, the sterility and drug and alcohol dependency of female street hustlers described by Miller, the arthritis and back problems of domestics described by Glenn and Romero are all part of the toll of women's work that often remains hidden from view, but must be taken into account as it slowly debilitates the women workers described here. The assaults to self-esteem experienced by all the workers described in the volume remains even more darkly concealed.

These factors appear in study after study collected for this volume. The overwhelming consistency makes it difficult for us to shrink from these conclusions. There were many things that troubled us about women's work experiences as we moved through our analysis — but many other things were heartening, as well. In providing the integration, and setting it within a policy context, we can hopefully move on to solving the problems and celebrating the successes of women's work. For, surely, we cannot live well without those who bring such strengths to their life endeavors.

REFERENCES

Berger, Peter L. and Thomas Luckmann. 1967. *The Social Construction of Reality*. New York: Anchor.

Marx, Karl. 1983. *The Portable Karl Marx*, edited by Eugene Kamnka. Middlesex, England: Penguin Books.

Schur, Edwin M. 1984. *Labelling Women Deviant: Gender, Stigma and Social Control*. Philadelphia: Temple University Press.

Simmel, Georg. 1984. *Georg Simmel: On Women, Sexuality and Love*. New Haven. Yale University Press.

Smith, Dorothy E. 1974. "The social construction of documentary reality," *Sociological Inquiry* 44:257–68.

Smith, Dorothy E. 1981. "The experienced world as problematic: A feminist method," Twelfth Annual Sorokin Lecture. Saskatoon: University of Saskatchewan.

Contributors

Sheila K. Collins received her M.S.W. in Social Work from Wayne State University and her Ph.D. in Adult Education from the University of Nebraska-Lincoln. She is currently on the faculty of the Graduate School of Social Work at the University of Texas-Arlington. She has published in the areas of women and work, women and divorce, and self-help. She is currently completing a book on the art of self-care.

Maureen Connelly received her Ph.D. in sociology from Ohio State University in 1980. She is Associate Professor of Sociology at Frostburg State College in Frostburg, Maryland. She has recently received an MSW from the University of Maryland. Her areas of interest are sex roles and deviant behavior.

Mary C. Corley, R.N., Ph.D. is a nurse/sociologist serving on the graduate faculty at the Medical College of Virginia School of Nursing, Virginia Commonwealth University. She has served as Project Director of a congressionally mandated study on Recruitment and Retention of Nurses in the Veterans Administration. She holds a bachelor's degree in nursing from Marquette University, a masters degree in nursing from the Catholic University of America, and a Ph.D. in sociology from the University of Kentucky.

Melinda Detlefs, M.A. received her masters degree in women's studies from the City University of New York in 1984. The article in this book is drawn in part from her thesis. She was the Women's Development Officer for the YWCA of Western Samoa and the Women and Development Coordinator for the Peace Corps of Western Samoa. She is currently teaching in the Cook Islands.

317

318 CONTRIBUTORS

Timothy Diamond received his Ph.D. in Sociology from The Ohio State University. He is a Research Associate of The Program on Women, Northwestern University. He is currently writing a book on the research reported in this volume. Tentatively entitled, *Making Gray Gold: The Everyday Production of Nursing Home Care*, the book will be published by the University of Chicago Press.

Anna M. Garcia is a research associate at the Center for U.S.-Mexican Studies at the University of California-San Diego. She has done extensive research on health delivery systems and their relation to minorities, particularly Hispanics; the labor market incorporation of Hispanics in California; and undocumented migration.

Evelyn Nakano Glenn is professor of sociology at SUNY/Binghamton. She is author of *Issei, Nisei, Warbride: Three Generations of Japanese Women in Domestic Service* and numerous articles on women and work with a particular focus on women in clerical occupations and on the impact of technology on women's work. More generally, her interests are in the areas of gender, race, and class.

Jane C. Hood is an assistant professor of sociology at the University of New Mexico in Albuquerque. She is the author of *Becoming a Two Job-Family* and has published articles on work and family life in the *Journal of Marriage and the Family*, *Family Relations*, *The Personnel Administrator*, and *Urban Life and Culture*. Currently, she is working on a qualitative study of nurses, shiftwork, and substance abuse, as well as a quasi-experimental study of images on gender tokens in work organizations.

M. Patricia Fernandez Kelly is a social anthropologist currently affiliated with the Department of Sociology at the Johns Hopkins University. She is the author of *For We Are Sold, I and My People: Women and Industry in Mexico's Frontier."* (Albany, New York: State University of New York Press, 1983). With June Nash, she is the editor of *Women, Men and the New International Division of Labor* (Albany, New York: State University of New York Press, 1983). With filmmaker Lorraine Gray, she is the co-producer of "The Global Assembly Line", an award-winning documentary film focusing on the impact of the internationalization of manufacturing on the United States, the Philippines and the U.S.-Mexico Border. For the last three years, she has been a principal investigator in "A Collaborative Study of Hispanic Women in Garment and Electronics Industries in Southern California."

Susan E. Martin has a B.A. in history from Swarthmore College, an M.A. in education from the University of Rochester, and a Ph.D. in sociology from American University. Since 1983 she has been a project director at the Police Foundation where she is currently working on studies of the status of women in policing and the police handling of child abuse cases. Previously she was a study director of the Panel of Research on Rehabilitative Techniques and the Panel of Research on Sentencing and a staff officer for the Committee on Research on Law Enforcement and the Administration of Justice at the National Research Council. She is author of *"Breaking and Entering": Policewomen on Patrol, Catching Career Criminals: A Study of the Repeat Offender Project,* and co-editor of *Research on Sentencing: The Search for Reform.*

Hans O. Mauksch is Professor Emeritus, University of Missouri-Columbia. He is currently Adjunct Professor at the University of Wisconsin-Milwaukee and Visiting Professor at the University of Wisconsin-Parkside. His research and publications focus on the health professions and on health care systems. This area of research has brought about extensive involvement in issues of gender and work as well as gender as it affects consumer patterns. Mauksch has also been extensively involved in faculty development and the sociology of teaching.

Eleanor M. Miller is an associate professor of sociology at the University of Wisconsin-Milwaukee. She is author of *Street Woman* and is currently working in the general area of economic development and the illicit work of women.

Ruth Needleman is Coordinator and Associate Professor of Labor Studies at Indiana University Northwest. She is the author of articles in *Labor Studies Journal* and several books, and was the guest editor of the Winter, 1986 issue of *Labor Studies Journal,* "Turning the Tide: Women, Unions and Labor Education." She received her M.A. and Ph.D. from Harvard University and has been active in professional labor organizations, including service as vice president, Northwest Indiana Coalition of Labor Union Women and past chair of the Women's Committee of the University and College Labor Education Association.

Anne Nelson is Director of the Institute for Women and Work at the New York State School of Industrial and Labor Relations, Cornell University. She is the author of numerous books and articles on sex discrimination in the workplace. She is the past president of the University and College Labor Education Association.

Barbara Katz Rothman is an associate professor of sociology at Baruch College and at the Graduate Center of the City University of New York. She has authored *In Labor: Women and Power in the Birthplace* (entitled *Giving Birth* in paperback) and *The Tentative Pregnancy: Prenatal Diagnosis and the Future of Motherhood.*

Patricia Rhoton received her Ph.D. in sociology from Notre Dame in 1981. She worked at the Center for Human Resource Research at Ohio State University from 1977 to 1986. She has published several articles related to occupational choice and the interaction of work and other types of human activity. She is currently self-employed, doing marketing research and consulting.

Mary Romero is Assistant Dean at Yale College and teaches in the Women's Studies Program there. She has published articles on Chicana workers, the impact of affirmative action and the appropriation of Chicano culture. She is currently writing a book on Chicana domestic workers.

Anne Statham is Associate Professor of Sociology and Director of Outreach for the Behavioral Science Division at the University of Wisconsin-Parkside. She has authored and co-authored numerous articles in the area of women and work. She is currently completing another co-authored book on gender differences in the teaching styles of university professors and is working on a book manuscript incorporating all of her material on men and women managers.

Dee Ann Spencer is Professor of Sociology at Central Missouri State University, where she has taught since the completion of her Ph.D. at the University of Missouri. She has received grants from the National Institute of Education to conduct qualitative research in schools and on women teachers' lives. She is continuing the latter research by comparing women teachers in the U.S. and those in Mexico and along the U.S.-Mexico border. She has published articles in *The Elementary School Journal, Urban Life, Semiotica,* and *The Teacher Education Quarterly,* and chapters in several books, most recently a chapter in *Contemporary Women Teachers: Balancing School and Home.*

Index of Names

Aadland, S.C., 148
Acker, J., 206, 221
Addams, Jane, 57, 61, 74
Adkinson, J.A., 175, 184
Adler, F., 109–10, 131
Alclay, R., 287, 288
Aldag, R.J., 147
Alexander, C.P., 40, 54
Allutto, J., 146, 147
Alonso, R.D., 146, 147
Apple, M.W., 170, 182, 184
Applegate, J., 172, 186
Arber, S., 110, 131
Ash, M.K., 252–53, 254, 262
Ashley, J., 135, 147
Astin, H., 188, 192, 194, 200
Auletta, K., 130, 131

Baca, R., 288
Bage, T.J., 246, 263
Banton, M., 220, 221
Barnes, Barry, 5, 8
Bastels, M., 288
Becker, H.S., 80, 90, 145, 147
Beechey, V., 41, 54

Benson, S.P., 246, 263
Benston, Margaret, 61, 74
Berger, Peter L., 311, 314
Bigus, O.S., 107
Biklen, S.K., 172, 184
Bittner, E., 208, 220, 221, 223
Blankenship, W.C., 207, 221
Bluestone, B., 287, 288
Blumstein, P., 260, 263
Boehm, Virginia, 227, 242
Bolin, W., 189–90, 200
Bonilla, F., 288
Bowker, L.H., 110, 131
Bradshaw, T.K., 265, 288
Brain, Robert, 227, 241
Braverman, Harry, 61, 74
Breit, B., 223
Brents, B.H., 54
Bridges, W.P., 205, 221
Brief, A.P., 147
Brockner, J., 146, 147
Broom, L., 77, 90
Broveman, Inge, 188, 201, 305, 306
Broverman, Donald, 188, 201, 305, 306
Brown, Linda Keller, 227, 241
Bullough, B., 138, 145–46, 148, 304, 306

Index of Concepts